Russia's Engagement

with the **West**

Russia's Engagement with the West

Transformation and Integration in the Twenty-First Century

Alexander J. Motyl, Blair A. Ruble, and Lilia Shevtsova, Editors

M.E.Sharpe
Armonk, New York
London, England

Library of Congress Cataloging-in-Publication Data

Russia's engagement with the west : transformation and integration in the twenty-first century
/ Alexander J. Motyl, Blair A. Ruble and Lilia Shevtsova, editors
    p. cm.
Includes bibliographical references and index.
    ISBN 0-7656-1441-3 (hardcover : alk. paper); ISBN 0-7656-1442-1 (pbk. : alk. paper)
    1. Russia (Federation)—Foreign relations. 2. Russia (Federation)—Foreign relations—
Europe. 3. Europe—Foreign relations—Russia (Federation) 4. Russia (Federation)—Politics
and government—1991–5. North Atlantic Treaty Organization. I. Motyl, Alexander J.
II. Ruble, Blair A., 1949– III. Shevtsova, Lilia Fedorovna.

DK510.764.T73 2004
327.4704′09′0511—dc22   2004005787

Contents

List of Tables and Figures

Tables

Figures

About the Editors and Contributors

Pilar Bonet has been the correspondent in Moscow of the Spanish newspaper *El Pais* from 1984 until 1997 and again since 2001 when she returned to Russia after four years as *El Pais* correspondent in Germany. She has been at the Kennan Center as a research scholar and has published three books on Russian topics, one of which, *Figures in a Red Landscape*, has been published in English. Bonet has degrees in Spanish literature from Barcelona University and in journalism from Barcelona Autonomous University.

Sophia Clément-Noguier teaches International Relations at the Institut d'Études Politiques in Paris. Earlier, she worked at the Delegation of Strategic Affairs of the French Ministry of Defense and was a senior fellow at the Institute for Security Studies of the (Western) European Union in Paris. She has published on crisis management and transatlantic security issues, notably "Tensions between Unilateralism and Multilateralism in U.S. Policy within the NATO Alliance" in *International Perspectives on U.S. Unilateralism and Multilateralism*, ed. David Malone and Yuen Foong Khong.

Philip Hanson is emeritus professor of the political economy of Russia and Eastern Europe, University of Birmingham, UK, and associate fellow of the Royal Institute of International Affairs, London. Previously, he has worked at the British Treasury, the Foreign and Commonwealth Office, the United Nations Economic Commission for Europe, Radio Free Europe/Radio Liberty, and at the universities of Michigan, Harvard, and Kyoto. His books include *From Stagnation to Catastroika* (1992), *Regional Economic Change in Russia* (co-edited with Michael Bradshaw, 2000), and *The Rise and Fall of the Soviet Economy* (2003).

Ania Krok-Paszkowska has a PhD in political science from the University of Leiden. She has been a visiting fellow at the Robert Schuman Centre for Advanced Studies (European University Institute in Florence). Her current work focuses mainly on the European Union and enlargement. Her recent publications include a report on "The Political Dimension of Enlargement" (2001), "Public Attitudes towards the EU in Candidate Countries" (2003), and "Poland's Road to the European Union" (with Jan Zielonka, 2004).

Stephan Kux is delegate for European affairs of the Canton of Zürich (Switzerland) and senior lecturer in political science at the University of Zürich. Educated at Columbia University and the London School of Economics, he has specialized in Soviet and Russian affairs and European integration. His current work is on domestic adaptation to European integration and transformation of political systems in the east and south in a comparative perspective. Kux has published several books on Soviet federalism and revolution, foreign affairs, and the fall of the Soviet empire.

Rajan Menon is Monroe J. Rathbone Professor of International Relations at Lehigh University and a fellow at the New America Foundation. He is also a senior fellow at the Council on Foreign Relations, and a senior adviser and academic fellow at the Carnegie Corporation's International Peace and Security Program. His chapter is part of a book project supported by a 2002 Carnegie Scholar award from the Carnegie Corporation of New York. His most recent publications include *Russia, the Caucasus, and Central Asia: The Twenty-First Century Security Environment* (1999) and *Energy and Conflict in Central Asia* (2001).

Jerzy Maćków is chair of comparative politics (Central and Eastern Europe) at the Institute for Political Science at the University of Regensburg. His fields of interest include the theory of totalitarianism and authoritarian rule, post-communist transformation, and country studies (Belarus, Poland, Russia, Ukraine). His recent publications include *Die Konstruktion politischer Stabilität. Polen und Russland in den Umbrüchen der achtziger und neunziger Jahre* (1998) and *Parlamentarische Demokratie und Autoritarismus. Erfolge und Misserfolge der postkommunistischen Verfassunggebung* (1998).

Alexander J. Motyl is professor of political science and deputy director of the Center for Global Change and Governance at Rutgers University-Newark. He is the author of six books, the latest of which is *Imperial Ends: The Decay, Collapse, and Revival of Empires*, and he is the editor of *The Encyclopedia of Nationalism*.

Oleksandr Pavliuk is an expert on European security. He has published widely on security in the post-Soviet space, Ukrainian foreign policy, and implications of EU and NATO enlargement. He is editor of the recent volume *The Black Sea Region: Cooperation and Security-Building* (2004) and co-editor of *Building Security in the New States of Eurasia* (2000).

Alexander Rahr is program director of the Körber-Centre for Russian and CIS Affairs of the German Council on Foreign Relations. He is also coordinator of the Council's EU–Russia Forum. Before joining the Institute in 1994, he was senior analyst at the Research Institute of Radio Free Europe/Radio Liberty, Munich, and project manager at the Federal Institute for East European and International Studies, Cologne. He has published biographical studies of Mikhail Gorbachev (1986) and Vladimir Putin (2000), and is co-author of the Trilateral Commission Report on Central Asia (2000). He was educated at the University at Munich.

Blair A. Ruble is director of the Kennan Institute for Advanced Russian Studies of the Woodrow Wilson Center in Washington, D.C., where he also serves as co-coordinator for comparative urban studies. He received his MA and PhD degrees in political science from the University of Toronto, and his undergraduate degree from the University of North Carolina at Chapel Hill. His book-length works include *Leningrad: Shaping a Soviet City* (1990), *Money Sings! The Changing Politics of Urban Space in Post-Soviet Yaroslavl* (1995), and *Second Metropolis: Pragmatic Pluralism in Gilded Age Chicago, Silver Age Moscow, and Meiji Osaka* (2001).

Yuri Senokosov is director of the publishing program of the Moscow School of Political Studies. He is editor-in-chief of *Obshchaia tetrad'* magazine and co-editor of the London-published, English-language tri-quarterly *Russia on Russia*. A graduate of the history department of Moscow State University, Dr. Senokosov served on the editorial board of the journal *Voprosy filosofii* (Problems of Philosophy) and is author of a book *Vlast' kak problema* (Power as Problem).

Lilia Shevtsova has been senior associate at the Carnegie Endowment for International Peace since 1995 and was on the faculty of the Moscow State Institute for International Relations from 1997 to 2003. Shevtsova is a member of the editorial boards of the journals *Polis, Pro et Contra, Journal of Democracy, Demokratizatsiia, Megapolis*, and *Moscow News*. She is a member of the Women in International Security Advisory Board, the Executive Council of the Russian Political Studies Association, the Council for Central and Eastern European Studies, and the Board of the Institute for Human Sciences at Boston University. Shevtsova is author and co-author of several books, including *Yeltsin's Russia: Myths and Reality* (1998) and *Putin's Russia* (2003), and co-editor of *Gorbachev, Yeltsin, and Putin: Political Leadership in Russia's Transition* (2001).

Angela E. Stent is director of the Center for Eurasian, Russian, and East European Studies and professor of government and foreign service at Georgetown University. She has published widely on U.S.–Russian relations and on Russia's relations with Europe. She has served as National Intelligence Officer for Russia and Eurasia on the National Intelligence Council and on the Policy Planning Staff of the U.S. Department of State.

Elizabeth Teague is an analyst of Russian politics with the UK Foreign and Commonwealth Office, currently on secondment to the UK Ministry of Defence. Earlier, she worked as an analyst of Soviet affairs with Radio Free Europe/Radio Liberty Inc. in Munich, as an advisor to the OSCE High Commissioner on National Minorities in The Hague, and as an analyst for the Jamestown Foundation. The views expressed here are her own and should not be taken as representing those of the British Government.

Dmitri Trenin is a senior associate at the Carnegie Endowment for International Peace and director of studies at the Carnegie Moscow Center. Prior to his retirement from the Russian military in 1993 he served as a liaison officer with the Western allies in Germany, staff member of the Soviet delegation to the Nuclear and Space Talks in Geneva, and was the first senior fellow at the NATO Defense College. He has authored several books on Russian foreign and security policy, including *The End of Eurasia: Russia on the Border between Geopolitics and Globalization* (2001, 2002) and *Russia's Restless Frontier* (2004).

Jan Zielonka is Ralf Dahrendorf Fellow in European Politics at St. Antony's College, University of Oxford. He previously taught at the European University Institute, Leiden University, and the University of Warsaw. His books include *Explaining Euro-Paralysis* (1998), *Europe Unbound* (2002), and two volumes on *Democratic Consolidation in Eastern Europe* (2001).

Russia's Engagement

with the **West**

Introduction

Russia's Reintegration into the West
The Challenges Before Russia

Alexander J. Motyl, Blair A. Ruble,
and Lilia Shevtsova

How can Russia become prosperous, well governed, and socially equitable—a country that is, to use the Western social-science parlance, "modern"?[1] The answers to this question—whether proposed by Russians or by analysts outside Russia—often fall into the two mutually exclusive camps already defined by similar debates in previous centuries. One side claims that Russia can become modern only if it adopts liberal values and democratic practices. The other insists that Russia must go its own way, relying on the national values, authoritarian traditions, and institutions that have both defined and been defined by Russia's history and culture.

This question and the answers are not new, and the fact that they have characterized debates over Russia's future for the past two hundred years strongly suggests that this binary opposition, while useful as a way of imagining stark historical alternatives, may have outlived its utility as a signpost for developing policy-relevant approaches to Russia's future. Accordingly, the Center for Global Change and Governance at Rutgers University-Newark, with the sponsorship of the Carnegie Corporation of New York, convened a group of U.S., European, and Russian observers of Russia to discuss how Russia's relationship with the West, broadly defined, has changed in recent years.[2] This effort was predicated on an assumption that President Vladimir Putin's support for the United States in the post–September 11, 2001, war against terrorism may have represented a sea change in how Russia interacts with the West, at least on the level of state-to-state relations. What new options did Putin's post–September 11 embrace of the West create for Russia's internal development? How does pursuit of those domestic options influence Russia's relationship with the world beyond its borders?

While the choices facing Russia and the West are rather more complicated than the binary opposition of Westernizers and Slavophiles would suggest, we do believe that Russia can become modern only if it proceeds along a democratic path— one that, naturally enough, must take into account Russia's historical and cultural

3

specificities. This is so, not because nondemocratic paths to modernity—prosperity, good governance, and social equity—are impossible, but because the peculiar conditions of Russian's post-communist institutional development virtually guarantee that a nondemocratic path to modernity will not only fail but also produce a dysfunctional, polarized, and ultimately impoverished country. While we acknowledge that the choice of democratic modernization must be made first and foremost within Russia itself, we believe that the West—the United States and the European Union—can facilitate democratic paths most conducive to economic growth and Russia's well-being.

This perspective explicitly shapes our evaluation of developments within Russia over the past decade and a half. Russia has experienced wrenching change over that period. A new state, political regime, economic order, and society have emerged in what was, in retrospect, a fairly orderly manner. The Russian Federation has neither collapsed nor broken apart. It avoided social revolution or widespread turmoil and has so far escaped harsh dictatorial rule. Indeed, the new Russia has many achievements to its credit, including having succeeded in stabilizing itself and generating economic growth. After years of uncertainty, most Russians have realized that they cannot attain general prosperity, social equity, and good governance—or modernity—without integration into Western society. Moreover, the Russian transition is still short-lived, under way only slightly more than a decade.

While Russian society appears ready for a dramatic breakthrough toward democratic principles, Russian elites remain unable to shake off the past. Most important, Russia's political system, however democratic its trappings, rests on personified power, bureaucratic measures, and the fusion of political power with business. In the years of Boris Yeltsin's stewardship, Russia became a democratically legitimated, paternalistic, and inefficient bureaucratic system. Under President Putin, Russia's democratic tendencies have weakened and its authoritarian ones have strengthened. In a word, Russia is moving away from the only kind of system that can succeed in making it modern.

Although the nature of Russia's system precludes the easy pursuit of democracy, the piecemeal introduction of democratizing measures is both possible and far more likely to succeed than centralization or authoritarianism, whether hard or soft. But a democratic form of modernization can work only if Russia is first weaned off its current authoritarian predilections. Insofar as the Russian government is unlikely to make the first move, the West could have an important role to play in this aspect of Russia's transformation. As we argue in the conclusion, the United States is ideally positioned to address Russia's "hard power" concerns and maintain a strategic partnership with it. But we believe that it is also time for the European Union (EU) to exert its "soft power" and reach out vigorously to Russia. Despite the many divisions that appeared within Europe as a result of the Iraq crisis, the European Union—if it is genuinely serious about becoming an influential global actor—has no choice but to settle its internal differences and reach out to Russia and its neighbors.

The Origins of the Contemporary Russian System

The Russia of today is not the one Boris Yeltsin and his allies intended to build when they assumed power in late 1991. Committed to transforming Russia into a liberal Western democracy with a prosperous market economy, they pursued two tactical goals. First, they desired to achieve supremacy over those elites opposed to rapid political and economic change. Second, they believed that top-down reforms in general and top-down economic reforms in particular would suffice to dismantle the institutions of the totalitarian Soviet state, including the Communist Party, the system of soviets, and the structures of the planned economy. Instead, Yeltsin's rule produced a quasi-democratic oligarchy resting on personal rule and a fusion of bureaucratic, political, and economic elite interests. It was the democratic legitimization of power through elections that became the most important means for preserving and generating this power in Russia. At the same time, power remained undivided, monolithic, and personalized. The democratically elected authorities increasingly pursued rent seeking rather than good governance as Yeltsin remained in power.

The bitter, inter-elite struggle for the spoils of the victory over communism, and, in particular, for the vast economic and financial resources up for privatization also led to the erosion, fragmentation, and privatization of state power, already dramatically weakened by the collapse of the Soviet state. Bold regional leaders exploited the disarray to seize assets and enhance their political and economic autonomy. Aggressive businessmen with political connections used it to appropriate enterprises and build empires across the country. Even timid regional leaders were compelled to assume more power in order to survive. Meanwhile, in Moscow, ministries fought ministries, the bureaucracy grew, and an erratic president became increasingly incapable of decisive action. The result was that the system itself encouraged contentious, institutionally unsettled, and poorly defined relations among central ministries; favored patronage over transparent civil-service guidelines in state employment; left many state employees undertrained, unmotivated, underpaid, and thus prone to rent seeking; and kept the technological level of state agencies low.

With so weak a state, it was small wonder that the rule of law was poorly institutionalized. Throughout the 1990s legal institutions in Russia were weak and politicized; law enforcement was poor; and private, including criminal, organizations routinely arrogated to themselves many of the police functions of the state. Property rights and investments were thus only haphazardly protected. Such an environment dramatically constrained incentives to invest and increased those to strip assets and extract cash from firms. It also bred corruption and extortion, generating barriers to imports, entrepreneurship, and the free movement of resources across regions, as officials, administrators, and managers collected rents through the rationing of permissions, allocations, and protections. The problem was particularly clear in the arbitrary and capricious system of taxes and tax collection at all levels and in the extortionate licensing and inspections policies of government agencies. Indeed, regions suffered from the same range of disabilities as the country as a whole, and the overall economic decline deprived them of the resources they needed to address those ills.

Contributing to the problem was a deeply rooted cultural predilection—the weak demand for state protection of basic rights and enforcement of contracts. As Jerzy Maćków argues (in chapter 2), the institutions of the legal system—the laws and legal procedures—were unused, as people remained wedded to the conviction that it was pointless to follow and turn to the law. The result was a vicious circle. Without the demand for law from the state, the Russian constitutional state became little more than a sham. Instead, a strong tradition of reliance on informal rules often appeared to dominate over formal judicial remedy.

The crumbling state accelerated Russia's economic decline by depriving the country of effective institutions to regulate economic activity, eroding the quality of public goods, such as health, education, and economic infrastructure, and creating openings for organized crime. Many of the institutional underpinnings necessary to any stable democracy were eviscerated as well. The economic decline, in turn, deprived the state of the resources it needed to rebuild its capacity to govern effectively and delegitimized democracy in the eyes of the population. A weak civil society did not produce support for rebuilding the system and state. In the end, a weak society and weak state resulted in systemic stagnation by the late 1990s.

Putin's Choice

After coming to power in 2000, Vladimir Putin developed a strategy consisting of two elements: first, concentrating power in his own hands, and second, promoting economic reform. The package appealed to Russians and foreigners alike, as it appeared to promise an end to weakness, vacillation, and misrule on the one hand and the emergence of a strong and stable Russia on the other. Within two years Putin established greater nominal central control over the regions and governors, marginalized the Federation Council, subordinated the fractious Duma to his will, weakened most opposition parties, established a pro-presidential bloc, reined in many of the oligarchs, and cowed the formerly boisterous media.

President Putin's centralizing tendencies did prove to have some reformist potential. Thanks to his pressure, the parliament passed important legislation on taxation, sale of land, and judicial reform. And in the aftermath of the terrorist strikes of September 11, 2001, he embarked on a pro-Western shift despite the resistance of the political class and his own entourage. Fortunately for Putin, the economy grew, thanks in large part to high oil revenues and an undervalued ruble. Strong economic performance enabled Putin to appeal to all major social and political groups. Some look at him as the great stabilizer, others view him as a modernizer or even as a transformer. Small wonder that his popularity ratings remain extremely high (above 70 percent), which made his reelection in 2004 a virtual certainty well beforehand.

As Lilia Shevtsova argues (in chapter 5), however, President Putin's accomplishments are likely to be illusory. While economic growth may prove to be sustainable—a point Philip Hanson (chapter 6) makes—the Russian economy still suffers from a variety of important weaknesses. First, its economic infrastructure is years behind that of developed countries and will require vast investments to be brought up to par. Second, many sectors of private business are stagnating. Third, the banking sector is thoroughly underdeveloped and will remain a brake on economic development for as long as that is the case. Fourth, crime and corruption are still rampant and also represent drags on economic growth. Fifth, the catastrophic state of the population's health affects Russia's potential for growth and its human capital. Last, Russia's excessive reliance on natural resources threatens to deform its economy and its state.

President Putin's political achievements are no less dubious. Four years of his admittedly stronger control of the state cannot conceal that the state is weak and disorganized in many important respects. Elites are at loggerheads, ministries promote their own interests and fight over budgetary outlays, and coordination and cooperation in the pursuit of policy ends is minimal. The formal subordination of the regions and governors to seven "super-governors" appointed by Putin, for instance, by no means signifies that the regions are any more beholden to Moscow's wishes. Quite the contrary, the regions are as avidly pursuing their own interests as they did in the past, but they are doing so less visibly and less vocally.

It is hard not to conclude that President Putin has tried to centralize the political system by means of antidemocratic methods. There exists a system of complicities between the political and economic elites, a system that emerged and crystallized during the privatizations of the Yeltsin years. Parliamentary debate has been reduced. The Federation Council, the upper chamber, barely functions as a forum for regional interests. The State Duma, the lower chamber, lacks the legal instruments to check the executive power. The judiciary is subject to the influence of the executive or—to put it mildly—material incentives, and corruption in the police and the army is rampant even if there is evidence of some decline in rent seeking by state authorities.

The arbitrary implementation of new laws limits the political opportunities for the emergence of a vibrant opposition to Putin. The political disciplining of the mass media, both electronic and print, recalls the atmosphere of self-censorship of the Soviet Union. There has been no basic change in the political leadership's attitude toward the law. Although Putin's programmatic statements claim that the rule of law is as important as economic reform and the "strong state," in practice the power of the state often has been placed above the law. This tendency finds expression in the growing strength of the secret police and, in October 2003, in the arrest of Yukos CEO Mikhail Khodorkovsky.

The contemporary Russian state is, like its imperial and Soviet predecessors, both overly ambitious in its goals and too inefficient for promoting modernity as defined above. The Russian people, who experienced difficult social-economic privations in the 1990s, have already begun to experience a change in mentality, from passivity and submissiveness to greater participation and self-assertion. But the post-communist political elite has not undergone significant change. As before, the Russian elite maintains the self-righteous notion that a large concentration of power is good for the country. At the same time, it translates that power into privilege and wealth. As a result, even Putin's economic successes will be ephemeral. Because the state remains weak and the rule of law has not been consolidated, economic growth will continue to benefit most a relatively small segment of the population.

President Putin has neutralized the oligarchic system's more individualistic and ambitious representatives (among them the media oligarchs Vladimir Gusinsky and Boris Berezovsky), but there is no serious hint that the fusion of power and business known as "crony capitalism" is about to change. The continuity with Yeltsin's traditions was brought to light again in December 2002 by the irregular privatization of the state-owned share of the Slavneft oil company, which was sold according to the worst traditions of the privatization auctions. As Grigory Yavlinsky put it, "A stagnant social corporate-criminal system with an extremely ineffective segmented market and without any mechanism for long-term reproduction and increase in economic resources is, unfortunately, the most realistic outlook for Russia today. We will not have a law-based state with an open dynamic economy and a responsible political and economic elite." According to him, the system does not have "a mechanism for the redistribution of benefits at the national level."[3]

What kind of political system is the Russian Federation? It consists of three formal democratic characteristics—the holding of regular free elections, a vibrant but increasingly less-free press, and forceful avowals by the leadership of its commitment to democracy. These, however, are outweighed by a slew of non- or even antidemocratic features. The political system of the Russian Federation utilizes democratic procedures to legitimize itself, but its essence is authoritarian. Elections, though free, are rarely fair. The press, though lively, increasingly kowtows to the president. The political leadership and the political class in general are made up of personalities who, despite their stated commitment to democracy, cannot be considered as having democratic convictions. The power of the president is barely constrained, and the constitutional organs are subordinate to the head of state. Political power remains fused with business, and regional authorities are just as nondemocratic as the Kremlin. Putin's Russia, like Yeltsin's, is a weak, paternalistic, quasi-authoritarian regime. But Putin's Russia has become worrisomely *less* democratic and *more* authoritarian as well. It may not yet be fully authoritarian, but that is clearly the direction in which it is going.

President Putin's pursuit of "vertical" power is understandable. There are many instances of successful top-down modernizations, ranging from Bismarckian Germany to the East Asian "tigers" of Taiwan, South Korea, Singapore, and Indonesia. Russia's own history—in the late nineteenth and early twentieth centuries as well as during the Soviet period—suggests that authoritarian regimes can modernize societies. By the same token, Communist China successfully modernized under Deng Xiaoping while remaining an authoritarian state ruled by the Communist Party. Even so, we do not see quasi-democratic oligarchy or authoritarianism as a viable option for Russia, which lacks a state strong enough to sustain authoritarianism. Indeed, if Putin continues to pursue an antidemocratic and increasingly authoritarian course, Russia will necessarily stagnate.

Authoritarian Stagnation and the Obstacles to Authoritarian Modernization

As we stated at the outset, Russia can achieve modernity only by means of democracy, and it is Russia's own historical peculiarities—and not just normative preferences or social science principles—that lead to this conclusion. Two points deserve mention. First, quasi-authoritarian regimes of the kind that Russia possesses are intrinsically disinclined to promote social equity and general prosperity; they are also the antithesis of good governance. Second, even if some quasi-authoritarian regimes—say those enjoying exceptional leadership—are able to resist these inclinations, they are a recipe for stagnation when joined in combination with a natural resource-based economy and a weak state. Under conditions such as these, the temptation is virtually irresistible for political elites to use the weak state for the pursuit of easy economic advantage and not for economic development, good governance, and the construction of a just society. The result is that the combination of authoritarianism, excessive dependence on natural resources, and state weakness perpetuates itself and ultimately leads to a stagnant society, polity, and economy.

Full-scale authoritarianism is no solution to this conundrum, precisely because Russia, like the other Soviet successor states, is a uniquely post-totalitarian and post-imperial entity that lacks the institutional preconditions of authoritarianism. The very weakness of the corrupt Russian state apparatus precludes effective authoritarian rule. Authoritarianism cannot rest on the Russian military, as it is in even worse condition than the state apparatus. Only the Federal Security Service (FSB) has retained much of the Committee for State Security's (KGB) capacity, but no authoritarianism can rest on the secret police alone, regardless of how formidable and fearful it may be. And even though President Putin has reintegrated many of the functions of the old KGB back into the FSB, the FSB is in fact much weaker than the fearsome KGB. Another obstacle to authoritarianism in Russia is that both the regions and society, which has become accustomed to certain freedoms, would resist.

This is not to say that misguided rulers cannot—or will not—employ authoritarian means to try to build a state and a military. But it is to say that they will necessarily fail. Authoritarian state building all too easily acquires pernicious characteristics, especially when social, political, economic, and cultural institutions are nonexistent or weak. Under conditions such as these, state building has a tendency to become the preponderant policy concern of elites and thus to run ahead of other institutions. In newly independent countries with weak economies, the staffing of states frequently becomes a source of political patronage for competing elites. When, as in post-communist circumstances, both conditions come together, the temptation to let state building develop pathologically can become irresistible. When the state becomes institutionally and numerically bloated, its efficiency and effectiveness invariably decline as lines of command become blurred, elites engage in localized empire building, resources are diverted from productive uses, and state employees begin to engage in bribe taking and corruption. The state apparatus, as it grows more corrupt, then becomes an obstacle to modernization.

A Democratic Alternative and the Role of the West

If authoritarianism is a nonstarter for Russia, then the only alternative is democracy. Unfortunately, Putin's overly centralized and bureaucratic course to date means that the move toward democracy entails more than deflecting Russia from its current trajectory. Russia must first be weaned off any hopes and illusions connected with authoritarianism. Most especially Russians, and those outside Russia concerned with its future, must abandon the notion that liberal democracy in Russia can be built from the top. Only after attempts to establish a "managed democracy" are abandoned will it be possible to nudge the country toward real democracy and democratic modernization.

Redirecting Russia in this manner can only be accomplished slowly. For one thing, democracy abjures rash moves; for another, modernizing a stable country is a time-consuming effort in the best of circumstances; for a third, the absence of a strong and effective state is as much an obstacle to a democratic order as it is to an oligarchic or authoritarian one. But, in contrast to the nondemocratic route toward modernity, which can only fail, the democratizing route can succeed—albeit slowly. Authoritarian rulers cannot command modern institutions into being. It is in the very nature of such institutions to resist authoritarian directives from above, especially in post-totalitarian circumstances.

Democratizing rulers, however, can coax such institutions into existence—not by commanding them to be, but by creating the appropriate incentives for people to determine, more or less freely, what works best for them and thus what is most likely to move them away from stagnation. In contrast, authoritarian rulers not only will fail, but also are likely to create dysfunctional institutions that will only entrench stagnation. Democratizing rulers can also avoid this pitfall, inasmuch as their endorsement and pursuit of "piecemeal social engineering" in conjunction with popular input from below is more likely to forestall the development of a parasitic state and a supine society. The democratizing approach provides no guarantees of success; but the authoritarian approach does guarantee failure.

As with all societal transformations, Russian democracy cannot originate either in the Kremlin or abroad—it must emerge from within Russian society broadly defined. Most worrisome from this perspective is thus the fact that strong rule—with its promise of a strong Russia—still appeals to those Russians who feel humiliated by the loss of the Soviet Union and their superpower status. As long as imperial nostalgia remains strong in Russia—and, as Oleksandr Pavliuk illustrates (chapter 9), it appears to be quite resilient—Russian democracy could well remain beyond reach.

In other words, there seems little reason to think that Russia—at least its elites—will suddenly abandon the authoritarian temptation any time soon. It is therefore incumbent upon the West to try to make a difference by providing Russia with incentives to abandon oligarchy—by integrating it into Western institutions. The rationale for such a move is obvious. Exposing Russia to and involving it in Western ways of pursuing prosperity and good governance could induce changes in Russia's own institutions and thereby move it toward democracy and modernity. The argument is hardly new, of course: indeed, it represents the core of the European Union's rationale for admitting the East Central European states and thereby creating a zone of democracy and stability in the region. Ania Krok-Paszkowska and Jan Zielonka (chapter 7), Sophia Clément-Noguier (chapter 12), and Stephan Kux (chapter 8) examine the receptiveness of European institutions to Russia. Rajan Menon (chapter 10), Alexander Rahr (chapter 11), Angela E. Stent (chapter 13), and Dmitri Trenin (chapter 14) look at Russia's place in the larger geostrategic relationship involving the United States, Europe, and NATO.

The good news is that both the Russian economy and Russian culture are less an obstacle to Russia's integration into the West now than they were in the past. Russia's economy is strikingly open. Merchandise exports plus imports equal more than half of GDP (when the latter is valued in dollars at the exchange rate). As Hanson points out, more than half that trade is with Europe, including EU accession countries and non-EU states like Norway and Switzerland. Moreover, although Russia's crony capitalism is an obstacle to marketization and democratization, it is a form of capitalism nonetheless and as such is testimony to the enormous changes that have taken place in the Russian economy. At present, some two-thirds of Russia's GDP is privately produced, entrepreneurship is vibrant even beyond Moscow, and the market is increasingly being accepted by most Russians.

Russia is, as Pilar Bonet (chapter 4), Yuri Senokosov (chapter 3), and Elizabeth Teague (chapter 1) suggest, far more European than most people acknowledge. After all, geographically, a third of Russia lies in Europe, and most Russians live in European Russia. Moreover, Russia has long been involved in European affairs and their cultural context. That did not change, even under the communists who attempted to destroy the national culture. Russians read the same classics of European literature that European and American students read. Educated Russians listen to the same music and enjoy the same pieces of artwork as educated Europeans and Americans. In addition, despite its Orthodox religious roots, Russia is no less secular than Europe. Besides, there is no monolithic European culture, but rather a multiplicity of European folk and national cultures. There is thus no reason to think that Russian culture is less European than the cultures of France, Hungary, or the Roma. Finally, Russia, like Europe, is also subject to cultural Americanization, and, like Europeans, Russians vehemently criticize the process in the abstract while simultaneously embracing it in real life.

The following chapters explore the themes raised in this introduction. A careful assessment of the factors that facilitate and impede Russia's integration into the West will produce a mixed picture. Our conclusion will suggest just how a win-win-win solution might be crafted that will achieve this goal with equal degrees of policy initiative by the United States, Europe, and Russia.

Russia's transformation and integration is not just good for Russia. We also believe that, despite the tensions affecting U.S.–EU–Russian relations in the continuing aftermath of the war in Iraq, now is the time for Russia, Europe, and America to appreciate that their own self-interest entails cooperation. Indeed, we argue that just as Europe and America can help Russia with its democratic transformation, so too Russia can help Europe overcome its growing division into east and west while both Russia and Europe can mitigate America's tendency to pursue go-it-alone policies. We understand that, at this point in time, the discursive practices of all three sides suggest that such a cooperative solution seems unrealistic. But we claim that, notwithstanding discourses, the reality of underlying self-interest points to what we believe is an ultimately more realistic—and certainly more mutually profitable—"win-win-win" approach.

We therefore contend that Russia's transformation into a prosperous, well-governed, and socially equitable country must be democratic in order to succeed and that a democratic transformation of Russia would be facilitated enormously by its integration into the democratic institutions of the West. But we go further and also claim that not only would Russia's long-term transformation into a democratic society be beneficial to Europe and America but that its short-term involvement in EU–U.S. relations would—ironically—help integrate the EU's new members into its institutions as well as keep the United States integrated in the world. In sum, the U.S.–EU–Russia "triangle" can—with some farsighted leadership—be made to work for everyone's benefit.

Notes

1. While the authors of this volume understand and appreciate the profound and controversial debates surrounding the use of the term "modern," we use it in this volume to represent no more and no less than as we define it here, namely, the capacity for a prosperous, well-governed, and socially equitable state.
2. The members of the project included Pilar Bonet (*El Pais*, Moscow), Sophia Clément-Noguier (Institute of Political Science, Paris), Philip Hanson (University of Birmingham, UK), Frederick Kempe (*Wall Street Journal Europe*, Brussels), Ania Krok-Paskowska (European University Institute, Florence), Stephan Kux (University of Zürich, Switzerland),

Jerzy Maćków (University of Regensburg, Germany), Rajan Menon (Lehigh University, United States), Alexander J. Motyl (Rutgers University-Newark, United States), Alexander Rahr (German Council on Foreign Relations, Berlin), Blair A. Ruble (Kennan Institute, Washington, DC), Yuri Senokosov (Moscow School of Political Studies), Lilia Shevtsova (Carnegie Endowment for International Peace, Moscow), Angela E. Stent (Georgetown University, Washington, DC), Elizabeth Teague (Ministry of Defence, UK), Dmitri Trenin (Carnegie Endowment for International Peace, Moscow), Jan Zielonka (Oxford University). Motyl, Ruble, and Shevtsova served as principal investigators. Bojana Blagojevic (Rutgers University-Newark) and Joseph Dresen (Kennan Institute) served as project assistants.

3. Grigory Yavlinsky, "Demodernization," www.eng.yabloko.ru/People/YAVL/o4–1102.html. Accessed: October 6, 2003.

Part One

Transformation:
Obstacles and Possibilities

1

Citizenship, Borders, and National Identity

Elizabeth Teague

When the Soviet Union collapsed in 1991, Russia gained its independence but lost both its superpower status and much of the empire over which it had ruled for centuries. As an independent state, Russia faced the challenges not only of building a democratic government and a market economy, but also of constructing a new national identity for its citizens. At the time of the last Soviet census, in 1989, ethnic Russians made up barely 50 percent of the population of the Soviet Union. By the time independent Russia held its first census in 2002, more than 80 percent of the country's population identified themselves in that way.

How do Russians perceive themselves now that the multiethnic Soviet Union is no more and Russians make up the overwhelming majority in their own state? Russians have for centuries had a strong sense of cultural identity, yet Russian national identity has traditionally been weak. That is to say, Russians have tended not to see themselves as the core component of a Russian nation-state, but rather to view the state as something alien, inimical, and hostile to their vital interests. Historians attribute this lack of trust between the state and the nation to the fact that Russia became, early on, the center of a vast multiethnic empire. This, historians argue, impeded the development of a specific Russian national consciousness. Then, during the Soviet period, the authorities deliberately discouraged any sense of Russian national identity. Only since independence has Russia had the freedom to shed its imperial legacy and become a nation-state.

The editors of this book ask what Russia must do in order to become prosperous, well governed, and just. They conclude that today's Russian state is too weak to pursue the authoritarian path successfully, and that Russia's route to modernity must accordingly proceed along the path of democracy. For democracy to flourish, Russia requires a well-functioning civil society, that is, institutions that facilitate a productive relationship between society and the state. This presupposes not only effective state institutions but also citizens with a strong sense of themselves, their culture, and the place they occupy in the nation-state.

Russians have for centuries asked themselves whether their culture and their place in history is unique or whether, in order to achieve the just society they desire, they need first to integrate into the European mainstream. This ongoing debate over Russian national identity is clearly reflected in the issue of citizenship with which Russia's leaders have been grappling ever since the country became independent. The fact that the country has, since 1991, operated under a succession of three quite different sets of citizenship legislation—and that President Putin in 2003 promised to make further revisions to the law—indicates that the dilemma remains a live issue. How it is resolved will determine how Russians see themselves, their society, and their neighbors, how they define their borders, and what kind of political system they develop. As this chapter attempts to show, the issue remains so far unresolved.

Russia's Search for Identity

Russia's attitude to the outside world, and to its own identity, has always been complex, and one issue over which Russians have long disagreed centers on the country's relation to Europe. Russia's most densely populated regions lie in Europe and it was in Europe that, in the ninth century, the first state of the eastern Slavs took shape. By the eleventh century, Kievan Rus was a major center of Christian civilization and a hub of European trade and manufacturing. To this day, the bulk of Russia's population is concentrated in the western- and southern-European regions of the country. Yet Russia has traditionally seen itself also as a Eurasian country with vital trade and security interests in Asia as well as in Europe. Today, even after Russia has lost many of its imperial possessions, two-thirds of Russia's territory and most of its natural wealth—oil, gas, timber, and precious metals—lie east of the Ural Mountains.

The question of Russia's borders is of vital importance. Borders are not just lines on a map; they are markers of cultural, social, political, and fiscal difference. Writing in 1911, Ambrose Bierce defined a boundary as an "imaginary line between two nations, separating the imaginary rights of one from the imaginary rights of the other."[1] More recently, Benedict Anderson has described nations as "imagined communities."[2] Once seen as primordial institutions, existing in embryonic form since the dawn of history, nations are now described by scholars as having been "imagined" or even "invented" only in the past few hundred years. By "imagined," Anderson means that the nation is bigger than the earliest human communities such as the extended family or the tribe, where each individual was personally acquainted with the members of his or her social network. The idea of the nation-state came much later, as individuals began to develop a sense of solidarity with people, most of whom they might never see or meet in the flesh, but in whom they nonetheless recognized a collective purpose and a shared set of values. In the nation, this sense of shared values cuts across differences of class, age, and sex. And, while a nation commonly shares a single geographic area, borders are political constructions, determined in the modern world less by nature or geography than by political, social, and economic considerations.

Historians argue that one reason why Russians were slow to develop a strong sense of national identity is that nature did not endow them with easily defended borders. According to Richard Pipes, an important role was also played by the extreme northern location of the dense forests that formed the cradle of the Russian people. The region suffered from poor soil, unreliable rainfall, and a short growing season. The solution favored by the early inhabitants was to put more and more land under cultivation. The early Russians were accordingly continually on the move in search of virgin land, and the borders of their territory were constantly expanding.[3] In addition, the early Russians had to defend themselves against numerous hostile tribes who dominated the steppes to the east and the south. Again, the solution they chose was to move into the steppe-land and to cultivate its rich black earth themselves.

This set in motion what Geoffrey Hosking has called a "perpetual dynamic of conquest" that fueled centuries of Russian imperial expansion.[4] First, the Russians expanded northward toward the Baltic. Then they moved eastward across the Urals into Siberia until, in the seventeenth century, they arrived at the Pacific. Next, they moved southward into the Caucasus. In the late nineteenth century, Central Asia came under Russian rule.

As the empire expanded, so it came to include people of increasingly diverse cultural and ethnic backgrounds. This was what the historian O.V. Kliuchevskii meant when he described Russia's premodern history as that of "a country that colonises itself." That is to say, Russian history is a history of colonization.[5] Russia was the center of the largest land empire history has known. For over four centuries, its territorial expansion averaged fifty square miles a day.[6] Hosking has stressed the profound impact this rate of expansion had on the formation of Russian national identity. In particular, he attributes Russians' abiding preoccupation with defining their identity to the fact that Russia became an empire before it had had time to become a nation. Hosking maintains that the demands of empire building obstructed the formation of the Russian nation and that, while Russia existed for centuries first as a Russian (*russkii*) people and later as an all-encompassing multinational Russian (*rossiiskii*) empire, it was only with the collapse of the Soviet Union that it was able to begin to establish itself as a nation-state.[7]

The fact that Russia was a land empire meant it was never clear where the boundaries were between the metropolis and the colonies, and the inhabitants of the former were governed in much the same way as those of the latter. In her study of the "invention" of the Russian nation, Vera Tolz argues that, while Russians have had a strong sense of ethnic and cultural identity since the sixteenth or seventeenth century, the fact that Russia retained autocratic rule and serfdom long after these institutions had been abandoned by Russia's Western European neighbors obstructed the development of the sense of common purpose that Anderson and Hosking identify as essential for nation building. Tolz points also to the lateness of Russia's industrialization and to the gulf that existed between the imperial elite and the masses. This situation was perpetuated under the Soviet system, Tolz argues, when Russian ethnicity was downplayed in favor of the creation of a new "Soviet people" and the gap between the leaders and the led remained as wide as ever.[8]

Tolz argues that Russians have traditionally seen the West as the "Other" by comparison with which they have defined themselves. Russians have accordingly tended to regard Western Europe with mixed emotions. The famous debate between "Slavophiles" and "Westernizers" that began within the Russian intelligentsia in the 1840s exemplified this ambivalence. The Slavophiles put the case for Russian exceptionalism, arguing that destiny had fated Russia to follow its own path. While the Slavophiles did not reject Western values in themselves, they insisted that Russia's unique combination of semi-Asiatic roots and Orthodox religious heritage could not be reconciled with the individualistic and materialistic values of the Western world. The Westernizers, for their part, did not deny the intrinsic value of Russia's cultural heritage. But they argued that, if Russia was to overcome its backwardness and realize its potential as a great power, it must adopt some Western customs and find ways of integrating with the rest of Europe. Otherwise, it would be condemned to isolation, exclusion, and impotence.

The collapse of the Soviet Union in 1991 injected fresh life into this debate, insofar as it forced Russia to choose a new path. Stripped of much of its former empire, post-Soviet Russia found itself forced back within borders that lacked historical precedent and national logic. That is to say, Russia's new frontiers were not coterminous with the space occupied by ethnic Russians; in 1991, 25 million ethnic Russians found themselves, overnight, living in one or another of the former Soviet republics on Russia's borders. Since then, the border issue has become more acute. This is partly because of the perceived threat of global terrorism, partly because of European Union (EU) enlargement, and partly because Russia feels threatened by the prospect of high immigration.

A New Concept of Citizenship

If Russia's development as a nation-state and a democracy is still a work in progress, it follows that developing a sense of citizenship will be crucially important. Citizenship is a key plank of any democratic society. It relies on members of a given society perceiving common interests and shared values and a sense of community even with people they do not know. If individuals do not perceive themselves as equal members of a wider community, each with a stake in the way that community develops and is organized, they are unlikely to believe that they can exert any influence over their leaders and shape their institutions to run for the benefit of the community. This is, of course, a problem that confronts many countries in addition to Russia.

Citizenship is the legal bond that connects the individual to the state and, through the state and its constitution, the individual to his or her fellow citizens, most of whom he or she will never meet. Being a citizen confers duties as well as rights, and in a democracy all members of the community on an equal basis share these.

In a democracy, the state acts in the name and interests and under the control of its citizens. This control, exercised through the ballot box, is at times a blunt instrument. Nothing better has yet been devised, however. The nature of citizens' rights and duties varies from state to state and is governed by no universal standard. But the bottom line is that a democratic state guarantees its citizens the power to determine national policy, gives them a claim to the community's resources, and promises to protect them in time of need. It follows that, for a democracy, nothing is more important than its relation to its citizens. Because the relationship is so fundamental, states demand considerable latitude regarding how and to whom they will give their citizenship. In Russia, the Yeltsin and Putin leaderships have approached the issue of citizenship in very different ways.

When the Soviet Union broke up in 1991, the leadership of President Boris Yeltsin found itself facing problems very different from those confronting the leaders of the other Soviet republics. Overnight, as noted above, an estimated 25 million ethnic Russian found themselves living "abroad," that is, outside the borders of the Russian Federation in one or another of the newly independent former Soviet republics.

The status of the ethnic Russians in the countries on Russia's borders became the focus of an impassioned debate both inside Russia and between Russia and the other newly independent states. At first, many Russian policy makers found it hard to come to terms with the idea that the new states were indeed independent and no longer a zone of automatic Russian interest and influence. Among other things, they claimed the right to protect the interests of the many ethnic Russians and Russian speakers living in what they called the "near abroad." (This term was always unpopular among Russia's neighbors, who saw it not only as demeaning but also as reflecting a Russian attitude that the former Soviet states remained within Russia's sphere of influence and should follow its lead in their own policy decisions; the term was formally abandoned soon after Putin came to power.)

Russia had adopted its first law on citizenship in November 1991, before the Soviet Union broke up, but this legislation became obsolete when the Soviet Union collapsed one month later. An amended law was adopted in February 1992, but this too was before most Russian lawmakers had had time to grasp the full implications of the Soviet collapse. Many at that stage still hoped to preserve and reconstitute at least part of the Soviet empire.

Like all of the former Soviet republics except Estonia and Latvia, Russia adopted a citizenship policy popularly known as the "zero option." Russia's citizenship law of February 1992 offered Russian citizenship to any citizen of the Soviet Union who registered with the Russian authorities within three years (this deadline was subsequently extended) and who did not in the meantime take the citizenship of any other Soviet successor state.[9] The law was amended in June 1993 to extend its application to the entire population of the former Soviet Union, that is, even to those former Soviet citizens who had already acquired citizenship in one of the other Soviet successor-states.[10] The right to dual citizenship was moreover enshrined in Russia's 1993 constitution. This alarmed Russia's neighbors, almost all of which saw Russia's claim to a legitimate interest in protecting its co-ethnics abroad as a threat to their sovereignty and to their own still fragile national identities. They viewed Russia's 1993 amendment of its citizenship law as a blatant attempt to entice their citizens into taking dual citizenship with the aim of restoring Russian influence in their internal affairs. Almost all of them strongly resisted Russia's efforts to persuade them to sign bilateral treaties on dual citizenship. (Turkmenistan, one of the few that agreed, revoked its agreement in 2003.) They put up equally strong resistance to Moscow's 1994 proposal for the creation of a common citizenship for the members of the Commonwealth of Independent States (CIS).[11]

In retrospect, some of Moscow's statements seem to have been merely vote-catching measures aimed at impressing domestic audiences. In most cases, Russia's promises of support for compatriots outside its borders were unrealistic because the Russian government could not afford to implement them. They did, however, reflect the instrumental way in which Moscow tended at that time to view Russian citizenship. They certainly influenced the way in which Russia's neighbors looked at both Russia and the CIS, and help to explain why the CIS has so far remained an organization confined largely to paper.

European institutions such as the Council of Europe and the Organization for Security and Cooperation in Europe (OSCE) offered advice on European norms and standards as they applied to the situation in the post-communist states. The OSCE's High Commissioner on National Minorities (HCNM) was particularly active in the countries on Russia's periphery, notably in the Baltic states, Ukraine, Kazakhstan, and Kyrgyzstan, all countries with large communities of ethnic Russians as well as representatives of other minorities. The fact that several of the states with which the HCNM was involved were keen to join institutions such as NATO and the European Union meant that they reacted positively to many of his recommendations. He had much less leverage in countries such as Russia that saw no immediate prospect of joining Euro-Atlantic alliances.[12]

Another important factor was that public opinion polls consistently showed that most ordinary inhabitants of Russia cared little about the fate of their compatriots outside Russia. Russian politicians who tried to use the issue as a rallying cry failed to muster popular support. It was of course significant that the ethnic Russians in the countries on Russia's borders were not a homogeneous group, were widely scattered, and did not appear to view themselves as sharing a common identity. Politicians inside Russia formed pressure groups and even political parties in their name, but the Russians outside Russia showed no sign of making an effort to influence Moscow's policies. They did not attempt to form or join a political party or lobby to represent their interests inside the Russian Federation.

Nor, initial expectations notwithstanding, did Moscow's moves attract huge numbers of expatriate Russians to apply for citizenship. Reliable data are hard to come by but the evidence suggests that no more than 4 million people (of the 25 million potential candidates) took Russian citizenship under the generous terms of

Russia's first citizenship law.[13] Even though substantial numbers of Russian-speaking residents of Estonia and Latvia were stateless, the prospect of higher living standards persuaded the majority of them to remain in those countries. Thus, Estonia was estimated in 2002 to be home to some 200,000 stateless persons and 70,000 persons with Russian citizenship[14] while Latvia was home to some 500,000 "noncitizens" and 17,000 Russian citizens.[15]

Building the Russian Nation

Gradually, as the anticipated millions failed to materialize, Moscow began to change its position. There were several practical reasons for this. One was that Russia faced a deteriorating demographic situation, resulting in the short term to a shortage of skilled labor and military conscripts, and threatening in the longer term to lead to a sharp decline in the size of the Russian nation. Official statistics suggest that, in 1992–2001, some 7 million people moved to Russia while 3 million left. This level of net immigration was not sufficient to compensate for natural decrease in the population caused by low birth rates and, equally important, unusually high death rates.

Fertility rates below replacement level are a feature of all European states. Albania, with a fertility rate of 2.28, is the sole exception; otherwise, the rate ranges between a high of 1.9 children per woman in Ireland to a low of 1.1 in Latvia.[16] This is attributed to female education and women's control over their fertility. In Russia, the rate is 1.14. Russia's situation differs from that of most of the rest of Europe, however, in that it is experiencing not only a low birth rate but also a high and rising mortality rate. President Putin noted in his annual address to the Russian parliament in May 2003 that the country's death rate had increased by 10 percent over the previous three years, leading to a fall in the average life expectancy from sixty-seven years in 1999 to sixty-four in 2002. Among the causes were high rates of illness, accidents, poisonings, and injuries. "New epidemics" such as drug abuse and HIV/AIDS infection were exacerbating the problem.

Russia's indigenous population is contracting and aging. As a result, Russia's population has been falling by an average of 750,000 people per year for the past decade.[17] This has led to a fall in the size of the population as a whole but, particularly worryingly, in the number of people of working age. According to preliminary results of the 2002 census (the full results will be published in 2004), the population had fallen by 1.3 percent since 1989, to 145.2 million. This surprised statisticians because it suggested that the population had not been declining as rapidly as had been thought, but the underlying symptoms remained the same. For every ten babies born, Murrray Feshbach points out, seventeen Russians die.[18] He predicts that, if present trends continue, Russia's population will fall to 100 million by the year 2050. Other statisticians predict even sharper declines. Feshbach warns that what he calls Russia's "demographic and health meltdown" will have a massive impact on both the workforce and the military.[19]

The threat posed by HIV/AIDS is especially acute. At present, this does not look so serious because Russia has a relatively low number of people infected. As several recent studies have pointed out, however, it is becoming an increasing threat. The problem is that Russia has a very high rate of infection. Together with neighboring Ukraine, Russia has the fastest rate of infection in the world. And it is important to note that while HIV was originally spread predominantly by means of intravenous drug use, it is now spreading faster through heterosexual contact. This is already having an impact on newborns.

The Putin leadership took this situation seriously. In an unusual move, Putin ranked population trends first among a list of threats to Russian national security when he made his first state-of-the-nation speech in June 2000; later he touched on the issue in his annual state-of the-nation addresses to the Russian parliament. The government approved a number of experimental projects aimed at boosting the birthrate, and said it was considering legislative changes to restrict women's access to abortion. The government recognized, however, that these moves would take time to have an effect. Accordingly, it focused its attention on the possibility of attracting immigrants, recognizing that merely to maintain its present population level. Russia needed to attract between 700,000 and 1 million immigrants a year.[20]

So far, legal immigration (as opposed to illegal, of which more below) has failed to compensate for the natural decrease in the population. In 1992–1995, legal immigration compensated for 72 percent of the natural decrease. In 1996–1998, the figure was 40 percent. In 2001, a sharp fall in the number of people (legally) moving to Russia meant that immigration offset only 7.7 percent of the decrease.[21]

The Putin leadership has made numerous attempts to deal with Russia's problems by amending Russia's citizenship law. As seen above, it inherited from the Yeltsin era an approach to citizenship that was both inclusive and instrumental, and that offered Russian citizenship to virtually anyone who wanted it. This was one of the first things the Putin leadership changed. In June 2001, the presidential administration submitted to parliament a draft of a new law on Russian citizenship. An explanatory note revealed, however, that the decision to draft the bill had been made in 1997, that is, when Yeltsin was still in charge and before Putin had been appointed to high rank. The existing law, the note went on, had been elaborated "in a transitional period when a new form of Russian statehood was coming into being." As a result, the note concluded, the law had taken account "neither of the way Russia and its legal system would develop, nor of the nature of [Russia's] relations with the newly independent states [the other former Soviet republics]."

The legislative proposals of 2001, by contrast, adopted a highly restrictive approach. Drafted by the presidential administration, they abolished the preferential fast-track procedure previously on offer to former Soviet citizens, and required such people to meet the same criteria as those from outside the former Soviet space if they wished to obtain Russian citizenship through naturalization.[22]

To qualify for citizenship, all applicants had to have lived legally in Russia for a minimum of five years, be in possession of an official residence permit, and submit an income declaration proving that they had a legitimate source of income and could maintain themselves and their families. Applicants were also required to be familiar with the Russian language and constitution. Anyone with a criminal record was liable to be rejected. The leadership remained keen to attract desirable immigrants and concessions were accordingly made for certain groups of people. The minimum period of required residence fell to one year for those with scientific and professional qualifications. And, as will be seen below, residents of certain strategically located trouble spots received special treatment.

The proposed changes met a stormy reception in parliament, where parliamentarians complained that it discriminated against Russia's co-ethnics in the CIS. It was also opposed by human rights activists, who warned that the new law would create fertile conditions for bribe taking by officials.[23] The law was nonetheless eventually approved and entered into force in July 2002.[24]

In denying ethnic Russians from the CIS an automatic right to naturalization, the drafters of the 2001–2002 citizenship and immigration legislation appeared to be drawing explicitly on Western models and bringing Russian legislation into line with European standards. They also appeared to be fundamentally revising what it meant to be "Russian." The new law seemed likely to result in a stronger notion of the Russian Federation as a conceptual unit; this in turn was likely to have important implications for Russia's relations, first, with its neighbors, and second, with the wider world. Where formerly the approach had been ambiguous, the scene seemed to be set for a stronger sense of Russian nationhood within set boundaries. If citizenship became harder to get, and if, at the same time, the penalties for working in Russia illegally became more severe, the value of Russian citizenship would rise and more people would want to acquire it. Russia would then be in the desirable position of being able to pick and choose which immigrants it wanted to invite to live and work on its territory. Not only that, but it would be able to make them pay taxes.

Russia as a Country of Immigration

The new laws also sent a signal that Russia was, for the first time in its history, seriously interested in immigration. The newspaper *Izvestiia* commented on February 21, 2002, that the new legislation should be seen in the context of the shortage of specialist labor already afflicting several Russian regions and expected to make itself felt throughout Russia as the years progressed. For this reason, the 2002 citizenship law stated that simplified procedures for acquiring citizenship would apply to those with scientific or technical qualifications, special skills, or knowledge useful to Russia. Such people would have to spend only one year's residence in Russia, rather than five.

The Putin leadership proposed a further special concession, that is, changes to the law to give Russian citizenship to young men from the CIS countries who volunteered for the Russian army. Such people would be offered fast-track citizenship after three years' military service.[25] Some of Russia's neighbors, including Belarus, Ukraine, Georgia, and Tajikistan, expressed shock at the proposal and made it clear they would do everything they could to prevent their young men from volunteering.[26] But Kyrgyzstan welcomed the opportunity, acknowledging that it had a high birth rate and insufficient job opportunities to keep all its young people in employment.[27]

There were some signs that Russia might use the law for political purposes. These came from Georgia's secessionist regions. In December 2000, Russia had introduced a visa regime with Georgia, citing the threat posed by Chechen terrorists who Russia believed were taking refuge in Georgia. Along with Turkmenistan, seen by Russia as a source of drug smuggling, Georgia was the only member-state of the CIS to which Russia did not grant visa-free status. To Tbilisi's anger, however, Russia maintained visa-free access to Russian territory for Georgia's two secessionist regions, Abkhazia and South Ossetia. In the period preceding the entry into force of Russia's new exclusive citizenship law, Russian officials moreover granted Russian citizenship to the residents of these two regions. The summer of 2002 saw thousands of residents of the two secessionist regions apply for naturalization under the old rules. By the time the new rules entered into force, some 150,000 of Abkhazia's 320,000 residents and half of South Ossetia's estimated 70,000 population had applied for Russian citizenship.[28] This provoked bitter protests from the Georgian government, which accused Russia of preparing to use the presence of Russian citizens as a pretext to intervene in Georgia's internal affairs.

Revising the Citizenship Law Again—and Again?

As mentioned above, the 2002 citizenship law aroused strong opposition from many sectors of Russian society. In September 2003, the presidential administration announced plans to relax the regulations.[29] The scale of the amendments was surprising and suggested a return to the earlier, inclusive citizenship regulations of the Yeltsin era. Citizens of other CIS countries who had been born on Russian Federation territory would be able to apply for Russian citizenship in line with a simplified procedure and would no longer be required to wait five years from the date of being granted the right to settle in Russia before doing so. Nor would they have to prove that they had a legitimate source of income and were proficient in the Russian language. People who had been married for three years or more to Russian citizens would also be eligible to apply for fast-track naturalization; so too would citizens of CIS countries who had received higher education or specialist training in Russia, and citizens of CIS countries who had completed three years' service under contract in Russia's armed services.[30] The Minister for Nationalities stressed that the aim of the changes was to attract skilled workers and to underline that Russia welcomed economic migrants.[31]

Even these changes did not resolve the controversy, however. Speaking on a nationwide television phone-in program in December 2003, President Putin declared that the present laws on citizenship and immigration were "excessively tough" and promised that his administration would be introducing further changes in order to attract to Russia the skilled workers that Russia needed.[32]

Tackling Illegal Immigration

The law on immigration, which came into effect on November 1, 2002, had tightened regulations governing foreign citizens wishing to live and work in Russia. Those wishing to stay on a medium- to long-term basis (as opposed to making short visits) would have to undergo screening. All foreigners entering Russia would receive an immigration card and be entered on a single, permanent computerized database.[33] After some initial hiccups, the new system appeared to work smoothly.

Quotas for foreign workers came into force in February 2003; each region decided its own quota, subject to approval by the federal government. Foreign workers–or their employers–were required to pay fees averaging $100 to register and receive a work permit. This enabled the Federal Migration Service (FMS), charged with administering the new system, to speak gleefully of earning $10 million for the treasury.[34] Entry would be refused to those with criminal records or serious diseases. In this case, applicants from the former Soviet republics were to be treated just the same as those from outside. The declared aim was to ensure that Russia attracted "high-class specialists, with good financial prospects, capable of building a house or starting a business." A presidential aide provoked an official complaint from the government of Tajikistan when he said the aim was to keep "Tajik beggars" out of Russia.[35]

For a while, the press was full of scare stories about massive numbers of illegal immigrants flooding unchecked into Russian territory, bringing crime and disease with them and provoking ethnic tension wherever they settled. Indeed, as Bettina Renz has pointed out, the adoption of the law bore all the hallmarks of the campaigning approach that in the Soviet period used to precede the announcement of a change of Kremlin policy.[36] As might be expected from a situation where state control had reportedly been lost, there was no consensus over the size of the problem. The figures given by various government agencies were confusing and contradictory, but Interior Minister Boris Gryzlov asserted that, in addition to the estimated 1.5 million illegal immigrants, up to 5 million seasonal workers from China, Vietnam, Afghanistan, and the South Caucasus were entering Russia every year.[37] They allegedly arrived on tourist or student visas and took temporary jobs to make ends meet. When their permits expired, they stayed on and became illegal immigrants.[38] They were in Russia illegally and had no interest in taking its citizenship. They were not, therefore, integrating into the community, and the state had virtually no control over them. They worked in the shadow economy, sent their earnings (estimated at some $7–8 billion annually) out of the country to their families back home, and paid no taxes to anyone.[39] Local officials complained, for good measure, that illegal workers were skewing labor markets and boosting joblessness among Russia's 7 million unemployed by taking menial or low-paying jobs that most Russians did not want to do. Other officials charged that they were contributing to rising crime and provoking interethnic conflict.

At the same time, Putin made clear that he was aware that Russia needed a massive injection of new workers to resolve the country's economic problems. He instructed the FMS to ensure that all those with the desired qualifications and expertise were able to enter Russia "without hindrance or delay."[40] The quota for foreign workers for 2003 was set at 500,000.[41] Taking part in a phone-in with members of the Russian public on December 19, 2002, Putin acknowledged that this figure was too low and predicted that it would soon rise to around 700,000. Demographers nonetheless expressed strong doubts that the legislation would attract immigrant labor in the quantities that Russia needed to overcome its demographic crisis. Much would of course depend on how the new rules were implemented. If they were implemented unfairly, and in a manner that relied too heavily on law enforcement and too little on creating attractive opportunities for personal prosperity and initiative, they were likely to be evaded and ineffectual.

There seemed meanwhile little doubt that the immigrant workers, so much desired by the planners in the federal government, were deeply resented by the indigenous residents of the regions in which they tended to settle. This was particularly true of the Russian Far East, where local leaders complained about improbably high numbers of Chinese immigrant workers, and of Krasnodar and Stavropol krais in Russia's North Caucasus.

Tightening Russia's Border Regime

Meanwhile, the Putin leadership began to try to come to grips with the issue of Russia's porous borders. This sprang partly from Russia's desire to stop illegal immigrants from entering the country, partly because of the threat posed by terrorists and partly because of the influence exerted by the EU on those of Russia's near neighbors that were keen to become EU members. Russia is also trying to develop a new border policy vis-à-vis the European countries. The need for tighter regulations was highlighted when Putin called, in August 2002, for visa-free travel between Russia and the European Union as a means of integrating Russia more closely into Europe.[42]

The Kremlin recognizes the enormity of the task. According to Interior Minister Gryzlov, "for the past ten years there has been no real border between the former Soviet states."[43] Parliamentarian Dmitri Rogozin compared Russia to "a yard with an open gate."[44] In September 2003, Putin acknowledged the lack of adequate infrastructure for Russia's land and sea borders, and the problems that this posed. The borders, he exclaimed, were "in no fit state. Why, nothing has been done for more than a decade!"[45] One of Putin's first moves was to transfer the Federal Border Guards back under the wing of the Federal Security Service (FSB, domestic successor of the Soviet-era KGB). Russia is already reviewing the documentation that visitors from the CIS countries may use to enter Russia and has stated that it will no longer accept pre-1991 Soviet identity documents ("internal passports").[46]

Russia has launched a series of consultations between the FSB and the security services of Russia's neighboring countries aimed at sharing information in order to reduce illegal immigration, cut down on drug smuggling, and deter terrorism. Russia began to cooperate with several CIS states, notably Georgia, jointly to patrol their common border, and with Tajikistan, which has no common border with Russia but whose border with Afghanistan is believed to be one of the major routes whereby heroin is smuggled both into Russia and through Russia to Western Europe. While still wary of their former big brother, many of the states on Russia's borders welcomed help in controlling their borders. Experts argued, however, that if border regimes were tightened up, it was likely to be small-scale traders, families, and ethnic minorities who would suffer, whereas drug smugglers, human traffickers, and money-launderers would find ways through even the most stringent borders.[47] They argued that increased cooperation between international police and security services would be a more efficient means of countering cross-border crime than investing in border police, barbed wire, and surveillance equipment.

Conclusion

The fact that legislation on so crucial an issue as citizenship has changed three times in the decade since Russia became independent, and that further changes are promised, indicates both the importance of the issue and the extent to which the Russian population and its leaders remain undecided over the kind of country they want to build. The Putin leadership originally oversaw the introduction of legislation that, while still fuzzy on some of the detail, could in the long term have led the country to think of itself no longer as a Eurasian empire with indeterminate borders but rather as a member of the European mainstream. This could in turn have enabled Russia's neighbors to feel more relaxed about living next door to so huge and potentially powerful a country. Russia's leaders also concluded that attracting immigrant labor was essential for Russia's future economic prosperity. They accordingly introduced new laws aimed both at encouraging immigration by suitably qualified people and at ensuring that, once in the country, immigrant workers promised likely, over time, to lead to a change in the way in which Russia viewed itself. However, these legislative changes proved highly controversial and President Putin promised personally that they would be reviewed. That in turn suggested that Russia still required time to come to terms with its loss of empire and meet the challenge of constructing a new nation-state.

Notes

The author is writing in a personal capacity and her views do not reflect those of the British government.

1. Ambrose Bierce, July 28, 2004, *The Devil's Dictionary*, www.online-literature.com/bierce/devilsdictionary/2/.

2. Benedict Anderson, *Imagined Communities: Reflections on the Origin and Spread of Nationalism* (London: Verso, 1991, passim).

3. Pipes, *Russia Under the Old Regime* (Harmondsworth, UK: Penguin, 1977), ch. 1, pp. 1–24.

4. Geoffrey Hosking, *Russia: People and Empire, 1552–1917* (London: HarperCollins, 1997), pp. 3–4.

5. Michael Rywkin, "Russian Nationalism Reassessed." Paper delivered at the annual convention of the Association for the Study of Nationalities, New York City, April 2004.

6. Richard Pipes, *The Formation of the USSR: Communism and Nationalism, 1917–1923* (Cambridge, MA: Harvard University Press, 1964), pp. 1–2.

7. "Can Russia Survive as a Nation-State?" Lecture delivered in London under the auspices of the BEARR Trust, November 6, 2002.

8. Vera Tolz, *Russia: Inventing the National* (London: Arnold, 2001, passim).

9. *Rossiiskaia gazeta*, February 2, 1992.

10. *Rossiiskaia gazeta*, July 14, 1993.

11. For discussion, see Lowell Barrington, "The Domestic and International Consequences of Citizenship in the Soviet Successor States," *Europe-Asia Studies*, no. 5: 731–63.

12. Walter A. Kemp, *Quiet Diplomacy in Action: The OSCE High Commissioner on National Minorities* (The Hague: Kluwer Law International, 2001).

13. *Diena* [Riga], February 22, 2002.

14. *Diena* [Riga], February 27, 2002.

15. *Jauna Avize* [Riga], February 22, 2002.

16. *Financial Times*, March 5, 2003.

17. Timothy Heleniak, "Russia's Demographic Decline Continues," Population Reference Bureau, 2002.

18. *New York Times*, May 23, 2003.

19. Murray Feshbach, "Russia's Demographic and Health Meltdown," in *Russia's Uncertain Economic Future*, ed. John P. Hardt for the Joint Economic Committee, United States Congress, pp. 283–306 (Armonk, NY: M.E. Sharpe, 2002).

20. *Izvestiia*, February 21, 2002.

21. *Interfax*, February 21, 2002; *Prime Tass*, December 9, 2002; Heleniak, "Migration Dilemmas Haunt Post-Soviet Russia."

22. For the text of the law, see *Rossiiskaia gazeta*, June 5, 2002.

23. *Moscow Times*, February 21, 2002.

24. *Rossiiskaia gazeta*, June 5, 2002.

25. *Nezavisimaia gazeta*, April 7, 2003.

26. *Nezavisimaia gazeta*, July 9, 2003.

27. ITAR-TASS, July 9, 2003.

28. Kavkasia-Press news agency, June 28, 2002; *Moscow Times*, July 1, 2002; PrimeNews [Tbilisi], June 10, 2002.

29. *Vedomosti*, September 25, 2003.

30. RTR Russia TV, October 19 and 29, 2003.

31. RIA news agency, October 8, 2003.

32. RTR Russia TV, December 18, 2003.

33. *Rossiiskaia gazeta*, April 4, 2002; RTR Russia TV, November 1, 2002; *Interfax*, December 15, 2002.

34. ITAR-TASS, August 23, 2002.
35. Tajik Radio, April 29, 2002.
36. Bettina Renz, "Regulating the Migration Process in Contemporary Russia: Securitisation or Normalisation," paper presented at the annual conference of the British Association for Slavonic and East European Studies, Cambridge, March 2003.
37. RIA news agency, March 19, 2002; *Kommersant*, April 25, 2002.
38. ITAR-TASS, June 28, 2002.
39. *Rossiiskaia gazeta*, April 4, 2002.
40. *Interfax*, February 26, 2002.
41. *Interfax*, October 1, 2002.
42. *RFE/RL Newsline*, August 28, 2002.
43. *Kommersant*, April 25, 2002.
44. *Interfax*, February 5, 2002.
45. ITAR-TASS, September 17, 2003.
46. ITAR-TASS, April 10, 2003.
47. Jan Zielonka, ed. *Europe Unbound: Enlarging and Reshaping the Boundaries of the European Union* (London: Routledge, 2002) passim.

Biblioigraphy

Anderson, Benedict. 1991. *Imagined Communities: Reflections on the Origin and Spread of Nationalism*. London: Verso.

Aron, Leon, and Kenneth M. Jensen, eds. 1994. *The Emergence of Russian Foreign Policy*. Washington, DC: U.S. Institute of Peace Press.

Barrington, Lowell. 1995. "The Domestic and International Consequences of Citizenship in the Soviet Successor States." Europe-Asia Studies, no. 5: 731–63.

———. "Rethinking the Triadic Nexus: External National Homelands, International Organizations, and Ethnic Relations in the former Soviet Union." Paper presented at the annual convention of the Association for the Study of Nationalities, New York, April 1999.

Bierce, Ambrose. *The Devil's Dictionary*, www.online-literature.com/bierce/devils dictionary/2/.

Feshbach, Murray. 2002. "Russia's Demographic and Health Meltdown." In *Russia's Uncertain Economic Future*, ed. John P. Hardt for the Joint Economic Committee, Congress of the United States, pp. 283–306. Armonk, NY: M.E. Sharpe.

———. 2003. "A Country on the Verge." *New York Times*, May 31.

———. 2003. *Russia's Health and Demographic Crises: Policy Implications and Consequences*. Washington, DC: Chemical and Biological Arms Control Institute.

Figes, Orlando. 2002. *Natasha's Dance: A Cultural History of Russia*. Harmondsworth, UK: Penguin.

Heleniak, Timothy. 2002. "Russia's Demographic Decline Continues." Population Reference Bureau.

———. 2002. "Migration Dilemmas Haunt Post-Soviet Russia." Migration Policy Institute.

Hosking, Geoffrey. 1997. *Russia: People and Empire, 1552–1917*. London: HarperCollins.

Kemp, Walter A., ed. 2001. *Quiet Diplomacy in Action: The OSCE High Commissioner on National Minorities*. The Hague: Kluwer Law International.

Miller, Jacqueline M. 2001. "Imperial Designs? Citizenship and Russia's Policies in the Former Soviet Union." PONARS Policy Memo No. 240, Washington, DC: Center for Strategic and International Studies.

Pipes, Richard. 1964. *The Formation of the USSR: Communism and Nationalism, 1917–1923*. Cambridge, MA: Harvard University Press.

———. 1977. *Russia under the Old Regime*. Harmondsworth, UK: Penguin.

Renz, Bettina. "Regulating the Migration Process in Contemporary Russia: Securitisation or Normalisation?" Paper presented at the annual conference of the British Association for Slavonic and East European Studies, Cambridge, March 2003.

Rywkin, Michael. "Russian Nationalism Reassessed," paper delivered at the Annual Convention of the Association for the Study of Nationalities, New York City, April 2004.

Thiesse, Anne-Marie. "Democracy Softens Forces of Change: Inventing National Identity." Le Monde diplomatique, June 1999.

Tolz, Vera. 2001. *Russia: Inventing the Nation*. London: Arnold.

Trenin, Dmitri. 2002. *The End of Eurasia: Russia on the Border Between Geopolitics and Globalization*. Washington, DC: Carnegie Endowment for International Peace.

Zielonka, Jan, ed. 2002. *Europe Unbound: Enlarging and Reshaping the Boundaries of the European Union*. London: Routledge.

2

Russian Legal Culture, Civil Society, and Chances for Westernization

Jerzy Maćków

The Russian Disregard for the Law

Legal cultures typically reveal both national and supranational ("legal families") as well as, within the nation concerned, regional and social characteristics.[1] Therefore, there is no such thing as a completely homogeneous, national legal culture. However, some national legal cultures are dominated by certain striking characteristics that determine the two central dimensions of any legal culture: first, knowledge and expectations of the legal system, and second, behavior within the legal system.[2] A weak demand for law is considered to be the central characteristic of the Russian legal culture.[3]

Thus, the infrastructure of the constitutional state (supply for law) existing in Russia—the institutions of the legal system, the laws, and the legal procedures—are not being used by the people. This weak demand for law makes the task of constructing a working constitutional state (*pravovoe gosudarstvo*) in post-communist Russia much more difficult. "As things stand now, citizens are unlikely to respond immediately to overblown rhetoric about the importance of establishing a *pravovoe gosudarstvo,* or even to changes in the letter of the law, whether legislative or institutional."[4] In other words, the Russian population remains locked within the conviction that it is pointless to follow the law. Many a Russian politician replies to the question of who is responsible for the lack of respect for the law by saying:

> The people. Not those elected, but the electorate. The intelligentsia, which sets moral norms and judges their observance. It is they who determine what is permissible in society and what cannot be allowed. For example, everybody knows that the town hall of a major Russian city is thoroughly corrupt, that all is rotten. I ask the voters: "Why do you put up with it?" They answer me: "It is true that bribes are accepted, but at least people work. If the others are elected, they will take bribes, but they won't work." This example gives an account of the norms at work in the society.[5]

Of course, it is a smug answer given too soon that suggests that the political elite in Russia handles the law in a more responsible manner than the people.

The weak demand for law is also responsible for the dysfunctionality of the Russian constitutional state: The Russians know that their constitutional state does not work well; therefore, they do not have high expectations of it. Consequently, they act above the law and do not use the opportunities that the legal system could offer. The dilemma is as follows. Without the demand for law, the Russian constitutional state can at best represent little more than a sham that hides the informal decision-making channels. If, however, the constitutional state is nothing more than a sham, the demand for law cannot be strengthened.

The weak demand for law, as well as the dysfunctionality of the constitutional state, also results in Russia's incompatibility with the European Union (EU). The creation of a constitutional state within a post-communist society, which has no recourse to the tradition of a constitutional state, requires a basic change in the legal culture. As long as this change remains uncompleted, it is impossible to develop a modern civil society, which is inconceivable without either institutions of a functional constitutional state (a supply for law) or a strong demand for law. It is the task of this chapter to clarify the destructive effect of the lack of respect for the law on the formation of Russian civil society. To this end, the structures of the young Russian civil society as well as the basic traits of Russia's political culture will be analyzed. Additionally, the problems and long-term chances of Russia's integration into the world of European civil societies will be investigated, while taking into account the possibilities available to the West to exercise its influence on these processes.

Western Civil Society

The fact that modern Western civil society includes a constitutional state is concealed by the narrow understanding of civil society that dominates its contemporary conception. According to this, the state does not belong to the civil society. Moreover, the state is seen as a threat to autonomous social associations, in other words, the nongovernmental organizations (NGOs).[6] The opposing position, the broad understanding of civil society, is by comparison none too popular nowadays. According to this understanding, civil society represents a "political society" because the state is still a part of the associations of which the civil society is comprised.[7] The broad understanding of the civil society relates more to reality as it describes the actual traits of modern Western society. Modern Western civil society (in this broad sense) is the type of society that emerged after the Enlightenment, first in Europe and then in the United States. In comparison to other types of contemporary societies it has several traits that cannot be overlooked:

- the incalculable diversity of autonomously acting players (the state included);
- ideological plurality and freedom of public expression;
- the autonomy of politics and the economy;
- state respect for the autonomy of the individual;
- a working constitution.

In Western civil society the expressly advocated ideological and associational pluralism unavoidably calls forth the need for a generally accepted consensus about procedures. Only the law can regulate the interactions of various societal actors with one another to achieve this. It is obvious that only a state that subordinates itself to the law is capable of protecting this procedural consent that is based upon a wholehearted respect for the law.

The Western democracies of Europe are the products of a civil society based on a constitutional state and a respect for the law. Already in medieval times the monarchs of Europe, from England and Spain right through to Poland, submitted themselves to laws that they had passed and that were increasingly being passed by parliament. The modern constitutional state has effectively limited the power of monarchs since the era of the constitutional monarchies of the nineteenth century at the very latest. The constitutional monarchies were authoritarian states under the rule of law. The increasing popularity of political equality brought about their slow evolution to the modern representative democracies of today.

The specifically Western respect for the law, which has the capability to control the massed power of the state, can, according to many, be traced back to the economic strength of actors in the civil society. The medieval monarchs of Europe already relied on the financial support of their subjects in order to carry out their political actions. The wealth of their subjects was in turn derived from private ownership of land. In the West, private ownership and the law, which establishes the norms, go hand in hand.[8]

The Russian Tradition of Autocracy and Noncivil Society

In comparison to this, the history of Russia from around the thirteenth century onward is the history of a reign without limitation by the law. Significantly enough, up until the second half of the eighteenth century, this history is also the history of patrimonial rule, which means that the whole land, including its inhabitants, was regarded as the possession of the sovereign.[9] But even the introduction of private land ownership by Catherine the Great and the reforms of the nineteenth century failed to create the kind of dynamic that Russia would have needed to bring it quickly on course for a constitutional monarchy.

In fact, every Russian monarch continued the tradition of retaining the autocratic regime of the tsar and refused to limit this influence through a constitution or other laws. This was also true for those rulers considered to be the greatest "reformers" or "modernizers" of nineteenth-century Russia: Alexander I, Nicholas I, and Alexander II. It is true that they sought to reform Russian society according to the European models. However, rather than employing the civil society for support, they relied upon the modern state bureaucracy they attempted to build up, with only limited success. In addition, they clearly refuted civil freedoms, which they regarded as a threat to the autocracy. They justified the *samoderzhavie* (autocracy) as an apparently inalienable precondition for successful reforms and stability. Within this form of government, autonomous societal actors remained weak. Two groups of such actors may be identified.

The first group comprised the idealist intellectuals, who were, however, out of touch with reality. They had enjoyed an education within a West-oriented school system, which had been expanded since the days of Peter the Great, and had studied at Western universities. Their attempts to cooperate with the state in modernizing the society had already been curtly rejected by Alexander I.[10] The Decembrists and later the socialists and the anarchists emerged from these intellectual circles.

The second group was made up of businessmen who, due to their direct connection to societal reality, may indeed be looked upon as a force of civil society. From the time of Alexander I onward, their activities increasingly called for the supply for law:

> Property relations were destined to play [a pivotal role] in Russian history from this time forward. Trade and the sale of rights to land and to the labor of others called for the clarification of existing laws governing property and persons. The need for a comprehensive code of law began to be felt. People understood that such a code need not concern itself with public or constitutional law but could focus exclusively on the private sphere. . . . [A] code of laws could be introduced without changing the social hierarchy or jeopardizing the existing political system.[11]

Even this hope—which seems small when compared to the constitutional monarchies in Western Europe—was not fulfilled in imperial Russia. By the nineteenth century, Russia was already the European land of the noncivil society. It was only after the Revolution of 1905 that the first attempts at introducing constitutionalism in Russia were temporarily institutionalized.

After the Bolshevik putsch in 1917, even this development was undone. The abolition of private property destroyed the economic basis of an already weak civil society. The physical elimination of the "propertied class" finished off the job. At the same time, the principle of judicial partiality was put into practice. While there had been a point in complaining about the immense discrepancy between the legal norms and actual legal practice in Russia during the imperial time of the tsars, the constitution and the law under the communist regime degenerated into a mere instrument of power. In this way, the imperial tradition of the patrimonial, autocratic rule and the noncivil society was continued and perfected under the red banner of the totalitarian regime.[12] At least two generations of people who had lived under Soviet rule were socialized within a hypocritical legal system that dealt with or applied the law arbitrarily and brazenly for political aims.

At the same time, the communists strove to construct a democracy without private ownership and a constitutional system. However, they understood the democratic idea of equality in terms of the social equality of a society alike in impoverishment and deprived of its rights. Developments during the communist era occurred only during the period of the New Economic Policy. Had they not been promptly undone by Stalin, in the long term they could have ushered in a civil society.

However, things were different in the second half of the 1980s, as the state attempted through the policies of perestroika and glasnost to create a kind of controlled public opinion. To achieve this, new organizations (among them "popular fronts") that were influenced mainly by the intellectuals were created by the state. They were supposed to widen the spectrum of the official organizations, through which Gorbachev expected the efficiency of the political system to increase. This naive aim was not fulfilled. Nonetheless, this policy initiated unintended developments, which can be seen as the run-up to Russian civil society. Many popular fronts became independent (which more or less directly caused the fall of the Soviet Union). In addition to this, many independent spirits vociferously expressed their opinions during perestroika, through which an embryonic public opinion came into existence. These developments were accompanied, particularly in the major Russian cities, by the spontaneous creation of small organizations and associations called *neformaly* (informal organizations). In the industrial areas, even free trade unions came into being in the wake of strikes.[13]

Despite all this, however, Russia managed to develop the rudiments of a civil society only after achieving independence and taking leave of socialism. These preconditions were attained after the failed August 1991 putsch and the dissolution of the Soviet Union in December 1991. At this time, Russia had no constitutional state, no adequate legal culture demanding such a state, and no representative democracy. On the contrary, Russia was a slightly battered noncivil society ruled by a dictatorial president. Still, Yeltsin officially proclaimed his plans to build a Western-style civil society as well as a representative democracy. To this day, these noble tasks remain unfulfilled. On the other hand, it would be naive to expect that many centuries of development can be reversed within a single decade.

Modern Western civil society (in a broad sense) contains an efficient constitutional state, autonomous societal actors (civil society in a narrow sense), and a passive social sphere, which in most Western countries is supported by the welfare state. The following two sections analyze the Russian equivalents of the components of the civil society that formed in Russia during the 1990s.

A Weak State Above the Constitution and the Law

When the Soviet Union relinquished its totalitarian claim to power—its attempt to direct and control the whole of society—the Russian state was also confronted for the first time with the problem of its inefficiency in its entirety. Without a fundamental reform of the state the chances of achieving the post-communist aim of transforming the communist system into a market democratic system are practically nonexistent. Despite the extreme weakness of the other societal actors, the state is to withdraw step by step out of those areas that society, reorganized as autonomous associations, is capable of forming. At the same time, the state is to create the basic legal and economic framework to enable society to act freely.

If Western civil society is indeed to be built in the post-totalitarian period, the inefficient state—whose structures must not be allowed to remain ubiquitous— has to be strengthened. Disregard for the law manifests itself in everyday life most clearly in the sweeping corruption at all levels of state administration. Under these circumstances, the political class must prevent a "privatization" of the state that would result in the state "becoming the arena for conflicting individual interests," which could weaken the executive structures.[14]

Russia is not the only country to experience problems with an inefficient state. This is a typical burden of all post-communist societies. The disastrous heritage of the destruction of law under communist rule also had a negative impact on the transformation of Central European societies. However, although they are also affected by the "privatization of the state," they deal with this danger in a completely different way than the Russians. This can be exemplified in the so-called Rywin affair, which currently occupies the Polish public.

In the summer of 2002, Lech Rywin, a film producer with strong political leanings toward the then ruling post-communist Social Democrats, made the following suggestion to Adam Michnik, the chief editor of Poland's largest daily newspaper, *Gazeta Wyborcza*. For $17.5 million Rywin, who claimed that he was acting on behalf of the "group that was in power," said he would arrange for a change in the media law that prevents control over the media from becoming too concentrated. This would enable the *Gazeta Wyborcza* to purchase a private television channel. Michnik secretly recorded one of these conversations with Rywin. However, it was only in December 2002 that the *Gazeta Wyborcza* published a revealing article about Rywin's proposal. On the basis of this, a parliamentary committee was formed, to which many journalists and politicians have since reported, not least about the characteristics of the actors in the political process in Poland: arrogance, self-interest, bending of the law, an obvious lack of understanding of the public good, and incompetence. Particularly painful for Polish citizens is the realization that even the moralizing *Gazeta Wyborcza,* including Adam Michnik, is also fully integrated into the idiosyncrasies of Warsaw politics. The Rywin affair has brought to light the cost of having a legal system in Poland—a cost that can be expressed in money.

Amazingly, the Warsaw correspondent from *Moskovskie Novosti* saw something positive in these events.

> They are not only interesting for the Russian reader because . . . [Rywin] is of Russian descent. At the core of the scandal there are people who we know [in Russia]: A media magnate, a prime minister, a film producer, "a group in the shadows," which is made up of representatives from media and business circles. They play an intimate game that is also familiar to us. . . . In this affair there are bribery, tape recordings, and, of course, an identifiable perpetrator. It is only the conclusion of the affair that is new to us. In Poland this constitutes a scandal that can cost the Prime Minister his office and land the film producer in prison. In Russia such affairs fizzle out [without any repercussions].[15]

These differences have also been confirmed in the area of small business. A series of interviews with managers in the Polish and Russian capitals "has reaffirmed that the rule of law has taken far greater hold in Warsaw than in Moscow. Warsaw shopkeepers expressed far greater faith in the police and in the courts to protect property rights than did shopkeepers in Moscow. In addition, Warsaw shopkeepers faced a regulatory environment that was far more conducive to running a business."[16] Without a doubt, prior to communist rule the demand for law had put down stronger roots in Central Europe than in Russia,[17] which explains, at least partially, the differences in dealing with corruption.

The "privatization of the state" in Russia could, on the one hand, be combated by strengthening the public's right to control the state. Here, the independence of the mass media plays a crucial role. The electronic state media are perhaps more important than private stations and publishing houses because they are generally accessible, inexpensive, and popular. On the other hand, the political leadership must pay strict attention to the law. If they do, the state media will be able to fulfill its mission. Also, the parameters of a new legal public culture will be established, and in due course this promises to end the tradition of Russian legal nihilism (*pravovoi nigilizm*).[18]

After the failure of the August 1991 putsch, the political leadership under Boris Yeltsin did not particularly excel in heeding the law itself. However, in the 1990s the institutional infrastructure of the constitutional state (the supply for law) was built up in a manner similar to that of the post-communist candidates for membership in the EU. The simultaneous legalization of private property was intended to help those who grew up in the Soviet system to develop into citizens aware of their own interests. In order to assert these economic interests, the people will have to create a demand for law and make use of the state's legal infrastructure. In this way, the constitutional state will function. Additionally, the partial privatization of the media sector promised to strengthen the public.

In reality, none of these hopes or expectations turned out to be absolutely without foundation, but they have proven to be unrealistically optimistic. It has quickly been revealed that despite all the improvements to the legal system the judiciary remains dependent upon politics. Yeltsin did not apply himself seriously to strengthening the parliament or the constitutional organs. Rather, he concentrated on securing his power. He did this with the legitimization that is anchored in Russian tradition, whereby the central power has to be "strong for the good of Russia." At the same time he hoped that the introduction of a market economy in early 1992 would lead to an economic wonder that would make up for the deficits in Russian constitutionalism.[19] In the autumn and winter of 1993 this strategy ended in disaster because the country had inherited the sad results of three generations of a centrally planned economy.

The economic shock therapy to which Yeltsin subjected Russia in 1992 led to the population's withdrawal of support from his reform team. No longer popular with the electorate, disregarding the constitutional institutions, and sure of Western support despite his breaks with the constitution, the president forced the country into a new constitution that was designed to secure his power. Even after the new constitution was accepted, Yeltsin demonstrated to the people countless times how it was exploited to secure his power. The regional executives followed this example, often at the behest of the Kremlin, causing lasting damage to the infrastructure of the young constitutional state as well as to the federal system. It is apparent that a democratic political system could not develop under these circumstances. But what kind of political system is the Russian Federation?

There are at least two formal examples we can draw on to argue for the classification of Russia as a democracy: the regular free elections that are held in the country and a political leadership that vociferously avows itself to be democratic. At the same time there are noticeable phenomena of political life that justify doubts about Russian democracy: The free elections in Russia cannot always (if at all) be regarded as fair; the political leadership and the political class in general are made up of personalities who, despite their stated commitment to democracy, cannot be considered as having democratic convictions; the power of the president's authority is hardly constrained in practice; the implementation of political decisions leaves much to be desired; the constitutional organs of Russian democracy are factually subordinate to the head of state; and finally, the regional organs of power multiply the diffuse power structures of the Kremlin.

Nowhere in the world has democracy been achieved through the introduction of free elections alone. Numerous experiences with democratization processes in the twentieth century have revealed there is no democracy that would not practice and protect the constitutional state. Authoritarian political practice in Russia cannot be traced back to a lack of experience and contact with democratic procedures, but is rather typical in a society that began to have free elections before a constitutional state had been established. The political system of the Russian Federation can be classified as a quasi-democratic authoritarian system. Like many contemporary authoritarian systems it utilizes democratic procedures to legitimize itself. The head of state who stands de facto above the law becomes the central regulative power of this system.

Corruption in the state administration was not subjected to any effective barriers under Yeltsin. Through politics the tycoons at the federal and regional levels divided the media market among themselves, and afterward they put their stations and papers to work for the central and regional executives. It was toward the end of the 1990s that some powerful businessmen first turned away from the weakened president. In this way his power, which had already been undermined by his rapid loss of popularity with the Russian population, was damaged once again. It is no wonder that, in observing and living through these developments, citizens have failed to evolve the demand for law that was required of them.

It is meanwhile clear how Putin wants to attempt to hold back the decay—the "privatization"—of the state. The direction of his measures is, to put it mildly, doubtful. He is aiming to centralize the political system. His reforms do not shy away from the antidemocratic orientation of the political system that was established in the Yeltsin era: the strengthening of the "vertical executive" at the cost of federalism; the passing of a new party law intended to limit the political chances of any party that could prove to provide real opposition; the forced registration of social organizations and associations.[20] The political disciplining of the electronic mass media demonstrates the head of state's attitude. The Duma put through limitations on the freedom of the media after the "Northeast" tragedy.[21] This decision sanctions the official way of dealing with information, which recalls the practices of the Soviet Union. Admittedly, none of this would be so bad, if it could at least be assumed that the central Russian power were bound to these new laws.

However, there was no basic change in the political leadership concerning respect for the law, although the president had energetically promoted overcoming general skepticism toward the law during his election campaign. According to his program, the rule of law is as important as the economic reforms and the "strong state."[22] In practice, the state is placed above the law as soon as it seems opportune. This tendency finds expression in the increasing strength of the repressive organs of the political system as well as the dependence of the judiciary on politics, which are obvious.

The notorious Pas'ko case can be seen as representative of these problems. In 1999 Grigorii Pas'ko, soldier and journalist, was sentenced by the military court of the Russian Pacific Fleet to three years in prison because he was alleged to have undertaken espionage for Japan. In 1993 he had sold a videotape for $100 to Japanese television. It showed military material that was obviously unusable as it had been thrown into the Japanese Sea from a ship of the Russian Pacific Fleet. He was released shortly after the first sentence, having spent nearly two years in custody, and moreover coming under the amnesty decreed by parliament. However, since then he has been sentenced several times in the same case, whereby the changing sentences and the reasoning behind them show the strong political dependency of the judiciary. It has been alleged that the Pas'ko case has been drawn into the conflicts between competing cliques of the presidential administration, thus explaining the mood swings of Russian legal organs,[23] which seem almost unbelievable from the perspective of a Western constitutional state.

The Russian state incorporates an omnipresence paired with deplorable inefficiency. In this sense, its striking continuity with the imperial and Soviet tradition is brought to light. There are still no recognizable efforts of the political center to unconditionally subject this state to the rule of law. Throughout the past decade, the Russian people were expected to withstand difficult privations in the social-economic area. This carried with it immense risks for political stability in the early 1990s. The political leadership argued that these privations would bring about the desired transition of the passive and state-oriented mentality of the people who had been socialized within the Soviet regime. The post-communist political elite itself, however, has not undergone such treatment. As before, the Russian elite maintains the self-righteous notion that a large concentration of power is good for the country. At the same time, they carry on the Soviet tradition whereby the exercise of power means privileges. Since the end of communism, that has meant wealth.

Putin's popularity in Russia proves that the resolute, though often illegal, actions of the political elite do not injure the predominant principles of legal culture, and neither does the condition of the constitutional state seem to shock the majority of Russians. In this context it is typical that at the turn of the year 2001–2002, 38 percent of Russians who were questioned stated that they were not interested in the Pas'ko case. Twenty percent of those questioned agreed with his sentence, and 8 percent of these considered the sentence to four years in a strict prison camp to be "too lenient." A full "15 percent expressed their mistrust in the Federal Security Service (FSB) and were of the opinion that the secret service had fabricated the charge. A further 10 percent support the idea of freeing Pas'ko, which should not be underestimated."[24]

The Pas'ko case not only illustrates the condition of the Russian constitutional state but also explains the specifics of what could be seen as Russian civil society (in the narrow sense) if it was not a small island in a huge sea of passivity. It is no coincidence that today many regard Pas'ko as a hero of this civil society.

Civil Society and the Passive Sphere: A Partial Demand for Law

In the meantime, around 300,000 social organizations have been registered with the Russian Ministry of the Interior. It is estimated that only around 75,000 of them are active. The number of their activists is stated to be a million.[25] The state's skepticism as regards the law and the accompanying weak demand for law among the majority of the population has allowed only enclaves of a civil society to come into existence, which are only partially similar to the Western model. In part it recalls the groups and the organizations that were created by the state during perestroika. At least this is appropriate with regard to today's so-called civil society of the president. On June 12, 2001, for the anniversary of Russian independence, Putin invited around thirty hand-picked representatives of various associations—stamp collectors, beekeepers, friends of the garden, artists, and some astronauts—to the Kremlin. During the meeting, the suggestion was made to the representatives of the associations

> to found a chamber for all social organizations—a chamber within the presidential administration, of course. Where else should the civil society be, if not near the president? The staff would be happy to help with premises, telephone connections and such things. And you'll even get a sign for the door reading: "Civil Society near the President of the Russian Federation."[26]

A large number of Russian societal actors admittedly cannot be classified as henchmen of the state. In the meantime, they are independent in terms of the economy insofar as they have to struggle their way through Russian capitalism (even if they are financially supported by the state, it is done only because they offer services in exchange). For this reason they may indeed be seen as (at least potential) harbingers of the Russian civil society according to the Western model.

In contrast to the situation under perestroika, they are no longer mere employees of the state, who either work for or—like the *neformaly* (informal organizations) previously—act against this employer who has been forced upon them. Despite this, the new civil society enclaves still consist of two major groups of actors who are strongly differentiated in terms of their distance from the state. Seen through Western eyes, the closeness to the state of the first group is just as worrying as the great distance from the state of the other.

The first group is made up of powerful representatives of private business (including the aforementioned tycoons), who by pushing through their interests also make use of the corrupt state bureaucracy. Their closeness to the state should not come as a surprise in a post-totalitarian society, where the economy is only slowly emancipating itself from the state. Neither is it surprising that the functionaries of the state, who merely pay lip service to the law, demand political and material services in return for their favors. This situation, which seems abnormal when seen from the Western point of view, can be overcome only if the businessmen among the young, and still weak, middle class gain in importance.

It is to be expected that, unlike the representatives of big business, the representatives of small to medium-sized enterprises will express a strong demand for law, because without the help of an effective legal system they will have no chance to realize their interests against the privileged tycoons. However, the results of an investigation that was carried out in the mid-1990s show how far the Russian middle class still has to go. In the framework of this investigation the employees in the free market sector of the Russian economy, among others, were questioned about what they tend to do when a debtor fails to repay a considerable loan. While 28.6 percent to 53.1 percent[27] of those questioned stated that they would try to find a compromise and another 1.9 percent to 9.4 percent replied that they would get help from "informal middle men," only 0.6 percent to 3.1 percent of the respondents admitted that they would put their case before the court.[28]

As to those business people who are today still privileged and close to the state, it can be assumed that their demand for law will not exceed that of the small and medium enterprises. The case of Mikhail Khodorkovsky reveals that the Kremlin under Putin will not accept any independent tycoons who get by without any support from the state. Whether the political pressure that Putin has placed upon the economic oligarchy will lead, at least in a small way, to a revision of this basic attitude remains to be seen. After the revision of the political course to the "strong state" that was put into effect after Yeltsin, the "new Russians" should have realized that the state is fully capable of changing its policies toward them. However, it would be too naive to expect that the *nouveaux riches* of Russia, in the face of this experience, would quickly develop into supporters of a state that respects the law and the constitution. Not only the legacy of the Soviet legal culture and the shortcomings in the new Russian legal system speak against this.[29] More important in this context is the fact that the power-holders of the Russian private economy owe their rise to exactly those activities that were built on the dominant weak demand for law. As long as decisive economic success can be achieved only with the help of the state, the latter will be corrupted and the law will be ignored.

The Russian Orthodox Church and the formerly state-run trade unions (as opposed to the *nezavisimye profsoiuzy*—free trade unions) also belong to those actors close to the state. They are trying to follow their noncommercial, and therefore long-term, interests with the help of the state. In return for this they offer the state long-term support for its policies. However, the more their privileges are secured by the law, the more these actors will be interested in a functional constitutional state, as has already been shown in the case of the Russian Orthodox Church. However, for ideological reasons even this church supports constitutional pluralistic order only to a degree. It distances itself from "formal" law and its claim to regulate "essential human needs."[30]

Russian Orthodoxy did not experience its Second Vatican Council. In its effort to relativize the constitutional state it has received support from among the intellectuals. There are even some political scientists who postulate a construction of Russian state and society based on the "traditional spiritual and cultural foundations of Russian Orthodox civilization." These foundations—"the service for fellow man"—allegedly formed the spiritual and governmental existence of Russia "in the course of a millennium."[31] This stance also illustrates that Russia, which has been involved in Europe since time immemorial, will nonetheless find it extremely difficult to establish a working constitutional state because of its specific non-Western tradition.

The political parties, which are closely connected with the state's oligarchy, represent a considerable problem for Russian civil society (as well as for the Russian political system), because they tend to serve as a part of "civil society of the president." They understand their closeness to the state differently than the political parties in the West, namely, in terms of subordination to the state's rulers. Under Yeltsin it was still possible to hope that the communists, who were always popular with the Russian people, and the liberals, who were favored by the intelligentsia, would, step by step, develop into real political opposition parties. In Central Europe, the communist, or rather the post-communist, parties lost the first founding elections after the end of the totalitarian system. Being now in parliamentary opposition, those parties insisted that the new rulers should uphold legal norms and procedures of democracy. The various societies' disappointment in the social consequences of post-communist transformation caused the more or less converted post-communist groups to win parliamentary elections. In this way they have reconciled themselves to the constitutional state, despite their own susceptibility to corruption.

Yeltsin prevented a similar development from taking place in Russia by outlawing, through an extremely questionable ukase, the Communist Party after the putsch in August 1991. Despite this, the communists have returned to the political stage. Ever since then, they have been able to count on the support of those who are disaffected as a result of the transformation. Under neither Yeltsin nor Putin have the communists been able to develop a particular demand for law. On the one hand, they want socialism back. On the other hand, they are always prepared to cooperate with the *partiia vlasti*—the "party of power" close to the Kremlin—when it seems opportune.

Under Putin, however, the impression is occasionally given that "Russian democracy" does not need political opposition—even liberal Yabloko (prior to December 2003, when it held seats in parliament) merely wanted to be a "constructive opposition" party. A Russian commentator made the following appropriate analysis:

> In a genuinely democratic country the citizens form parties to fight for victory in parliamentary elections, which in turn enables them to participate in the government. Here, in contrast, the *partiia* [*vlasti*—J.M.] is founded by the government in order to obtain an obedient parliament. All the other parties are then confronted with a choice: Either come to terms with their own irrelevance . . . or become a "service party" for the Kremlin.[32]

It is not political competition but cooptation that increasingly regulates access to the *partiia vlasti*. Just how much danger this represents for the alleged attempt at political democratization will be revealed at the latest when the president loses his popularity and his "party of power" Edinaia Rossiia either collapses or drastically loses significance, without a different party available to replace it. Also, the tendency toward the formation of the *partiia vlasti* could be counteracted, especially through strengthening the demand for law. However, as long as the most important political actors dedicate more attention to participation in the "party of power" than to the struggle for guaranteeing fair political competition, the Russian political parties can hardly be seen as actors of civil society according to the Western model.

The second large group of Russian societal actors consists of the noncommercial NGOs, which are independent from the state. Many of these organizations are ideologically oriented toward the West, engaged in the area of human rights, and they have many contacts with various Western institutions, through which they are partially financed. They differ from their nineteenth-century predecessors in that they do not tend toward antibourgeois, utopian thought.

In contrast to the "civil society of the president" including the party of power and the representatives of big business and the middle class, the noncommercial NGOs have a strong demand for law. This is linked to their desire for autonomy, because they suffer gravely under legal insecurity, which not least touches on their economical foundations. It is true that the formally valid system of legal norms provides them with an adequate legal basis. However, the way that central and regional state authorities deal with these organizations (especially those organizations that focus on human rights) intimates that there have been attempts to rein them in—the raising of bureaucratic obstacles against registration being an example.[33]

In addition, it is impossible to overlook the state's most recent attempts to bring these organizations under its influence. In the obsessive unifying that has been dominant in the Kremlin since Putin, the president's administration has actually attempted to classify the NGOs as better ("more important") and worse ("less important") based on the criterion of their closeness to the president. It is true that the employees of the president's administration, which organized the "'citizens' forum" of the Russian associations, had second thoughts over time and also accepted the representatives of the autonomous NGOs into the organizational committee of the "'citizens' forum." Still, the fatal impression of the "forum" as a fig leaf intended to improve the undemocratic image of the political leadership was not completely dispelled. At the "citizens' forum," held in November 2001 in the Kremlin and attended by 3,000 representatives of the NGOs, "civil society was apparently discussed as communism was once discussed: as a bright and distant aim."[34] During the forum, the prime minister, Kas'ianov, had to listen to Pas'ko's short speech (Pas'ko had only just been released from jail), illustrating symbolically the obscure reality of the relationship between the autonomous NGOs and the executive in today's Russia. It is obvious that a state having the *Gestalt* and behavior of the Russian state cannot be seen as a reliable partner for the autonomous social actors.

The potent actors of the new Russian society—the big associations, the economic tycoons, the large trade unions, the Russian Orthodox Church, some political parties—combine a weak demand for law with an orientation toward the state. In this respect they are similar to the broad, underprivileged masses, although this may seem paradoxical. The passive sphere represents the majority of Russian society today. People in this sphere during the communist era were poor but accustomed to being on social security. In today's Russia they must fight for their economic survival and are therefore susceptible to populist claims.

The indifferent attitude of those in the passive sphere toward the law therefore contradicts their own interests, because only a narrow minority is capable of using a state that does not take the law too seriously. Nonetheless, it is understandable that the passive sphere relies on an authoritarian power that does not necessarily respect the law. The "firm hand" of the president promises to take up their cause swiftly and decisively. Moreover, the majority of the Russian population regards the liberal NGOs, which are worried about their autonomy, as a "foreign Western body" that disrupts the "natural hierarchical order."

The majority of Russian society is anti-European, anti-American, and, in fact, is generally oriented against the West—in the sense that the European Union (EU), the West European states, and the United States are seen as enemies, at least potential ones. For this majority, Putin is an extremely credible president in whom the badly educated, older, and poor people not living in the major Russian cities show the most confidence. He benefits from the fact that most Russians apparently support those institutions that are not legitimized democratically, such as the Russian Orthodox Church and the army. Dmitrii Furman summarizes: "The transition from Yeltsin to Putin was carried out practically without the participation of the people, and the elections of the president were marked by the practical absence of an alternative candidate. These elections were like the ritual of the oath on the new monarch. This oath legitimizes his power completely."[35] The same can be said of Putin's reelection in March 2004.

This constellation of Russian societal actors demonstrates the depressing continuity of conditions that have always been characteristic of Russian noncivil society. The "alliance" between the majority of the population and the political leadership, which is derived from the conviction that the state's efficiency is more important than its regard for the law, also has consequences for both Russia's political culture and for the way Russia deals with others.

Russia's Political Culture and Demand for Law

The fact that most Russians prefer an all-responsible state controlled by a firm hand to a constitutional state should not be neglected when analyzing the legal culture or when examining Russia's political culture.[36] The latter's transformation can at the very least influence the knowledge and expectations of the legal system and the behavior within it. It goes without saying that not every change in a political culture will strengthen the demand for law and a constitutional state.

It is apparent that, after communism, the areas of Russia's political culture to be changed were those essential to the very existence of the society and the state. It was in this context, at the end of the Soviet Union, that the question was posed as to whether Russia would structure its future as a kind of multinational empire or as a Russian (nation-) state.[37] Both options implied a serious transformation of the political culture that had been inherited from communism.

At the turn of the 1980s and 1990s, a number of surveys about Soviet society still created the impression that the Russian population's political culture was in the middle of just such a fundamental transformation. Iurii Levada, who, in the years 1989–1991, carried out the most revealing empirical study into Soviet society, analyzed the "sociocultural type of the 'simple Soviet man' (*prostoi sovetskii chelovek*): a deeply frustrated and divided person, who is not capable of coping with his own everyday relationships or of changing them."[38]

According to Levada, this type of person, who is also to be found in other modern societies, dominated Russian society in the era of Soviet rule. The "simple Soviet man" was defined by antinomy. He combined a conviction of his own historical uniqueness with a latent readiness to place foreigners in higher esteem than himself; he was capable of hoping for a public welfare system while at the same time concealing his suspicion of the state; he recognized the state's hierarchy while at the same time latently believing in egalitarianism; and finally, he was characterized both by an imperial attitude and a hidden frustration of a suppressed ethnic identity.[39] The Soviet governmental and societal structures of the Stalin and Brezhnev eras were complementary to this personality type. Because these structures collapsed in 1989 to 1991, Levada interpreted the data he had collected as the "abolishment of the Soviet man."

Levada, however, did not lapse into cheap optimism. Although he tended toward the premature assumption that the young generation—in contrast to their parents and grandparents—had already overcome the characteristics of the "Soviet man," he regarded the future of Russian society as being uncertain. On the one hand, Russians still felt driven toward collectivism and had problems with their national identity as well as with their (somewhat strange) historical consciousness.[40] On the other hand, Levada left it in no doubt that the belief held by many respondents, namely, that the differences between the Western world and Russia were not too great to be bridged, should not have too much importance attached to it. According to the Russian opinion pollster, this belief merely represented "the primitive expectation of a Western miracle" and not the readiness to tread the difficult path that would lead to the realization of their own human potential.[41]

More recent empirical findings dating from the second half of the 1990s[42] verify nothing of the profound change expected by the optimists, but rather a consolidation of Russia's political culture. Even the "aggressive" Russian youth, to whom Levada had attributed a significant potential for transformation a few years before, had, in the meantime, accepted the history of the Soviet society as its own.[43]

In Central Europe, despite the disappointment in the consequences of postcommunist transformation, the end of communism was considered as being a (very slow) "transition to normality." Unlike this, even in 1995, 17 percent of all Russians questioned contended that the Brezhnev period of the Soviet Union should be regarded as the period in history that the Russians should be proud of. At the same time, the overwhelming majority of Russians were proud of imperial Russia (a total of 77 percent).[44] In this respect, the statistic 17 percent, is witness to an unusual bond with the era of communist "stagnation."

All in all, it is not possible to talk about a break of today's political culture with the heritage of the "Soviet man." This disappointing finding should not, however, be interpreted one-sidedly. The durability of the political culture was one of the main reasons that Russian society did not utterly disintegrate during the social and political upheavals of the 1990s.[45]

Acceptance of the communist past goes hand in hand with the transformation of ethnic consciousness that could be seen in the 1990s. Even those Russians who, during the communist era, attached no importance to ethnic identities, or for whom ethnic identity played a less important role, have become aware of their own national identity. Nowadays, Russians regard themselves increasingly as the ethnicity that constitutes the state. While doing this, they positively recognize their "national idiosyncrasies," which they comprehend in terms of the uniqueness of their history and civilization.[46]

Finally, turning to the empirical findings that reveal information about the concrete political attitudes of Russians toward the constitutional state, one is confronted with a diffuse picture. The majority of Russians highlight the close connection between democracy and a constitutional state, for instance. In this context, they particularly support equality before the law and the independence of the courts. At the same time, however, they show extraordinary indifference when it comes to supporting the rights of the individual, local self-administration, and compliance with legally established political procedures.[47]

The public opinion of the Russians when regarding the Russian relationship to the EU, to Europe, and the West as a whole demonstrates yet another antinomy of their political culture. In 1998, some 20 percent of those questioned declared that they would trust the EU. At the same time, only around 2 percent of the respondents stated that they would support a movement to join the EU. These statistics would not be regarded as inconclusive if at the same time 70 percent of those questioned had not categorized Russian culture as belonging to the Western end of the "Eurasian scale" (44.3 percent even saw Russian national character as being "Western").[48]

Naturally, the interpretation of findings about the political culture of any given society will throw up contradictions. It would be extremely naive to believe that one could form a coherent conception of politics and polity from such findings. Even with the generous assumption that Russian opinions are not distinguished by an unusual level of contradiction in international comparison, these opinions do not provide a basis for the hope that the change in Russian political culture could strengthen the weak demand for law. Indirectly, these findings support the thesis that the political leadership and the elites as a whole play a central role in the Russian transformation process.[49] Through their consistent actions the political class is able to consciously establish parameters for cultural continuity and cultural transformation. It is not only in Russia that the political class is failing miserably in this task.

Without Respect for the Law:
A Misguided Understanding of the EU

Russia has had a lot of experience in incorporating foreign cultures. The imperial history of Russia and the Soviet Union is a history of the assimilation of societies that starkly differed from Russia, above all in their legal culture. In order to achieve this, imperial Russia or the Soviet Union normally relied on the destruction of the traditional legal institutions in the societies it wished to assimilate. Still, this forced assimilation was not completely successful and in some cases it failed completely. However, it must be said that the Soviet Union was more successful in this respect than imperial Russia.

Based on the example of the Commonwealth of Independent States (CIS), it can be seen that Russia has apparently learned little from its own history. Among the CIS states, not one of which is a functional constitutional state, Russia appears as a hegemonic power. Russia knows two methods for advancing the integration of neighboring foreign countries. In a conflict of interest between Russia and one of the former Soviet republics (even if it is not a CIS member), the Kremlin relentlessly makes use of political, economic, or military pressure.[50] If, on the other hand, no conflicts of interest arise, Moscow can grant quite generous political, economic, and military support.

The process of European integration, as it has developed since the 1950s, is based on the fundamental compatibility of the participating subjects. This compatibility relies on the one hand, on the structural similarity of integrated subjects as constitutional states and on the other hand, on the similarity in their legal cultures. It is therefore possible to talk about a "European family of legal cultures." These similarities make possible serious conflicts of interests between the concerned states without threat to the framework of the European Union.

Under these circumstances, it is common for stronger (larger or more economically developed) members of the European Union not to be able to prevail over supposed "weaker" states should conflicts of interest arise. This is the indirect result of the fact that the "weak" as well as the "stronger" actors act within a supranational legal framework, which is considered legitimate by all players. This framework arose out of the voluntary renunciation of important parts of the sovereignty of all the states concerned, which then developed further in terms of federal principles. Both the smaller European states and the former European global powers (England and Spain) and the would-be global powers (France and Germany) have proved themselves capable of giving up this sovereignty. None of this would have been possible if the EU states did not share the same legal culture. The transfer of principles from the constitutional state to the supranational level eases the slow departure from world power or great power status for the largest European states, which in practice has long since been completed.

The Russian legal culture of arbitrary rule could not lead to a similar accomplishment after the loss of global power status. On the contrary, in Russia the fear prevails that the enormous country would ultimately have to give up its dreams of global power as a member of the EU. This fear is as justified as Russian hopes of reattaining world power status are unjustified, because if there were to be a new power in Eurasia in the near future, then it would be neither Russia nor China. The only possible candidate for a new Eurasian global power is the European Union.

Without the positive experience of a constitutional state of their own, Russia and the Russians will remain incapable of subjecting themselves to current European laws and the coming "European constitution." Even the Europe-friendly Russian politicians who plead for an institutional rapprochement toward the EU understand "Brussels" as the power center of the European Union. They would prefer to bring their own country into this center as a decision-making authority. The partial dissolution of the Russian state through the transfer to the EU of sovereign rights such as financial or—in future—foreign policy matters would be out of the question. They assume that Brussels could be brought to share its power with an integrated Russian state. This completely unrealistic point of view reflects not only the inability to accept the legitimate legal power structures of the European Union as their own, but also the conception prevailing among Russians that every power structure is centralized, which they use to explain EU federalism. The Russian misunderstanding of federalism and European integration is based on the same underlying cause, namely, the anti-Western legal culture.

Russia's Westernization

Of all the possible factors that could help to answer the question of Russian compatibility with the European Union—geography, its affiliation with European culture, the elites' willingness to integrate, its level of modernization, and its degree of integration in world markets—the presence of a functional constitutional state is of prime importance. The development of such a state represents the central scenario of Russia's adaptation to the structural and cultural reality of the EU. Alternative scenarios, which are repeatedly named in this context, often distract from Russia's most important problems. These scenarios, which would indeed ease the development of a functional constitutional state but cannot replace it, are the following: "Europeanization," "Americanization," "integration into the global market," and "modernization."

We begin with Europeanization. What is meant by this? Should Russian culture, which has developed over centuries, be traded in as quickly as possible and replaced with European culture? This is not possible. First of all, geographically, a third of Russia lies in Europe and was always involved in European affairs and their cultural context. That has not changed, even under the communists who attempted to destroy the national culture. The Russians read the same classics of European literature that Western and Central European (as well as American) students are supposed to read (but usually do not). Educated Russians listen to the same music and enjoy the same pieces of artwork as educated Central and West Europeans and Americans. Aside from this, and their Christian origins, there is no single "European culture," but rather a connected multiplicity of European folk and national cultures. This multiplicity allows the Russian culture to be considered just as European as the cultures of France, Hungary, or the Roma.

Does it then refer to the issue of the Europeanization of Russia in a religious context? Must the Russian Orthodox Church be replaced with the Catholic or Protestant churches? It is true that the claim to religious monopoly in Russia, which is still represented today by the Russian Orthodox Church, is reminiscent of the times before the Reformation in Western Europe. It is also true that the closeness of the Russian Orthodox Church and the state appears quite peculiar to Westerners. However, it cannot be forgotten that, despite the peculiar characteristics of the Russian Orthodox Church, Russia has secularized in a fashion similar to the other "Christian" societies in Europe. The rather unconscious religiously motivated moral pretensions are always subordinated to self-interest, both in those "Christian" societies and in Russia, usually at the expense of the politically weak. The tacit approval of genocide in Chechnya by the majority of Europeans, Russians, and Americans demonstrates this most vividly today.

Turning to the Americanization of Russia, it makes little sense to create an artificial contrast to Europeanization. Americanization, which is without a doubt observable in Russia, concerns superficial changes in lifestyle. Russian students wear the American cap and gown during their graduation celebrations; Russians watch more and more products of the American film industry and go to McDonald's en masse. In fact, while this Americanization depicts an interesting cultural phenomenon, its earthshaking significance apparently exists only for intellectuals. Incidentally, these Americanizing changes in lifestyle are just as vehemently criticized in Russia as they are in France, Germany, and elsewhere in Europe. In this regard, Russians already hardly differ from Europeans, so that there is no need for Europeanization in this area.

Nowadays, there is a tendency to overestimate the importance of material, and above all economic, factors for societal development. This appears to be the most important reason why many observers call for Russia's integration into the global market and Russia's economic modernization as the central prerequisites for integration into the EU. In doing so it is often forgotten that good economic development and successful economic cooperation with the outside world can exist even if a functional constitutional state is lacking—Saudi Arabia and the Asian Tigers provide clear examples.

With regard to modernity, it cannot be overlooked that Russia underwent an intensive communist modernization, with the result that today it is not a traditional, that is, an agrarian, rural, or uneducated society, but is by all means a modern society, though not in the Western sense. In this book modernity is defined normatively as general prosperity, some degree of social equity, and good governance.[51] This definition is closely connected with the societal development of Western countries and this is the reason for its normative connection of "efficient" and "modern." It is no coincidence that even today's Russian *zapadniki* (Westernizers) understand modernization as a process through which Russia can decrease its shortfall in terms of development.[52]

To do justice to the particularities of Russian development, however, it is helpful to complement the normative understanding of modernization with an empirical concept, defining the latter in terms of economic, social, and cultural processes based on industrialization, division of labor, rational state bureaucracy, growing prosperity, and so on. From this empirical point of view, the numerous social, economic, and political developments during the Soviet era must be understood as processes of modernization that the state forced upon a society deprived of its rights.

The state's confiscation of society's rights, a characteristic of national Russian tradition as well as of Soviet totalitarianism, is to blame for the seemingly paradoxical fact that Russia today can be regarded as being at once quite modern and in dire need of modernization. This apparently modern Russia has shown itself today as incapable of realizing the principles that are important for a modern Western civil society—namely, the autonomy of economics and politics as well as the primacy of the individual over the collective. These principles are not even rudimentarily realizable without an effective limitation of political authority through laws and a constitution.

In sum: Russia is European, integrated into global markets, in some way modern, and, if need be, also "American" enough, to be considered seriously for integration into the European Union. The fact that it differs culturally in many respects from the other European nations does not necessarily have to be a barrier to its integration. The European nations are also culturally different from one another in many respects. At the same time, they are culturally similar insofar as they all respect their respective laws and legal systems. The same is true of other nations that are considered to be Western. Thus the functional constitutional state is the common core of Western society. The creation of a functional constitutional state essentially means therefore the Westernization of society. Russia must Westernize itself in order to become compatible with Europe.

It is common knowledge that fundamental changes in legal culture take a long time. However, it should not be ignored that societies undergoing profound system transformation have better chances of furthering cultural change than do saturated Western societies. Meanwhile, despite the completed consolidation of the political system in Russia, its transformation into a modern constitutional state can still be consciously pushed ahead. While the quasi-democratic authoritarian political system has been consolidated, Russian society remains, as before, in an ongoing process of change. The political leadership could use this situation to increase the demand for law to facilitate the emergence of civil society.

Unfortunately, it is not expected that the following measures, which would serve these aims, will be put into practice by today's political leadership:

- a constitutional amendment that separates the constitutional court from the Kremlin (the appointment of judges only by the parliament);
- the dissolution of the *partiia vlasti*, which prevents the expansion of the Russian party system and a strengthening of Russian parliamentarianism;
- most importantly, the practice of self-constraint by the Kremlin, expressed in a respect for the law at all costs.

There are, however, signs that the political leadership could improve the economic conditions for the development of civil society. It can be assumed that the state's slow and unwilling retreat out of the economy cannot be held back. This would contribute toward solving

> the fundamental problem behind the weak legal system in Russia . . . that the state extracts too great a proportion of resources, redistributes too much, intervenes too much in enterprises, and is too strong in relation to both enterprises and the public. At the same time the state does not represent sufficiently the public interests but is overly concerned instead with the private interests of a few large and politically favored enterprises. The state is weak, in the sense of representing the interests of the public, since, because it is too large, society is unable to control it through legal and political means.[53]

The introduction of the flat tax shows that even the authoritarian leadership is capable of improving this situation. Although this reform also served the political center and in reality only superficially lowered the tax burden, it has proven itself to be a fiscal success.[54] Simplification of the tax system has obviously taken place as a reaction to companies' increasing need for legal security. The "Western" principle, whereby private property increases the demand for law, already functions in Russia today. The demand for law would increase even more if the Russian middle class expands. Generally it must be assumed that the important impulses for a functional Russian constitutional state will come primarily from the economy. The growing use of the *arbitrazh* courts that deal among others with disputes between enterprises and the state can be traced back to a new state policy of "dictatorship of law."[55] But nonetheless it shows a new trend that may lead to an increased independence of the judicial system.

The state remains the main problem for Russian society. Conversely, Russian society remains the state's main problem. Only Russia can get itself out of this dilemma. The West cannot exercise any direct influence. The indirect medium- and long-term influence of the West should not be regarded as irrelevant.

What Can the West Do?

Unless a country is occupied by a foreign power over a long period, we cannot expect its culture to be changed enduringly by an outside force. This holds true for the inability of Western actors (among them the United States, the EU, and the international institutions dominated by the West) to Westernize Russia. Still, they can transmit selected impulses for the desired institutional and cultural changes. In order for this to happen, four requirements must be met.

- First, it is necessary for the West to recognize Russian reality for what it is: a state and a society that are neither democratic nor civil. Western politicians and analysts hurt Russia especially when, out of arrogance or ignorance, they use different criteria to judge the Russian constitutional state from those they use for their own states. The debate among Western politicians, academics, and journalists about "Russian democracy" only helps the enemies of constitutional democracy within Russia. If the West wants to foster Russia's modernization, it must not harm Russian constitutionalism by taking it for something it is not.
- Second, Western actors must give top priority to the aim of Westernization (i.e., the development of a functioning constitutional state) concerning their policies toward Russia. In practice, this means that these actors in their respective relationships to Russia will have to subordinate their own short-term interests, which are sometimes contradictory, to this most important aim. Western politics toward Russia are often legitimized through the complacent claim that it will profit from any form of cooperation with the West. This

claim will have to be given up. For example, it would help to abandon the self-righteous notion that Western companies active in Russia provide considerable impulses toward the creation of a Russian constitutional state. The truth is, rather, that these companies adapt to the realities of any market—even those of the "Russian market"—as soon as they see a chance for profit.
- Third, the efforts of the West to provide impulses for the desired changes in Russia will be futile if the Russian side sees no hope that change in certain areas would serve Russian interests. Only once this requirement has been met can we expect that efforts will be made to tackle difficult reforms in Russia.
- Fourth—and finally—these reforms should aim to create equality between the partners. As a result of these efforts, Russia should be able to enjoy the same rights and be obliged to fulfill the same duties as its Western partners.

These four requirements may be analyzed through the example of the long process that was supposed to prepare Russia for membership in the World Trade Organization (WTO). First, the principle of realistic perception: The West is well aware that Russia still has a nonmarket economy. Second, the principle of highest priority: It is of vital interest to the West (especially the United States and the EU) for Russia to create a working market economy, as this would drive forward the country's Westernization. For this reason, the West is urging the Russian economy to liberalize both internally and externally, a process that should make Russian membership in the WTO possible. Third, the principle of safeguarding interests: The Russian leadership understands quite well that the status of a nonmarket economy costs their country billions of U.S. dollars per annum. In 2003, some 120 costly antidumping actions from Western countries were in place against Russia. Fourth, the principle of equality: Membership in the WTO would confirm that Russia has attained the status of a market economy that Western countries, who are long-standing members of the General Agreement on Tariffs and Trade and the WTO, already enjoy. The antidumping actions would consequently be referred to the WTO's dispute settling mechanism, considerably lowering Russia's expenses in settling conflicts over access to the Russian market and the dumping prices of Russian products.

It is evident that the Russians themselves will have to deal with the most difficult parts of the efforts to join the WTO:

> Implementation and enforcement of existing rules is likely to represent a significant problem for Russia's WTO accession. Russia's customs administration is notorious for inefficiency and corruption. The government has undertaken steps to make the system more transparent and to reduce opportunities for bribe-taking. But change will be slow as long as salaries of less than $20 per month effectively force customs officials to seek alternative sources of revenue. The situation is similar in other branches of administration, with the result that legislation is often arbitrarily enforced. Seeking remedies in court can be time-consuming and frustrating.[56]

Still, this example illustrates not only the problems but also the chances for an externally induced process of Westernization in areas important for Russian transformation.

Yet another important area today in relation to cooperation between the West and Russia is embodied in the "war on terror" led by the United States. However, in this regard, Western actors are proving themselves to be utterly unable to provide any impulse at all for Westernization of Russia.

- First, the realistic view of Russia's role in this war has been consciously repressed due to political opportunism. This is because the Kremlin wants to have its war against the Chechens acknowledged as a part of the global war against terrorism. Because the American administration occasionally needs support from Russia in its struggle against international terrorism, George W. Bush has demonstrated a willingness to turn a blind eye to Russian policies toward Chechnya. Paris and Berlin go even further. In their policies toward Russia, German Chancellor Gerhard Schröder and French President Jacques Chirac completely neglected its internal developments because they wanted to win Putin over in order to form a kind of alliance against the United States.
- Second, there can be no doubt that the war against terrorism currently receives much higher priority than the Westernization of Russia in both the United States and the EU.
- Third, facing such a constellation of interests, it is not possible for Russia to find a reliable partner in a quarreling West. Moreover, it is successfully attempting to exploit this contentiousness for its imperial Caucasian policies and other aims.
- Fourth, in the "war on terror" the West has from the start refrained from demanding that Russia comply with the norms that the Western states reproach each other for infringing.

In summary, the limited opportunities available to the West to exercise influence over the cultural changes in Russia are wasted whenever they act against their own values and norms. Because a significant change in this behavior is not to be expected, Western assistance with long-term aims, especially from the EU, must lie in the advancement of education in Russia. As many students as possible should have the opportunity to become acquainted with the Western legal system firsthand, in the hope that they would then return to Russia after their studies in the West and, for idealistic reasons, not adapt to the realities of their homeland.

New members of the EU cannot have a sizable positive influence on the Russian legal culture. They are culturally too far apart and politically too weak for this to happen. However, the Polish influence on Ukraine and Belarus, which the Russians considered to be their "Slavic brothers," should not be completely overlooked. Certain impulses from below are necessary for cultural change in Russia, which historically has always been influenced by extensive exchange between Poland on the one side and the Ukrainian and Belarusian lands on the other. Therefore the EU, acting out of egocentricity, made the mistake of compelling Poland to introduce a visa for the Belarusians, the Ukrainians, and the Russians during the negotiations for Poland's entry to the EU. Whether this measure is withdrawn will depend on the extended, freedom-loving EU.

Notes

1. Roger Cotterrel, "The Concept of Legal Culture" in *Comparing Legal Cultures*, ed. David Nelken (Aldershot: Dartmouth, 1997), pp. 13–39, 16.
2. The legal culture can accordingly be understood in terms of both ideas and behavior. In the first case, it comprises the knowledge as well as the attitudes toward and expectations of the law and the legal system. In contrast, the behavioral concept can be taken to mean at least partially institutionalized patterns of behavior in relation to the law and the legal system, which have evolved over time. See Cotterel, "The Concept of Legal Culture," pp. 15, 21–22. The analysis of the mutual relations between the two concepts is not the aim of this chapter. In this context it is enough to point out that knowledge, attitudes, and expectations with respect to the law and the legal system represent a predisposition to ways of behaving within the respective legal systems.
3. This discussion is mainly carried out in *East European Constitutional Review* 8, no. 4 (Fall 1999): 88–108.
4. Kathryn Hendley, "Rewriting the Rules of the Game in Russia: The Neglected Issue of the Demand for Law," *East European Constitutional Review* 8, no. 4 (Fall 1999): 89–95, 90.
5. "Zashchita Chubaisa," *Moskovskie novosti*, no. 28, July 23–29, 2002.
6. This concept of the civil society, which goes back to Hegel, was designed by the anticommunist resistance in Central Europe in the 1970s and the 1980s to cope with the task of analyzing the totalitarian claim of unlimited control of the society. The narrow concept of the civil society often appears in a utopian version, if it postulates the establishment of a state-free society. It gains analytical traits, especially when referring to independent actors of the civil society (which is conceptualized in the broad sense).
7. The "civil society" (as a political society) has been discussed in the West only since the eighteenth century. Ernest Gellner is among the few authors in the 1990s who have supported the broad concept of the civil society (including the state). However, he does not mention the constitutional state in his concept. See Ernest Gellner, *Conditions of Liberty: Civil Society and Its Rivals* (London: Hamish Hamilton, 1994).
8. See Richard Pipes, *Property and Freedom* (New York: Vintage Books, 1999), pp. 121–57.
9. For the definition of patrimonial rule see Pipes, *Property and Freedom*, pp. 159–61.
10. Marc Raeff, *Understanding Imperial Russia: State and Society in the Old Regime*, trans. Arthur Goldhammer (New York: Columbia University Press, 1984), pp. 141–42.
11. Ibid. pp. 122.
12. Jarosław Bratkiewicz, *Wielkoruski szowinizm w swietle teorii kontynuacji* (Warsaw: Instytut Studiów Politycznych, 1991), pp. 108–35.
13. Jerzy Maćków, *Die Konstruktion politischer Stabilität. Polen und Russland in den Umbrüchen der achtziger und neunziger Jahre* (Baden-Baden: Nomos Verlagsgesellschaft, 1998), pp. 167–99.
14. T.E. Vorozheikina, "Gosudarstvo i obshchestvo v Rossii," *Polis*, no. 4 (2002), pp. 60–65, 62.
15. Valerii Masterov, "Magnat poprosil o rasstrele," *Moskovskie novosti*, no. 1, January 21–27, 2003.

16. Timothy Frye, "Keeping Shop: The Value of the Rule of Law in Warsaw and Moscow" in *Assessing the Value of Law in Transition Economies*, ed. Peter Murrell (Ann Arbor: University of Michigan Press, 2001), pp. 228–48, 245–46.

17. Georg Brunner, "Rechtskultur in Osteuropa: Das Problem der Kulturgrenzen," in *Politische und ökonomische Transformation in Osteuropa*, ed. Georg Brunner (Berlin: Berlin Verlag, 1996), pp. 91–112.

18. Not even the apologists of the Russian path to development contest the justification of using this term. Viktor A. Kulinchenko and Aleksandr V. Kulinchenko, "O dukhovno-kul'turnykh osnovaniiakh modernizatsii Rossii," *Polis*, no. 2 (2003): 150–56, 155.

19. Maćków, *Die Konstruktion politischer Stabilität*, pp. 120–25.

20. Vorozheikina, "Gosudarstvo i obshchestvo v Rossii," p. 61.

21. Viktor Loshak, "Perevod strelok vruchnuiu," *Moskovskie novosti*, no. 43, November 5–11, 2002.

22. Jerzy Maćków, "Jelzins Erbe: Die präsidentielle Staatsgewalt im politischen System Russlands," *Zeitschrift für Parlamentsfragen* 3, no. 4 (September 2000): 635–56, 654.

23. Jens Siegert, Ökoheld oder Vaterlandsverräter? Der Fall Pas'ko–Ein ehrstück über Russlands defekten Rechtsstaat," *Osteuropa-Spezial* (April 2002): 41–54.

24. This group of replies presupposes that the sentence does not yet have the force of the law behind it. See Siegert, *Ökoheld oder Vaterlandsverrpäter?* p. 52.

25. Elke Fein, "Zivilgesellschaftlicher Paradigmawechsel oder PR-Aktion. Zum ersten allrussischen 'Bürgerforum' im Kreml," *Osteuropa-Spezial* (April 2002): 19–40, 20–22.

26. These are the words of the astronaut Leonov, during the said meeting in the Kremlin, quoted from Elke Fein, "Zivilgesellschaftlicher Paradigmawechsel oder PR-Aktion," pp. 19–40, 23–24.

27. Depending on the income status of those questioned, they were placed into one of four categories according to this criterion.

28. M.K. Gorshkov et al., *Rossiia na rubezhe vekov* (Moscow: RNISiNP ROSSPEN, 2000), p. 290.

29. Hendly, "Rewriting the Rules of the Game in Russia," pp. 92–94.

30. Viktor A. Kulinchenko and Aleksandr V. Kulinchenko, "O dukhovno-kul'turnykh osnovaniiakh modernizatsii Rossii." *Polis*, no. 2 (2003): 150–56.

31. Ibid., p. 156.

32. Boris Vishnevskii, "Ten', znai svoe mesto," *Moskovskie novosti*, no. 16, April 29–May 4, 2003.

33. Anita Bister, "Handlungsspielräume der zivilen Gesellschaft in Russland," *Zur Demokratisierung Russlands. Vol. 2. Leadership, Parteien, Regionen und Zivilgesellschaft*, ed. Gerhard Mangott (Baden-Baden: Nomos Verlagsgesellschaft, 2002), pp. 117–60, 124–25.

34. Leonid Radzikhovskii, *Nezavisimaia gazeta*, no. 222, November 28, 2001. Quoted from Fein, "Zivilgesellschaftlicher Paradigmawechsel oder PR–Aktion," p. 38.

35. Dmitrii Furman, "Ia ochen' doveriaiu prezidentu," *Moskovskie novosti*, no. 473, December 3–9, 2002.

36. Here, political culture is understood in the classical sense, as the "subjective side of politics," as "the particular patterns of [cognitive, affective, and evaluational] orientation toward political objects of the nation." Gabriel A. Almond and Sidney Verba, *The Civic Culture: Political Attitudes and Democracy in Five Nations* (Princeton: Princeton University Press, 1963), pp. 14ff.

37. Gerhard Simon, "Russland: Imperiale Restauration oder national-staatlicher Neubeginn," in *Osteuropa zwischen Nationalstaat und Integration*, ed. Georg Brunner (Berlin: Berlin Verlag, 1995), pp. 91–104.

38. Juri Lewada (Iurii Levada), *Die Sowjetmenschen 1989–1991. Soziogramm eines Zerfalls* (Munich: Deutscher Taschenbuch-Verlag, 1993), p. 295.

39. Ibid., p. 170.
40. Ibid., pp. 302–3.
41. Ibid., p. 295.
42. Gorshkov et al., *Rossiia na rubezhe vekov.* In this book the results of sociological studies carried out in 1995–2000 by members of the Russian Independent Institute for Social and National Problems (RNISiNP) have been collected. These studies were undertaken on behalf of the Friedrich-Ebert-Stiftung.
43. Refer to Gorshkov et al., *Rossiia na rubezhe vekov,* pp. 116, 129–73.
44. A full 54 percent of those people asked stated that they felt proud of the era of Peter the Great. Cf. Gorshkov et al., *Rossiia na rubezhe vekov,* p. 12.
45. Ibid., pp. 242–43.
46. Ibid., pp. 243–44.
47. Ibid., p. 247.
48. Ibid., pp. 230, 228.
49. See chapter 5 in this book, by Lilia Shevtsova, "Political Leadership in Russia's Transformation."
50. See chapter 9 in this book, by Oleksandr Pavliuk, about the relationship of Russia to Belarus, Moldova, and the Ukraine, "Russia's Integration with the West and the States 'in Between.'"
51. See the introduction and conclusion in this book, by Alexander J. Motyl, Blair A. Ruble, and Lilia Shevtsova.
52. In this context Leontii Byzov talks about the "adherents of catch-up modernization" (in contrast to the supporters of an "organic modernization," which takes into consideration the path of development that evolved naturally in the course of Russian history). Leontii Byzov, "Stanovlenie novoi politicheskoi identichnosti v postsovetskoi Rossii: Evolutsia sotsial'no-politicheskikh orientatsii i obshchestvennogo zaprosa" in *Rossiiskoe obshchestvo: Stanovlenie demokraticheskikh tsennostei?* ed. Michael McFaul and Andrei Riabov (Moscow: Moskovskii Tsentr Karnegi, 1999), pp. 43–86, 52.
53. Anders Åslund, "Law in Russia," *East European Constitutional Review* 8, no. 4 (Fall 1999): 96–101, 98.
54. Jacob Fruchtmann, "Steuern durch Macht–Macht durch Steuern. Die russische Steuerpolitik unter Putin," *Osteuropa-Spezial* (April 2002): 85–100.
55. Kathryn Hendley interprets this tendency more optimistically. Kathryn Hendley, "Suing the State in Russia," *Post-Soviet Affairs* 18, no. 2 (2002): 122–147, 137.
56. Katinka Barysh, "Russia's Long Road to the WTO" (2003); available at www.agendapublishing.com/onlinepastpubs/093–barysh.pdf (April 20, 2004).

3

Russian Culture and Integration into the West

Yuri Senokosov
(Translated from Russian by Mark Dadian)

> Every culture is an island. It communicates with other islands,
> but ultimately it can only experience tragedy and
> laughter in its own climate.
>
> Arthur Koestler, *An Autobiography*

Russia never went through the Reformation, which fostered the spiritual renewal of Europe. And Russia never had its age of Enlightenment. Why? The shortest explanation is that serfdom was abolished only in 1861 and the system of Russian autocracy collapsed only in 1917 with war and revolution. It was then swiftly restored after the civil war in the form of a totalitarian regime.

Hence today, when we speak about Russia's transition to a new, more Western phase in its history—one with rule of law and freedom of intellectual expression—it is important to consider both the distant past that shaped the psychology and culture of the Russian people (their mentality, lifestyle, and modes of perception of the outside world), and the seventy-year legacy of communist rule.

In other words, one must remember that at the beginning of the twentieth century, at the time of the Bolshevik coup and the civil war, the balance of Russian history see-sawed between centuries of autocratic slavery and short-lived decades of young political freedom, which appeared in Russia after the abolition of serfdom. At that time the balance tilted in favor of totalitarian dictatorship.

Today Russia is going through a difficult, torturous, but, in my opinion, final, stage of this historical tragedy, a stage characterized by the totalitarian legacy, and, simultaneously, the gradual restoration of the once substantive liberal-democratic values and institutions. As time passes Russia will change. The lessons of recent history when the Soviet Union and the West were equally dependent on the ideology of threats and confrontation tell us that this has to be the case.

The Burden of Greatness

Why is it that some nations originate, become vassal states, and remain small, while others become victorious and create empires, thereby winning a right to greatness? In the context of macrohistorical processes the answer seems obvious: Empires are created by the might and craft of their rulers. But then another question arises. Why do empires collapse, and, in the twentieth century, transform into modern developed democracies? This question might also appear rhetorical because history suggests an answer. As George Orwell aptly remarked in an article on Kipling, an empire is primarily a militant "money-making concern," and the very motives that call empires to life become the cause of their ruin.[1]

Nonetheless, as the Soviet Union lost its race with the West, the Western countries in the post–World War II period, leaning on the traditional values of European culture and the achievements of scientific and technical progress, were able to modify the former "imperial" institutions, thus resolving a fundamental dilemma between human rights and national sovereignty. In the meantime Russia, still nostalgic for its Soviet past, is on a toilsome road to progress and is experiencing difficulties in realizing its place in the world.

During a transition period, the chief indicator of social development is the state of mass consciousness. Therefore, let us consider Russia from the standpoint of the dilemma noted above: the contradiction between human rights and the idea of national sovereignty. For the purposes of this analysis we take as a starting point a sociologic poll conducted jointly by the All-Russian Center for the Study of Public Opinion (VTsIOM) and the Moscow School of Political Studies in 1999.[2] One should also bear in mind that the Soviet Union was a self-contained system whose main goals were the construction of communism and the buildup of military potential for purposes of the preservation and global proliferation of communist ideology. In postwar Europe, however, national defense problems did not eclipse human rights issues in domestic and foreign policy. The reasons are obvious: the final collapse of the colonial empires and the gradual weakening of Europeans' "imperious ambitions."

Given that less than ten years had passed since the breakup of the Soviet Union, the poll produced a well-expected pattern. Even though the majority of respondents (72 percent of 2,000 sampled) in 1999 no longer thought of Russia as a great power, almost the same number felt sorry about the breakup of the Soviet Union. In the meantime 65 percent (in March 1999) and 54 percent (in August 2000)[3] of respondents still perceived the West—and specifically the United States—as a threat to Russia's national security. After September 11, 2001, the general Russian attitude toward the West changed dramatically, yet this did not result in any notable integration progress because of the country's persistent dogmatic belief in the inviolability of state sovereignty.

What is the situation of human rights in Russia? How prevalent is this problem today? According to the 1999 poll—and this is not surprising when we consider

Russia's communist past and the economic conditions in the country following the financial crisis—social rights occupied the top position (68 percent of respondents gave priority to free education, health care, and social welfare in general). As to those who opted for civic rights (the right to information, elected representation in the power structures, freedom of speech, conscience, and movement), their aggregate share was much lower. Still this number was slightly higher than the share of those respondents who were ready to support the reforms, "to force the state to serve their interests" (almost one-third of the country's population). In this connection consider another figure. To the question "What idea could best unite society?" 31 percent of respondents replied "a decent life." In other words, the idea of a life appropriate for a free citizen. With all the semantic connotations of the word "decent," I think that the respondents had this in mind.

Yet what is the impediment to such a life? And why do I associate the life of a man cognizant of his rights with the idea of national sovereignty, placing them in a mutually dependent relationship? Is there a contradiction here? This contradiction exists in contemporary Russia. It is noteworthy that some of those Russians who "yearn for the past greatness" still express sound civic views. I do not regard the situation as hopeless: First, because people's aspiration for change is at the same time an aspiration for stability that can evolve in the new Russia on the basis of human rights and freedoms; and second, because life itself shall resolve this contradiction, although this will take time. Here I am tempted to draw an analogy.

It is known that in the twentieth-century scientific community there was a period of misunderstanding and even animosity between the supporters of classical and nonclassical physics—until modern technologies proved that Newtonian and quantum mechanics do not negate each other. Deriving from this analogy and the results of the sociological poll, I am emphasizing that Russia's incorporation into the Western community directly depends on the understanding by the country's population that civic rights and political freedoms will not destroy the country. In this connection I cite data from another poll.

When answering the question, "In your opinion, what is the first characteristic of a great power?," 39 percent of respondents surveyed by VTsIOM in October 2000 were inclined to associate their country's greatness with the observation of human rights and freedoms. Usually, in a crisis situation, a human being is either trying to adjust himself passively or, conversely, imposing himself, seeking personal gain, that is, enrichment, power, or publicity. Either way a man is always looking for a way out (the original meaning of the Greek "crisis" implies the search for an escape, a solution, an outcome, an argument). In this connection, a passage from the memoirs of Otto von Bismarck is relevant:

A state that is governed by the greedy, by the *novarum rerum cupidi* [those who strive for innovations] and by the orators, who are most capable of deceiving the unreasonable masses, such state shall always be consigned to impetuous development, which cannot but cause bad damage to an organism of such huge weight as the body politic. The cumbersome masses of the great nations in the process of their life and development should only advance carefully, since the road that they follow to an unknown future is not smooth. Any large state community that has lost the rational and decelerating influence of the propertied classes—influence of whatever nature, material or spiritual—will inevitably attain such a speed that, as in the case of the first French revolution, the state chariot will be broken. As the time passes the greedy element acquires preponderance if only because of its mass. It is for the interest of that same element to avoid the dangerous precipitation.... Unless this speed is checked, then within a relatively short period of time the historical cycle shall revert to dictatorship, despotism, absolutism, for even the unreasonable masses eventually bow down to the necessity of order.

It is a matter of political tact and prudence to define the limits that have to be observed in this battle—in order to provide for control over the government (which is required for the benefit of the country), and, at the same time—to prevent this control from transformation into overlordship.[4]

While they relate to a different historical period, these thoughts of Bismarck highlight the essence of the problem posed in this article. To what extent can thoughtful and enlightened people influence the current situation in Russia when it is not possible either to ignore the "mass, inclined toward stability and order" or to neglect the "greed of the wealthy" and insufficiency of political culture? This is the key to the solution of the present concerns in Russia.

Again, I emphasize that crossing the social divide in Russia is in the hands of persons who are *politically enlightened*, that is, those who know the limits of the "art of what is possible" and can deliver this knowledge to the people of Russia. The problem of the relationship between the people and the state, that is, the means that could allow people to control the state as expressing the will of the sovereign (the tsar), first entered Russia's political agenda at the end of the nineteenth and beginning of the twentieth centuries. A prominent Russian jurist and sociologist B.A. Kistiakovskii thus commented on the issue of sovereignty, which in those years had become a subject of intense European discussion.

Sovereignty has been conclusively defined as a supreme authority that as a judicial and dogmatic notion does not tolerate any degrees and divisions. The notions of limited sovereignty, reduced sovereignty, semisovereignty, or divisible sovereignty are all contradictory, and hence inapplicable to a scientific explanation of state and legal issues. Furthermore, the solution of the next issue—whether sovereignty is an inalienable distinction of statehood—appears quite hopeless. The resolution of this problem is nevertheless of utmost importance in defining the nature of a federative state, that is, in defining the legal status of both the union state and its member countries.[5]

The story of establishing the "legal status" of the Soviet state—ten years after these lines were written—is well known. Bolsheviks, as distinct from Kistiakovskii, were convinced that their sovereign proletarian authority (which represented to them an absolute historical value) could be preserved only through force and class propaganda for the sake of state survival. Hence it is not surprising that a significant proportion of Russians, having found themselves in a situation of "survival" once again, persist in thinking that Russia's sovereignty and security are in danger, and they hope for a restoration of the dubious Soviet greatness—an era of greatness when, in the words of a French philosopher and diplomat, Jacques Maritain, sovereignty was placed "above the moral law."[6]

As a religious thinker, Jacques Maritain saw an alternative to totalitarian "sovereign" dictatorship in medieval notions of splendor and the grace of divine power. And it is not accidental that it took Europe a whole era—the Enlightenment—to rethink this medieval heritage in terms of philosophical analysis (in the works of Montesquieu, Hume, Kant, and the American federalists). It was the Enlightenment that lay the foundation for the contemporary Western concept of democracy and human rights, in contrast to the despotism that, according to Kant, is a rule based on condescension that treats people as if they were minors who cannot discern what is good and bad for them and are therefore forced into passivity.

In the history of every nation, especially during a transition period, human passions play a key role in shaping the political landscape: the passions find their resolution in historical symbols such as the struggle for national independence or the struggle for civic rights and freedoms. In fact, these two symbols—national sovereignty and human rights—appear in the modern world as the moving forces of Western history, and as such, Russia's way out of its crisis. The two symbols call for duty and duty-induced thinking, which do not imply any outside guarantees, insofar as both duty and free will *exist*: they never *were* and never *will be*, unless *I* make a choice.

It is pertinent to recall that the word *modern* first appeared in European languages on the eve of the Reformation, against the background of medieval notions about man. The word traces back to Latin where *modo* served as an adverb signifying "just now." Here we are dealing with the notion of general *newness* of life, which differs from the ancestral lifestyle in the sense that Europeans came to regard their past as an indispensable part of contemporaneity. Of course, man has always lived in a contemporary epoch, yet never was surprised about it. While the Humanists—after they discovered the classic heritage and rediscovered the Bible—developed a metaphysical doctrine that portrayed history as a permanently modern or a permanently new concept.

History contains this permanent modernity, permanent *newness* in the spatiotemporal continuum, as a physicist might put it. We tend to associate the *past*, the *present*, and the *future* with spatial concepts of reality. That is, we perceive space as something that separates us from the outside world. Hence space is not directly controllable, it is out of our reach. What about time? We depend on time when we say: "I was like that five or ten years ago"—in making this pronouncement we demonstrate a wish to become detached from our own self. Yet this is a concept of physical, concrete time, while *contemporaneity* appeals to time that is not subject to physical measurements, since in this case a man attempts to understand his *self*—and time, in its spatial manifestations, is devoid of quantitative identifiers.

Therefore, the concept of duty, which allows a *self* to locate its position in the continuum of traditions and survival is born through the act of a "temporal" thought.

"As for me, all I know is that I know nothing," Socrates told his opponents.

This intense desire to grasp something that lies on the border of the unknown comprises the drama of human freedom. This drama is enacted in relation to a person's capabilities and efforts toward a creative existence. It implies man's "recollection in civilization," his readiness to accept the ancient heritage and Christian values: before Christ the world knew the Law and the prophets, but "until this very day the Kingdom of heaven has suffered violent attacks and violent men seize it" (Matthew, 99:12). It is man's spiritual labor that wins the Kingdom. Every endeavor is justified by man's personal courage and is based on man's inner voice. Therefore, the issue of the law is first and foremost an expression of the human right to freedom, where our existence is represented in the public space by direct, personal actions rather than by an all-rejecting bureaucratic machine. Only then will our hopes and aspirations correspond to what can be termed a "catalyst" of public life, that is, law and ethics as a totality of principles that lay the foundation for our mutual relationship and our relation to the world.

Modern democracy, as well as friendship—and I would like to emphasize this analogy—are very special phenomena in the life of a human. What is real friendship? Plato said that friendship preconditions the well-being of the body politic, and its absence leads to civil strife. Friendship, according to Plato, is a voluntary choice of consimilar lives, a benevolent companionship. Friendship originates when two people accept each other unconditionally—without a passionate desire to possess, without envy, fear, or suspicions. A friend is good for a silent walk or a hearty conversation. You may know all about your friend's weaknesses, but you accept him in toto. Friendship does not survive grudges and arrogation. A developed democracy is essentially based on a similar mental pattern—it can survive only through compromise, trust, mutual understanding, and solidarity between people. A human being is a selfish creature with animal, biological needs that can be sanitized only through his "second birth" and upbringing, and after law makes its way into history.

We live in an era of mass media, mass consumption, and mass societies, which makes it logical to imply the existence of a "mass" man as an object of social research. The emergence of mass consumer, voter, reader, and viewer does not erase the professional, social, or individual distinctions between people, yet it causes the formation of a special type of social space, or a new arena for social action,[7] one that exists beyond or above the borders of the existing states. This alone means that a "mass," unlike a crowd or a totality of state subjects, may contain an "unnoticed minority" and even an independent person who is able to elect at his own discretion a behavioral pattern. The latter means that a person always has a chance to upgrade to an independent level, capable of free thinking, that is, to be a citizen in a sense that transcends the notion of a sovereign state.

Hardships of Transformation

The prosperity of today's Western nations is rooted in their economic development and the changes that took place in the history of European culture—the evolution of parliaments, political parties, and civil society, as well as high social mobility of the population. Jeffrey Sachs observes that only "a few societies have displayed this combination of political, cultural and economic institutions."[8] (It is pertinent to note that we imply here whole epochs in modern European history, as characterized by the resolution of seemingly unresolvable contradictions in society's religious and socioeconomic life. This became possible thanks to scientific and geographical discoveries, natural processes of differentiation of labor, and the emergence of new political institutions.)

As far as Russia is concerned, such a "combination" remained historically alien to society, first and foremost because of its cultural inability to change internally through peaceful means—when changes did take place in Russian history, they were characterized by cabal, riots, and schism, none of which was likely to encourage the process of democratic change.

Everything comes to him who waits. Nothing is impossible to a patient heart. With time and patience the leaf of mulberry becomes satin. There will be our turn to triumph. These are rough English equivalents for some of the Russian proverbs that reflect people's hope and have been traditionally favored by the country's authorities for manipulation purposes—to suppress social conflicts and contradictions rather than to resolve them.

Let us turn to the historical sources of the hardships that post-Soviet Russia confronts in its attempt to overcome the inertia and legacy of the past.

The Schism

The schism has always presented the greatest danger to democratic reforms in Russia, as the schism revealed the depth of socioeconomic, political, and cultural contradictions that engender distrust between people. This starts with suspicion, envy, and prejudice and ends with violence (unless there are social institutions that can stop it).

This refers primarily to the contradictions pertaining to the era of dissension of the "Old Believers" in the sixteenth century. In the opinion of Sergei Zen'kovskii, a prominent historian of Russia's spiritual culture, the dissension originally manifested itself not as *secession from* the church of a considerable part of the clergy and laymen, but rather as an *inner split within* the church itself.

In other words, unlike the Reformation in Europe, the dissension did not start as a radical opposition movement. Only when convinced that the profession of active faith and spiritual renewal met with no response from the Orthodox hierarchs, the Old Believers, in the words of Zen'kovskii, doubted the episcopate itself. Other motives of a personal or social nature, played "a part in the dissension

. . . but it was not for those that the Old Believers [after the repressions started—Yu. S.] suffered agonies, mounted the scaffold, or perished in the torturer's fires."[9]

The psychology of religious martyrdom was inherent in many religious doctrines, including Christianity, and greatly influenced first the establishment of the Catholic Church in Europe and later its renewal in the form of reformist churches. In Russia, this psychology, vehemently suppressed by the autocratic regime, not only weakened the position of the Orthodox Church but resulted in the emergence of a *radical centaur* (combining, in a tragic way, state violence and the hatred of Old Believers), who was far removed from the Christian scriptures of tolerance and, consequently, from developing civic elements in social life. It is to be remembered that the state as such is unable to create a civil society. No government has the power to immediately convert a subject into a citizen. In the end this depends on a people's ability to resolve emerging conflicts, conduct discussions, and arrive at mutually agreeable decisions. In other words, the process of establishing a civil society depends on people's understanding of their rights and of the imposed laws, thereby implying mature civic consciousness with regard to the social links strengthened by mutual effort. Only in such a case will there emerge some germinal "civic form" that originates from a metaphysical perception by humans of their freedom "boundaries."

Another tangle of contradictions that played a fatal part in Russian history relates to Russia's embarking upon a European path of development.

Deciding to lead Russia along the road of progress, Peter I completed the process of creating the concept of Russian statehood that was initiated by the Moscow tsars. Yet how was this process conducted? It was based upon an assumption that people have to show initiative yet be obedient at the same time. Is it possible to combine initiative with obedience?

It is clear that the main condition for Russian-style progress was the intensification of bureaucratic despotism and preservation of serfdom. "When it comes to openness, then to deny all prejudice or to recognize it are two extremes equally dangerous. There exists national prejudice, which needs to be respected; educational prejudice, which needs to be handled delicately; and religious prejudice, which needs to be encouraged."[10] These are the words of the Russian empress Catherine II.

However, as Peter's idea of creating a "window on Europe" was established in the minds of Russia's educated society, Catherine's tolerant views were gradually sinking into oblivion, and the gap between the "reformers" and supporters of autocracy grew deeper. The fact that the French peasants who participated in the Revolution of 1789–1799 wanted to become noblemen, whereas the Russian noblemen who participated in the Decembrists' revolt of 1825 wished to become peasants supports the above-mentioned thesis about Russia's reaction to its frustrated Enlightenment. Hence it was not incidental that soon after suppression of the Decembrists' revolt and the appearance of Petr Chaadaev's "philosophical letters," Russian educated society went through a second split—this time between the "Slavophiles" and "Westernizers."

The country then saw the emergence of a new type of ideological radical who started to call for the overthrow of the government.

The latter statement may be illustrated with a passage from a book by Baron B.E. Nol'de, *Yuri Samarin and His Time*, dedicated to the argument that occurred during a meeting in London in July 1864 between Alexander Herzen, a Westernizer and Samarin, a Slavophile, prominent Russian historian, and public figure, who was an active proponent of the Great Reforms of 1861.

> For him [Samarin] Herzen personified the phenomenon in Russian life that he hated most—he personified the Russian Revolution. . . . Samarin decided to tell Herzen his mind. After his departure from London he wrote Herzen a long letter in which he restated his accusation, explicitly and harshly . . . "I am repeating to you," he wrote, "the words that I said to you in London: Your propaganda affected a whole generation as an unnatural habit would affect a young, tender organism. You have dried up its brain, weakened its nervous system, and made it completely incapable of concentration and moderation. As an indentured man of the revolution, you are quite indifferent to its origins—whether it comes from a university, a village, a church, or a nobleman's castle. You are not asking it where it is headed and what actuations it causes on its way."[11]

Concluding his story, Nol'de comments: "Now—when decades have elapsed— this meeting has acquired the meaning of a historical symbol. Some time ago, at the end of the winter of 1849, when Samarin met Emperor Nicholas I at the Winter Palace—their meeting signified two different Russias, a new Russia and an old Russia—and even so now Samarin and Herzen personify two Russias—the Russia of revolution and the Russia of historical tradition. Their argument is still not over."

Alas, this dispute remains open, even after decades have passed. Is Russia capable of entering the nonviolent historical tradition? The deep socioeconomic contradictions, related to the public's negative attitude toward property, have not been resolved in Russia, and have led first to the revolution of 1917, and then to the social breakdown of society in today's Russia. With a huge part of Russia's population living below the poverty line, people do not consider the redistribution of the country's social wealth in the 1990s as fair, and they are even less inclined to put up with economic redistribution, ten years since privatization has ended.

At present, the number of poor in Russia is five times the number of wealthy. The Institute of Complex Social Studies of the Russian Academy of Sciences reports that the wealthy constitute about 5 percent of the country's population (up to 7 million people, including family members). While the well-off are generally dissatisfied with the quality of the Russian state, the poor are primarily concerned about their socioeconomic condition.[12]

Evolution of Power

When describing power one is inclined to talk about the power of authority, the power of ideology, and the "power of the revolver," that is, violence, insofar as it is widely held that to retain power is possible only through force. Force is then perceived as the epitome of power. Whereas it is obvious that the establishment of contemporary democratic institutions was accompanied by the reconceptualization of the notion of force and its efficiency in politics, the modern democracy that exists in the West in the form of civil society implies a space of freedom in which every member of society is capable of defining his priorities and making choices. One person can inspire another with anything but the thought conceived by that other person. One can impart a semblance of accord, the illusion of understanding, and good intent, yet thought and will can never be imparted. It is only in the space of freedom that human aspirations and hopes—those that require publicity, social resonance, and good intent on the part of the authorities—can produce a catalyst of social life.

Russia's political class faces the immediate task of realizing the cultural mechanisms that can transform the above-mentioned contradictions into a positive philosophy and change the very nature of power.

During Brezhnev's "stagnation" period, the power of the nomenklatura in Russia reached its apogee. Shadow business became part of the administrative bodies that, together with the party apparatus, were distributing and redistributing the national wealth. Yet an important issue remained unresolved—the nomenklatura could not pass on their ill-gotten privileges to their heirs. This was almost impossible in a society without private property. The problem became acute only toward the end of the 1980s, when the extensive Soviet economics were depleted and exploitation mechanisms weakened—due to softening of the regime and pervasive corruption.

Force and violence may help a politician to achieve temporary success, but never a strategic goal, if a strategic goal is associated with the public good or perceived in relation to an ideal.

It is beyond any doubt that under the influence of external and internal factors the traditional structure of "Russian power," already transformed in the 1990s, will undergo further changes. The future of Russia depends to a large extent on the mode of this transformation process.

The major concern for Russia today is to decide whether it can develop a social and cultural system with a foundation other than the existing power structure. Is it possible if we take into account five centuries of serfdom during which the Russian people developed a special psychology that was far removed from the recognition of human rights, civil society, and free entrepreneurship?[13] The slow progress Russia has made to democracy is often attributed to the so-called traditionalist standing of its population, also known as the "Russian system," its main characteristics being authoritarian government, paternalism, international isolation, the domination of state interests over individuals, and imperious ambitions in foreign policy.[14] Such notions of statehood are often cited as being innate to Russians. This runs in tandem with their respect for collective values and Orthodox morals, and their inclination toward a benevolent autocracy. Yet is this really the case?

Scenarios for Russia—2015

The ancient philosophers claimed that there has to exist in the world something beyond visual things: something invisible has to be active because otherwise it would have been impossible to *foresee* the future. Yet what does *foresee* mean?

Foresight is a thought directed at something already assumed—something that Kant defined as practicability without practical ends or a rational plan. In socially meaningful historical processes (under conditions of freedom), there is always some kind of "plan," realized at the level of a substantialized metaphor of infinity, which is the *ratio*—a planned proportion between the finite and the infinite—when even after an unlimited period of time man is still free and can think freely of what *is* and what cannot be different. For freedom in ourselves is a rigorous inner necessity, and we are attracted to it by factors that transcend external circumstances. Beyond itself, beyond the act of its existence, freedom has no other raison d'être, or other foundation. This may be understood in the sense that man is born with an aspiration toward something that can be glimpsed only through mental effort— effort that cannot be arrested. Scenario planning developed out of this desire for foresight and became a common way of studying trends of social development. The known cannot breed the unknown. A scenario (within the boundaries of rational behavior) responds to the issue of what would happen under various developments, imparting a vector to these developments and to human behavior.

This is exactly the task pursued in Russia by Club 2015, which was set up by a group of young entrepreneurs and senior managers after the financial crisis of 1998. They realized that it would be a mistake to restrict their priorities to their own professional needs. They also had to devote their attention to the overall development of the country. In their first "scenarios" discussion papers, published in 1999, the club founders felt the necessity to understand the challenges of tomorrow and to communicate their conclusions to their compatriots. In two years' time and in cooperation with the Social Contract National Project Institute, headed by Alexander Auzan, Club 2015 launched a project called "Scenarios for Russia—2," directed by Vladimir Preobrazhenskii. The goal of this project is to formulate a positive view of Russia in 2015 and to define a path toward achieving a renewed Russia based on a wide spectrum of studies performed by over a hundred professionals in various fields of knowledge.[15] The year 2015 was chosen by the club members in the belief that by that time the Russian people will have had a chance "to see a different, transformed country."

Traditionalists and Modernists

One of the sociological studies conducted under the scenario project titled "Russians—Identity and National Interests in the Information Age" (September 2001), has demonstrated that while some Russian people are indeed traditional in their view of society, they constitute a minority of the country's population.

According to this study, most Russian citizens today hold a modernist view of life to one degree or another.

Firm believers in the "Russian system," with its domination of the state over the individual, paternalism, and isolationism accounted for only 7 percent of respondents. Their "support echelon," in terms of sympathy for the individual and paternalism within the "Russian system," is not very significant either. This group of "sympathizers" comprises 29 percent of those sampled and is dominated by the older and less-educated segment of the population. Meanwhile the supporters of the modernist alternative to the "Russian system" (priority of an individual's interests, aspiration toward independence and responsibility for one's life, and openness of the country) constitute one-third of the population with a slightly larger "support echelon"—totaling more than 60 percent of Russians.

Thus, contrary to a widely held opinion, the development vector of Russian society within people's consciousness is evidently opposite to traditionalist trends. The majority of people do not regard themselves as passive objects of the government, under the thumb of the state. This is primarily a result of urbanization. The withdrawal of an individual from the state and expanded psychological freedom occurred in Russia over several postwar decades, undermining the foundations of the communist regime.

Two Myths About the Nation

In the opinion of the project authors, further modernization of the society is impeded not by people's mentality, but mainly by the Russian elite, which is not prepared to govern free people. In an attempt to compensate for that inability the elite has reanimated two age-old myths about the Russian people. The first myth treats Russians as an Orthodox God-chosen nation that possesses unique spiritual qualities and is destined for a Messianic role in world history. The second myth is that of a "vegetable nation" made up of passive and inert people who have an unfortunate desire to be "molded" by means of propaganda and the political devices of a "governed democracy." It is then inferred that paternalistic care from the state is necessary to lead the people to the market economy that is allegedly alien to Russians. These two myths are mirror images: The first myth is that the people are essentially traditionalists; the second that the people are an obstacle to modernization.

Yet it is evident that a passive and reflective attitude toward the world was eradicated from the Russian consciousness during the decades of Soviet rule, with its orientation toward atheistic values of earthly life: this, however, did not affect the nation's morals as such. Contemporary Russians (spontaneous "Protestantism" testifies to their self-identification with values of earthly existence) do not identify with a distant communist future, but recognize the need for individual freedom and are willing to abide by moral and legal restrictions that are required to maintain social order.

Collectivists and Individualists

The trends noted here can also be traced to Russian preferences for collective and individualist principles, albeit with lesser evidence. After centuries of pre-Soviet (communal) and decades of communist collectivism, the 1990s saw a shift toward individualism with its priority of personal over collective interests. The total share of respondents who opted for an individualist position in a minimum of three of the five proposed questions came to 53 percent, with 44 percent "collectivists." The study shows that even those who voted for "collectivism" did not see it as a means to equality, but rather as some abstract concept that allowed private and group interests to combine.

The collectivist orientation of a significant part of Russian society is predominantly a sign of the population's reaction to the inability of the elites, state officials, and officers to provide for the harmonious coexistence of individual freedom with universal legal norms. This is a reaction not to individualism as such, but to the weakness of Russia's social institutions and to the negative experience of essentially antisocial acts on the part of elites.

Attitude Toward Reforms

High levels of support by society of modernist approaches is also revealed in the socioeconomic orientation of the country's population. This refers to people's attitudes toward the actual problems associated with reforms in Russia and their outlook, including attitudes toward private and state property, state control over citizens' income, state interference with business, free access to information, and many others. The aggregate percentage share of respondents who opted for a reformist position is twice as high as the share of conservatives.

It is beyond any doubt that throughout its history Russia has never enjoyed more favorable conditions for modernization and Westernization. However, the traditionalist wing of the Russian elite is willing to return to the former vertical integration that would feed upon total state control. On the other hand, the reformist elite is striving to expand horizontal freedoms in society, while preserving the state's vertical autonomy. The main obstacle on this path of development is the Russians' distrust of regional and other branches of power, as well as of each other. Half of the population today is convinced that it is impossible to fight the high-handedness of Russia's authorities. Yet the overwhelming majority of respondents would prefer to live in a country that enjoys a greater degree of trust.

Thus, by the end of the twentieth century, there emerged in Russia a qualitatively new nation—not because of propaganda, but thanks to a change in historical milestones. And the burning matter today is the formation and enlightenment of an elite that is able to match people's hopes and expectations.

A New Political Class

Immediately after World War II and well into the 1950s a young educated professional in the Soviet Union stood a good chance of getting into the nomenklatura at some level within two to three years of finishing graduate studies. By the beginning of the 1980s, that period had stretched to twenty-two years. In other words, a university graduate of 1960 could attain some position of authority by about forty-five years of age, while a college graduate at the beginning of the 1980s could not expect any serious promotion earlier than 2000. Absence of competition was the chief psychological and social motive of Gorbachev's perestroika, which, in turn, resulted in a short period of meteoric careers.

In Russia of the 1990s the appropriation of capital, the occupation of political posts and managerial positions, and the acquisition of modest yet formerly unobtainable material comfort, that is, personal success, became mass phenomena. As a result of active economic transformation and political change more than half of Russia's population entered the "achievement paradigm" (a term used by V. Preobrazhenskii—see note 15). That said, it has to be taken into account that many people were forced into it by dire necessity, so that the "achievement race" was for many quite involuntary and dictated by social clichés rather than by shared values. Hence the emergence of "forced achievements" involved inevitable recoil. After the radical shortening of career terms from Brezhnev's twenty-two years to Yeltsin's five minutes, these terms began to stretch out again, and by the end of the 1990s, achievement motivation had weakened significantly. The country experienced the return of ideologists who were nostalgic for a privilege-based society. Moreover, whole social strata and geographical regions were excluded from the achievement paradigm.

With Vladimir Putin's advent to power the process of change in Russia's political class revived. Yet one can expect that the flushing out of the "Soviet stratum" from the element of bureaucrats, managers, and intellectuals will conclude by 2010, by which time the political class will mainly comprise people who have never lived under communist rule or have only obscure memories of the Soviet era.

From the viewpoint of Club 2015 members the most essential result of the 1998 crisis was the emergence in Russia of people whose work and success could be regarded as independent and socially useful. Presently, since the arrest of Mikhail Khodorkovsky, the former chief executive office of Yukos, problems of further transformation of the Russian political and social system are associated with realizing the potential of this independent and socially useful work. What we mean here is a fundamental human right to property—the basis of democratic development. In modern Russia, property rights, far from being merely restored, are rather created as a special branch of the law. Property rights must be converted into a vital necessity, supported by expansion of economic and political rights and freedoms.

As deregulation processes deepen, as business income enters the legal zone, and as the social sphere evolves dynamically with the development of the private sector, "we will see the 'other Russians' . . . who will play a crucial role in developing an efficient elite that gains its status in an ethically acceptable way."[16]

Therefore, Russia's immediate future depends on the resolution of an important contradiction—that between the "Russian system" (as described above), with its political elite, and the segment of Russia's society that aspires to modernization and rejects authoritarian rule. Resolving this contradiction will be key to Russia's development both domestically and internationally.

"Many Cultures, but Only One Civilization"

The words of A. Koestler, "Every culture is an island," in the epigraph to this chapter, reflect a widely held conviction about the originality and unique identity of cultures. A national culture is perceived as some substantialized potency of human abilities and skills that are reproduced in the form of customs, habits, preferences, aesthetic tastes, behavioral patterns, and so forth.

Yet it is equally obvious that any modern culture also includes the domains *invented* of knowledge as science, art, and philosophy where man continues to experiment with self-fulfillment. This is the focus of the conclusion of this chapter.

A culture can develop, that is, undergo historical changes in its own environment, to the extent it is allowed to materialize and preserve the products of man's free, "nondimensional" efforts, or, in other words, to the extent it is open to the existing "background" of free and creative entities that are *not* culture. In this sense Western man's aspiration to freedom and creativity transcends the borders of that same Western culture. Otherwise it would be impossible to explain the emergence of various cultures and to solve the problem of the existence of multiple cultures.

We express the answer as follows: For the very reason that there exist domains beyond culture where it is possible to experiment with a *potential* image of man (in religion, art, science, and philosophy), we witness the plurality of cultures, the fact of their multiplicity. For that matter, the culture-breeding function of modern science can be understood only through realization of the hidden mechanisms of production of that scientific (and philosophical) knowledge. Otherwise we risk entering into an irresolvable contradiction with our intuition. Our intuition tells us that such understanding is independent of thought that is conceived and elaborated in a particular culture. Such is the paradox of cultural plurality that we witnessed for the first time in the history of modernity when the European nations passed the limit of their antecedent cultures, and their aspiration to freedom was expressed in the universal principles of economic liberalism, political democracy, and personal privacy. Democracy was no longer perceived as polity, but as a process of social development and the liquidation of compulsion, and dependence upon the state started to be considered as an absolute necessity for the freedom of every man.

There followed the issue of "developing" (within the framework of religious tradition) feelings that would be adequate to that freedom—feelings more perfect and sublime than the unexceptional, "natural" sensations. This, in turn, found its symbolic expression in art. The very possibility of developing a unique personality came to be dependent on one's ability to overcome one's nature—which implied, in scriptural terms, one's "second birth."

This project of creating a new democratic culture is well under way—expanding human abilities in a globalizing world that attains new levels of freedom with unprecedented progress in media and communications.

As mentioned earlier in this chapter, Russia as we see it today also has cultural prerequisites for entering the new world. However, for these prerequisites to materialize, the authorities in Russia must change, first by giving up the ideology of state paternalism, and the people must accede to this change in ideology by accepting the overarching transformation of the society. Is this possible? Can we hope for it even if we take into account the modernist trends in Russian society? This will mean a profound change in Russia's age-old, multifaceted social arrangements and will affect the interests of the country's huge bureaucracy. Is this possible politically, in the absence of the necessary political culture? economically, with a meager budget? psychologically, under the conditions of a social split? business-wise, in a country lacking professional managers? ideologically, when Russia does not have a clearly defined reform plan? These issues await resolution. Yet there are certain grounds for optimism.

Notwithstanding the social split and contradictions, corruption, the age-old mentality of the people, today's Russia has won its chief victories—freedom, an emerging multiparty system, a developing market economy, and a plurality of opinions. These are the victories of the past decades. And if we, as observers and participants in this process, can discern Russia's success, then we will have a certain understanding of the world in which we engage ourselves with political enlightenment, economic education, formation of social opinion, and the upbringing of a new generation.

"There are many cultures, but only one civilization," wisely observed Merab Mamardashvili, a Georgian philosopher.[17] Freedom breeds only freedom. This makes dialogue, information exchange, and contacts between people possible. This is the civilization that is "older than our state."[18] Through communication we come to live in a civilized world, or, in other words, in an open society that is free of formal borders.

The ability to master life's complications is the main precondition for the development of a democratic culture—where competition and solidarity do not exclude, but complement each other, opening new vistas for wider cooperation, dialogue, reforms, transformation, and integration of Russia into the Western community.

Notes

1. George Orwell, "Rudyard Kipling," in *The Collected Essays, Journalism and Letters* (New York: Penguin, 1970), p. 217.
2. For analysis and related data, see "Sapere aude," *Vestnik moskovskoi shkoly politicheskikh issledovanii* 13 (1999).
3. See *Obshchestvennoe mnenie-2000. Po materialam issledovanii* (Moscow: VTsIOM, 2000), p. 89.
4. Otto von Bismarck, *Mysli i vospominaniia*, vol. 2. Trans. from German (Moscow: OGIZ, 1940), pp. 56–57.
5. B.A. Kistiakovskii, *Filosofiia i sotsiologiia prava* (St. Petersburg: Izdatel'stvo russkogo khristianskogo gumanitarnogo instituta, 1998), p. 244.
6. See Jacques Maritain, *Man and the State* (Chicago: University of Chicago Press, 1956).
7. See Iurii Levada, *Ot mnenii k ponimaniiu. Sotsiologicheskie ocherki, 1993–2000* (Moscow: Moskovskaia shkola politicheskikh issledovanii, 2000), p. 254.
8. Jeffrey Sachs, "Notes on a New Sociology of Economic Development," in *Culture Matters: How Values Shape Human Progress*, ed. Lawrence E. Harrison and Samuel P. Huntington (New York: Basic Books, 2000), p. 34.
9. Sergei Zen'kovskii, *Russkoe staroobriadchestvo. Dukhovnye dvizheniia semnadtsatogo veka* (Moscow: Tserkov, 1995), p. 489.
10. *Zapiski imperatritsy Ekateriny Vtoroi* (Moscow: Orbita, 1989), p. 624.
11. Baron B.E. Nol'de, *Iurii Samarin i ego vremia*, 2d ed. (Paris: YMCA-PRESS, 1978), pp. 183–84.
12. See Vladimir Ryzhkov, "Ob'iavim voinu bednosti," *Izvestiia*, June 19, 2003.
13. See *Razmyshleniia o Rossii i russkikh. Shtrikhi k istorii russkogo national'nogo kharaktera.* 3 vols. Comp. S.K. Ivanov, ed. Yu.P. Senokosov (Moscow, 1994–2003).
14. See Iu.S. Pivovarov and A.A. Fursov, "'Russkaia sistema' kak popytka ponimaniia russkoi istorii," *Polis*, no. 4 (2001).
15. See Vladimir Preobrazhenskii, "Stsenarii dlia Rossii-2015," *Obshchaia tetrad'* 24, no. 1 (2003). See also *Bazovye tsennosti rossiian: Sotsial'nye ustanovki. Zhiznennye strategii. Simvoly. Mify*, ed. A.V. Riabov and E.Sh. Kurmangaleeva (Moscow: Dom intellektualnoi knigi, 2003).
16. Vladimir Preobrazhenskii, *Stsenarii dlia Rossii-2015*, p. 60.
17. Merab Mamardashvili, *Kak ia ponimaiu filosofiiu*, Comp. and ed., Iu.P. Senokosov (Moscow: Progress-Kul'tura, 1992), p. 334.
18. A. Toynbee, "Civilization on Trial," (Oxford, UK: Oxford University Press, 1948)

4

Public Opinion and Pro-Western Interest Groups in Russia

Pilar Bonet

Archaic Politics and Modern Ethnologies

Russian authoritarian political culture has not disappeared since the collapse of communism, but is alive and well. Once again Russia, which in the past transplanted Marxist ideas to its soil, has proven itself capable of assimilating Western elements, whether ideas, social doctrines, or technical innovations, but only to mold them into local traditional patterns that operate and interact according to rules of their own.

At the end of Vladimir Putin's first presidential term, the strength and survival capacity of the local cultural elements vis-à-vis those imported from the West was obvious even to those reformers who at the beginning of the 1990s categorically refused to consider historical and cultural factors in their analysis, convinced as they were that the transition to a market economy in Russia was no different than other transitions in post-communist countries of Eastern Europe.[1]

But the disintegration of the Soviet state, the crumbling of the social and political system, and the lost points of reference had devastating effects on the feelings of identity of people who once regarded themselves as citizens of one of the two superpowers of the world. The loss of the empire has been and still is especially hard for those Russians serving in institutions whose raison d'être was precisely the maintenance of the superpower, such as the army, security bodies, and organizations linked to the military and the military industry.

It is not the purpose of this chapter to find out what lies at the origins of the Russian reinterpretation or assimilation of Western elements, but to stress that this reinterpretation exists and is seen in the results of polls and public opinion today. Public opinion in Russia has gone a long way from the acknowledgment of its existence during perestroika (as opposed to its being repressed and hidden before) to its manipulation during the Putin era.[2]

In the late 1980s the Soviet leader Mikhail Gorbachev found it hard to accept the first polls that openly questioned his popularity and because of them he clashed with sociologist Iurii Levada, the former director of the All-Russian Center for the

Study of Public Opinion (VTsIOM). Nevertheless, Gorbachev either got used to polls that he could not control or the magnitude of the problems he had to cope with was such that polls were very much a secondary matter.

In 1996, when the popularity of the first Russian president was at a record low, Boris Yeltsin reacted by pooling all available resources in order to be reelected. At enormous cost in terms of energy, sharing of influence, and money, the president managed to raise his rating for long enough to achieve his aim.

In their approach to public opinion, Putin and his team are more manipulative than their predecessors. The presidential administration attentively controls television and decides who and what should be ignored, banned, or put into a given context. Representatives of the presidential press service phone news agencies and newspapers in order to prevent certain information from being published and they have also managed to purge all independent and critical journalists from the selected pool of reporters covering Kremlin events.

For Putin, public opinion probably matters much more than it did for his predecessors, because, unlike them, Putin consciously uses polls as a replacement for political democratic institutes. These institutions did not go on developing but have even somewhat atrophied during Putin's first mandate.

We must thus operate with a combination of archaic politics and modern technologies. Opinion polls replace a modern democratic system of checks and balances and function as advisory mechanisms similar to those used by preconstitutional monarchs to tune their rule to the needs of the people. The opinion polls speak instead of institutions and instead of real people.

For Putin it is important to be at the head of trends coming from society and to be able to lead and control these trends himself. While the president reacts to the mood of society and takes it into consideration, he reacts on his own terms, inside the pyramidal structure of power and according to the rules of the so-called vertical of power. In spring 2003 during the war in Iraq, local Moscow authorities banned attempts by nongovernmental organizations (NGOs) to organize protests in front of the American Embassy, but they strongly supported an ill-timed large rally organized by the pro-presidential party *Edinaia Rossiia* (United Russia), very much in Soviet style, just hours before the hot phase of the war was over. The Kremlin took into account the antiwar mood in Iraq, but it wanted to decide on its own how and when that mood should be expressed and who was to take credit for it.

In order not to confront public opinion, the Kremlin did nothing to soften the anti-American mood during the war in Iraq and even fueled it slightly, allowing the first and second television channels to display a very aggressive anti-American attitude.

Public opinion in Putin's era is essential, because the second president of Russia is himself a product of public opinion. The VTsIOM polls carried out in the 1990s had shown the growing demand for a strong leader. Russian society wanted a leader capable of guaranteeing stability and welfare, who would be able to bring order to the unstable society inherited from the Yeltsin years. On the international front, it wanted a leader who would be respected and able to restore the country's lost prestige in the world.

In 1993, the pro-Western attitude of the first post-communist years started to shift because of the negative social results of the reforms and the complicated privatization process, which resulted in impoverishment of the population, the vanishing of people, savings, and the destruction of the Soviet intelligentsia as a possible catalyst and generator of civilized interest groups and parties.

The "besieged fortress" mood, which made a strong comeback in Russian society at the end of the 1990s, was a result of frustration because of the lack of success of the reforms. Public opinion has become extremely volatile and hypersensitive toward the West and tends to interpret unfavorable events concerning Russian interests in terms of discrimination, threat, lack of respect, or indifference toward those interests.

The Russian media expressed bitterness and frustration when Russian athletes did not reach the success they expected in Salt Lake City at the Winter Games in 2002, when the pop group TATU did not win the Eurovision singing contest, and when the filmmaker Aleksandr Sokurov (again) did not win the Cannes Film Festival in 2003 for his film *Russian Ark*. In all three of these basically unconnected events, Russian commentators tended to see a common ill will from the West toward their country.

Confronted with the "lost empire syndrome" Russian authorities can choose: either to tell their subjects the bitter truths of Russian decline in the hope that the painful realities will accelerate the recovery of the nation or to create false illusions with the purpose of extending the virtual existence of the empire beyond its real one.

Putin has chosen a mixed hybrid approach. He conveys simultaneously the hard realities of post-imperial times and superpower rhetoric. On the one hand, he proclaims a strategic commitment with Europe, and on the other, he announces that Russia will strive for "moral and military superiority" as well as economic and intellectual superiority.[3]

Only in being superior will Russia be able to maintain its position "among the main superpowers of the planet," he stated. Nostalgia is visible in the reintroduction of old state symbols: the Hymn of the Russian Federation with the music of the old Soviet anthem, the flag of the army whose combination of stars and eagles reflects a mixture of the Soviet and pre-Soviet periods.

Putin is concerned about public opinion and does not take risky steps that could endanger his rating. The president seems determined not to be trapped between conflicting foreign and internal policies, as Gorbachev was. After the initial success of the U.S. war in Iraq, the military factor made a comeback into the official Kremlin rhetoric. Judging from the comments of experts, for Russia one of the lessons of the Iraq war is that a country needs good weapons to be strong. In contrast, in 2001, only 17 percent of people polled thought that nuclear weapons were needed for a country to be great.

Table 4.1

How Did Putin, the Political Establishment, and the Mass Media React to U.S. Military Action? (as percent)

	Putin		Political establishment		Mass media	
	Afghanistan	Iraq	Afghanistan	Iraq	Afghanistan	Iraq
They support the United States	46	2	35	2	29	2
They refrained from judging the United States	40	39	43	30	43	25
Negatively	4	53	6	56	10	63
Don't know	10	6	16	12	18	10

Source: All-Russian Center for the Study of Public Opinion polls, November 2001 and April 2003 (www.wciom.ru/?pt=54&article=116).

Note: The poll on Iraq was carried out on April 2003 among 1,600 people. The poll on Afghanistan was taken in November 2001.

Putin committed himself to the West clearly after September 11, 2001, but his position has developed over time. By supporting the U.S.-led antiterrorist campaign, Russia was also looking for an external justification of its war in Chechnya. September 11 came in handy for Moscow because it happened when public opinion in Russia had started to weary of the conflict in the Caucasus, which had contributed to Putin's popularity in 1999. Against the background of the Kremlin's inability to solve the conflict, Putin exploited the idea that international terrorism can affect anybody and tried to link Chechen fighters to international terrorist networks.

Russia's support of the United States during the war in Afghanistan did not apply to American policy in Iraq. Two polls conducted by VTsIOM in November 2001 and in April 2003 concerning Afghanistan and Iraq, respectively, show very different reactions among the Russians (see Table 4.1). The question was: In your opinion, how did Putin, the political establishment, and the mass media react to U.S. military action?

Russian elites have a mainly pragmatic Western orientation. They want to be as close as possible to the sources of money, technology, and power, and, whatever their judgment of American actions, they understand that Washington is a key factor in Moscow's relations with other parts of the world. In the Iraq crisis Russia has refrained from playing divisive games among the Europeans and among the European and the Americans, although it aligned itself more with the Europeans.

Nevertheless, Moscow has not yet learned to make credible proposals for a stronger Europe and is not yet in a position to think creatively on the European field. This is so partly because it lacks a new stable feeling of identity adapted to the new post-Soviet realities, partly because of the country's internal situation, and partly because it has not achieved new relations free of imperial suspicions with its neighbors, as demonstrated in the border conflict that arose around Tuzla Island in the Azov Sea in October 2003. Historical reconciliation between Germany and its neighbors was key to a new European configuration after World War II. Historical reconciliation between Russia and the former "small brothers" of the Soviet empire is also key to positive and fruitful development in this region of the world.

The carriers of Western values described in this chapter are not very numerous, but are of utmost importance in preparing the ground for the long-term task of integrating Russia into Europe in a nonconfrontational way with the United States. They do not represent the opinion of the majority of the society, but they influence and shape opinion and soften imperial moods. They also provide ideas for integration into the West, denounce the recidivism of the past and the deformations of the present, and show that being respected in the West is not only a question of weapons of mass destruction.

One might have assumed that the attitudes toward the West would be more constrained among those who suffered more from the disintegration of the empire, especially in those sectors that have yet to undertake painful reforms. But this is not necessarily so. Part of the staff in the Ministry of Defense might simply be anti-Western because it defends privileges and the old habits based on the Cold War, but there is also a demand for reform and modernization coming from the military institution itself. A poll among 300 career officers showed that *Soiuz pravykh sil* (the Union of Right Forces), a pro-Western liberal party that made military reform its main asset, has a popularity of 12 percent, running second after the amorphous *Edinaia Rossiia* with a 24 percent preference.[4]

The example of the Spanish army, which underwent a complete transformation and modernization by joining NATO, could also apply to the Russian army, if cooperation between NATO and Russia provides real opportunities for young people to enhance their capabilities and learn new skills.

Russian culture is one of the members of the European family of cultures but Russians still have to overcome the syndrome of the lost empire, a process that other European countries have experienced, and that in the case of Spain, for instance, went on for several centuries.

Carriers and Users of Western Values

In strict terms, the pro-Western sectors in Russia can be defined as the carriers of liberal democratic values, who believe that the individual (and not the state as in traditional Russian authoritarian thinking) is the main subject and object of political and social activity as well as the main agent of rights. For these sectors, the West is the political, social, and cultural environment that offers the best possible practical conditions to implement those rights.

The carriers of Western values in Russia look to the West as means of democratization (as an equivalent of modernization). They operate in a two-track dynamic: They want transformation or systemic change and integration with the West. Both processes interact as inseparable sides of the modernization-democratization drive.

Russians are still divided about feeling European, although the number of people who declared themselves as such has increased and their share is more than 50 percent, according to VTsIOM data. Judging from a survey carried out in January 2000, 46 percent of those polled did not feel European, whereas 54 percent did consider themselves as such. In 1999, to the questions: Do you feel European? Do you feel an affiliation with the culture and history of the European Community? 56 percent replied negatively, 27 percent positively, and 17 percent did not know.[5]

Russia has become global without solving its nineteenth-century dilemma between East and West. When asked about the path of development they would prefer for their country, Russians show a new orientation toward an eclectic model, a postmodern mixture of elements belonging to different experiences worldwide, including their own traditions.

In 1992, 24 percent of Russians favored an orientation toward Western Europe, 28 percent toward the United States, and 25 percent toward Japan. In 2000, when asked what should be the path of the reforms, 63 percent felt that Russia should explore its own historical experience, traditions, and particularities rather than follow alien patterns. Only 14 percent expressed a preference for the United States and Europe.

In 2000, 19 percent of the population considered the Western system as a model for Russia, 37 percent believed it was not at all valid for the Russian way of life, and 30 percent considered it valid in part. According to the sociologist Leonid Sedov, only 16 percent of the population can be considered as real, true, committed, consequent liberals in Russia, where the total liberal sector of society amounts to 35 percent of the population, including those not so consequent in their liberal convictions.

The slogan "Russia for the Russians" strikes a chord for more than half of the Russian population. According to Sedov, 16 percent support this slogan directly and 40 percent are prepared to support its implementation up to a certain extent, whereas 25 percent of the population dismisses it as "fascist."

When talking about pro-Western orientations, within the Russian political, social, and economic sectors, one has to distinguish between the carriers of Western liberal values (in the strict sense mentioned above) and those using a pro-Western orientation in an instrumental way to promote goals other than the democratization of internal political, economic, and social relations in Russia.

For some, the West is a basic reference. For the majority, the West is an instrument for other purposes, including the restoration of a hypertrophied state more interested in military, industrial, and material capacities than in protecting human rights or civic freedoms. Thirty percent of Russians consider the restoration of superpower status as the main task of Russian politics for the next ten or fifteen years. In 2002, those identifying this status with high living standards (67 percent) and high industrial development (66 percent) exceeded those who identified it with the observance of basic human rights and freedoms (34 percent).

Sociologists and scholars are divided on whether a strong pro-Western sector has already developed in Russian society. In my opinion, the cause of lack of protection and guarantees of democratic rights in this country is the weakness of the liberal sector and does not confirm the thesis according to which liberalism is vigorously developing and consolidating.

The absence of a dynamic social impulse for democratic transformations and weak or nonexistent grassroots pressure on political institutions show that there is not a strong pro-Western sector in Russia (understood as a carrier and generator of values and not as a user or consumer of those values for other aims).

Democracy as a By-product?

The current Russian leadership is making an effort to adapt to the West, but it cannot be seen as strictly pro-Western (in terms of carrier of values). A key subject for discussion is how much of its adaptation to the West is in fact an imitation of Western values, as Lilia Shevtsova (see chapter 5) puts it.

Democratization of political life deserves a skeptical assessment, as shown by the dubious legal procedures begun in 2003 by the office of the public prosecutor against the oil tycoon Mikhail Khodorkovsky, one of the main proponents of integrating Russia with the West.

The Russian leadership uses and abuses the so-called administrative resources to channel political processes and to get the needed results in elections at different levels. It practices a restrictive information policy (as the official coverage of the Chechen War and other crises shows) and has managed to get rid of the few accountability mechanisms inherited from the Yeltsin period.

Parliamentarian debate has vanished. The Federation Council, the upper chamber, has been fully distorted in its function of representation of regional interests and has instead transformed itself into a safe haven for persons involved in dubious affairs. The State Duma, the lower chamber, lacks the legal instruments to control executive power (e.g., to appoint an effective investigation commission with faculties to summon the executive and make it accountable for its deeds), judiciary power is influenced by the moods of the executive or by material factors (to put it mildly), and corruption in the police and the army are rampant.

Formally there is a democracy, but the relations behind the formal division of powers is of a quite different nature. We deal here with a system of complicities between the political and economic elites. That system emerged and crystallized during the privatizations of the Yeltsin years.

After he came to power, Putin got rid of the more individualistic and ambitious representatives (the oligarchs Vladimir Gusinsky and Boris Berezovsky) of the inherited system. Nevertheless, in spite of Putin's statements about the equality of all citizens before the law, there is no serious hint that the methods of crony capitalism sponsored by political power will end.

The foggy practices of the Yeltsin period continued during the Putin era. In December 2002, the state sold its control package in the oil company Slavneft according to the worst traditions of the privatization auctions. It is quite possible that we are watching in Russia the consolidation of a perverted system, much along Latin American models, and not a transition toward the West.

Politician Grigory Yavlinsky wrote:

> A stagnant social corporate-criminal system with an extremely ineffective segmented market and without any mechanism for long-term reproduction and increase in economic resources is, unfortunately, the most realistic outlook for Russia today. We will not have a law-based state with an open dynamic economy and a responsible political and economic elite.

According to Yavlinsky, the system that has arisen in Russia does not have "a mechanism for the redistribution of benefits at the national level."[6]

The Russian leadership does not pursue democratization as an aim. Putin's foreign policy is less based on values than on the acknowledgment that Russia needs the West in order to become a superpower again. Democratization as a goal was lost during the systemic transformations of the 1990s, when, for fear of a communist comeback, Western countries closed their eyes to the violation and distortion of democratic procedures in the referendum to approve the constitution in 1993, and in the presidential elections of 1996.

Power in Russia was usurped by a small number of people, the oligarchs who gathered around Yeltsin in 1996. Together with the main sources of national income, they privatized the state for themselves. Administrative positions were allocated in exchange for money and rival groups fought to ensure their interests at the top of institutions dealing mainly with natural resources. After Boris Berezovsky and Vladimir Gusinsky, the most outspoken oligarchs, left the country, Putin and the tycoons who had supported Boris Yeltsin enjoyed a period of relative stability, but as presidential elections in 2004 approached, Putin alarmed the liberal sectors by producing a new populist policy inspired by the *siloviki*, his colleagues from the security services, apparently aimed at least to a partial revision of the privatizations of the 1990s. The arrest of the oil tycoon Mikhail Khodorkovsky, the richest man in Russia, in October 2003 marked the beginning of a new era, the consequences of which are still difficult to foresee.

Democratization (real westernization and not the cloning of Western rules) is taking place in Russia, not as an item on the state agenda, but as a collateral product, as an achievement of forces acting outside the bodies of political representation. Democratization today in Russia is a by-product of other processes.

A Foreign Policy to Everyone's Taste

Putin is enjoying unique support as a Russian leader. In foreign policy, the area of broadest consensus in society, the Russian leader has managed to satisfy almost everyone. He is perceived as a defender of Russia's interests in his own country, and he was perceived as a supporter of the pro-Western line in the West, at least until the prosecutor's office campaign against Khodorkovsky became clear in July 2003.

Putin's popularity rose to 83 percent after the Dubrovka hostage crisis in October 2002 and remained well above 70 percent afterward. In contrast to Gorbachev and Yeltsin, who in the eyes of Russians made too many concessions to the West, Putin is seen as someone who defends the interests of their country. As far as the war in Iraq is concerned, 45 percent of Russians thought Putin did his best, and 38 percent believed that he should have shown more determination against the United States.[7]

The Russian attitude toward the United States has been generally positive in recent years, with two exceptions: in 1999 in connection with NATO and war in Yugoslavia and at the beginning of 2002. When the Kosovo conflict occurred, Russia was weakened and isolated by the 1998 default, and Russians were afraid of Western "humanitarian" intervention on their territory similar to the one in Yugoslavia. The second decline in the positive approach concerned the alleged discrimination against Russian athletes at the Olympic Games in Salt Lake City.[8]

From 1991 onward, VTsIOM has calculated the index between positive and negative attitudes toward the United States. The best marks (from 62 up to 65) were calculated at the beginning of the 1990s. At that time, high hopes were pinned on the West, and Western advisers were not yet identified with depredatory privatization tailored for the benefit of a few insiders at the expense of the Russian rank-and-file citizens.

The Russian approach toward the United States nowadays is highly volatile, but free of dreams and unrealistic expectations. Data from August 2002 indicate that up to 62 percent of Russians consider relations with the United States friendly, good, normal, and peaceful.

The events and aftermath of September 11 prompted a temporary upsurge of solidarity and identification with the United States. Up to 80 percent of Russians thought that the attack on the World Trade Center in New York affected all humanity, and 77 percent believed that Putin acted correctly when he supported the U.S. antiterrorism campaign.

The Cold War and its stereotypes as well as previous Russian traditions have left their mark. Russians still see themselves as potential victims of evil intentions from abroad. President Putin personally is not alien to these views in spite of reacting positively to the presence of the United States in Central Asia and Georgia after September 11. In January 2000, 48 percent considered the United States a substantial threat to the security of Russia, well above China (23 percent), and the European Union (EU) (22 percent). Russians see EU criticism of the Kremlin's policy in Chechnya as an attempt to interfere in the internal affairs of their country and to weaken it (46 percent). They prefer to think that the West does not understand the real situation in Chechnya (20 percent) rather than to accept that it acts out of a desire to stop the bloodshed and to ensure the observance of human rights (13 percent).

From the Russian perspective, the United States wanted to attack Iraq not so much in order to deal with international terrorism (21 percent), but to show "who the boss is" in the world (43 percent), to control Iraqi oil (34 percent), or to boost the American economy with military contracts (19 percent). More than a fifth of Russians thought their country should have condemned the actions of the United States and helped Iraq (21 percent were in favor of diplomatic help to Baghdad and 2.8 percent favored military help).[9]

Russians have become more positive toward NATO. In November 2002, 49 percent of Russians did not see the Atlantic Alliance as a threat to Russia, whereas 32 percent did. NATO is a more familiar reality for Russians than the EU. Sixty percent know that NATO is "an American-led military alliance with Western Europe and Canada," whereas only 31 percent know that "the capital of the EU is located in Brussels." But even if they are not so familiar with the European construction, 48 percent would vote in favor of Russian integration in the EU if a referendum on this matter were to be organized (14 percent were against it).

Democratization Versus the Vertical of Power

The fundamental embryonic elements of democratization and Westernization in Russia are not in the state institutions, but in the NGOs, consumer associations, interest groups, independent media, and other elements of civil society, that took up the defense of human rights listed in the Russian constitution, but not guaranteed in practice by the legislative, judiciary, and executive powers.

The state institutions, largely weak, bureaucratic, or, in the worst case, corrupt, are not in a position to work for democratization without external help. They can be forced to act or react, but they cannot lead the process. Their agenda is not to democratize but to form the hierarchical structure known as the "vertical of power."

Putin's political will for the democratization, transparency, participation, and accountability of representative organs—provided it exists—would not be enough to change the system. For Russia to move more energetically along the path of democratization, a strong drive for change in society is necessary. But the impulses toward Westernization and democratization are fragmented and local. They lack backbone and synergy. Classical institutions, such as parties or trade unions, fail to win support for urgent national problems such as a radical reform of the armed forces or the end of the war in Chechnya.

A Pragmatic Dialogue

The network of NGOs in Russia is very extensive and diversified. By early 2001, 450,000 organizations were registered and more than half of them were independent civic associations.[10] They represent a wide range of interests, from philanthropy to hobby associations and only some of them are dedicated to promoting democracy, a state of law, and Western values. The lack of a developed political environment often results in a confusion of roles among NGOs, political parties, and political institutions.

In the field of human rights, democracy, and institution building, the NGOs criticize the political institutions, but also help them. The Union of Committees of Soldiers' Mothers, for instance, works with the Ministry of Defense during levy periods, and the International Federation of Consumer Associations provides expertise for new laws, as was the case with the legal package against bureaucracy. The presidential administration has frequently used NGOs for feedback on public opinion or to detect problems, but it has kept them at bay in the decision-making process.

In 2001 a new dialogue was launched between political and social institutions. For three years the so-called Civic Forum brought together representatives of Putin's political administration and the patchy spectrum of NGOs and social institutions that promote democracy and Western values. Basic problems concerning democratization and the implementation of Western values have been conveyed to the president, from restrictions on freedom of information to the situation in Russian jails, from the problems of Chechen refugees to the abuses of the military or the bureaucrats' resistance to implementing legislation to protect the independence of private agents in civil society.

The relation between NGOs and the political administration of Russia has become more pragmatic and closer. This coming together was reflected in the Civic Forum. In November 2001, this event, which was attended by Putin, gathered 5,000 representatives of NGOs in the Kremlin and opened new paths for dialogue between the administration and the representatives of civil society. The third Civic Forum, which took place in the town of Nizhnii Novgorod in October 2003, showed that the effects of the dialogue were nevertheless limited and might have reached their peak.

Today there is a more or less regular dialogue between the presidential administration and some of the most prestigious and influential NGOs such as the Memorial Society, the Union of Committees of Soldiers' Mothers, the Civil Rights Committee, the Glasnost Defense Foundation, the Moscow Helsinki Group, and the Confederation of Consumers Societies. These NGOs have some features in common: they are well connected in the West, they have experience and know-how, and they are respected. In some cases, their leaders have been in jail or suffered repression for their Western views during the Soviet period.

The dialogue between the Kremlin and the NGOs, which started on the occasion of the first Civic Forum in 2001, has been channeled (and to a certain extent institutionalized) through President Putin's Human Rights Commission. In July 2002, the president appointed Ella Pamfilova as head of the commission, which is an advisory body consisting of thirty members, among them representatives of the NGOs mentioned above.[11]

In December 2002, on the occasion of International Human Rights Day, Putin met the commission in full for the first time and had a lively exchange of views with its members. They complained of the Kremlin's policy toward Chechnya, the emigration and refugee policy, as well as the abuses of the military. The president and human rights activists met again in December 2003.

The NGOs give advice, make proposals, and give help, but, since they are outside the decision-making mechanism, they cannot control the implementation of their ideas in case they manage to get them through. They influence the political process mainly through Western channels. By endorsing the activities of NGOs, by using their information, and trying to get replies to their questions, Western political institutions remind the Russian leadership of its international commitments. As a member of the Council of Europe, Russia ratified the European Convention on Human Rights in 1998 and its citizens are increasingly taking their complaints to the European Court of Human Rights in Strasbourg, France. In May 2004, the court received about 15,000 complaints, of which 200 referred to Chechnya.

If job allocation mechanisms in the administration or the executive were ruled by principles of efficiency and not by the crony patronage inherited from the Yeltsin period, one could imagine that some leaders of Russian NGOs would be very useful to Russian democratization as incumbents of high positions of responsibility, but this is not the case and they remain somehow on the periphery of the decision-making process.

The Sources of Financial Support

Russian NGOs have a chronic lack of financial support from domestic sources and are mainly funded by grants from Western institutions. Primarily through TACIS programs, the EU is the largest donor of technical aid to Russia. TACIS, which was launched by the EU in 1991, provides grant-financed technical assistance to twelve countries in Eastern Europe and Central Asia.

State institutions have also benefited from Western programs to develop civil society and democratization, like those generously financed by tycoon George Soros. This fact does not prevent Putin feeling suspicious about foreign aid and Western funding of NGOs. The Kremlin has tried to impose its own agenda on foreign organizations working in Russia. That refers to the mission of the Organization for Security and Cooperation in Europe (OSCE) in Chechnya or humanitarian NGOs helping Chechen refugees in Ingushetia. "There is no such thing as Western philanthropy toward Russia, but intelligence service priorities," Putin said on one occasion.[12] The leader might have his own views about the aims of Western funding, but as a pragmatist, he is prepared to reap the benefits of foreign investment in Russian democracy building. In his meeting with the Commission of Human Rights at the Kremlin in December 2002, he showed real interest in practical solutions being offered by their partners, mainly by Valerii Abramkin, director of the Moscow Center for Prison Reform.

The still limited Russian financial support for institution and democracy building has had one of its best examples in the figure of oligarch Mikhail Khodorkovsky, the former head of the oil company Yukos, who was imprisoned on October 25, 2003, and accused of evading taxes as well as other charges that may be punishable by a 10-year jail term. Khodorkovsky, a former Communist Youth leader and the richest man in Russia, was implementing a systematic and ambitious agenda, which could be considered a very important contribution to the integration of Russia in the West and to the promotion of Western values.

By the end of 2002 Yukos had devoted $45 million of net profits toward charitable and social purposes, an amount equivalent to 1.5 percent of its profit, according to Mikhail Trushin, deputy chairman of the company in charge of educational, cultural, and philanthropic projects.[13] They include the Federation of Internet Education (FIE), which has been training tens of thousands of teachers in all regions of Russia. The FIE was planning to open up to 50 centers all around the country and to train up to 250,000 teachers all together by 2006. Yukos runs the foundation Open Russia, which implements social, educational, and cultural programs, a club of local journalists (*Ot pervykh ust*), and an organization (*Novaia tsivilizatsia*) to help teenagers to adapt to democratic society. It also runs a program to draft legislation together with the Parliamentary Foundation and different projects in the fields of foreign policy research and publishing. Yukos also sponsored the publication of a monthly page devoted to civil society in the newspaper *Izvestiia*.

The New Agenda

The events of September 11 gave broader scope to Putin's foreign policy, which had already proclaimed integration with Europe as one of its "key directions." The president has renewed his European commitment, but the Americans' concerns about security dictate the agenda and make the West less sensitive to democratic problems in Russia and Russia more assertive of its authoritarian traditions.

Putin's main objective is "to make Europe a continent of peace without dividing lines, which presupposes Russia's deep integration into the common European economic, legal and humanitarian space."[14]

The problem of Kaliningrad, which will become a Russian enclave in the EU territory after its next enlargement, has prompted Putin to proclaim "freedom of movement" in the "European space" as one issue on his agenda. A broad number of subjects (among them Russia's own borders) have to be defined before the Russian and European spaces can be fully compatible. There is more than a demagogic note in Putin's defense of freedom of movement in the European space, if we take into consideration that the Russian government has closed vast territories of Siberia to foreigners in the past year and that requirements to invite foreigners have been hardened since the issue was transferred from the Ministry of Foreign Affairs to the Ministry of Interior.

Russia and the EU

The EU and Russia are already exploring their compatibility in the economic, political, humanitarian, security, and military fields. The Partnership and Cooperation Agreement (PCA), which came into force in 1997 for an initial period of ten years, together with the Common Strategy on Russia of 1999, are the pillars of this cooperation. To them we can add the new mechanism of cooperation between Russia and NATO, signed in May 2002.

The EU and Russia are trying to draw the outline of A Common European Economic Space (CEES). By October 2003, a working group, chaired by Commissioner Chris Patten and Russian Deputy Prime Minister Khristenko, had produced a concept for closer economic relations between the two entities. To this end, the business community and the representatives of civil society were asked for contributions. Academic and economic entities such as the Working Center for Economic Reforms under the government of the Russian Federation launched a debate on the CEES, which ultimately deals with the construction of a united Europe as far as this is possible in the present circumstances.[15]

The aim of the CEES is a privileged relationship, focusing on regulatory and legislative convergence and trade and investment facilitation. Therefore, the search for compatibilities between Russia and the European Union is of a different nature than the adoption of the *acquis communautaire* by EU candidate members, although both processes might have specific elements in common. After all, creating the CEES will be a step toward the integration of Russia in the West.

Slowly, Russian-European relations are becoming deeper, diversified, and more technical. The EU leadership (the president of the commission together with the EU rotating presidency) meets with the Russian leadership twice a year, and, meanwhile, joint committees and expert groups up to the governmental level deal with specific issues such as the future of the Kaliningrad enclave, the energy dialogue to ensure supplies of gas and oil in exchange for long-term investments, the market economy status, or the CEES.

The increasing number of Russian institutions involved in one way or another with the European realities reflects the progressive articulation of the relationship. This may be extended to the European television space. Russian progressive involvement in the management of EuroNews, a multilingual channel covering world news from a European perspective, is mainly a political goal: Russia has given a place to Europe in its information space and has conquered a platform to project its own image into Europe.

In 2001, the Russian State Radio and Television Company (VGTRK, or second channel) bought a share in the international consortium SECEMI, which is a combination of twenty public television broadcasters and runs EuroNews. By buying up to 16 percent of the shares of the consortium in 2002, Russia became one of the four main shareholders (together with France, Spain, and Italy) and got a seat on the administration board. EuroNews started broadcasting in September 2001 in Russia, where its audience quota is larger than in Europe.

Global Aims

In contrast to the EU candidate countries or Ukraine, Russia has not reformed its executive and legislative organs for better adaptation to the EU. Russia has neither a minister of European affairs in the government nor a Europe commission in the State Duma. Russia is not striving to join the EU under the current terms of this organization. The main horizon of Russian global integration is the WTO.

At the governmental level, the technicalities of economic integration in the world are handled by the Ministry of Economic Development. There the vice minister, Maksim Medvedkov, a respected specialist in Western law who has worked in Brussels, has been in charge of negotiating his country's membership in the WTO. He was one of the authors of the PCA between Russia and the EU.

Economic legislation being passed by the Duma in order to catch up with the external world does not explicitly refer to "Western," "European," or "American" standards, but to "international" standards. When looking for legislation models, Russian experts look for benchmarks in the whole legislative spectrum available worldwide. Russian legislators and legal experts are more experienced and in a stronger position today than during the first years of the transitional period. Gone are the days when the legislative process was influenced by American and European lobbies competing among themselves to leave their mark on the banking system or the organization of the land cadastre.

As far as legislative power is concerned, the Foreign Affairs Committees of the Duma and the Federation Council have been involved in negotiations with the EU, mainly because of the impact of EU enlargement on Kaliningrad.

The adoption of legislation to adapt the Russian legal system to international standards is proceeding very sluggishly and for the most part without particular pressure from the president or the government. To complete its adaptation to international standards Russia must pass more than a hundred laws, among them the long delayed Customs Code and further legislation to protect intellectual property and fight against intellectual piracy.

The pro-Western tendencies had limited representation in the Third Duma (1999–2003). Of the nine groups that make up the 450 seats of the lower chamber of Parliament, only two (the Union of Right Forces, or URF, with thirty-two legislators and Yabloko with seventeen) have a proven pro-European orientation. Yabloko acted as the most homogeneous team in defending Western democratic values. The URF was weakened by its heterogeneity, although its leaders, at that time Boris Nemtsov and Irina Khakamada, were clearly pro-European. Neither URF nor Yabloko were represented in the Fourth Duma, since both parties failed in the December 2003 elections.

The pro-presidential party United Russia, which resulted from the union of Fatherland-All Russia and Unity, follows Kremlin indications whatever they are. To the traditional anti-Western positions of the Communist Party and the Liberal Democratic Party of Vladimir Zhirinovskii, one has to add the extreme anti-Western position of Gennadii Raikov, of Popular Democracy(ND). Raikov has been the main force behind legislative initiatives against Catholicism and homosexuals and initiatives in favor of the reestablishment of the death penalty, a punishment that was subjected to a moratorium after Russia joined the Council of Europe in 1996. Polls indicate that almost 79 percent of Russians are in favor of capital punishment. ND is now integrated into the United Russia majority in the Fourth Duma.

To Kill or Not to Kill

Since rejection of capital punishment is one of the main features of the European model (as opposed to the U.S. model), the ratio for/against capital punishment in the Duma might be used to identify genuine pro-European tendencies in legislative power.

In February 2002, 266 deputies (out of the total 450 legislators of the chamber) signed a request calling on Putin to abolish the moratorium on the death penalty. In other words, they urged the president to reestablish the implementation of capital punishment in Russia. As the matter still stands, the Russian Constitutional Court ruled that courts cannot impose death sentences until the system of jury trials is fully established on the whole territory of the Russian Federation.

The president, who has declared himself against the death penalty, did not give in to the legislators' petition. If he had, he would have had to confront the Council of Europe, of which Russia is a member.

Putin avoided confrontation at home and abroad by using a shrewd Machiavellian scheme. He managed to put off the full introduction of jury trials until 2007 (instead of enacting it in the whole Russian Federation from January 2003 as initially foreseen). This delay extends the validity of the Constitutional Court decision blocking death sentences until 2007. In the State Duma, only the liberal parties Yabloko (in full) and the Union of Right Forces (with a few exceptions) are opposed to the death penalty. The pro-presidential groups are split on this matter.

The different sectors involved in the rapprochement between Russia and the West form a patchy spectrum. On the think-tank front, the Institute of Europe and the Institute of World Economy and International Relations (IMEMO) devote themselves to scholarly research and eagerly fulfill political advisory functions, if required. Others, like the Committee For Russia in a United Europe (RUE) or the Council of Foreign and Defense Policy, concentrate their efforts on the debate of the hot topics between Russia and the EU. The Moscow Political School has embarked on the creative propagation of pan-European ideas both in seminars and publications. On the business front, the Russian Union of Industrialists and Entrepreneurs (RUIE) or the European Business Club help in shaping the Russian economic agenda toward Europe.

In the fragmented world of Russian civilian society, a convergence of representatives of business and defenders of human rights seems to be emerging for the sake of defending common interests. Some elements of this convergence of interests were apparent in the summer of 2001 when George Soros met with representatives of civil society such as Arkadii Roginskii (Memorial Society), Liudmila Alekseeva (Moscow Helsinki Group), and Aleksei Simonov (Glasnost Defense Foundation), as well as with young managers of the Club 2015. Aleksandr Auzan and the Confederation of Consumers Societies play a pivotal role in this convergence.

Some Institutions Working for the Integration of Russia and Europe

The Think Tanks

Russian think tanks played a significant role in the pro-Western orientation under Gorbachev, who looked for theoretical backing in centers like the IMEMO and the Institute of Economics of the World Socialist System headed by Oleg Bogomolov. Yeltsin put an end to that cooperation and partially replaced it with informal brainstorming sessions, which took place under the auspices of his advisers in the Kremlin or in the Security Council. With Putin, more secretive small format meetings have replaced the former gatherings of a large number of specialists.

Experts in the Institute of Europe who were consulted for this chapter see a return to traditional consultation practices between political decision-making bodies and think tanks, which existed before Yeltsin changed the format of the relationship. Under Putin, the decision-making organs show no regularity, no systematic approach, and no commitment to cooperating with the think tanks. The Institute of Europe gathers a very competent group of young specialists and produces a large amount of literature to disseminate information on the European building process. The Institute works to spread this knowledge in the Russian provinces too. Its director, Nikolai Shmeliev, is a member of the president's Commission on Human Rights and his vice director, Sergei Karaganov, is a respected and articulate analyst.

The Committee for Russia in a United Europe (RUE)

This debate forum has been the center of the most dynamic discussions on European matters in Moscow since its creation in November 2001. With systematic analysis of current European topics affecting Russian interests, such as the future of Kaliningrad or the consequences of a common European currency, RUE has broken new ground in exploring current European affairs from a plurality of perspectives. Member of Parliament Vladimir Rizhkov is the executive secretary of the committee and also the main driving force of the twenty-three founding members, politicians, businesspeople, and experts with a pro-European orientation. Among them, we can list the former vice president of the Defense Committee of the Duma, Aleksei Arbatov, the head of the Kaliningrad administration, Vladimir Yegorov, the governor of Novgorod, Mikhail Prusak, the president of Chuvashia, Nikolai Fedorov, as well as Sergei Karaganov and Boris Nemtsov. At the founding session, Nemtsov raised the possibility that Russia would become a member of the

EU in a decade. Mikhail Khodorkovsky is a member of the committee and has also been one of its main sources of financial support.

Managers of large companies and banks, think-tank experts, economists, EU representatives, foreign service officials, and diplomats from EU countries meet regularly in order to promote a common vision of Europe. Among the subjects under analysis is a roadmap for a visa-free regime for Russians in Europe.

According to Rizhkov, tourism (from 4 million to 5 million Russian visitors to Europe every year), the economy (Europe as the main trade partner), and anti-Americanism (a desire to be part of the West but rejection of the United States), as well as the strong performance of the euro are the elements that define the pro-European landscape in Russia.

Moscow School of Political Studies

This institution, established in 1993, has been a formidable tool for the penetration of Western and European ideas throughout Russia. The students (politicians, members of public administrations, economists, and journalists) are members of national, regional, and Commonwealth of Independent States (CIS) elites. The basic cycle of seminars gives the students a chance to become familiar with European and national institutions in Strasbourg, Brussels, and in EU countries in a very short time.

Over the years, the structure of the school has become more and more sophisticated. Yuri Senokosov, former editor of the journal *Problems of Philosophy*, is responsible for the school's large publications program, which includes a series of specialized and basic reference books in political science, philosophy, and the history of ideas, as well as leaflets and a journal, *Obshchaia tetrad'* (General Notebook).

Members of the State Duma and numerous officials, from local levels of the administration to the Kremlin, are among the school's graduates, which has promoted contact among the more than 5,000 students by creating an Alumni Association. As far as funding is concerned, the school has relied upon foreign sources, mainly the Council of Europe, but also the USAID, and national and regional organizations in different countries of the EU where seminars take place. According to a poll conducted by VTsIOM, 95 percent of the school's graduates state that the school has seriously influenced their perception of the world and mainly of Europe, and that the school has helped them to overcome Soviet complexes, the feeling of isolation, and the mentality of "great power" and "besieged fortress." It has also helped them to understand the need for Russia to be integrated with European civilization.

Russian Union of Industrialists and Entrepreneurs

The Russian Union of Industrialists and Entrepreneurs (RUIE) is the largest association of employers in Russia. It was created in December 1991 and according to its president, Arkadii Vol'skii, it joins 320,000 juridical and physical persons producing altogether more than 50 percent of Russia's GNP. The association began to play a new political role in 2001 after its board was reshuffled to make room for representatives of the main economic and financial sectors. Arkadii Vol'skii, a veteran official who worked with Yurii Andropov and Mikhail Gorbachev, remains at the head of the organization, but the positions around him have been taken by the oligarchs striving to co-shape the rules of a democratic market-oriented economy in Russia. After Putin's victory in the showdown with the oligarchs Vladimir Gusinsky and Boris Berezovsky, the RUIE became the president's main partner in his new civilized and more or less regular dialogue with the business sectors. This dialogue became more tense after Khodarkovsky's imprisonment. In an effort to raise the reputation of Russian entrepreneurs, the RUIE approved in 2002 a chart of corporate and business ethics and a declaration of principles. The RUIE is in favor of a "strong democratic State" with "developed institutions of civil society."

The RUIE contributes with its own experts to the Russian-EU working groups on different topics. They produce drafts for pieces of reform legislation in the financial, industrial, and banking fields. They also put pressure on the government to speed up the harmonization of laws with European standards and to prepare Russia's accession to the WTO. And they blame the EU and the WTO for being discriminatory toward Russian products.

The RUIE represents a wide range of interests. When frustrated by European bureaucrats, its members can become as outspoken as Anatolii Chubais, the head of the electric power monopoly Unified Energy System of Russia (RAO EES Rossiia). "Russia will become a world economy without the help of the Europeans," if the EU does not open its markets to Russian products and services, said Chubais in Turin.[16] "We should learn from what the Americans have attained in a century and what the Chinese have attained in a decade," said Vol'ski, who admires the Chinese for their capacity to attract a much higher level of foreign investment than the Russians.[17] The RUIE works in close cooperation with the European Business Club. This independent organization, founded in 1995, represents the interests of members (mainly European companies) to the Russian and European governments at the highest level. It is very active in organizing seminars on practical and technical topics (e.g., the WTO, introduction of the euro, and specific legislation).

The Energy Sector

Since Europe is the main market for Russian energy, the representatives of oil companies as well as the gas (Gazprom) and electricity monopolies play a role in shaping the European policy on Russia. In October 2001, Russia and the EU launched an energy dialogue with the aim of working toward the definition and arrangements for an energy partnership to be established within the legal framework of the EU–Russia Partnership and Cooperation Agreement (PCA).

The oil companies and Gazprom are key in the reintegration processes between Russia and the Western members of the CIS (Ukraine, Moldova, Belarus) and major players in the energy markets of Poland and other former Soviet allies in Central Europe. The oil-companies as well as Gazprom and RAO EES are all objectively interested in European integration, but with variations. In the oil sector, Yukos, the company formerly headed by Mikhail Khodorkovsky, wants to become a global player, with high standards of efficiency, diversified interests, and stakes in other oil-producing countries. Eager to sell electricity to Western Europe, Anatolii Chubais is the most passionate advocate of energy market liberalization in the EU. Linked to several European countries by long-term bilateral supply contracts, Gazprom is resisting liberalization, and, together with its economic partners in Western Europe, sticks to practices that contradict the principle of the single market in Europe. Being afraid of a drop in prices, Gazprom is one of the pillars of Russian bilateralism that contemplates a privileged role for Germany, the first market for Russian gas on the continent. Europe is not responding to the projects of the Russian energy sectors with the commitment those sectors would like to see. Frustrated by the European attitude, the Kremlin has launched an energy dialogue with the United States, which for the moment has a symbolic political character.

The Orthodox Church and the European Constitution

The new American agenda since September 11 increases Russia's chances of playing a more prominent role not only in security or the antiterrorism fight, but also in the definition of Western civilization.

Curiously enough, the Russian Orthodox Church has been one of the most active institutions in exploring the new opportunities for co-shaping the Western world. In recent years, this organization has expressed firm anti-Catholic and anti-Western views as well as very closed patrimonial conceptions concerning the missionary activities of other churches on Russian territory. But the Russian Orthodox Church has claimed a place in the discussion on the future of Europe and has contributed its own views to the European Convention, which, under former French president, Giscard d'Estaing, has drafted a new Constitutional Treaty (or Constitution) for the EU. The Russian Orthodox Church seems to have been encouraged by the president of the European Commission, Romano Prodi of Italy. Patriarch Aleksei of Moscow and All Russia wrote to Prodi:

> The Russian Orthodox Church is prepared to cooperate with the EU agencies in the field of developing an integral dimension of a united Europe. We can take part in discussing the problems of inter-ethnic and inter-religious relations and in elaborating legislation which would regulate the status of religious communities.[18]
>
> The attitude of the Orthodox Church, however, toward the united and enlarged Europe is based on protectionist considerations as far as its interests are

concerned. What is new, however, is that this time Russian Orthodoxy is acting as a European institution with a specific interest in Europe (spiritual, human, and material) and not from a marginal position outside Europe.

In 2002 Metropolitan Kiril visited Brussels where he met with high-ranking officials of the European Union and NATO. After hearing his report, the Holy Synod of the Russian Orthodox Church decided in July 2002 to establish a permanent representation to the European institutions with the aim of participating in the theoretical discussions on the future of Europe.[19]

These discussions are a "timely opportunity to reflect more generally on the role of the Orthodox tradition in a united Europe and to share its reflections with European political institutions."[20]

One of the proposals made by the Department for External Church Relations of the Russian Orthodox Church is that the future Constitutional Treaty makes the status of religious organizations the prerogative of national governments.

In November, Bishop Hilarion Alfeyev spoke against the secular model "based on Western post-Christian humanism," which separates religion from the state and from society. "Now the processes currently taking place in Europe are somewhat similar to those in the Soviet Union. Militant secularism becomes as dangerous for religion as militant atheism."[21]

Notes

1. As an example of this trend see E.G. Yasin, *Modernizatsia ekonomiki i sistema tsennostei* (Moscow: Gosudarstvennyi universitet, Vyshaia shkola ekonomiki, 2003).

2. See the introductory article "Ogliadyvaias' na proidennoe i neprodumannoe, 1987–2002," in *Ezhegodnik obshchestvennogo mnenie 2002*, (Moscow: Vserossiiskii Tsentr Izuchenia Obshchestvennogo Mnenie, 2002).

3. Putin's annual address to the nation, May 16, 2003.

4. According to a VTsIOM poll, quoted in *Nezavisimaia gazeta*, June 4, 2003.

5. Unless otherwise stated, opinion poll results quoted in this work are from the VTsIOM Website and the 2002 report cited in note 2 as well as from Iurii Levada and Leonid Sedov, former director and senior expert, respectively, of that institution until they quit in August 2003 as a result of the Kremlin policy toward the center.

6. See Grigory Yavlinsky, "Demodernizatsia" *Novaia gazeta*, November 11–13, 2002.

7. According to a VIsIOM poll conducted April 24–28, 2003.

8. See Iu.A. Levada, "Sotsial'no-politicheskaia situatsia v Rossii v avguste 2002," www.oldpoloru/documents/503225.latml.

9. Leonid Sedov, "Strana i mir," draft of an article given by the author in spring 2003.

10. See www.usaid.gov.

11. For the whole list of members see the presidential decree of October 19, 2002, published in *Rossiiskaia gazeta*, October 22, 2002, www.rg.ru/oficial/doc/ykazi/1208.shtm.

12. According to sources available to the author of this chapter.

13. See www.Yukos.com/pdf/YUKOS_BLAGO.pdf.

14. See Vladimir Putin's Messages to the President of the Commission of the European Communities and Heads of the Member States of the European Union, Ministry of Foreign Affairs of the Russian Federation, *Daily News Bulletin*, August 28, 2002.

15. See *Common Economic Space: Prospects of Russia-EU Relations, White Book* (Moscow: Russian European Center for Economic Policy, October 2002).

16. *Kommersant Daily*, February 18, 2002.

17. See interview with Arkadii Vol'skii in *Delovie liudi*, Moscow, February 17, 2002.

18. Letter from the Patriarch to Romano Prodi, October 3, 2002.

19. See www.orthodoxeurope.org.

20. Bishop Hilarion Alfeyev, "Christian Witness to Uniting Europe. A View from the Russian Orthodox Church" (paper delivered at the International Symposium on Wisdom as a Source of European Unity) Rome, Chamber of Deputies, Italian Parliament, November 15, 2002, www.orthodoxeurope.org/page/14/21.aspx.

21. Ibid.

5

Political Leadership in Russia's Transformation

Lilia Shevtsova

Among the various factors contributing to the post-communist transformation in Russia—which includes institution building, democratization, the evolution of public opinion, the formation of civil society, economic reform, and the interrelationship between the center and the periphery—the institution of political leadership plays a particularly significant role. Political leadership, in fact, is the core of the political regime that is a form of interaction between the leader, on the one hand, and the elites and society at large, on the other.[1]

In all societies in transition the role of leadership is all the more important because the leader compensates for the lack of sound and viable institutions and often turns out to be the crucial transformational variable. The historical tradition of autocracy and the personification of power in Russia have turned leadership in this country into the decisive factor for change. Moreover, whether the transformation of Russia is ultimately successful will depend on the ability and readiness of political leadership, the main political institution in Russian society, to lay the ground for the formation of other independent political institutions, which in turn should weaken the pivotal role of leadership. Thus, the degree of Russia's liberal democratic transformation and its real, not virtual, integration into Western civilization depends not only on radical restructuring of its personified power, but also on making leadership an important political institution that should not replace other institutions.[2]

I will discuss in this chapter the following questions: What is the nature of the evolution of the Russian political regime under Vladimir Putin? To what extent does this evolution mean radical transformation of the traditional "Russian system," which relies on personification of power and domination of the state, and which subjects society and individuals to its will?[3] What are the major outcomes of Putin's activity and what are the crucial challenges Russia faces? To what extent do Putin's reforms facilitate Russia's integration into Western civilization?

Vladimir Putin: Forming his Own Leadership

Vladimir Putin became the new master of the Kremlin by using the contradictory aspirations of Russian society for change and continuity at the same time. On one hand, at the end of Yeltsin's rule Russia tried to close the chapter on Yeltsin once and for all and was ready for renewal. But, on the other hand, Russian society was apprehensive about new shocks and the unexpected, and therefore was eager to extricate itself from the previous revolutionary cycle and to secure stability at any cost. This meant sticking to the status quo. Putin virtually repeated the formula for coming to power that had been successfully tested by Boris Yeltsin in 1991, when Yeltsin used society's yearning for more radical reforms as well as the desire to put an end to the uncertainty and zigzags of Gorbachev's rule.[4] Putin's ascendancy to power thus potentially entailed an opportunity for Russia to move toward different ends: first, to stabilization of the oligarchic type of capitalism and Yeltsin's elected monarchy[5] that had emerged in the 1990s; second, to reliance upon power structures (the Ministry of Interior, Defense Ministry, special services) and state apparatus to strengthen the authoritarian vector; and third, to more radical reform, not only of the economy but of political rule itself.

In 2000–2001 the new Russian leader practically began refashioning the Yeltsin regime by taking apart its most important building blocks. Instead of the Yeltsin principle of mutual connivance, shadowy checks and balances, tolerance for opposition, and the maintenance of power by redistributing and decentralizing it and provoking constant revolutionary shocks, Putin turned to the principle of subordination, hierarchical submission, quelling opposition, control over alternative ways of thinking of the elite, and centralization of the federation. In essence, Putin began to build a "conveyer belt" political regime. However, the conservative elements of his support base (representatives of the power ministries—*siloviki* as they were dubbed in Russia) were counterbalanced not only by big business— "the oligarchs," but also by liberal-technocrats who became the major driving force behind Putin's modernization project. This type of regime somewhat resembles the bureaucratic-authoritarian political regimes that existed in the 1960s and 1970s in Latin America and were analyzed by David Collier and Guillermo O'Donnell[6]— they also relied on a mix that included the army, the oligarchy, and technocrats with dominant roles of the state apparatus and the leader.

Having changed some characteristics and the style of leadership, Putin did not change the system of governance—it remained a hybrid consisting of incompatible blocks: monolithic, personified power and its democratic legitimacy through regular elections. This system shows the continuing presence of the Russian tradition of rule and at the same time an attempt to rupture with it. It allows us to determine what is essential and central to Russian authority: the preservation of power and its continuity, and simultaneously the need to make it legitimate. On the one hand, the inevitable conflict between democratic and authoritarian beginnings creates the opportunity, or the illusion, that it could develop in the most diverse directions—authoritarian as well as democratic. On the other hand, this conflict turns into a source of internal instability for the political regime and prevents authorities—and the society—from rallying around a single system of values. Moreover, the combination of democracy and personified rule with elements of the tsarist tradition cannot help but lead to the discrediting of democracy and its conversion into a facade that hides an entirely different substance inside.[7]

Preserving a hybrid system, Putin has succeeded in projecting the image of a leader who could at once appeal to all sectors of society and political groups—an image of Everybody's Man. It is precisely this image that helped him form broadly based social and political support for the new rule, and various elements of this base of support expected that the president would carry out their objectives, which had often been mutually exclusive.

From the very beginning the new president aimed to get beyond the limits of Yeltsin's reliance on tycoons and regional leaders and instead set the goal of depending on the federal bureaucracy and coercive organs. He was sufficiently flexible, however, and tried not to become hostage either to his praetorians or to other bureaucratic clans, which to a large extent he succeeded in doing.

In 2001 President Putin demonstrated that power and its consolidation were not his goals per se. Unexpectedly for many who had predicted that the former KGB officer would think only about his power and its consolidation, the president achieved two breakthroughs—in the field of economy and foreign policy. He restarted the economic reform that had stalled under Yeltsin and after the tragic events of September 11, 2001, in the United States, he made a pro-Western shift in Russian foreign policy. Moreover, the latter occurred at a time when a significant part of Russian society was taking a "wait and see" approach, when anti-Western and, more specifically, anti-American sentiments were relatively strong among the political class. In September 2001, 54 percent of those Russians polled preferred Russia to be neutral; 20 percent were in favor of the Taliban; and 28 percent supported the inclusion of Russia in military activities against terrorists. For the first time, Putin openly went against the mainstream.

By the end of 2002, the framework of Putin's regime became more or less clear. The new Russian president appears to be a traditional Russia modernizer: he definitely wants to stop the decay, to strengthen the state, and to include Russia in the West. But at the same time, he apparently believes that he has to consolidate Russian society on the basis of the same old rules and traditions of personified power and state primacy. That means Russia's integration into the Western structures as an autonomous subject still hostile to Western principles.

Gradually, political experience under Putin has demonstrated that he has failed to go beyond dilemmas that had rocked Yeltsin's authority. One of them is the necessity to preserve personal rule with strong patrimonial features in a new historic situation and pluralistic society, which entails elections. In this situation the leader even without much reflection attempts to maximize his power (concentrating it in the presidency) and at the same time to minimize responsibility for that power. But here we encounter a paradox, one of many in Russian political practice: sharing responsibility without sharing real power is possible under one condition—if the division of responsibility becomes a sharing of irresponsibility. This leads to the development in Russia of authority, at the head of which is an all-powered leader, who thinks only of how to control all levers of power, but who is not accountable for anything. The same occurs on all other levels of authority—at the level of subjects of the federation, at local levels, and at city levels, where local barons and apparatuses come to power but refuse to accept responsibility for their actions. Both civil society and the judicial system are too weak to make them accountable.[8] In short, the system of governance in Russia continues to reproduce unaccountability.

Russia Turns to the West

At the end of the first Putin presidency the fundamental challenges facing Russia have become apparent, as well as the means available for dealing with them.[9] For the first time, the new, post-communist Russia is taking on a shape and a substantial part of Russian society already knows what it wants. It looks as if Russia is finally turning in one definite direction—toward the West. It is not clear, however, how long it will take the country to throw off the last waverings and suspicions concerning the West, and what price it will have to pay for its final break with the past.

It is not true anymore that the communist vestiges are the major obstacle to deep and systemic Russian transformation. Quite the contrary: Russia unexpectedly easily and amazingly fast has made a break with the institutional and ideological characteristics shaped by communism. They may still influence the behavior of 15–20 percent of the electorate voting for the Communist Party.[10] But even those who are voting for communists do not always support a return to the communist past—they reject the present. Paradoxically, the communists themselves have adopted—at least formally—all the major democratic ideas. They have learned to function within the framework of parliamentary democracy and now they are in favor of free media and opposition (ironically, communists are sometimes even more supportive of political freedoms than some liberals who openly call for a Pinochet regime) in Russia simply because these democratic principles create the possibility for communists to survive. True, the Russian Communist Party has failed to undergo the same positive evolution that former communist parties have in Central and Eastern Europe. But at least it has succeeded in adjusting to political pluralism and parliamentary democracy.

In any case, Russia's modernist trajectory is much more constrained not by the communist legacy per se, but by the traditional, centuries-long logic of personified power and the relationship between the state and the individual. This logic is still reflected in the preservation, though in modified form, of the "Russian system," that is, autocracy, domination of the state, and the fusion of politics and property.

On the positive side of the balance sheet, we see that Russian society after years of coming to grips with the new reality has realized that it cannot modernize itself relying only on its inner resources, without help from the outside, and that a breakthrough to the twenty-first century is impossible without the help of the West.

(I mean "the West" not in the geographical sense, but rather the whole civilization that is ordered around the concept of liberal democracy.) Though Russia under Yeltsin attempted to get the financial assistance and economic support of Western countries, nurturing hope for a new Marshall Plan, under Putin a significant part of the population has come to understand that only integration into Western society can help Russia become a modern state.[11] For them, the West is not only *a means* of modernization and a mine of resources that Russia lacks but also *a goal* in itself—an altogether new phenomenon in Russian thinking.

After the tragedy of September 11, 2001, Vladimir Putin forced the ruling class to accept, not without grudges, his pro-Western shift. Opportunistic elites followed the leader, as is usual in Russia. But to move the presidential choice into the realm of concrete decisions, to make the pro-Western choice durable, a new bureaucracy is needed, one that will leave provincial backwaters and servility behind and think in the imperatives of the modern competitive age. Unfortunately, one can count such bureaucrats in Russia on the fingers of both hands. That is why the president has so few to rely on as he tries to channel Russia's relations with NATO in a new direction, to gain Russia membership in the World Trade Organization, and to move closer to Europe and toward more constructive relations with the United States. He has to make policy on his own, which is what he did during his first presidency. But gradually, the lack of sufficient support of his pro-Western course within the ruling class started to constrain his foreign policy, which revived old suspicions and irritants.

Thus, the Kremlin's choice in favor of the West is not solidified. It is not yet supported by the national consensus. It has not become Russia's ideology and its elites' key mission. It is based on the wishes and desires of the leader and his understanding of the weakness of other options, and the interests of advanced social groups. The choice still lacks content, a deeper substance. Moreover, the leader remains the classic Russian modernizer, operating within the limits of the triad of autocracy, Western resources, and a market economy. This means that both President Putin and Russian elites hope to join the West on their own terms—that is, while preserving at least some elements of the Russian system.

Russia still has to turn this rhetorical, often hesitant Westernization into concrete political decisions, and economic mechanisms—into everyday life. Besides, there is still no nationwide accord regarding the agenda of integration for Russia and to what extent transformation has to become a major prerequisite and guarantee of this integration. One of the best-known analysts following the U.S.-Russian relationship, Robert Legvold, correctly defined Putin's shift toward the West after the September 11 tragedy as "strategic choice without strategy."[12] Thus, the complicated interdependence between integration and transformation has not been understood within the Russian political class and society at large. There is still hope, at least among the elite groups, that Russia can integrate without adaptation to Western values because adaptation by many politicians and pundits is considered to be a weakness, a rejection of Russian identity, and even a betrayal of Russian state interests. There is still an illusion that while integrating into the Western structures Russia can preserve its full sovereignty and old rules of the game, the same prejudices and complexes—so strong is the longing to retain traditional state attributes as the guarantee of survival.

True, as events after the Iraqi war in 2003 have proved, Russia, despite its contradictions of the United States, has preserved its pro-Western choice. The same people who not so long ago blasted the West for the first NATO enlargement and Kosovo crisis this time behaved in a reasonable way. One may conclude now that a major part of the Russian political class has finally rejected claims of Russia as the pole of an alternative civilization and even the Primakovian formula of "multipolarity." Movement toward the West has become Russia's major direction. But Russians still have to overcome the new temptation to pursue what seems the easiest road to integrate with the West: imitating the market and democracy in their surface aspects while underneath preserving patron–client relations, the rule of the few, and governance without accountability. In fact, during Putin's tenure, the imitation of liberal democracy, imitation of the rule of law, imitation of the political pluralism, and imitation of pro-Western policy are becoming the most dangerous traps for Russian transformation.

Paradoxes of Westernization

In the meantime, the alliance that Russia concluded with the West and first of all with the United States in the aftermath of September 11, 2001, contains not only the possibility of real partnership and Russia's integration with the West but also the threat of a new Russian alienation. True, if there were a new misunderstanding or clash of interests with the West, Russia would hardly revert to its previous hostility toward Western civilization. One can hardly envisage militarization of Russia and its isolation from the outside world: there are not enough resources or readiness for this option among society and even on the part of elites hostile to the West. Another scenario much more plausible for Russia: descending to a murky zone of disenchantment with everybody and everything—including Russia itself.

So far, the alliance President Putin has struck with the West has taken the form of a Faustian bargain.[13] The essence of the bargain is simple. The West is including Russia in the implementation of some of its geopolitical interests—the war on terrorism, strengthening the security agenda, promoting an energy dialogue—while shutting its eyes to how far Russia still is from being a liberal democracy. Moreover, the majority of Western leaders continues to view Russia's leadership as the major guarantee of its cozy relations with the West, thus endorsing Russian rule through personified power and Russia's traditional state based on the domination of power over the individual. In its turn, Russia is solving the problem of external resources for its modernization while retaining the old rules of the game domestically.

The Faustian bargain has its supporters both in the developed democracies and in Russia. In the West, supporters of the bargain include first of all those who do not care about Russia or see its possible impact on the world, those who continue to view Russia as a hostile country, an embodiment of evil, and those who prefer to see Russia where it is now—at the perimeter of Western civilization, as a curtain dividing the West from rising China.

In Russia, the Faustian bargain is supported by the advocates of authoritarianism (including liberal authoritarianism) and Russia's "uniqueness." Thus, the new axis between Russia and the West is endorsed and promoted first of all by the traditionalist part of the establishment on both sides. Paradoxically, the current alliance between Russia and the West is an ideal means for preserving the bureaucratic-authoritarian regime that has emerged in Russia during Putin's tenure.

It is true that European political circles are rather critical of the new "axis" and they have become quite vocal in publicizing their concerns about the real nature of the alliance with Russia, which serves as legitimization of Russia's "pragmatic autocracy." In 2001–2002 there were signs that the American administration was interested in promoting the "axis" in an attempt to keep Russia on board in the antiterrorist campaign. But in 2003 the moods in Western capitals, including Washington, have changed. Deepening authoritarian trends in Russian politics, the Kremlin attack on one of Russia's oligarchs Mikhail Khodorkovsky, and the defeat of the Russian liberal democratic parties Yabloko and the Union of Right Forces have triggered real concern in the West and forced Western leaders to think about possible outcomes of the fact that Russia continues to pursue a different set of values.

Events of 2003–2004 amid growing mutual frustration in Russia and in the West demonstrated that the inclusion of Russia in the Western orbit on the basis of certain coinciding geopolitical interests could be situational and merely temporary. Only common values would guarantee the genuine integration of Russia into the Western community. Russia would have to fully embrace liberal democratic principles, rejecting attempts to tailor democratic institutions to the needs of personified power and the bureaucratic state. Only then could Russia join in a *constructive partnership* with the West. Furthermore, the Russian alliance with the West cannot be an alliance of leaders who may share personal sympathy for each other—this alliance should have a broader national and political base.

One has to admit that the Iraqi crisis also complicated Russia's movement toward the West: with the Western community split on the issue of Iraq, and, moreover, with this split making other divides within the West more apparent, not unexpectedly Russia has found herself at a loss as to which West to join. Rifts and squabbles within the West concerning the new world order and international priorities increased the ground for Russia's vacillations and zigzagging. Besides, a split Western community could not exert pressure on Russia to pursue a more radical transformation path.

A constructive partnership between Russia and the West would at first inevitably have aspects of benevolent asymmetry, at least in the economics field. A serious challenge for Russia is to give up the notion of military parity with the United

States, recognize its current limited capabilities, and channel its resources into building an affluent and "normal" society based on a different principle—first the individual and then the state. Cutting excessive global ambitions now would not preclude the possibility of Russia's emergence in the future as an economically prosperous regional and, perhaps, world power. But for the sake of its future, Russia—and the West—will have to end the imitation game, which is humiliating for all participants and destructive for Russia.

Are Russians Ready for Liberal Democracy?

Russia's future trajectory depends on whether Russian society and its political class are prepared to reject attempts to combine the incompatible: Westernization with Soviet-style superpower ambitions, democracy with personified power, the market with a regulatory role of the bureaucracy, inclusion in Europe with curbs on a free press. Is it ready to reject attempts to preserve great-power status based on military might? Numerous surveys suggest that by the late 1990s many Russians had matured enough to favor integration into a system of liberal values.[14]

In 2001–2002 only a portion of the population—about 24 percent according to polls conducted by the All-Russian Center for the Study of Public Opinion (VTsIOM—has retained its open allegiance to the traditional Russian state based on military might, imperial aspirations, and one-man rule. And 22 percent of Russians are trying to combine elements of the traditional "Russian system" with liberalism. But one can expect that at some point they will be ready to move further to accept the liberal democratic agenda (for instance, under the influence of the leader).[15]

A major part of the Russian population has in fact rejected key components of its previous identity—messianism and expansionism, Russian Orthodoxy as the state religion, and anti-Westernism as the official ideology. Polls in 2001–2003 indicate that 33 percent of the Russian population fully support the liberal democratic agenda, with another 37 percent who hesitate becoming more and more inclined to accept the Western alternative. All this demonstrates that Russia has enormous reformist potential.

But while a significant and growing number of Russians can throw away the crutches imposed by the political regime and walk independently, many in the ruling political class are not ready to give up their attempts to regulate, to reject patrimonialism, to leave behind the shadow networks, and to overcome nostalgia for the imperialist past—and finally to support the rule of law. Those who consider themselves Russian elites have been afraid to let go of the controls. They have no experience living in a free society. They are terrified of competition and have a fear of their own people and of any alternatives. They lean heavily on the police, the security services, the army, and the state apparatus, which they look on as their safety net and as guarantors of their survival. Their own helplessness, inadequate education, and lack of experience living in a culture of consensus and dialogue drive them to destroy any opposition, keeping potential rivals down. It is the political class in Russia, obsessed with self-preservation, that tries to reanimate the archaic elements of the public subconscious and heighten suspicion of the West, fear of openness, and nostalgia for the lost empire. Superpower status and authoritarianism are the last bastion of those who do not know how to live and rule in a new way. In fact, the majority of the ruling class understands that they have to deal with an imitation of great power and one man and they are happy with inventing the semblance.

It is a curious political phenomenon when intellectual and political establishments lag behind a nation. If at some point at least part of the elites fail to understand the urgency of eliminating the mythology, the emergence of a classical Marxist-style revolutionary situation in Russia is not entirely excluded.

Does the West Need Russia?

The West, for its part, has not yet decided how much it needs Russia. Western governments are still not prepared to integrate Russia into their space. This is understandable, for no one knows what it would do to Western civilization to bring in a weak (at the moment) giant, with all its complexes and pretensions, its murky past, still-vague desires, and huge ambitions, its enormous potential coupled with the vestiges of Soviet and pre-Soviet legacies. Besides, integration always means that the integrated subject accepts the rules of the game of the new entity and there is no evidence that Russia is ready for that.

Yes, there is an understanding, especially in Europe, that fundamental issues confronting the world community cannot be resolved without Russia. But Europe seems bothered that Russia is at a different level of development than itself.[16] Europe is creating a polity of a new kind—fashioning transnational governance, liquidating some functions of the nation-state, and destroying borders between countries, expanding its economic and political space. Russia continues building a traditional state with all its attributes and has been trying to lace civil society into a tight corset. There is a serious question: How can Russian modernism and European postmodernity coexist? It may not be realistic to anticipate the easy integration of entities with radically different views about the very substance of future development, that is, of elites that are building different types of states.

In addition, broad political groupings in the West are currently out of sympathy with Russia. Western liberals resent Russia's global aspirations, Moscow's Chechen war, the Kremlin's desire to stifle pluralism and freedom, the Kremlin's attempts to preserve its dominance in other new independent states, and every Russian leader's attempt to rule in a monarchic manner. Western conservatives, however, are prepared to engage Moscow in dialogue, but within the framework of realpolitik, avoiding mention of Russia's domestic problems and regarding the country as innately alien and incorrigible. Thus, unlike during the Gorbachev and early Yeltsin periods, there are no influential forces in the West prepared to more fully engage with Russia and to strive to influence Russian progress toward liberal democracy. Former British Ambassador to Russia Rodric Braithwaite, in his book *Across the Mosco River*, wrote: "When the facile optimism was disappointed, Western euphoria faded, and Russophobia returned. . . . The new Russophobia was expressed not by the governments, but in the statements of out-of-the-office politicians, the publications of academic experts, the sensational writings of journalists. . . . It was fueled by those who argued that the Russian Orthodox civilization was doomed to remain apart from the civilization of the West."[17]

Even those in the West who favor embracing Russia are still undecided about whether they should wait for Russia to complete its transformation into a democracy or start integrating without waiting for the outcomes of Russia's transformation. For the majority, first transformation, then integration is the most appropriate policy toward Russia. Western political circles hesitate, and many have almost reached the conclusion that it is better to wait. They still have to absorb Eastern Germany into Western Germany, to incorporate Central and Eastern Europe, and the Baltic states—and there is neither time nor money for new worries. Liberal democracies outside Europe have even less incentive to think about a sustainable marriage with Russia.

But Russia can transform itself only if it is part of the dialogue with the West. The impulses from the outside world might even become the crucial factor needed for change, especially in a situation where the domestic impetus for liberal and democratic reform is so weak. Russia's integration into the community of postindustrial nations should not necessarily mean membership in NATO and the European Union. Integration is a multistage process, and various forms of cooperation are possible—cooperation in strictly defined areas, adaptation, affiliation, mutual dependence, and strong bilateral relations. Analysts are correct in saying that Russia's setting its heart on full membership in Western international institutions in the nearest perspective could bring new disappointments to both sides if Russia is unable or unwilling to meet the requirements of that membership and these institutions do not seek palliatives like "special status" for Russia. But at the same time I believe that both Russia and Europe should find ways to set a goal of membership in the Western institutions or a goal of closer affiliation with these institutions as a stimulus for future Russian transformation. True, the time is not ripe to elaborate on details of this membership, but the time has come to discuss and set down the vector of development.

This time, Russians must avoid illusions that integration with the West will solve their problems. United Europe is still evolving and trying to find the optimal pattern for its common destiny. Western democracies continue to search for solutions to their domestic and international problems—growing unemployment, mass disenchantment with democratic institutions, and the rise of the extreme right.

What does Russia have to offer, critics ask, besides headaches, a bureaucracy that needs neutralizing as badly as it needs modernizing, and practice dealing with the whims and tantrums of politicians? Until quite recently, Russia was the center of attention because of its nuclear warheads. Once it became clear that Russia would not fight a war with the West, interest in it cooled. Yet Russia remains a microcosm in which a series of challenges to the West come together. All these challenges—strengthening European, Asian, and world security, combating terrorism and crime, building effective world markets, and diversifying energy resources—require Russian cooperation. And that is hardly the end of the list.

Do Russians Still Harbor Anti-Western Feelings?

Sociologists have discovered that a significant portion of ordinary Russians, despite surges of frustrating emotions, are essentially pro-Western.[18] According to polls conducted at the end of 2001, the vast majority of Russians—87 percent—thought that Russia should orient itself toward Western nations, and only 8 percent (most of them Muslims) preferred an orientation toward Muslim countries. Longing to preserve "uniqueness" was forgotten—unexpectedly for observers. When asked, "Partnership with which countries best responds to the interests of people like you?," a strong majority (63 percent) named the countries of Western Europe, 45 percent Belarus, 42 percent the United States, and 40 percent Ukraine. Only 6 percent considered cooperation with Iraq, Iran, and other "states of concern" useful. Cooperation with China was considered desirable by 22 percent.

Some social groups in Russia, though, retained exaggerated expectations: 34 percent still considered Russia a superpower no less than the United States. But a breakthrough in Russians' relinquishment of the superpower complex was apparent. Forty-three percent considered the status of France, Germany, or Japan to be desirable for Russia. The vast majority of Russians wanted a country that was not a military power but a "comfortable country, convenient for living, where top priority is given to the interests of people, their well-being, and opportunities." The shift toward the West and its values in Russia has been more widespread than many observers thought. Russians are more ready than they themselves thought to live a normal life in a normal country. It seems that the great-power factor is no longer the only consolidating force in Russia.

Perceptions of Russia as a bastion of anti-Americanism turned out to be mistaken as well. According to polls that the Public Opinion Foundation (FOM) conducted in October 2001, 35 percent of Russians had a good opinion of Americans, 44 percent were indifferent, 15 percent had a bad opinion, and 5 percent had no opinion. According to VTsIOM polls in November 2001, 65 percent of Russians wanted Russia and the United States to become allies, 13 percent did not care, 12 percent were against the idea, and 10 percent had no opinion.

But suspicions about America's intentions remained. In November 2001, 37 percent of those polled thought the United States was a nation friendly to Russia, 44 percent thought it was not friendly, and 19 percent had no opinion. Yet when questions were posed about specific things, it became clear that Russians did not perceive Americans as the enemy. For instance, in answer to the question, "Would you give blood for Americans wounded in a terrorist act?," 63 percent said yes and only 10 percent said no (25 percent said they could not be blood donors, and 3 percent had no opinion).

According to FOM public opinion polls at the end of 2002, 56 percent of Russians would like to strengthen cooperation with NATO (45 percent of respondents expressed the same attitude in 1999) and 23 percent did not think this cooperation is necessary (in 1999, 32 percent thought so). Now every fourth Russian is in favor of Russia's membership in NATO. This is really a breathtaking change in Russian moods toward the former enemy.

True, during the Iraqi debacle in 2003 Russian public opinion underwent significant changes: During this crisis only 20–25 percent of respondents were still favorably disposed to America, whereas the majority were strongly against the American-led war in Iraq. This fact has demonstrated that Russian public moods can be strongly affected by the media and official rhetoric. At the same time, there is evidence that Russian society at that moment was critical first of all of the American administration and its course but was not hostile to America as a nation. In any case, such changes in mood had happened during the first NATO enlargement and the Kosovo crisis when Russian was split in its attitude toward the United States. But after the crises the mood returned to favorable attitudes toward America—at the end of 2003 about 60 percent of respondents again viewed the United States as a benevolent power.

However, parliamentary elections in December 2003, when approximately 50 percent of voters supported the parties and movements with strong statist and nationalist bent (the Communist Party, the Liberal Democratic Party of Russia of Zhirinovsky, and Rodina [Motherland]), have demonstrated a worrisome trend. It appears that the Kremlin, in order to strengthen support for the pro-Kremlin movement United Russia and to create a basis for Putin's victory during the presidential elections in March 2004, has intentionally unleashed a nationalistic campaign, which the authorities themselves later had problems controlling. Defeat of the liberal democratic minority and the weakening of political pragmatism have increased the danger that newly awakened, but previously dormant, nationalistic and statist moods within part of the society may become increasingly vocal, which only proves how unstable and still vulnerable the Russian political scene is.

Thus, there are things to give one pause and force some hard thinking. It is also worth mentioning that the majority of those who consider the United States a potential ally base their attitude toward America primarily on the existence of a common enemy of the two countries. That is typical Soviet Russian logic: Against whom will we be friends? If the common enemies are to vanish, what would the two countries have left in common? Russia and the United States could once again find themselves, if not in different camps, then at a distance, at which point mutual suspicions or at least mutual irritation may flare up with renewed vigor.

The Imitation Game

Russian international behavior continues to be influenced by Russia's internal political developments.[19] A crucial question here is: When will the ruling class and the leader, who is the only viable political actor in Russia, realize that the bureaucratic-authoritarian regime has to be dropped? In the 1990s, during Yeltsin's tenure Russia rejected society's total subordination to the state. Having no other legitimacy, the authorities were forced—at least to some degree—to depend on the society and the election process. But the essence of the political regime remains the power of the leader—the monosubject who has all the levers in his hands and can rule unchecked, with no accountability before the society. That personified political regime perpetuates the existence of the Russian system, preventing its final burial and generating attempts to save its leftovers disguised by a democratic shell.[20]

At the end of the first Putin presidency it became clear that the Russian ruling class was trying to recreate in Russia the entire system of Western institutions, leaving out what it did not like and what really mattered: *definite rules of the game and uncertain results*. What Russian political elites consciously or unconsciously— it does not matter—have tried to build is just the opposite: *uncertain rules that can be changed at will, and predictable, certain results* guaranteeing that they remain in power. Not only Putin and his team but also a part of Russian society have decided that a democracy managed from above by a small group of people is perhaps not just the best but the only form of government possible in Russia—at least at this stage.

Russian society still has to decide, on the basis of painful experience, whether Russian-style "democracy," or rather *imitative democracy*, is an effective tool for modernizing the country. True, in two years, Putin's regime has created opportunities for stabilization and moderate economic reform, for ordering politics to some extent, and for strengthening the state. That fact has proven that pragmatic monosubject rule in Russia still has some reformist potential. These achievements practically guaranteed Putin's reelection in 2004. A substantial portion of society is quite satisfied with what it has—a limited modernist scenario—fearing other options and alternatives.

The probability of serious structural crises in Russia that would bring collapse of the system in the next few years—if basic developmental trends continue—is rather small or even nonexistent. The regime has no serious foes. Nor is there a substantial gap between expectations and fulfillment, if only because society's expectations are so low, basically reduced to a wish that things will not get any worse. Very little is needed at the moment to retain stability in Russia aside from paying salaries and pensions regularly.

Yet in the longer run, stability based on the absence of alternatives, on low expectations, and cn oil prices and presidential approval rating (which in 2004, skyrocketed to 83 percent of popular support) must be detrimental. The multiparty system, the government, the parliament, and the power of regional bosses all depend on loyalty to the leader, who in turn depends on his ratings. But let us imagine what could happen if the president's ratings plunged. It would shake the entire vertically built system or even trigger its avalanche-like collapse. A system built on shadowy deals and one-man rule is much more vulnerable than a system formed on the foundation of strong and viable institutions. Russia still must come to this conclusion, and this is the major challenge it faces.

A combination of mild authoritarianism packed into pragmatic wrappings and economic liberalization is perfectly adequate for dragging a peasant country onto the road of industrialization. To meet postindustrial challenges, however, to move toward a high-technology society, a new type of system is needed, one that makes room for social initiatives, local self-government, individual freedom, and independence of political institutions.

Russia's Traps

In 2004 Putin's reelection and his second presidency became a reality, which nobody has ever doubted. But at the beginning of his new tenure issues that need answers have been accumulating. How could a dialogue with the West coexist with the desire to "seal up" society, depriving it of the freedoms to which it had grown accustomed during the Yeltsin years? How could Moscow get out of the second Chechen war and stabilize the Northern Caucasus?[21] How could the Kremlin keep stability from again turning into deep stagnation? And how could Russians achieve a new reform breakthrough while avoiding chaos and disintegration?

So far, the Kremlin's policy has created traps for Russia and for the presidency that might turn out to be disastrous both for the political regime and the country at large. This is a most dramatic trap. On one hand, the Kremlin's policy permits the natural, albeit slow, growth of the middle class, of the new Russian generation ready to live and compete in the modern world. On the other hand, it hinders political pluralism and the competition for power in the country. Sooner or later, conflict would be inevitable between the new and dynamic social groups that strive for parliamentary democracy, local self-government, freedoms, and decentralization of power, and those groups that support the current regime, that is, the bureaucracy, the power ministries, and the oligarchs loyal to the Kremlin. Without legal channels of regulating the clashes of interests, this could lead to an unraveling of the political structure or at least to severe political instability.

What form that conflict between the longing to preserve the status quo and the demand for political freedom will take is not clear. Would it result in pressure from the bottom, a gradual reform from the top, or a combination of both? The key would be to solve the conflict without bloodshed or major social upheaval. No less important is avoiding the growth of nationalist forces, which as "old Europe" during Putin's second tenure has found can happen even in stable, mature democracies. This will be Putin's task or the task for another leader if Putin proves that he cannot reform Russian politics. In any case, the challenge of changing Russian mechanisms of governance—the "Russian system"—is unavoidable.

One more systemic trap became apparent at the end of Putin's first presidency: the attempt of the ruling class to secure succession and reproduction of its power. This is not an issue that president Putin can afford to put off until the end of his second presidency. The political elite and Putin's own team turned their thoughts to ensuring the continuity of power even before the presidential elections were over. The Kremlin entourage has started to pressure Putin to change the constitution so as to allow him to run for a third term. It was clear that if he resisted this pressure the elite groups would start to look around for a new leader, leaving Putin dangerously isolated. Whatever the case, Putin will have little time for reform during his second presidency being preoccupied with another problem—organizing the self-reproduction of power and the survival of personified power.

The Leader's Mission

Russia's leader is still the major actor on the Russian political scene. He is influencing Russia's future, and at some moments he is creating the future even if he is often reluctant to take a position. Is President Putin capable of comprehending that the rule—"presidential verticality of power"—he has created will not allow him to realize his goal to form a civilized market economy and a modern state? And if he realizes that, is the founder of bureaucratic authoritarianism prepared to restructure his rule accordingly? In any case, after achieving victory in the parliamentary and presidential elections in 2003–2004, President Putin has all the levers of power under his control and he is no longer dependent on the political corporation that helped his ascendancy to power. He is free to move in any direction and theoretically can undertake any bold reforms.

Coming to power, Putin initially did not risk going beyond the traditional pattern of trying to be Everybody's Man and trying hard to appeal to various interest groups. But then, quite unexpectedly for many observers, in summer 2003, the president let one group in his entourage—the representatives of the power structures —attack one of the most powerful Russian tycoons, Mikhail Khodorkovsky, which was interpreted as an attack on big business as a corporate group.[22] This step ruined the old balance in the Kremlin and created a threat that in the end the leader might be taken hostage by his *siloviki*. Putin smartly avoided this trap. But the events of 2003, with the crackdown on one of the most transparent Russian companies and the political crisis that followed this crackdown, resulting in a change of balance in the Kremlin, have once more demonstrated that Russian power is not consolidated and is torn from within by unresolvable conflicts of interests. And in the end, authority might become a major source of instability for the country. Unless the leader and political class finally decide to restructure the political regime and start building independent institutions, new political crises in Russia will be unavoidable. The events of 2003 have also proven that the struggle for succession and a search for Putin's heir has begun. At the same time, the growing role of autocratic ways of governance has demonstrated that the Russian political regime has been moving backward, toward traditionalism.

Sooner or later, however, the Russian president will have to think about his historical mission. And then he will have to solve a dilemma: whether to remain a stabilizing leader of corrupt capitalism—either oligarchic or state capitalism—or to become a transformer and start building a new system that would allow Russia to become a full-fledged liberal democracy and enter the postindustrial world as an equal.

The first choice would mean a continuation of imitation and the construction of a Potemkin village, that is, the usual pastime of Russia's leaders and political class. It would be a life of pretending. The authorities pretend to rule and the people pretend to obey. That choice would mean slow degradation and no chance for Russia to get on its feet. Avalanche-like collapse, unexpected ruin, disintegration—all these theatrical and frightening options are not for Russia. The gloomiest scenario for the country is the slow spreading of rot, which might not always be visible but in the end would lead to further degeneration of power and the state, disintegration of the society, and muddling through for years and decades. That is the price of trying to refurbish the current system and stabilizing the current Russian reality.

For Putin personally, this first scenario would end with a repeat of Yeltsin's story—that is, with the "privatization" of the leader and the regime by a band of Kremlin clans. Any leader in Russia will be doomed if he has no strong institutions to support him. In fact, there is nothing unusual or typically Russian about that option. Guillermo O'Donnell has demonstrated that this is the usual end of all "delegative democracies"—impotent omnipotence.[23]

The second possible path for President Putin—reform of the regime and final dismantling of the Russian system—is riskier, without guarantees of success, and with a likelihood that he might break his neck. If the political steering wheel is not turned wisely, reform could end up in Gorbachevism, with the leader losing control of power and events. But Vladimir Putin could be lucky. If he decided to de-hermetize the regime, gradually undertake the most essential antibureaucratic reform, strengthen the legal system, return freedom to the media, and manage to cross thin ice without falling in, he would accomplish what no Russian or Soviet leader ever had. He would begin building a responsible system of governance based not on the irrational and mystical power embodied in the leader but on the rule of law. That would be a new chapter in Russian history.

Is President Putin capable of taking that step? It could be tantamount to political suicide for him—to dismantle what he has created during his first term. No one in political history has done such a contradictory thing—no one has ever created an authoritarian regime only to consciously destroy it. True, Gorbachev committed political suicide—but it was suicide of a different kind. The last Soviet leader tried to restructure an already existing system not knowing at the moment that the system had not been reformable. Could President Vladimir Putin perform the unthinkable?

We may be demanding the impossible from Vladimir the Modernizer. We reproach him for his rule through personified power and his attempts to control the country's fate single-handedly. But at the same time, there is no sign that influential forces have formed in Russian society that could offer enough support for a completely new, democratic regime. Even the liberals are supporting pragmatic authoritarianism. Yet we expect the authoritarian leader to democratize "from above" and voluntarily give up power to institutions in Russian society that appear to be happy with Putin's authoritarianism. I admit that this seems beyond the limits of realism. Besides, Putin's evolution at the end of 2003 and beginning of 2004 shows that Russia is drifting toward more harsh authoritarianism.

But is this movement President Putin's initiative only and could he have prevented this shift? The answer is—hardly. What could force Putin to start this process of giving power away if there is no pressure in Russian society to start political reform from the bottom, if the liberal democratic alternative is so weak? But leadership presupposes vision and the ability to see beyond the present day. At some point Putin could come to the understanding that building independent institutions and strengthening the rule of law are not only the ways to reenergize Russia but are the only ways for his own and elite survival. If Putin understands that, he will enter Russian history as Leader-Transformer, the politician who stopped a long Russian tradition of modernizing the same patrimonial power and started to transform it.

But if there is a transition from autocratic rule to the rule of institutions, the leader has to consider how to prevent the young Russian democracy from succumbing to angry populism and destroying the market, using Bolshevik means to redress injustices by taking from the rich, renationalizing private property, and returning to suspicion of the West. We admit that it is thanks in great part to Putin's authoritarianism that Russia has revived economic reform and has entered into an alliance with Western countries. Has Russia matured enough to put an end to civilized tsarism? We will not be able to answer this question until Russia begins that transition.

Rethinking the Old Truths

During a time of historic transformations, many things must be regarded in a new light. What seems to be an obstacle in normal development may turn out to be a blessing when a transitional society is seeking a new identity. Thus Russia is saved by the fact that a complete consolidation of society and rule is still impossible there. Today's reality, including the bureaucratic, quasi-authoritarian regime, cannot be cast in concrete. Both the regime and the system, which include not only the political structure but the economic mechanisms, continue to remain hybrid and contain outwardly incompatible principles and trends: state regulation and market, spontaneity and state apparatus pressure, centralization and fragmentation, pro-Western shift and state power rhetoric, pragmatism and many mystical attitudes. In fact, the reality—social, political, and economic—continues to be amorphous, fluid, and hard to fit into any strict category. Therefore, movement in a more positive direction is possible.

Yet we cannot rule out temporal retrograde movement completely. One cannot entirely exclude even totalitarian syndromes as an attempt of the ruling team to preserve its power or to solve an urgent problem. In any case, leadership, under both Yeltsin and Putin, has proved that it has learned to deal with a stable and more or less favorable situation. But it is unclear what those in the Kremlin will do if threatened, if they are confronted with severe crisis. Are they going to kick over the chessboard?

At the same time, even totalitarian syndromes will hardly bring a real totalitarian regime. Russia is lacking at least three of the crucial variables that make such a regime possible: an effective state apparatus loyal to the center; a strong repressive mechanism, first of all an army; and readiness on the part of the provinces to be subordinated to the center. In this context all harsh syndromes will ultimately end as a new imitation.

The conflicts and the struggle that have revived in Russia despite the Kremlin's attempts to control everything are more good than bad. The conflicts show that the country is alive, and interests are formed through the conflicts. Struggle does not permit the regime to ossify. An even more positive factor is the spontaneity present in the populace and its growing independence. When polled, 45 percent of the population said that the state plays no role in their lives at all.

Of course, it is not good for society and the state to travel on parallel tracks. But it is good that people are coming out from the shadow of the state Leviathan and living independently. Soon they will have to build a new kind of statehood, based on different principles, and the product will be their own state serving their interests. In the meantime, Russia retains a certain unruliness and spontaneity that allow society to breathe. The more spontaneity, the better—for now.

Prospects for Transformation and Integration

It would be too trivial to conclude that Russia's transformation is still incomplete— of course it is. Moreover, Russia has gotten into difficulties in trying to combine moderate market reforms, mild authoritarianism, and pro-Western orientation. The inconsistencies and even the conflicts among the three goals have already become clear. The way that the Russian ruling team is trying to solve these conflicts is evident as well—through limitation, controlled adaptation, and imitation. Russia's imitation game on the domestic front inevitably triggers imitation on the foreign policy field—in the field of cooperation and partnership with the West.

The West is so tired of Russia's problems and zigzagging that it prefers to turn to "wait and see" politics toward Russia or some form of bargain with the Kremlin, preferring Russia's stagnant stability to uncertainties of its further transformation. In Russia itself we do not see viable democratic forces ready to pursue more vigorously the liberal democratic alternative. Moreover, there is an impression that with the vocal nationalist and great power elite contingents waiting in the wings, Putin is virtually the only obstacle to Russia's sliding toward a new totalitarianism that is unfriendly to the West. This is a negative side of the story.

There is a positive side of the story as well. First, both Russia and the West are gradually overcoming unjustified hopes and illusions concerning Russia's rapid transformation and painless integration—there is growing understanding of the complexity of the process. More analysts on both sides have also realized the irreversibility of some changes in Russian society, which make a U-turn impossible and also made the emergence of a pure authoritarian or totalitarian regime hostile to the West rather difficult. There is also a mutual understanding that while Russia's membership in Western institutions (NATO, EU) is not a realistic goal today, there are other forms of cooperation that may develop and lead to discussion of the membership issue in the not so distant future.

Second, there is growing understanding in Russia and even within the Kremlin that in order to be integrated Russia has to build a new institutional system. The problem is that Putin apparently hopes to construct such a system from the top and keep it under control. This means that the Russian president and his team still have to understand that imitative democracy cannot help Russia to modernize itself and enter the Western world. It is hoped that such an understanding is gradually taking root among some—albeit not all—elite groups.

Third, despite all the vacillations during the 1990s and in recent years under Putin, Russia has preserved its pro-Western orientation of development and this is crucially important for future Russian transformation. It is true that this orientation is currently based mainly on Russia's participation in the antiterror campaign, but even this limited alliance is acquiring a logic of its own, forcing even the Russian traditionalist establishment to learn new ideas and become accustomed to new principles. In any case, it is now difficult to envisage a sharp turn by Moscow in the opposite, anti-Western direction.

Fourth, Russia's future developments will be influenced first of all by its domestic events. But at some point Russia's pro-Western orientation will become the factor that could influence the choice of new domestic goals or the next leader.

Fifth, modernization from the top will hardly bring Russia into the world of developed nations. But at least part of the Russian political and economic class has begun to understand the limits and constraints of the traditionalist pattern of modernization agenda. There are concerns as to the future of reforms "from the top" even among some of the oligarchs (Mikhail Khodorkovsky is one of them). True, there is still no sign that the ruling class is ready to change the old pattern. Moreover, the events of 2003–2004 may mean that Putin's second presidency will be more authoritarian with simultaneously growing pressure on parts of the state apparatus. The existence of liberal technocrats in the Kremlin entourage will not change this picture due to the fact that Russian technocrats have long ago learned how to play the role of regime decoration. But developments in Russia, including getting rid of illusions, are evolving much faster than one can anticipate. We cannot exclude that at some point the political class or the part of it trying to survive and prevent the collapse of stability and unraveling of the regime will try to gradually de-hermetize the system and start to build independent and legitimate institutions.

Sixth, there is the role of the West. At the moment the West demonstrates a quite understandable "Russia fatigue." Besides, the West cannot stimulate regime change in Russia and there is no clear understanding of what can be done to help Russia to make one more step toward liberal democracy. At the same time, sooner or later the Western community will understand that only with Russia on board can the West answer the various challenges of the twenty-first century concerning global and European security, world terrorism, nonproliferation, drug trafficking, volatile emerging markets, energy supplies, rising China, and so forth. Only Russia's active cooperation can breathe new life into some Western institutions, such as NATO, now in search of new missions. This means that the West hardly has the luxury of observing quietly and from a distance the current stagnation of Russian stability. I am not excluding the possibility that the West at some point may come with a new initiative toward helping to integrate Russia institutionally and socially. It may take the form of a breakthrough initiative to help Russia with its administrative or military reform, or stabilization (including arranging the "peace money") in the Northern Caucasus, or helping to reenergize the Far East and Siberia, or opening borders and easing the Schengen visa regime. In any case, Russia is too important a global factor to be left alone with its transformation. The success of this transformation is not only the major challenge for Russia, but for the West as well.

But it is also true that the future of Russia will be decided by Russian society and Russian elites. The most important guarantee and prerequisite of the next step in Russian transformation is the leader's ability to use the potential of leadership and its crucial role in Russia's history to lay the ground for other independent political institutions.

Notes

1. On leadership in times of change see *Governing Through Turbulence: Leadership and Change in the Late Twentieth Century*, ed. David F. Walsh, Paul J. Best, and Kul B. Rai (Westport, CT: Praeger, 1995); *Leaders of Transition*, ed. Martin Westlake (New York: St. Martin's Press, 2000).

2. On the role of leadership during the Russian post-communist transformation see George W. Breslauer, *Gorbachev and Yeltsin as Leaders* (New York: Cambridge University Press, 2002); *Gorbachev, Yeltsin, Putin: Political Leadership in Russia's Transition*, ed. Archie Brown and Lilia Shevtsova (Washington, DC: Carnegie Endowment for International Peace, 2001).

3. The term Russian system belongs to Andrei Fursov and Iurii Pivovarov. See *Ocherki istorii russkoi obshchestvennoi mysli, 19—pervoi poloviny 20 veka* (Moscow, 1997).

4. Lilia Shevtsova, *Yeltsin's Russia: Myths and Reality* (Washington, DC: Carnegie Endowment for International Peace, 1999).

5. The idea of "elected monarchy" was first used by Alexis de Tocqueville in his *Democracy in America*, where he described political power in Poland. My co-author, Igor Kliamkin, and I used this term when we analyzed the political regime that had been formed in post-communist Russia under Yeltsin. See Igor Kliamkin and Lilia Shevtsova, *Vnesistemnyi rezhim Borisa vtorogo* (Moscow: Moscow Carnegie Center, 1999). One interesting attempt to define the nature of Yeltsin's regime was made by Richard Sakwa, who introduced the definition of the "regime system." While not agreeing with his understanding of the systemic nature of Yeltsin's regime (I do not think that this regime constitutes a system), I fully support his view of its essential characteristics. Sakwa wrote: "The August regime was a peculiar hybrid of democratic proceduralism and authoritarian patterns of leadership politics" (Richard Sakwa, "The Regime System in Russia," *Contemporary Politics* 3, no. 1 (1997): 13).

6. David Collier and Guillermo O'Donnell in *The New Authoritarianism in Latin America*, ed. D. Collier (Princeton, NJ: Princeton University Press, 1979), p. 292.

7. There are numerous attempts to define such hybrid systems—these systems are defined as "authoritarian democracies," "elected democracies," "delegative democracies," and "illiberal democracies." Larry Diamond uses the term "twilight zone." Thomas Carothers uses the term "gray-zone" countries. These terms try to describe what Diamond defines as presence "in the zone of persistence without legitimation or institutionalization." See Larry Diamond, *Developing Democracy: Toward Consolidation* (Baltimore: Johns Hopkins University Press, 1999), p. 22; Thomas Carothers, "The End of the Transitional Paradigm," *Journal of Democracy*, no. 1 (2002).

8. Lilia Shevtsova, "From Yeltsin to Putin: Evolution of Power," in *Gorbachev, Yeltsin, Putin*, ed. Brown and Shevtsova, p. 78.

9. This section is partially drawn from Lilia Shevtsova's *Putin's Russia* (Washington, DC: Carnegie Endowment for International Peace, 2003).

10. During the parliamentary elections in December 2003, only 15 percent of voters voted for the communists.

11. See dialogues about Westernizers and nationalists in *Zapadniki i natsional'isty: vozmozhen li dialog?* (Moscow: Liberal Mission Foundation, OGI, 2003).

12. See Robert Legvold, "U.S.–Russian Relations Ten Months After September 11," paper presented at the 27th Conference of the Aspen Institute, U.S.–Russia Relations: A New Framework, Washington, DC, August 15–21, 2002, p. 72.

13. Angela Stent and Lilia Shevtsova, "America, Russia and Europe: A Realignment?" *Survival* 44, no. 4 (2002–3): 72.

14. On the nature of Russian democracy see Timothy J. Colton and Michael McFaul, "Russian Democracy under Putin," *Problems of Post-Communism* 50, no. 4 (July–August 2003).

15. Tatiana Kutkoveits and Igor Kliamkin, "Remontu ne podlezhit," *Novaia izvestiia*, September 25, 2002.

16. On Russia and the West see Dov Lynch, "Russia Faces Europe," Chaillot papers, no. 60 (Paris: Institute for Security Studies, 2003).

17. Rodric Braithwaite, *Across the Moscow River: The World Turned Upside Down* (New Haven, CT: Yale University Press, 2002,) pp. 338–39.

18. On Russian anti-Western feelings see *Zapadniki i national'isty.*

19. On paradoxes of the Russian political system see Gerhard Mangott, *Zur Demokratisierung Russlands* (Baden-Baden: Nomos Verlagsgesellschaft, 2002).

20. On the nature of the system at the end of the Putin's first presidency see Grigory Yavlinsky, *Demodernization: Russian Economic and Political Perspectives* (Moscow: Yabloko Party, 2003; available at www.yabloko.ru (April 21, 2004).

21. Endorsement of the new Chechen constitution and election of its new president in 2003 could not end the civil war in the region—for that negotiations with moderate separatists and massive economic assistance to rebuild Chechnya together with international monitoring are needed.

22. Lilia Shevtsova, "Whither Putin after the Yukos Affair," *Moscow Times*, August 27, 2003; published by Vlast' i Biznes: Lieto 2003. Liberal Mission Foundation, Moscow, 2003, available at: www.liberal.ru.

23. Guillermo O'Donnell, "Delegative Democracy," *Journal of Democracy* 5, no. 1 (January 1994): 59–62.

6

Making a Good Entrance

Russia's Reengagement with the World Economy and, Unfortunately, with Europe in Particular

Philip Hanson

Russia is not, at the time of writing, a member of the right clubs. It is not in the World Trade Organization (WTO), it is not in the European Union (EU), not in the Organization for Economic Cooperation and Development (OECD), not in NATO, and counts for only a half in the G-7½. For a country that is reentering society after seventy years of semi-isolation, and one that is economically small (0.8 percent of world output at the exchange rate, 2.6 percent of world output at purchasing power parity in 2000, according to the World Bank), this is an economic handicap.

It is probably more of a handicap than it would have been in an earlier age. Individuals may have taken to "Bowling Alone," but countries have become more clubbable. From 1868, when the Meiji Restoration ended Japan's centuries-old seclusion, the Japanese were able to turn their country into a successful, late-industrializing, catching-up nation without having to submit to a set of rules devised by a club of wealthy states. They put up trade barriers, kept out foreign direct investment, brought in foreign science and technology, and started new industries with state investment. Even their successors as late industrializers a century or so later, such as Korea, Taiwan, and Singapore, also largely set their own economic rules.

In contrast, Russia is at present growing, opening up, and changing economically, but its policy makers believe with good reason that it is essential to seek membership in the WTO and a closer relationship with the EU; in both cases Russia is being asked to rearrange its affairs to meet rules set by others. For WTO accession it is being asked to raise domestic energy prices, cut tariffs, restrict farm subsidies far below U.S. or EU rates, and open its more attractive sectors more fully to foreign business. To develop with the EU a Common European Economic Space, it is being asked (as things stand at present) to adopt a great deal of the EU's commercial and social legislation—the *acquis communautaire*—and is not being offered free trade in return.

Russia's situation as an outsider looking in has clear economic disadvantages.

Outside the WTO it cannot make use of the organization's machinery for resolving trade disputes. Dealing at arm's length with the EU, it confronts EU protectionism, restricting its sales of farm products, chemicals, and steel to the largest nearby market.

The more successful ex-communist countries of Central Europe and the Baltic region have joined the OECD, the WTO, and the EU. The process by which they qualified for EU membership brings out clearly the analogy with an individual joining a club, right down to the ritual humiliation inflicted on would-be members of fraternity houses: in this case, being beaten over the head, for several years, with thirty-one chapters of the *acquis*. A milder version of this hazing seems to be the best Brussels can offer Russia, as a condition of becoming merely a slightly closer outsider.

This preamble may suggest that I want to present Russia as a victim. That is not the case. Nations, like individuals, may be kept out of the best clubs for good reason. The desirability of WTO membership and of a Common European Economic Space for Russia is clear, and Russia's readiness to benefit from these associations remains to be judged. The aim of this chapter is to review Russia's changing economic links with the outside world and to consider ways in which policy makers inside and outside Russia might act to alter those links so as to promote Russia's development as a capitalist, market economy.

The Russian Economy Since 1998

I have assessed the recent performance and medium-term prospects of the Russian economy at length elsewhere (Hanson 2003). This section is a summary of the main points in that assessment that are relevant to Russia's international economic integration.

The August 1998 financial crisis was a punishment for poor Russian economic policy making. From mid-1995 the ruble had been "stabilized" within a slowly descending exchange-rate corridor; the authorities had stopped financing budgetary deficits by printing money; they had not, however, stopped running deficits; these were financed chiefly by three- or six-month securities known as GKOs; foreign investors were allowed into the ruble-denominated GKO market, and for a time made very high returns in it; much of manufacturing industry was kept from closure by being allowed to underpay taxes and energy costs; the government deficits were directly and indirectly a reflection of these tacit subsidies; in effect, the natural-resource sector was used to prop up a large population of manufacturing enterprises that were thereby spared the sink-or-swim pressures of real market competition.

In August 1998, that curious collective animal, the market, decided that neither the ruble exchange rate against the dollar nor the redemption of the mounting pyramid of GKOs was sustainable. The exchange rate was allowed to fall, and quickly went from 6 rubles to the dollar to about 25. It is at the time of writing about 31. Russia defaulted on part of its sovereign debt.

After the crisis Russia experienced its first officially recorded output growth since 1989 (apart from a brief, marginal upturn in 1997). In 1999–2002 inclusive, GDP growth averaged just under 6 percent a year. The trigger for the recovery was the huge devaluation of the ruble. This made imports suddenly much more expensive. That in turn offered Russian processing industry—engineering, food-processing, clothing, and the like—an opportunity to come back from the dead and use their large, underutilized capacity for the production of import substitutes. This, to the surprise of many, they managed to do. A mass of previously moribund enterprises, kept alive hitherto by large and systematic nonpayment, overvalued barter settlements, and other ingenious and government-tolerated deviations from standard market behavior, began to generate cash again. In this way, a policy failure, resulting in a forced devaluation, kick-started recovery.

In 1999 an upturn in oil prices provided further assistance. Therefore, the recovery was led by net exports (exports less imports). This led many analysts to argue that the unexpected Russian growth spurt would fade away either when oil prices fell again for a prolonged period or when the real appreciation of the ruble against the dollar and the euro (ruble depreciation insufficient to offset the higher rate of inflation in Russia, or even nominal ruble appreciation while Russian inflation stayed comparatively high) eroded the boost to Russian competitiveness provided by the devaluation.[1]

In 2001–2003, however, Russia survived some dips, admittedly brief, in oil prices, and net exports declined as the ruble appreciated in real terms, but domestic demand (household consumption, government spending, and investment) continued to drive the economy. The growth of investment—by as much as 17 percent year on year in 2000 and 12 percent year on year in 2003—was a particularly striking change from the past.[2] Capital flight, meanwhile, fell in 2001–2003. The importance of Cyprus as a source of inward foreign investment rose, indicating the return of some Russian-controlled offshore funds.

All of this occurred against a background of cautious macroeconomic policies and some acceleration of institutional reforms in Russia. The government has been running surpluses, paying down debt (in late 2003 foreign public debt was a modest 22 percent of GDP), moderating the growth of the money supply, and limiting inflation: still in double digits (12.0 percent for consumer prices in 2003), but coming down. Gold and foreign exchange reserves rose strongly, and are at levels almost sufficient to pay for a year's merchandise imports. Reforms of the tax system, of the land code, of business regulation (reducing the burden of registration, licensing, product certification, and inspection), and of the judiciary have been pushed through a compliant Duma under an active president. Russians and foreigners doing business in Russia mostly report an improved business environment.

How sustainable is this progress? Skeptics maintain there are major obstacles to Russia maintaining in the long run a trend rate of growth much above 3 percent a year, sufficient to keep the country on a catching-up trajectory.

The following are the main stylized facts that are usually cited in support of this view. The investment share of GDP (about 18 percent) remains modest; much infrastructure has decayed and needs large investment; the surge in import-substitute production has used up spare capacity in manufacturing but new investment there is lacking; the banks do little lending to the real sector, which might facilitate restructuring; large subsidies remain to electricity and housing, distorting resource allocation; small-firm development has stagnated; above all, this remains a society in which informal rules prevail, allowing reforms to be legislated but not implemented, private interests to capture state agencies, and property rights to remain blurred and insecure. Therefore, competitive market forces do not work strongly and this is not the kind of well-ordered society that can get out from under the natural-resource curse as, for example, Norway and the Netherlands have done.

The case for a more optimistic view rests not on a denial that these are indeed the obstacles to Russian prosperity, but on evidence that changes are under way that are reducing their importance. In other words, it is a matter of assessing the nature and direction of change. The changes include the growth in investment and decline in capital flight referred to above. These suggest that the Russian business community is itself taking a more positive view. There are also signs of growth in small-firm employment in 2002 and 2003; survey evidence that legislation to reduce the regulatory (and therefore the corruption) burden has really changed things on the ground (six-monthly surveys by Cefir: see www.cefir.ru); the firm-level data indicating that leading Russian businessmen have after much delay tended to become real majority stakeholders in their firms, increasing their interest in the strengthening of property rights; the growth of bank lending to nonbank companies; the evidence of improved tax compliance by business. None of this evidence is yet conclusive, but whether the Russian economy really is, at last, modernizing, is an open question.

It is true that lessons from world history are not encouraging. The institutional quality of national economies appears to be remarkably stable over time. Argentina does not (despite signs in the 1990s to the contrary) easily become Chile. But for ex-communist countries the relevance of the very-long-run historical evidence is not clear. Most of them have already changed their economic institutions massively since the fall of communism. The great differences in their initial conditions around 1990 may go a long way to account for the wide variations among them in the rapidity of that change. It is possible that the long-delayed experience of domestic economic growth in Russia has had a benign effect: stimulating Russian businesspeople to take a longer-run view than before, and, in effect, to have incentives to demand better economic institutions.

So far as relations with the outside world are concerned, the changes for Russia have been massive. In the depths of Stalinism, in the late 1930s, links with the outside world were minimized; merchandise exports were as little as 0.5 percent of GNP (Holzman 1963, 290). After World War II trade expanded but chiefly with satellite countries. Intra-Council for Mutual Economic Assistance trade was extremely inefficient, and the location of activity and geographical flows of transactions within the Soviet Union were probably even more so. Part of post-communist change is the massive reorientation of Russian trade flows that has already taken place (see the next section).

For much of the 1990s the International Monetary Fund, the World Bank, and to a smaller extent the European Bank for Reconstruction and Development (EBRD) worked on institutional change in the Russian economy by means of conditional aid—the success of which is much disputed. Now market pressures operate more strongly. Large Russian companies increasingly have incentives to improve their financial reporting and their business practices in general. This applies whether they are hiring senior Western executives (as many are now doing), issuing American Depositary Receipts on Western equity markets, making direct share issues on foreign markets, issuing bonds, or raising syndicated loans. Foreign portfolio and direct investment into Russia tend on the whole to exert similar pressures.

It is possible to argue, as some Russian critics do, that these growing market links operate to confine Russia to the role of "natural-resource appendage" to the established Western economies. One thesis of this chapter is that Russia's exclusion so far from the WTO and its arm's-length relationship with the EU make it easier for Russian isolationists and proponents of a unique Russian way to argue at least somewhat plausibly along those lines. Conversely, reducing the barriers to Russian international economic integration weakens the Russian-way isolationists.

The Present Economic Links Between Russia and the West

Russians (more precisely, Russians mainly resident in Russia) have three main kinds of business and economic dealings with the West: trade in goods and services, cross-border investment (in both directions, and both direct and portfolio), and travel for business, tourism, and education. Within the trade category, transactions concerning fuel and energy are sufficiently important for both parties to be looked at as a special subset.

Merchandise Trade

Foreign trade now looms large in the Russian economy. In 2002 merchandise exports plus imports were $152 billion and GDP at the exchange rate was $350 billion. The ratio of merchandise trade turnover to national income was therefore 43 percent. That measure is appropriate as an indicator of the importance of trade in generating income and absorbing expenditure, and it shows Russia to be, by world standards, a rather small and rather open economy. If GDP were reckoned, however, not at the exchange rate but at purchasing power parity, the trade:GDP ratio would come down to well below 20 percent. This measure is more appropriate for indicating the external world's role in the allocation of Russian resources; it suggests a rather larger and only moderately open economy.

The partner composition of Russian trade has changed dramatically over the past

Table 6.1

Russian Merchandise Trade in 2002 (by trade partner group)

Total trade ($bn)	
Exports	105.8
Imports	46.0
Total turnover	151.8
Of which, with (% of turnover)	
Other CIS countries	16.9
Central and Eastern Europe	12.9
EU15	36.6
Norway and Switzerland	4.2
Asia-Pacific	16.4
United States	4.6
Other	8.4

Source: www.customs.ru [accessed April 23, 2003].

decade. Trade with the other members of the Commonwealth of Independent States (CIS) was just under 17 percent of the total last year—a remarkably low level when it is considered that in early December 1991 these were all part of one country.

Table 6.1 gives a snapshot of the composition of Russian merchandise trade by trade-partner group in 2002. It will be seen that "Europe," in the sense of the present EU of fifteen nations (EU15) plus Central and Eastern Europe (most of which joined the EU in 2004) and Norway and Switzerland, accounted for 54 percent of Russia's total merchandise trade, and two-thirds of its non-CIS merchandise trade. The gravitational pull of the United States on the Russian economy, so far as merchandise trade is concerned, is small. The U.S. economy may be somewhat larger than that of the EU15: $9.6 trillion against $8.5 trillion in 2000, according to the World Bank. But the U.S. economy is much farther away. More precisely: it is much farther away than Europe from European Russia, where Russian population and income are concentrated.

It should be added that the data on Russian trade used here understate trade volumes. The Russian Central Bank calculates merchandise trade in 2002 at $107.2 billion for exports and $61 billion for imports—the latter including an estimate for "shuttle" (informal) trade (www.cbr.ru). Unfortunately, only the customs data give a country breakdown. Russian and EU sources give slightly different figure for Russia–EU trade, but its significance for Russia is clear from either set of figures.

The importance of Europe in the sense used above (EU15 + Central and Eastern Europe + Norway + Switzerland), not merely to Russian trade but to total Russian economic activity, is considerable. From the Russian customs data and dollar GDP at the exchange rate, exports to Europe were 15.4 percent of GDP in 2002 and imports 6.5 percent.

Table 6.2

Russia–EU Merchandise Trade in 2000 ($bn and %)

	$bn	% Change year on year	Source
1. Total Russian exports	103.0	41	Russian Customs
2. EU15	36.9	48	Russian Customs
3. Total Russian imports	33.9	12	Russian Customs
4. From EU15	11.1	–0.4	Russian Customs
5. Total EU exports	867.6		Eurostat
6. To Russia	18.2	34	Eurostat
7. Total EU imports	945.5		Eurostat
8. From Russia	41.6	73	Eurostat

Memorandum Items	% Share	
RF exports to EU as % RF GDP	14–16	GDP and exchange rate from RECEP
RF imports from EU as % RF GDP	4–7	GDP and exchange rate from RECEP

Sources: UN ECE, *Economic Survey of Europe*, 2001: 2: 31; www.europa.eu.int/commm/eurostat/datashop; RECEP, *Russian Economic Trends. Monthly Update*, February 2002.

Notes: In the last two rows the alternative figures for Russia–EU trade flows from previous rows are presented as proportions of the official ruble GDP converted at the average ruble-dollar exchange rate for the year (total Russian GDP = $260.7 bn).

The "mirror trade statistics" here give distorted reflections. In a tidy world, row 2 should equal row 8 and row 4 should equal row 6. Divergences of this order are not uncommon and do not necessarily indicate a peculiarly Russian data problem. Countries often differ in their methods of valuation, their recording of countries of destination and of origin, and in the time at which a given flow is logged.

From the point of view of Brussels, this trade is in aggregate rather insignificant: 2–4 percent of total EU foreign trade and even smaller proportions of EU GDP—on a par with EU transactions with Norway.

One might therefore infer from these aggregate figures that if either party were the *demandeur* in the Russia-EU relationship, it would be Russia. I think this really is, on balance, the case. But the composition of the trade is such that this conclusion needs to be modified. The relationship is not so heavily one-sided as the total merchandise trade figures suggest.

Oil and Gas Trade

The reason for this is simple: the EU's heavy dependence on Russian energy, in the form of oil and gas. From figures on production, trade, and usage given by Kari Liuhto for 1999, it can be deduced that Russia supplied about 11 percent of the oil used in the preenlargement EU of fifteen countries and about 16 percent of gas consumption (N.B., *not* imports but total usage; from Liuhto 2002). Of course, the dependence is two-way: the seller needs the income, just as the buyer needs the product. Russia exports about a third of its gas production and almost two-thirds of its oil output. For both fuels, the dimensions of trade with Europe are substantial. Figures 6.1 and 6.2 illustrate this for the preenlargement EU15. The shares are higher (on both sides of the energy balance) for the enlarged EU.

The locations of pipelines, oil terminals, and gas reservoirs make it difficult for the supplier to switch markets in the short to medium term. To that extent Russian dependence on West European markets is strong in the medium term. In the longer run, it might be argued, Russia as a supplier may have more flexibility than Western Europe has as a customer. The other sources of supply to Western Europe offer little alternative in the longer run. As EU15 oil and gas consumption increases, Russia is the most likely source of additional supplies (conversation with executives of a major energy company, April 2002). One study cites a projection of Russian gas exports to the EU (apparently the EU15) almost doubling by 2008, to about 200 bcm p.a. (Samson and Greffe 2002, 11).

Does the United States constitute an alternative energy market for Russia? It certainly does not in the foreseeable future, despite recent U.S. administration interest in exploring energy cooperation between the two countries. Transportation costs are higher to the U.S. market, in part because of a remediable lack of large, deepwater oil terminals in Russia that would take large tankers. The present, experimental direct oil deliveries to the United States by Yukos and Lukoil are based on transshipment from small to big tankers at sea. In January–July 2002 they amounted to only 0.7 percent of U.S. oil imports, and of course even less of total U.S. oil consumption (derived from the *Russia Journal*, October 10, 2002).

The project to build a deepwater terminal at Murmansk and a pipeline to it, could in the medium term enable Russian oil companies to supply about 1 million b/d to U.S. markets, at a transport cost below that from the Gulf to Houston (Ariel Cohen, in a roundtable on Russia and the Middle East at the Association for the Study of Nationalities Annual Convention, New York City, April 3–5, 2003). That would still, however, be only about 5 percent of *current* U.S. levels of oil consumption. With U.S. usage and imports rising, it might in the medium term amount only to perhaps 5 percent of U.S. oil imports (Telhami et al., 2002). Gravity rules again.

The United States matters much more to Russia for its influence in strategic developments in world oil and gas than for its foreseeable role as a trade partner in the usual sense. The U.S. administration and U.S. oil majors, for example, have a considerable role in Caspian Basin developments, even where those do not involve direct Russia-U.S. transactions.

Foreign Investment

Russia has attracted relatively little foreign investment. Of the foreign investment that it has attracted, however, more than half has come from the present EU coun-

Figure 6.1   **The Dimensions of Russia–EU Oil Flows in 1999**

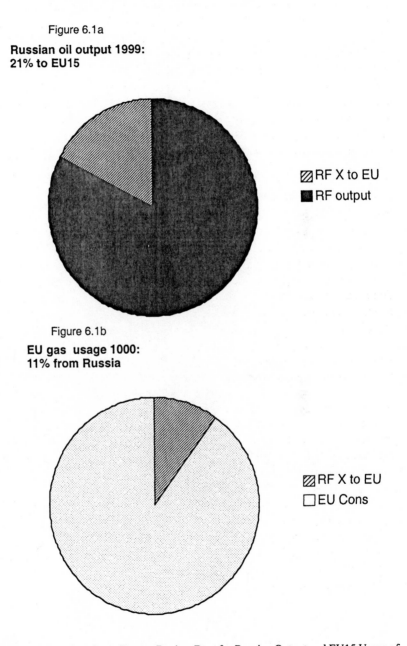

Figure 6.1a

**Russian oil output 1999:
21% to EU15**

RF X to EU
RF output

Figure 6.1b

**EU gas usage 1000:
11% from Russia**

RF X to EU
EU Cons

Source: British Petroleum Energy Review Data for Russian Output and EU15 Usage of
Oil, 1999.

Figure 6.2 **The Dimensions of Russia–EU Natural Gas Flows in 2001**

Figure 6.2a
**Russian oil output 2001:
14% to EU15**

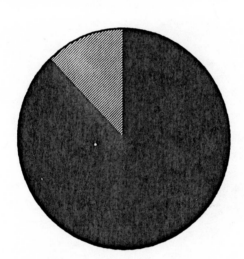

RF X to EU
RF output

Figure 6.2b
**EU gas usage 2001:
20% from Russia**

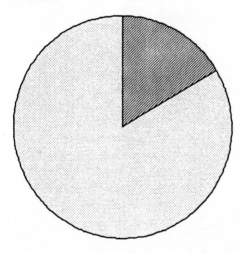

RF X to EU
EU Cons

Source: British Petroleum Energy Review Data for Russian Output and EU15 Usage of Oil, 1999.

Table 6.3

Inward Foreign Investment into Russia (cumulative totals to end-September 2002; in $bn)

	Foreign investment[a]	Of which foreign direct investment[b]
Total	39.80	19.39
Of which, from		
Germany	6.84	1.58
Great Britain	4.81	2.10
France	3.39	0.27
Netherlands	2.81	2.42
Italy	1.51	0.19
Luxembourg	0.94	0.15
All identified EU countries	20.30	6.71
United States	5.48	4.13

Source: Goskomstat, *Sotsial'no-ekonomicheskoe polozhenie Rossii* (January–September 2002).

[a]Foreign direct investment + foreign portfolio investment + other (mostly loans).

[b]Foreign direct investment defined as the acquisition of a stake of 10 percent or more in a business.

tries. Table 6.3 gives the cumulative totals of inward foreign investment to end-September 2002. (It should be added that Russian Central Bank statistics, www.cbr.ru, show a net inflow of capital into Russia in the second quarter of 2002—a major change.)

There are numerous problems of definition and identification in foreign investment statistics. For what the Russian official numbers in Table 6.3 are worth, they indicate that the EU15 countries loom even larger in inward foreign investment into Russia than they do in Russian merchandise trade (see Tables 6.1 and 6.2).

The role of the United States as a source of investment, particularly of direct investment, is more significant than it is as a trade partner. Indeed the role of multinational companies with headquarters in the United States may well be understated in Table 6.3. For example, the famous first McDonald's in Russia was opened by the Canadian McDonald's.

The destination of Russian outward capital flows is worse documented—not surprisingly, since part of those flows is illegal. It is safe to say, however, that the present EU is an important destination for Russian flight capital: not only in the form of houses in London and villas in the south of France, but in the form of businesses, share portfolios, and bank accounts, as well. Such financial links with Western Europe may not matter to the great majority of Russians, but they matter to more than just a tiny elite. Russian scholars of my acquaintance seem without exception to have bank accounts in Western Europe.

Movement of People

It is a commonplace in Britain that just about every "public" (fee-paying) school has a Russian pupil or two. There is a scattering of Russian students at British, French, and other West European universities, and Russian researchers and (mostly young) business people are present in modest numbers, too. Reportedly, the EU15 countries were in 2001 issuing about 1 million visas a year to Russian citizens (the Belgian ambassador to Russia speaking on November 13, 2001, quoted in *RFE/ RL Newsline*, November 14, 2001).

Compared to the movement of people across national borders within the EU, this is not a large number, out of a Russian population of 144 million. No doubt many of the visas issued each year are repeat visas issued to the same people. But if, for example, a total of 4 million Russian citizens had visited countries in the present EU over the past decade, that would be a more-than-negligible part of the population (just under 3 percent). A rather substantial chunk of the Russian business and political elite would appear to have some contacts with, and experience of, Western Europe. Contacts with the United States are much less: in fiscal year 2001 the U.S. Immigration and Naturalization Service recorded 20,413 immigrants from Russia and 126,564 nonimmigrant admissions (www.ins.usdoj.gov/graphics/aboutins/statistics/TEMP01yrbk/TEMPExcel/ [accessed February 5, 2003]).

All in all, Europe matters economically to Russia much more than any other part of the world. "Europe" in this context means the enlarged EU of twenty-five nations plus countries closely associated with the EU, namely, Norway and Switzerland. Norway, as a member of the European Economic Area (EEA), has undertaken to adhere to the EU *acquis* except for the part specifically to do with membership. Switzerland is outside the EEA but has seven sectoral agreements with the EU, the breaching of any one of which would render the others null and void, so it, too, is closely associated with, and in many respects inside, the single market.

Russian policy makers and businessmen may find dealing with the United States easier than dealing with the EU, because "Brussels" is not a single state, and has cumbersome decision-making procedures. But economic relations with the United States are, for Russia, superficial. The next section, therefore, is focused on Russia's relations with the EU.

Russia-EU Economic Issues

Issues Not Related to EU Enlargement

Russia has until recently been in the peripheral vision, at most, of European Commission staff. They have had more pressing concerns: the single market, the euro, enlargement. And, oil and gas apart, Russia is of little significance as a trade partner (Table 6.2). This may be changing, but the attention of Brussels to Russia still wavers; so, it seems, do its intentions. The rapidity of change, lately, in EU official positions about Russia, is striking.

In January 2002, Pascal Lamy, the EU trade commissioner, observed that Russia was becoming a priority in future EU economic policy (*BBC Global Newsline FSU Economic*, January 13, 2002). This somewhat implausible declaration was based, according to Lamy, on three concerns: the implementation of the EU–Russia partnership and cooperation agreement (which dates from 1994); negotiations for Russian accession to the World Trade Organization; and the declared EU aim, formally stated in 1999, of establishing (at some unspecified date) a unified economic area embracing an enlarged EU and Russia. To this list one might add the question of EU recognition of Russia as a market economy. This had not taken place at the time of Lamy's statement, but it did later in 2002.

There is a logical sequence of developments in Russia–EU economic relations: the according by the EU to Russia of market-economy status (which took effect in autumn 2002), Russian accession to the WTO, which is unlikely before 2005, and then some more systematic formal relationship between the EU and Russia—perhaps the establishment of a single economic space linking Russia and the EU. Indeed, in a Russian assessment of Russia's relations with the EU, WTO accession is treated as a step toward the common economic space (Mau and Novikov 2002).

In December 2002 European Commission President Romano Prodi made a key speech on "A Wider Europe—A Proximity Policy as the Key to Stability" (as cited in Gould 2003); he called for a debate to establish "where the limits of Europe lie," and to develop policies for relations with neighboring countries not currently expected to join the EU. The subsequent policy debate has interpreted this as offering some approximation of European Economic Area arrangements to at least some of those neighbors.

I shall review the issues between Moscow and Brussels, excluding those arising from the present EU enlargement, starting with WTO accession and moving on to the aim of a common economic space.

One key issue between Russia and the EU in the negotiations for Russia to join the WTO is the level of Russian domestic energy prices. Many EU officials see these as providing hidden subsidies to Russian producers. In December 2001 Trade Commissioner Lamy said that the EU would recognize Russia as a market economy only if it ceased levying export duties (which are mainly on oil) and ended its two-tier pricing of energy (*RFE/RL Newsline*, December 6, 2001).

These were and still are very difficult conditions for any Russian leadership to meet. For a start, the situation is different in different parts of the fuel-energy sector. Oil export volumes are constrained by pipeline capacity, so producers cannot freely switch from home to foreign markets across the whole range of oil production, and domestic prices are comparatively low, but not controlled. Domestic gas prices are controlled, on the basis that Gazprom is a monopolist, but it is not necessarily the case that domestic prices are below long-run marginal cost. Domestic electricity prices have indeed been controlled (again on monopoly grounds) and in this case the prices clearly have been below both market-clearing and cost-recovery levels.

The predominant interpretation by specialists—not just by Eurocrats—of Russian domestic energy prices has been that they incorporate a large quasi-subsidy to Russian producers of manufactures and services (for assessments see OECD 2002, Kuboniwa 2002, and Tabata 2002). Gas and electricity are the instances usually cited. However, there is now some evidence that gas prices are not "artificially" low. And domestic electricity prices were partially decontrolled in early 2003, in ways that may turn out to be quite damaging to households and producers in some regions (Rubchenko and Sivakov 2003).

There is also a problem with the logic of any demand that Russia's internal energy (or any other) prices should "equal" world prices. Russia, like other developing countries, has a medium-term equilibrium exchange rate that is much less favorable to the ruble than purchasing power parity. To insist on its domestic energy prices being equivalent at the exchange rate to world prices means requiring them to be high relative to other prices, in international perspective.

Energy prices remain a contentious issue between Russia and the EU, but in any event they did not block official EU (and U.S.) recognition of Russia as a market economy in 2002. This ought to have brought benefits for Russia, especially from Europe.

In early 2002, before Russia's change of status, the EU had twenty antidumping measures in force against Russian products, about half on steel and other metals and about half on chemicals; and it retained the power to impose quotas on Russian textiles and clothing (Hamilton 2003). Politicians and businessmen in Moscow saw this as EU protectionism, helping to lock Russia into its place as a natural-resource supplier. The change of official status to a market economy should have made antidumping measures, in particular, more difficult to bring into play.

Early signs, however, were not good. Russia's status as a market economy came into effect, so far as the EU was concerned, on November 8, 2002; meanwhile the European Union was adopting amendments to its antidumping legislation that reduce the benefit of having market-economy status. Previously, calls for antidumping (AD) measures against products from companies in a market economy would have to be tested against the costs of those producers, whereas similar complaints about products from a nonmarket economy could be tested against costs of supposedly similar producers in third countries. Now the amended AD legislation allows the European Commission to raise the prices of supposedly dumped goods from market-economy producers more or less unilaterally if the commission decides that the original prices are "artificially" low or the country of origin has significant barter trade (*Moscow Times*, November 11, 2002, 7). EU protectionism is deeply ingrained; so is suspicion of Moscow on the part of Brussels.

Russia's WTO accession is not reducible to EU-Russia bilateral negotiations. There are more than sixty WTO members in the working group on Russia's accession. These include the United States, Japan, and India. All have their own priorities. Reportedly, the United States is the most insistent, for example, on the Russian aerospace sector being opened up (one of the trickier accession demands for Russia to accommodate) (Cooper 2002; see also Hare 2002). However, the EU is reported to lead on several key demands.

Accession to the WTO is not merely a matter of working through a list of minor technicalities. The time devoted to it both by President Putin and by Russian industrial lobbies is one indicator of its real significance. It has enormous potential importance for the character of the Russian economy. The key outstanding issues, so far as the EU is concerned, are tariff levels; the opening of Russian financial services and telecoms to foreign companies; energy prices; and agricultural subsidy levels (*Vedomosti*, April 14, 2003). Behind these lies the general question of whether or not the Russian economy will be opened up to foreign business rather than kept as the preserve of the existing Russian business elite—with large implications for the level of competition.

Some specific issues and possible deals include the following. Some state support for domestic aerospace continuing, but not by means of tariffs; decontrol of domestic gas prices over a transition period; ending restrictions on the nationality of chief executive officers and chief financial officers of companies; export taxes on oil and gas to be replaced by wellhead taxes on all production; and agricultural subsidy levels to be allowed to increase, but by less than Russia has been seeking.

Compromises are likely be negotiated. But when? In 2002 President Putin was saying that Russia ought to be able to join the WTO in 2003, ahead of both parliamentary and presidential elections. But the sticking points mentioned above remained sticky well into 2003 (compare Hare 2002 with *Vedomosti*, April 14, 2003). The WTO members, meanwhile, ran into delays in the Doha round of trade liberalization negotiations (*Economist*, March 29, 2003, 75–77). It may be difficult to wrap up Russian accession until Doha is sorted—2005, at best, according to German Gref, the economy minister (*RFE/RL Newsline*, August 14, 2003). And one of the most active WTO groups pushing for Russian concessions in the accession negotiations has been the European Union. Indeed, the European Commission's determination to require changes in Russian domestic gas and electricity pricing goes beyond normal WTO requirements.

Yet the establishment of a single EU–RF economic space, if it makes sense at all, is hardly conceivable before Russia is admitted to the WTO. Moreover, WTO accession may be a necessary step toward a single EU–Russia economic space, but is hardly going to be sufficient. Indeed, many knowledgeable people treat the idea of this single economic space as something so remote from practical possibilities as not to be worth discussion. The EU policy makers may wish to treat it as a focus for EU–Russia cooperation. Some critics take the view that this rather remote aim is merely an unhelpful distraction from the practical question of a Russia–EU free trade area.

Commission pronouncements tend to treat a Russia–EU common economic space as something akin to the existing European Economic Area, combining the

EU with Iceland and Norway. That entails an emphasis on approximating laws and policies, with no permanent derogation from the EU's *acquis communautaire*, and it would probably, for Russia, exclude free trade in farm products.

In Western Europe, views on this approach vary substantially. One view is that such an EU-dominated arrangement would probably be unacceptable for Russia and a comprehensive free trade area would be more helpful (Hamilton 2003). Hamilton points out, among other things, that success for any country in selling to the EU is attributable primarily to that country having strong, competitive producers: he cites the example of the Asian newly industrialized countries. Harmonizing legislation and regulations is not the point—unless the country engaged in such harmonization is a candidate to join the EU.

Jacques Sapir (2002) argues almost the opposite: that genuinely free trade will lock Russia into a raw-materials-and-energy-supply role, and that an active industrial policy should first be pursued in Russia; he doubts, however, the European Commission's capacity to contribute effectively to such a policy.

Gould (2003, 10), writing with the experience of the European Free Trade Association (EFTA) member countries in mind, observes: "For countries not interested in or eligible for EU membership there is no clear rationale for an approximation to the *acquis*." He points out that acquiring EEA status has meant adopting almost all the *acquis*; having done that, a country should be qualified for membership.

Samson and Greffe (2002), writing as semiofficial advisers to both Brussels and Moscow, argue for the harmonization of legislation and the establishment of a single economic space, rather than the pursuit of a free trade area, but they accept that not all the *acquis* is appropriate to Russia now, and its adoption should be selective—though they imply that eventually complete harmonization is desirable. They cite econometric results purporting to demonstrate that the creation of a single market would benefit Russia more than a free trade area would. Since the calculations assume productivity-enhancing effects from a single market, this is not a surprising conclusion.

If a Common European Economic Space included a genuinely and completely free trade area between Russia and the EU, much of this discussion would be superfluous. The oddity of the present situation is that Brussels seems, as far as Russia is concerned, to envisage institutional approximation that would be appropriate for joining a single market—which goes beyond the removal of tariffs and quotas that constitutes the establishment of a free trade area—without an apparent readiness to envisage free trade as part of the plan.

The trouble therefore with Brussels's notion of a common economic space is that it seems to entail much "harmonization" by Russia toward rules and regulations unilaterally set by Brussels, together with less than free trade in (presumably) those sectors in which EU producers fear cheap competition, such as steel, some nonferrous metals, textiles, basic chemicals, and farm products.

The problem for any neighboring, nonmember state is that the EU is protectionist. Its common external tariff is modest: a 7 percent simple average of tariff rates. But, as Åslund and Warner (2003) have shown, EU protectionism on agricultural products (17.5 percent tariff average, with variable levies and technical-standards barriers complicating the picture), steel, chemicals, and other "sensitive" sectors (antidumping measures readily used, and acting as a deterrent to investment in capacity to export to the EU), particularly affects the CIS countries.

Meanwhile, some Russian policy analysts are taking a robust view of the relationship between Brussels and Moscow. Mau and Novikov (2002) consider the steps toward first a free trade area and then a single market. They treat institutional compatibility as the key issue. But they advocate a highly selective Russian adoption of the European Union's *acquis communautaire*. They argue that much of what is being required of the EU applicant countries is either not relevant to Russia or would be positively harmful. In particular, they contend that adoption of the *acquis* on labor and social legislation, consumer protection, agriculture, and environment would damage Russia's development as a competitive market economy and is not needed for the creation of a single economic space in which goods, services, labor, and capital move freely. Other chapters of the *acquis*, on transport, energy, statistics, telecoms, would be useful but are not necessary. Russia, in their view, can become integrated with Europe, in the sense of the EU, without either joining or even adopting most of the *acquis* like Norway. Their classification of the *acquis* chapters from the point of view of Russian institutional adaptation, is shown in Table 6.4.

The Mau-Novikov view of the *acquis* has its supporters outside Russia. Paul Hare, for example, in an analysis of institutional change in transition, notes in passing that the *acquis* has been influential, but perhaps not always in desirable ways (Hare 2001). Hamilton's 2003 paper, already cited, makes the point that harmonization of the kind espoused by the European Commission entails an unequal jurisdictional relationship—problematic for Norway and no doubt even more problematic for a state that twelve years ago was the core of a superpower.

European Commission officials and most governments in EU member states will not agree. If there were to be an EU-Russia single economic space in which people move freely, for example, there will be demands that the Russian state also take on EU member-state obligations on social policy and on cooperation in justice and internal affairs. A free trade area that extended to farm products and services would be mutually beneficial but would not raise such difficult issues for Russia.

It may be that Russia has little option but to pursue some sort of "modified EEA" arrangement. Bordachev (2003) argues this. Starting with the implicit assumption that closer economic links with Europe are desirable, he considers three possibilities: EU trade preferences such as are provided to North African countries; "perpetual candidate" status, like Turkey; and modified EEA association. The last he treats as the least bad, and tolerable for Moscow provided interparliamentary cooperation can be used to give Russia a say in "pre-draft" discussion of legislation and Russian business groups establish themselves as serious lobbyists in Brussels.

138

Table 6.4

Does Russia Need the *Acquis*? The Mau-Novikov View

Irrelevant	Inappropriate	Useful but not essential	Desirable
11. European Monetary Union	6. Competition*	9. Transport policy	1. Free movement of goods
15. Industrial policy	7. Agriculture	12. Statistics	2. Free movement of people
16. Small- and medium-sized enterprises	8. Fisheries	14. Energy	3. Free trade in services
17. Science	10. Taxation	19. Telecoms, IT	4. Free movement of capital
18. Education	13. Social policy	20. Culture, etc.	5. Company law
21. Regional policy	22. Environment	26. External relations	6. State aid*
24. Justice, etc.	23. Consumer protection		
27. Foreign policy			
28. Financial control			
29. Finance and budget			
30. (EU) institutions			

Source: Mau and Novikov (2002), p. 142.

*Within Chapter 6, EU competition policy is treated as inappropriate but EU limitations on state aid are accepted as necessary.

But is a so-called Common Space that does not include genuinely free trade in everything really such an attractive deal? Is it possible that the European Union is too *étatiste* for an emerging liberal, dynamic Russian economy to be integrated into it to Russia's advantage? The question may seem far-fetched. Where is this dynamic, liberal new Russian economy at present? If analysts and policy advisers like Vladimir Mau—a close associate of Egor Gaidar and formerly head of the government's Working Center for Economic Reforms, now rector of the Academy of the National Economy—have their way, however, it could yet materialize. That may indeed be rather more likely than a liberalized European Union.

The single economic space, though a long-term and uncertain prospect, should be taken seriously, but it should not be an arrangement dominated by the EU and its problematic *acquis*. Working toward a comprehensive free trade area is more promising. Even that, however, raises additional questions. Could a Russia-EU free trade area work, for example, regardless of conditions in the countries that would abut it and that straddle many of the transport routes between Russia and an enlarged EU? Russian territory will adjoin an enlarged EU along borders with Finland, Estonia, and (around Kaliningrad) Lithuania and Poland. Elsewhere Belarus, Ukraine, Moldova, and Romania intervene. Can these inconveniently located transition laggards simply be ignored?

The United States must, by contrast with the EU, seem a more straightforward partner: its elite thinking is more in harmony with that of Russia both on terrorism and on free markets. It is, however, far less economically engaged with Russia, and is likely to remain so. The notion of Russia joining a Free Trade Area for the Americas (Videman 2003) does not look a starter. If Mercosur countries would not be welcome in such a trade bloc, what price Russia? What is striking is that the Russian establishment's impatience with Europe is strong enough to give such ideas an airing.

The dilemma for Russia is that nobody sees it as a potential EU member in the foreseeable future, but being simply a neighbor of Europe is awkward and (so far) rather unrewarding. Europe is just about prepared to swallow Poland, writes Vladimir Videman, but that is the limit; Ukraine, let alone Russia, would be too much: "it is desirable to absorb into the European order small national enclaves, but certainly not large-scale, multi-cultural blocs" (Videman 2003, 62). The problem, writes Svetlov, is not even the economic instability of Ukraine and Russia, but the fear that they "will pull the blanket over to their side" (Svetlov 2002, 56).

Such speculations about thinking in Western Europe may not be entirely convincing, but they reveal an understandable fear: that Russia will have to fend for itself (Khisamov 2003).

EU Enlargement and Russia

In many respects, the accession of eight Central and East European countries to the EU in 2004 changes very little so far as Russia is concerned. (The accession of

Cyprus and Malta can be ignored here, except to note that a large amount of off-shore Russian capital has joined the EU with the first of these two Mediterranean islands.)

The main economic effects, potentially, for Russia are the following. The EU market has become larger—but only by about 4 percent in dollar terms (9 percent if the combined GDP is measured at purchasing power parity, but for trading purposes it is the exchange-rate measure that counts). Accession may enhance the prosperity of the new members (over and above growth that would have occurred outside the EU), bringing trade-creating effects for third parties. This enhanced prosperity could come from increased productivity in the new members through improved static efficiency, scale effects, and possibly competition effects, and also from dynamic effects through the stimulation of investment. Insofar as the enlargement confers similar benefits (net) on the EU15, there would be similar trade-creating effects there, too. Accession may alter the terms of Russian market access to the accession-candidate countries. Finally, the eastward movement of the EU changes the character of the Russian border around Kaliningrad (on both sides, if Poland and Lithuania both accede in 2004 or thereabouts): this will affect border trade and therefore the economy of Kaliningrad.

On the whole, these effects cannot be very large. In any case, they had in part already come to pass before 2004. The change in the size of the EU market is minor. Åslund and Warner (2003) present enlargement as highly significant for Russia and the other CIS countries, but what they have to say is not in fact at odds with the assessment here. Their argument is that the protectionism of the EU has significant costs for the CIS countries (see the previous section), and that the enlargement highlights the difference in treatment between the new insiders (the accession countries) and those that remain outside. Their analysis and evidence do not bear on the cost of enlargement itself. In fact they speculate that enlargement might operate as a stimulus to accelerate reform in the CIS countries—a conjecture that might just as easily be stood on its head: exclusion could breed a defiant rejection of attempts to be more like those included.

The main point here is that much of the effects of enlargement for Central Europe—and indirectly for Russia—have already begun to appear. Most trade between the leading accession candidates and the EU is already free. The Central and East European countries' (CEECs) trade shifted sharply westward after the collapse of communism. This re-orientation has been assisted by the CEECs' associate status with the EU and the elimination of most trade barriers. Still, it must be largely attributed to the reassertion of the force of gravity after the removal of central planning: the influences of competitiveness, market size, and transport costs were allowed to operate on the CEECs' economies after the collapse of the Soviet-dominated Council for Mutual Economic Assistance.

In some cases, transport systems have been or are being reshaped to facilitate this. For example, the CEECs' electricity grids, formerly integrated with the Soviet grid, are now linked with the Scandinavian (Nordel) or West European (UCPTE) grids—and these two are now being joined up; this increases the urgency of Russia's interest in linking its grid with the new TransEuropean Synchronised Integrated System (*Kommersant–Daily*, March 20, 2002, 1).

Similarly, the stimulation of foreign direct investment into the CEECs (including from Russia), to be expected from accession, must to a large extent be already in operation.

Thus some of the effects associated with accession are already being felt in the accession countries. The static-efficiency effects of freer trade, worth probably only about 1 percent of GDP (see Dyker 2001), have mostly been captured. The ending of EU contingent protection against imports of so-called sensitive items is still to come; so are the mixed blessings of the Common Agricultural Policy— from which the new members will get comparatively little in the way of additional subsidies but more competition.

The benefits of operating in a larger market (scale effects that can be distinguished from pure resource-allocation improvements on the assumption of constant returns) have also been in part already captured, and are not large.

Competition effects could be positive or negative. Joining the EU is not automatically good for a nation's economic health. A previously backward country may thrive, and rapidly narrow the gap between its own development level and that of the most advanced EU members. Or its businesses may struggle and make little headway against strong competition in the new single market. Ireland and Greece, respectively, exemplify these two outcomes.

Joining a single market and, in due course, the Eurozone as well, should stimulate investment by reducing country risk. Dyker (2001) cites an estimate of an output boost of up to 19 percent resulting from this. It does seem likely that the eight leading CEEC accession candidates, whose growth already exceeds that of the EU15, should if anything be more Irish than Greek in this respect. But again, this is a benefit already being received. The prospect of accession has already stimulated inward foreign investment into the CEECs—and probably domestic investment, too.

In short, the trade-creating effects, for Russia, of a Central and Eastern Europe rendered more prosperous by joining the EU are not huge, and in any case are already operating in part. The small economic size of the CEECs suggests that corresponding net gains for the EU15 from the enlargement will also not be very large. And by the same token, any such benefits have already been partly captured.

What about trade diversion? Could Russian products suffer from the accession states' adoption of the common external tariff of the EU in place of their own tariffs? Two Russian specialists, Zakhmatov and Fomichev, (2001) address market access issues in the case of Poland. They observe first of all a possibly positive consequence for Russian exports to Poland: on joining the EU, Poland will adopt the EU general system of preference (GSP); Zakhmatov and Fomichev calculate that for sixty out of sixty-two four-digit tariff headings, the GSP tariffs on Russian goods are lower than Poland's present tariffs; on the other hand, they note, the

GSP will lower Polish tariffs for third world exporters even more, so Russia faces lower tariffs but intensified competition.

Hamilton (2003) reaches the same conclusion with respect to Poland, but finds that accession and the adoption of the EU common external tariff would slightly raise the trade-weighted average tariff on Russian goods entering Hungary and the Czech Republic. It looks as though any net effect of tariff changes will be close to zero.

Zakhmatov and Fomichev also draw attention to the fact that Poland in 1999 took 87 percent of its oil imports [and therefore presumably 87 percent of all its oil usage—PH] from Russia and 75 percent of its gas. These proportions may be subject to downward pressure because of the EU energy-sourcing policy (unquantified "diversity"). However, they judge that, while proportions taken from Russia may be gradually reduced over time, absolute amounts may be little changed or could even grow.

The two other consequences they note may be mutually offsetting. Russian problems with EU technical standards will be extended to the Polish market. On the other hand Russian access via Poland to the EU15 market may be eased; this is because Russia's Partnership and Cooperation agreement with the EU requires EU member states to allow free (administratively unimpeded) access across their territory to markets in other EU countries. And funding from the European Investment Bank may be drawn on to improve these transport routes.

The Russian leadership understandably, therefore, wants to develop a constructive relationship with Poland. Speaking in Poznan on January 17, 2002, President Putin said, "Both our countries are interested in the construction on this continent of a single space of stability and progress." He went on to speak of Poland's accession to the EU as providing opportunities for greater economic cooperation between Russia and Poland, observing that Poland's present 5 percent share in Russian merchandise trade could and should be larger (www.president.ru/events/436.html [January 25, 2002]).

The Kaliningrad border issue is significant, though perhaps more for diplomatic and even symbolic than for economic reasons. A new EU border on either side of Kaliningrad will differ from the existing Russia–EU border in Karelia in two ways.

First, the neighboring states were not long ago in the same economic bloc (in the case of Lithuania, in the same country). In contrast, when Finland joined the EU, it had long been at arm's length in its dealings with Moscow. The Karelian border has become softer since then, as things have changed on the eastern side. The new Schengen borders round the Russian exclave impede a thriving legal, semilegal, and illegal cross-border trade between Kaliningrad and its neighbors that has grown in the past decade and probably (no reliable measurement yet exists) matters a great deal to Kaliningrad.

Second, these borders are around a piece of Russian territory already physically separated from the rest of Russia, and whose past as Königsberg contributes to Moscow's sensitivity about it. President Putin has taken it upon himself to call for visa-free travel for Kaliningrad residents through Poland or Lithuania to Russia. By saying this himself, he made it harder for Russia to back down. Yet neither Lithuania nor Poland considers such an arrangement as workable (*RFE/RL Newsline*, June 11, 2002)—quite apart from the objections of existing EU member states. Indications of a readiness to compromise have come from the Russian prime minister (ibid.), but a deal could take a long time.

Despite these hints from the prime minister about a possible compromise, the tougher line taken by the president still predominated in late summer 2002. The defense minister, Sergei Ivanov, speaking on July 30 in Lithuania, repeated the call for visa-free travel (*Itar-Tass* from Palanga, July 30, 2002). Dmitrii Rogozin, the chairman of the Duma International Affairs Committee and a hard-liner on Kaliningrad, was appointed as special presidential envoy in international negotiations about the region; he repeated the demand around the same time (*Interfax* from Moscow, July 30, 2002). Moreover, he contended that visa-free travel to and from Kaliningrad should be a right of all Russian citizens; some Western proposals for special electronic cards to be issued to Kaliningraders, allowing them visa-free overland access to and from the Russian "mainland," would be discriminatory (Radio Russia, August 11, 2002).

The more conciliatory (unofficial) Western suggestions did not go beyond a soft visa regime or special ID cards, for residents of Kaliningrad, facilitating cheap and frequent cross-border travel for legal trading.

A compromise was reached at the Russia-EU summit in Brussels on November 11, 2002. This entailed the adoption of "simplified transit documents" (*uproshchennye tranzitnye dokumenty*, or UTD, in Russian) for transit across Lithuania between Kaliningrad and "mainland" Russia. This was a fudge. The UTDs are visas by another name. EU taxpayers will cover the cost of the system, so the UTDs will be free to Kaliningraders and (at the Lithuanian border) to Russian family members heading to see relatives in Kaliningrad. (See www.strana.ru; www.izvestiya.ru of November 11, 2002.) Details remain to be worked out, but it is not clear how, if at all, these documents will help cross-border traders—who are, after all, not transiting Poland or Lithuania. The Russian media treated the outcome as a victory for Putin. Some European commentary emphasized, on the contrary, that it was a concession by Putin and that in return the EU had soft-pedaled issues of human rights in Chechnya (notably *Le Monde*, November 12, 2002).

More serious and constructive decisions could be made about Kaliningrad. One possibility—ambitious but not necessarily impracticable—is suggested by Evgenii Vinokurov (2003): Kaliningrad as a free trade area within the EU (requiring effective administration of certificates of origin, so that Russian production in total does not flow freely into the EU) and cheap and convenient travel between Kaliningrad and the EU, restricted to Kaliningrad residents on the one hand, and EU citizens going only to Kaliningrad, on the other. Some such special status could bring real benefits for the residents of Kaliningrad and also build confidence between Moscow and Brussels.

Conclusion

Russia's economy has been growing quite strongly. The sustainability of that growth is a matter of dispute. A case can be made that economic institutions are improving and the growth is not reducible to a favorable exchange rate and high oil prices. In some respects, the Russian economy is now rather open. More than half Russia's trade, much of its investment (inward and outward) and much of Russian people's cross-border contacts are with Europe. Trade is otherwise rather dispersed across trade partners. The United States is a minor trade-partner of Russia, but rather more important with respect to investment into Russia and more broadly as an influence on the world trading environment, including in oil and gas.

Russia is economically already quite strongly intertwined with the present EU. Those linkages are likely to strengthen further. The EU's eastward enlargement may not radically alter the scale of Russia–EU trade and investment flows. Some of the economic consequences for Russia of that enlargement, in fact, were already operating ahead of the enlargement itself.

The main economic issues between Russia and Brussels are EU support for Russian WTO accession, and the terms demanded for that support in access to Russian markets and further Russian structural reform; the long-term prospects of a unified economic space spanning Russia and an enlarged EU—which almost certainly requires Russian WTO accession as a precondition; and the handling of Kaliningrad in the present enlargement. It has been argued here that Brussels's notion of a common economic space is probably too one-sided, especially in its emphasis on EU partners adopting the *acquis* and its lack of a clear commitment to genuinely free trade.

Negotiations for WTO accession have been arduous and prolonged. Members of the WTO want all sorts of commitments by Russia that they could not be bothered to demand when they admitted Moldova, Kyrgyzstan, Georgia, and Armenia. Yet there are other ways of looking at what is at stake: just as Russia's entry has significant consequences, so does its continued exclusion.

Russia's interests are probably not best served by the development of a Common European Economic Space as presently envisaged in Brussels. Current thinking in the European Commission is long on Russian "harmonization" with the EU and short on opening EU markets to "sensitive" products from Russia—which now include grain. Only the prospect of eventual EU membership would provide Russia with the incentive to harmonize institutions. Is such a prospect conceivable? If the lesser objective of a free trade area were to be entertained, what would Russia have to do to make it feasible, and what would the EU have to do? EU protectionism and Russian administrative weakness combine, on a skeptical view, to make either form of closer economic cooperation difficult.

Two scenarios could be envisaged. The first would entail long delays over the WTO, relegating the single economic space or free trade area to some never-never land. The second would be at least a rate of progress on the WTO that kept Russian interest in it alive, and that made the achievement of a free trade area within (say) ten to fifteen years a serious possibility. Just how Kaliningrad is handled is a separable issue. But EU, Polish, and Lithuanian generosity over Kaliningrad—stopping short of foolish giveaways creating a border porous to all kinds of *biznes*—would help promote the second scenario.

The first scenario appeals to those West Europeans who are so suspicious of Russia that they fear the consequences of getting close to it, even in its post-communist form. The case for the second scenario rests on a belief that Russia and Europe both gain from closer mutual contact. In choosing between the two, one gets little help from history. An opening up of Russia to Europe and Europe to Russia has never been tried before.

The United States is unlikely to play a significant part in Russia's integration into the wider world economy, purely as a trade partner. Its importance to Moscow is above all political—that is, geostrategic. The role of the U.S. administration and U.S. oil companies in shaping oil and gas development in the Caspian Basin and in the Middle East is also significant for Moscow. But there could be another role for the United States in Russia's economic emergence on the world stage: that of a politically powerful interlocutor who goads others, including the EU, to open up their markets more than they currently do. As a small, open economy outside a major trading bloc, Russia needs powerful friends of this kind. To play this role, the United States does, however, need to be serious itself about freer trade.

Notes

The author is indebted to colleagues in the Transformation and Integration project and to Judy Batt for comments on earlier drafts.

1. In principle, changes in oil prices and in the real exchange rate could neatly offset one another. This has not however happened in practice. See Rautava 2002.

2. The growth of fixed investment slowed markedly in 2002—officially to 2.5 percent. There are reasons however to doubt the reliability of this figure (Hanson 2003). In January–June 2003 it was 11.9 percent up, year on year (Ministry of Economic Development and Trade, www.economy.gov.ru [July 24, 2003]).

Bibliography

Åslund, Anders, and Andrew Warner. 2003. "The Enlargement of the European Union. Consequences for the CIS Countries." Carnegie Endowment for International Peace, Working Paper no. 36 (April).
Boone, P., and D. Rodionov. 2001. "Rent Seeking in Russia and the CIS." Paper presented at the tenth anniversary conference of the EBRD, London, December.
Bordachev, Timofei. 2003. "Proshchai, starushka Evropa," *Vedomosti*, April 16.
BP (British Petroleum). 2002. *BP Statistical Review of World Energy June 2002*, London.
Cooper, Julian. 2002. "Russia and the WTO." Presentation at the Royal Institute of International Affairs, March 21, 2002.
Dyker, David. 2001. "The Dynamic Impact on the Central-Eastern European Economies of

Accession to the European Union: Social Capability and Technology Absorption,"
Europe-Asia Studies 53, no. 7 (November): 1001–21.

EC Green Paper. 2000. *Toward a European Strategy for the Security of Energy Supply,*
www.europe.eu.int/comm/energy_transport/en/lpi_en_3.html [April 20, 2004].

EU-Russia Energy Partnership. 2002. www.europe.eu.int/comm/energy_transport/en/
lpi_en_3.html [April 20, 2004].

Gould, Tim. 2003. "The European Economic Area as a Model for the Wider Europe." Background paper prepared for the EFTA meeting of Members of Parliament and their social
partners, Kristiansand, Norway, June 26, p. 10.

Grabbe, Heather. 2001. *Profiting from EU Enlargement.* London: Centre for European Reform.

Hamilton, Carl B. 2003. "Russia's European Economic Integration: Escapism and Realities." Centre for Economic Policy Research (CEPR) Discussion Paper 3840.

Hanson, Philip. 2003. "The Russian Economic Recovery: Do Four Years' Growth Tell us
that the Fundamentals Have Changed?" *Europe-Asia Studies* 55, no. 3 (May): 365–82.

Hanson, Philip, and Michael Bradshaw, eds. 2000. *Regional Economic Change in Russia,*
Cheltenham, UK: Edward Elgar.

Hare, Paul G. 2001. "Institutional Change and Economic Performance in the Transition
Economies." UN ECE, *Economic Survey of Europe 2002,* no. 2: 77–94.

———. 2002. "Russia and the World Trade Organization." Draft, July; the published version, together with contributions by negotiators Lamy and Medvedkov, and by E.G.
Yasin, is put out by the Centre for European Reform. Available at: www.cer.org.uk/
publications/394.html [April 20, 2004].

Holzman, Franklyn D. 1963. "Foreign Trade," in *Economic Trends in the Soviet Union,* ed.
A. Bergson and S. Kuznets, pp. 283–333. Cambridge, MA: Harvard University Press.

Khisamov, Iskander. 2003. "Vybor kontserta," *Ekspert,* no. 9 (March 10): 65.

Kuboniwa, Masaaki. 2002. "The Hollowing Out of Industry and Expansion of the Trade
Service Sector in Russia: Domestic Factors Determining Russia's Presence in the International Markets under Globalization." Paper presented at the AAASS National Conference, Pittsburgh, PA, November 21–24.

Liuhto, Kari. 2002. "Russian Oil and Gas—A Source of Integration." Research Report,
Dept. of Industrial Engineering and Management, Lappeenranta University of Technology, Finland.

Mau, V., and V. Novikov. 2002. "Otnosheniia Rossii i ES: prostranstvo vybora ili vybor
prostranstva?" *Voprosy ekonomiki,* no. 6: 133–45.

OECD (Organization for Economic Cooperation and Development. 2002. *Economic Survey of Russia 2002.* Paris.

Rautava, Jouko. 2002. "The Role of Oil Prices and the Real Exchange Rate in Russia's
Economy," Bank of Finland, BOFIT Discussion Paper no. 3.

Rubchenko, Maksim, and Dmitrii Sivakov. 2003. "Reforma bez pravitel'stva." *Ekspert,* no.
9 (March 10): 16–22.

Samson, Ivan, and Xavier Greffe. 2002. *Common Economic Space: Prospects of Russia–
EU Relations. White Book.* Moscow: TACIS/RECEP.

Sapir, Jacques. 2002. "Russia's Economic Growth and European Integration." Paper presented at the AAASS National Conference, Pittsburgh, PA, November 21–24.

Sulamaa, Pekka, and Mika Widgren. 2003. "Eastern Enlargement and Beyond: A Simulation Study on EU and CIS Integration." Centre for Economic Policy Research (CEPR)
Discussion paper 3768.

Svetlov, R.V. 2002. *Druz'ia i vragi Rossii.* St. Petersburg: Amfora.

Tabata, Shinichiro. 2002. "Flow of Oil and Gas Export Revenues and Their Taxation in
Russia." Paper presented at the AAASS National Conference, Pittsburgh, PA, November 21–24.

Telhami, Shibley, et al. (2002). "Does Saudi Arabia Still Matter?" *Foreign Affairs* 81, no. 6 (November/December): 167–79.
Videman (Widdemann), Vladimir. 2003. "Okno v Evropu ili dver' v Ameriku?" *Ekspert*, no. 9 (March 10): 59–65.
Vinokurov, Evgeny. 2003. "What Russia and the EU Can Do for Kaliningrad and What Kaliningrad Can Do for the European-Russian Dialogue." Brussels: draft CEPS working document, March.
Zakhmatov, Nikolai, and Viktor Fomichev. 2001. "Integratsiia Pol'shi v ES i interesy Rossii." *Sovremennaia Evropa* (October–December).

Part II

Integration:
Obstacles and Possibilities

7

The European Union's Policies Toward Russia

Ania Krok-Paszkowska and Jan Zielonka

This chapter sets out to give an overview of European Union (EU) policies toward Russia from an institutional perspective.[1] In our view, the fact that the EU is a very peculiar if not unique international actor largely determines its external policies. We will therefore first describe the nature of the EU as a multifaceted international actor and how it may evolve after enlargement to twenty-five member states. This will be followed by a short history of EU–Russia relations pointing to the preconditions of any meaningful cooperation on both sides. The form and substance of the EU's policies toward Russia will be analyzed next. We will try to evaluate the extent to which those policies have an impact, either positive or negative, on Russia's domestic transformation. Special attention will be devoted to the political and economic agendas of the EU and Russia with a view to ascertaining what kind of a relationship between the two is emerging and what form of integration with the EU is likely to develop after enlargement. In the conclusion we will reinforce our initial claim about the dominance of the institutional rather than political or economic logic in the EU's policies toward Russia.

The EU as a Multifaceted International Actor

There is a general tendency to view EU policies toward Russia in terms of state-to-state relations. We talk as if the EU had interests, instruments, and strategies similar to typical states such as the United States or Germany. This chapter will argue that this is a mistake. The EU is not a typical state, but a complex international institution in search of purpose and legitimacy. It is an actor of multifaceted character, full of paradoxes and contradictions. The EU is aspiring to become a powerful international actor without turning itself into a super state. It aims to have a strategic impact in Europe without behaving in a strategic way. It has ambitions of stabilizing its external environment, but its policies are being guided by internal rather than external pressures. The role of the EU as a single actor in the external field rather than as a number of individual states has been reinforced by recent treaties, in particular that of Amsterdam, and this has prompted a more serious engagement vis-à-vis Russia. Nevertheless, we will argue that the EU's current attempts to use and even widen its increased competencies in foreign affairs are still being countered by the ambiguity of its basic aims and functions and by other internal institutional characteristics. This is likely to remain so even after adoption of a European constitution, and the enlargement of the EU to twenty-five member states will only reinforce the ambivalent nature and complexity of various arrangements. In fact, a Union of twenty-five states is likely to resemble a multifunctional, multilayered, and highly diversified empire rather than a classical Westphalian state with clear borders, coherent institutional structure, and a single foreign policy (Zielonka 2001). This may further undermine the Union's ability to develop any sound strategy toward Russia. Nevertheless and paradoxically such a scenario may make it easier for Russia to integrate with the EU, especially at the grass-roots informal level. A Union resembling a complex empire will have fuzzy and soft borders that are easier to cross by neighbors than the fixed and hard borders of a Westphalian state. The distinction between members and nonmembers will also be less sharp in a Union resembling an empire. If the enlarged Union will not closely resemble a Westphalian state, then Russia will be able to get closer to it in certain selected fields without necessarily having to meet the entire set of Copenhagen criteria for accession. Regional actors both in Russia and the EU would not always need to handle their mutual relationship via central authorities in Moscow and Brussels. And cooperation in individual functional fields could develop without the need for a comprehensive strategic deal between the EU and Russia. Indeed, the key to Russia's integration with the EU would be the intensity of informal cross-border regional exchanges rather than the intensity of official exchanges on major strategic issues. The Union's ability to shape the external world in a strategic fashion is rather limited. Its external influence is largely based on its normative appeal and its ability to export regulatory frames, institutional solutions, and cultural habits. Let us take a closer look at the peculiar and still evolving nature of the EU as an international actor.

The EU has always been ambivalent and vague about many of its basic aims and functions because of the persistent lack of consensus about the very nature and functional scope of integration. The debate about federal vs. intergovernmental models, with differing views about legitimacy and sovereignty, is as lively as ever. At times, the EU seems to be more concerned with institutions than with the substance of its policy. The most contentious matters in the Convention on the Future of Europe centered on the institutional balance of the EU. Views differ on issues such as whether there should be a powerful executive president of the EU, how the president of the European Commission should be chosen, and how to institutionally restructure EU foreign and security policy.

In practice, the EU has long been a strong and dynamic actor in the fields of economics and trade. Indeed, a single internal market has been established as well as economic and monetary union, with a single currency having been adopted by the majority of member states. However, its track record in the fields of foreign policy, security, and diplomacy has been far weaker.

Even among the current fifteen member states, there are significant differences of opinion with respect to the development of medium- and long-term policy aims in both foreign affairs and defense. Views differ with respect to the range of tasks to be performed as well as the geographic scope of these tasks. A great deal of time and effort is spent on finding a "common denominator" for foreign policy positions. Individual member states have specific and sometimes conflicting agendas. The Balkan war in the early 1990s and the Iraq war a decade later have shown how sharp those disagreements and conflicts can be. This will only increase with the enlargement to countries that formed part of the former Soviet bloc. Although new treaty provisions and instruments provide the framework for the pursuit of a more robust Common Foreign and Security Policy (CFSP) and the establishment of a European Security and Defense Policy (ESDP), EU member states find it hard to accept the limits on national freedom of action that this entails. As a result, the CFSP, ESDP, and individual mechanisms such as strategies and joint actions have so far proven unable to transform the EU's enormous normative power of attraction into effective operational capability that would allow the EU to shape the external environment in any strategic fashion. In this sense, the EU is very different from the United States or other traditional state actors.

The EU is basically a civilian power with far greater competencies in the field of "soft" rather than "hard" security. Security is perceived more in terms of fighting organized crime and controlling the stream of illegal immigration than worries about a military threat. Although the EU aspires to prevent and manage conflict, it remains ambivalent about acquiring the military means to do so. All this has an impact on the EU's relations with Russia.

Thus in its relations with Russia the EU does not act simply because certain political or economic developments demand such action. The instruments the EU has at its disposal are not fully utilized due to the difficulty its member states have in reaching agreement upon collective goals. Moreover, the EU lacks institutional capacity to identify and then express its strategic interests.

The EU's institutional characteristics must therefore be taken into account in any analysis of the policies it pursues. When the EU does reach agreement on common goals, its complex institutional set-up merely adds to the difficulty in undertaking concrete action. The various EU institutions (Council, Commission, and Parliament) all have their own institutional interests, instruments, and capacities. The EU's decision-making procedures are slow and unwieldy. Budgetary procedures are too slow to respond to rapidly developing needs. Policy design and implementation are made more complicated by the so-called three-pillar structure, which places different policy areas under different institutional regimes, either more communitarian or more intergovernmental. The first, communitarian pillar, is mostly governed by qualified majority voting while unanimous decision making prevails in the EU's intergovernmental second pillar. Thus trade and economics (first pillar) is separated from foreign policy (second pillar). Policies broadly defined as justice and home affairs (JHA) covering asylum, immigration, external border management, judicial cooperation, and cross-border crime fall under different pillars and pose one of the most confusing areas of integration. The EU's parallel use of communitarian responsibility and intergovernmental cooperation in the field of foreign and security policy has also led to a lack of clarity on budgetary arrangements (Rummel, Reinhardt, and Wiedemann 1998).

This complex institutional set-up and the division of competences were discussed in the Convention on the Future of Europe, which prepared a draft treaty establishing a constitution for Europe (Draft Treaty 2003). There is general agreement that the various treaties making up the EU should be simplified and that the EU should have a unique legal personality, which would mean that the present three-pillar structure would be replaced by a unified institutional structure, making the EU more comprehensible as an international actor. It is recognized that decision making in an enlarged Union needs to be streamlined and made more transparent. There is far less consensus about the institutional balance of the enlarged EU. The main fault line lies between those who want a more federal or communitarian structure and those who would prefer a more intergovernmental model. This also reflects a struggle between larger and smaller member states. Smaller states are worried that certain institutional reforms will be forced through by the larger members. They see proposals to have fewer European commissioners (reduced from twenty to fifteen) and a president of the European Council chosen by heads of government for a two and a half year term as favoring candidates from large countries. They want to make sure that the European Commission is powerful enough to protect their rights against pressure from larger countries and to represent the wider EU interest. There are also divisions between old and new members, and in particular the original six members who tend to favor closer cooperation. The draft treaty allows for the possibility of enhanced cooperation by a small group of members willing and able to cooperate more closely in certain policy areas. New members have expressed worries that such cooperation could lead to their being relegated to a second or outer tier in a "two-speed" EU. There is also tension between net budget contributors (generally in northern and western Europe) and net budget receivers (generally in southern and eastern Europe).

Opinion polls show no great enthusiasm among the general publics of the member states for an integrated "federal" EU, but there is majority support for greater cooperation in foreign and defense policies (*Financial Times*, September 18, 2003). Electorates as well as elites are sending mixed messages about the type of EU they want. It is still unclear what kind of polity will emerge. Conflicting demands and interests were not reconciled during an intergovernmental conference held in October–December 2003. Even so, agreement on the constitution was reached in time for the EU summit in June 2004. The finalized draft treaty then still has to be approved unanimously by the twenty-five member states. Some of the states will have to hold referendums, making the ratification process rather problematic.

Such a state of affairs is nothing new. The EU is and will continue to be in flux:

"... the Union is always in the process of *becoming*—its constitution, institutions and policy remit have not yet reached, and may never reach, a stable equilibrium" (Latham, O'Donnell, and Smith 2000, 73). Given the differing views and the huge diversity of actors and their interests, but also the desire to find some kind of a solution, the outcome in the end is likely to be a compromise, and may well result in an institutional structure that has unexpected consequences. Actors will continue to find original and innovative ways to change or circumvent institutions to realize their goals.

This all means that the EU's external policies, including those toward Russia, will continue to be driven by institutional rather than political or economic logic. This has at least two important implications. First, the EU acts toward Russia only when equipped with a mandate and instruments in the form of a treaty. The EU is not geared toward ad hoc or rapid responses to political or economic developments. When the EU institutions are not given a legal framework for engagement, the EU responds to various developments in its relations with Russia by mere rhetorical statements, rather than any significant action. Individual members can then pursue their own agendas.

Second, the type of response by the EU to various political and economic developments concerning Russia is determined by its internal institutional characteristics. In other words, the EU is a very peculiar international actor with complex decision-making rules, and economic rather than military means of action. Its policies toward Russia are not so much a response to the peculiarities of Russia as such, but they are shaped by the peculiarities of the EU as international actor. Here, one ought to look beyond the detailed institutional set-up of the Union, and consider the evolving nature of the European polity being prompted by the EU's constitutional process and the ongoing process of enlargement. Does the EU increasingly resemble a traditional Westphalian state or an empire with fuzzy borders, divided sovereignty, and multiplicity of various institutional arrangements over different fields and territory?

Development of EU Policies

The fall of the Soviet Union did not automatically lead to closer cooperation between the EU and Russia. In the early 1990s, there was little interest in and understanding of EU integration issues among Russian politicians (Leshoukov 1998; also for an analysis of Russia's political leadership see Lilia Shevtsova, chapter 5 in this volume). The ongoing political and economic instability of the new Russian state left little time for the development of a coherent policy toward the EU. Politicians were preoccupied with maintaining the territorial integrity of Russia and controlling regional separatism. In 1998 came a severe financial crisis, which prompted Russia to focus on its internal economic issues. Until 1999, when Russia's medium-term strategy document was published, there was thus little attempt to define an overall strategy toward the EU. Moreover, traditionally Russia had focused its activity on the larger member states such as Germany, France, or Britain and concentrated on bilateral relations. Relations with the EU were seen as an economic issue and as largely technical in nature, rather than political. There was limited understanding of the complex EU machinery (even among the Russian delegation in Brussels).

But neither was the EU ready to be Russia's partner in the first years following the fall of the Soviet Union. The entry into force of the Maastricht Treaty in 1993 produced some changes in the structure and competencies of the EU. The Maastricht Treaty set forth a series of objectives, including the establishment of a single currency and a more assertive international role for the EU. The external dimension of the EU has grown in importance, partly through the process of eastward enlargement, partly through the second pillar laid down in the Maastricht Treaty (CFSP and defense) and justice and home affairs. However, ratification of the Maastricht Treaty proved to be a very complex and difficult process. As a result, the EU has been for years preoccupied with its internal institutional structure and unable to devote sufficient attention to external problems. Moreover, the mandate and the instruments provided by the Maastricht Treaty proved inadequate to cope with some of these external problems. This was particularly striking in the EU policies toward the wars in the Balkans, but in fact also applied to several other areas of EU foreign policy.

A new impetus for EU–Russia relations came with the signing of the Amsterdam Treaty and the commencement of accession negotiations with five Central and East European countries in March 1998 (Estonia and Poland sharing a common border with Russia), and a further five in March 2000 (again with two, Latvia and Lithuania, directly bordering Russia). The 1997 Amsterdam Treaty provided for the progressive establishment of an area of freedom, security, and justice, and extended the scope of communitarian policy making in justice and home affairs. More important for the EU's external dimension, it stated the EU's determination to assert its identity on the international scene through the implementation of a common foreign and security policy and "the progressive framing of a common defense policy" (Article 1, para. 3, Treaty of Amsterdam). The European Council conclusions in Nice in December 2000 proposed stepping up dialogue, cooperation, and consultation on security and defense issues with third countries such as Russia. All these developments had an effect on Russia's relationship with the EU. For the first time, Russia appeared to be reorienting its interests and priorities toward the EU, especially in the fields of trade and investment, rather than developing a special relationship with the United States in the old superpower mode. There have been regular EU–Russia summits since 1997, including contact not only between EU heads of states and government (rotating European Council presidency) and the president of the Russian Federation, but also increasingly between the European Commission and Russia. The dialogue has been broadened from mainly trade and investment issues to include foreign policy and security issues of joint concern.

The entry in 1995 of Finland and Sweden into the EU also led to a greater focus being placed on the EU–Russia relationship. Finland in particular pushed the Northern Dimension, aimed at providing new incentives for cooperation in northern Europe, the Baltic Sea region, and Russia, by improving security (migration and crime, border management) and dealing with energy and transport issues in the area (see Arter 2000). At the time, other regional relationships with Russia were neglected. A report by the European Parliament (European Parliament 2000a) argued that the EU and Russia also have common foreign policy interests in southeastern Europe (stability in the Balkans) and in combating international terrorism and violent Islamism in the Caucasus and Central Asia. Without a member state interested in taking up a cause, such initiatives take more time to evolve. Nevertheless, the EU side has pressed the Russians to undertake new initiatives and to work together with it to resolve the conflicts in Moldova (Transdniestria) and the South Caucasus (Abkhazia and Nagorno-Karabakh).[2]

With general agreement among member states about the need to assist Russia's integration into the world economy and about the necessity of cooperation in security politics, the most controversy has taken place at the level of EU institutions themselves and what their relative roles and powers should be in the context of the EU–Russia relationship. This has increasingly been shown up as EU competencies have spread to policy fields that have traditionally been within the realm of national politics. In justice and home affairs, the very proximity of Russia and especially the Kaliningrad enclave (with crime, social problems, etc.) has brought to the fore the interdependence between JHA and policies toward Russia—". . . threats, real or perceived of Russian illegal immigration and mafia, have become a factor behind the ongoing europeanization of home and justice affairs . . ." (Jensen 2001, 5). Moreover, cooperation within the framework of the Common Action Plan for Russia on Combating Organized Crime agreed upon in April 2000 is based on the establishment of transgovernmental networks in policy areas traditionally controlled by the national state. One of the ways the Commission has tried to overcome the inter-pillar rivalry and the setting of priorities and improve coordination between member states policies has been to elaborate Country Strategy Papers.

Indeed, small, incremental steps are taken at EU summits consolidating the EU's international role and new institutions, programs and policies are constantly being put in place. Some of this is, of course, a reaction to external pressures and events. The conflict in the former Yugoslavia, and especially Kosovo, highlighted the shortcomings of the EU's fledgling foreign policy and the danger that regional conflicts represent for neighboring countries. For instance, in reaction to the EU's lack of capacity to act in the Kosovo crisis, rapid progress was made in establishing civilian and military structures for ESDP.[3] This took place under the Swedish presidency, a traditionally neutral country. Despite the rotating presidency with overfull agendas and the different priorities set by presidencies with different historical alliances, interests, and geographical location, each new presidency takes on tasks agreed upon under previous presidencies.

Thus, despite the ambiguities and different visions of the EU, its increased competencies under the Amsterdam Treaty provide an institutional logic for developing them and filling them out. At the same time, the EU's external policies are determined by the nature of the EU as an international actor, with elements of national interests as well as the EU's institutional interest affecting decisions.

Form and Substance of Cooperation

When the Soviet Union collapsed, the Trade and Cooperation Agreement signed with the Soviet Union in 1989 had to be renegotiated. Negotiations on a new Partnership and Cooperation Agreement (PCA) were started in 1991 and the PCA was signed in Corfu in 1994. The signing coincided with the outbreak of war in Chechnya, which led to a delay in the ratification procedure. The ratification was further complicated by the accession of Finland, Sweden, and Austria and the need to add a special protocol. For the first time, Russia became a direct neighbor to an EU member state. In the meantime, relations between the EU and the Russian Federation continued under an interim agreement until the PCA came into force in December 1997. Summits between the EU and Russia had been held since 1995, although not on a regular basis, with some of the meetings being subject to President Yeltsin's state of health.

With the entry into force of the PCA, two summits are held annually and a Cooperation Council is held at the ministerial level once a year. A Cooperation Committee may meet at senior official level as often as necessary, but in practice it has so far met once a year. There are nine subcommittees at a technical level. There is also a Joint Parliamentary Committee made up of representatives of the European Parliament and the Duma. Outside the formal framework, the external affairs commissioner visits Russia at least once a year for bilateral European Commission–Russia meetings.

At the signing of the PCA, the EU presidency referred to "a mutually beneficial partnership of trust" that would help to consolidate democratic and economic reforms and improve respect for human rights in Russia. Russia's view as expressed by Prime Minister Primakov's speech at the EU–Russia Cooperation Council in January 1998 showed an emphasis on the economic character of the PCA. This reflected worries about Russian exporters' access to Central and East European markets and the consequences of enlargement.

Cooperation under the PCA is aimed at stimulating trade and investment, cooperating on energy, environment, and nuclear safety, and reinforcing dialogue on JHA as well as dialogue and cooperation on security issues, that is, it stretches across all three pillars. Another important part of the PCA is the fact that cooperation can be suspended in case of violation of fundamental human rights—a course of action that the EU has not carried out even in the light of the serious violations in Chechnya. Although for the EU the PCA is rather low in the hierarchy of international agreements (unlike Association Agreements with candidate countries or

Stabilization and Association Agreements with southeastern European states it does not anticipate EU future membership), for Russia it represents "one of the most detailed and advanced documents with a western institution ever signed" (Leshoukov 1998, 9). Having said that, the ambitions declared in the PCA tend to reflect wishful thinking and political correctness rather than political and economic realities and its implementation has fallen short of (probably unrealistic) expectations. Nevertheless, successive summits have had increasingly ambitious and complex agendas, and, while trade and economic issues form the core of EU–Russia relations, there has been an increasing emphasis on political and security issues reflecting the EU's newly acquired competencies in these areas and its willingness to promote them.

The third EU–Russia summit in June 1999 saw the introduction of the EU Common Strategy on Russia (1999–2003). Its key priorities include support for the consolidation of democracy, rule of law, and public institutions in Russia, the integration of Russia into a common European economic and social space, and the promotion of stability and security in Europe and beyond. However, the Common Strategy has been criticized for being too broadly defined to be effective and lacking substance. A report by the Foreign Affairs Committee of the European Parliament on the implementation of the Common Strategy has noted that its adoption was not accompanied by any decision to increase financial resources in order to achieve objectives and argues that it has had very little practical effect so far.[4] Although the Common Strategy adds little to the cooperation mechanisms already in existence under the PCA, it does signal a shift in emphasis from largely economic issues to the more political and strategic ones.[5] It also provides a forum for the high representative, shifting the emphasis somewhat from the commission to the council (the high representative is also secretary general of the council).

There has been a slow and incremental increase in the scope and density of EU–Russian relations within the past few years. At the fourth EU–Russia summit in October 1999, the then Prime Minister Putin officially presented the Medium-Term Strategy for the Development of Relations of the Russian Federation with the European Union for 2000–2010. This was the first comprehensive document to define Russia's policy toward the EU. Before the publication of this document, Russia had dealt with the EU on a rather ad hoc basis, concentrating on various issues of importance to them as the need arose, such as textiles, steel, or Siberian over-flight rights. At the fifth EU–Russia summit in May 2000, President Putin outlined the new Russian economic program aimed at sustainable growth, progressive solution of urgent social problems, and further integration into the world economy. In October 2000 in Paris, the EU–Russia summit adopted a special declaration on strengthening dialogue and cooperation on political and security matters. The intention was to institutionalize consultations on security and defense and to promote cooperation in operational crisis management. This reflected not only the EU's potential competencies arising from the decision at the Helsinki summit in fall 1999 to launch ESDP but also Russia's view that the EU's military-political dimension should be given particular attention.[6]

It is clear that following on from Maastricht and Amsterdam and with greater Russian engagement under Putin, political dialogue has been stepped up. In addition to the summits, cooperation councils, and committees, political directors at senior official level now meet four times a year. Experts meet in some fifteen CFSP working groups. The so-called Troikas (representatives of the current presidency and the CFSP High Representative/Council secretariat, the future presidency, and the Commission) meet with Russian counterparts twice a year. A High-Level Group has been set up to more fully elaborate the regulatory and legal implications of the concept of a common European economic space. Monthly meetings between an EU political and security committee Troika and Russia are held to assess consultations on crisis prevention and management. There has been mention of possible Russian participation in civilian and military crisis management operations as the ESDP develops. This reflects the "new" security agenda, which focuses more on nonmilitary aspects of security and therefore JHA, that is, through the EU rather than NATO. All in all, dialogue with Russia is more frequent than with any other third party.

The rhetoric and increased institutionalized activity has masked, however, the lack of real progress on the ground. Despite a plethora of "dialogues" (regular energy dialogue and dialogue on political and security matters initiated in October 2000)[7] and "action plans" (to combat organized crime, on justice and home affairs, to improve intellectual property rights in Russia, to cooperate on environment and nuclear safety, to fight against international crime, and focus on Kaliningrad [within the Northern Dimension framework]) agreed upon at various summits and Cooperation Councils, most of the action remains planned rather than implemented. For instance, an Opinion by the European Parliament (EP) Committee on Citizens' Freedoms and Rights, Justice, and Home Affairs notes that the action plan to combat organized crime is unlikely to be implemented given that "the Russian Federation's internal administration and criminal prosecution system are plagued with rampant abuses." Moreover, ". . . no adequate acknowledgement of that state of affairs is to be found in the action plan" (EP 2000b, 25).[8] From the Russian point of view, it is the EU's preoccupation with its internal problems of constitutional reforms and enlargement that stands in the way of progress (*Financial Times*, September 16, 2003, 7).

There is a tendency to create ever more institutional mechanisms to upgrade EU–Russia relations as a way of compensating for the underuse of existing mechanisms by both sides. One of the problems is the complexity of the mechanisms: the Russians have repeatedly asked for more informal structures and simplification of procedures, but EU member states find the formal mechanisms easier to follow and influence. However, the large number of high-level political meetings is not that well suited for dealing with more technical and implementation details and a better targeting of subcommittees has been suggested by the Commission. Another recommendation has been to make the EU–Russia Cooperation Council, which normally meets once a year, more flexible. It should involve top officials rather than only ministers or commissioners to deal more swiftly with issues requiring attention. The evolution of EU–Russia relations well reflects what Héritier (1999) has called the simultaneity of deadlock and development in EU policy making. The ongoing development and intensification of EU–Russia relations is based more on structure than substance, but the increasing institutionalization of exchanges and the very complexity and fragmentation of decision-making processes offers the opportunity to bypass potential deadlock by creative and innovative policy initiatives. The EU (more specifically, the European Commission) works through a process of ongoing negotiation and renegotiation with member states on the "boundaries" of communitarian competences and how its policies relate to the actions and interests of member states (Latham, O'Donnell, and Smith, 2000).

Political and Economic Agendas of the EU and Russia

So, given the peculiar nature of the EU, what kind of a relationship is emerging between it and Russia, and how is this relationship likely to evolve after enlargement? The EU, due to its very proximity to Russia, is affected by all manner of developments there. This relates not only to traditional trade and security issues but also to protection of the environment (especially nuclear environmental problems) and social problems (people trafficking, illegal immigration, refugee migration, and organized crime). There is, or should be, a common interest in dealing with these problems at their source. Indeed, Javier Solana has referred to the partnership with Russia as presenting a challenge to the EU "in the economic, the political, the social and the security spheres at one and the same time" and being "the most important, the most urgent and the most challenging task that the EU faces at the beginning of the 21st century" (Solana 1999).

Nevertheless, in its relations with Russia the EU usually emphasizes economic aspects. This is understandable in view of the relative economic importance of Russia to the EU, both in terms of energy imports, and export opportunities. However, the EU has taken a comprehensive view of how to assure closer economic cooperation. As External Affairs Commissioner Patten has pointed out, greater trade and investment and the creation of a stronger and more balanced commercial relationship are dependent upon the right legal climate (Patten 2001). The EU's agenda thus includes development of a proper legal and regulatory framework in Russia, integration of Russia within international institutions (not only economic but also political ones such as NATO), and promotion of human rights and democracy. However, Russian membership in the EU is not on the agenda.

The EU has advocated the adoption of the EU model for economic and legislative integration, and in January 2000 new Technical Assistance to the Commonwealth of Independent States (TACIS) regulations were passed aimed at supporting PCA implementation and targeted more toward "export" of a regulatory framework based on EU norms and standards. However, many experts have found this approach insufficient in view of structural deficits such as the lack of an efficient civil service, an independent judiciary as well as the weakness of civil society, the overlap of political and economic interests and insufficient economic modernization. For instance, the EP foreign affairs committee report argued that technical assistance under TACIS should be targeted more at democracy- and institution-building than simply market regulation and that significantly more resources should be made available. According to the EP report the influence of the TACIS program on socially and economically balanced development in Russia has been minimal and its budget is only a fraction of that allocated to other regions bordering the EU. The report recommended that the Commission should place greater emphasis on civil society projects and concentrate more on democratization of state and society, rule of law and respect for human rights, press freedom, and federalization of the Russian administration. It should adopt more of a double-track strategy of condemning human rights violations while cooperating with Russia to strengthen rule of law and democratic structures.

A more integrated EU policy toward Russia was outlined in the Country Strategy Paper 2002–2006 adopted in December 2001. The enlargement of the EU has brought the issues of borders, migration, and cross-border crime to the fore. While trade and economic relations form the core of the strategy, political and security issues are also prominent. The Strategy Paper underlines the need for effective and consistent implementation of legislation to protect human rights and civil liberties, and to stimulate investment. It notes that actual respect for human rights lags behind formal commitments and identifies the strengthening of civil society as a major objective. Russia is seen as a key actor for stability and security of the entire European continent and its importance is expected to increase with enlargement.

Following its experience with candidate states, the EU increasingly emphasizes *effective* implementation of the PCA and various strategies. The EU sees the Russian state as being yet unable to provide a stable political, institutional, and social environment for economic development and investment and stresses the need for effective and independent legal institutions to be established as a prerequisite for implementation of many of the "action plans" and initiatives agreed upon at various summits. At present, Russia simply lacks the administrative capacity to effectively implement the PCA.

Russian policy has been largely a response to what has been offered by the EU. But in the first years following the fall of the Soviet Union, Russia's main reference (and preference) has always been the United States, and its willingness to cooperate with the EU is colored by its interest to counter American domination (Leshoukov 1998). EU issues have usually been of a secondary nature for Russian politics, which has encouraged an instrumental approach, although in the past couple of years there have been signs of a Russian reorientation toward the EU. In other words, the place of the EU in Russia's foreign policy priorities has been upgraded. While Prime Minister Primakov stressed that Russia was a self-standing entity and a neighbor to Europe that had its own interests and mission, President Putin's administration is more interested in consolidating Russia's role in Europe and preventing, or at least mitigating, any developments that might marginalize Russia (Baranovsky 2002). Russia's Medium-Term Strategy[9] took up many of the priorities and proposals of the EU's Common Strategy toward Russia. Its declared aim is to create the basis for "advanced partnership relations" with the EU, to establish "a reliable pan-European system of collective security" and to mobilize "the economic potential and managerial experience" of the EU with a view to developing a "socially oriented" market economy and a democratic rule of law state. Despite the positive tone of the Medium-Term Strategy, a number of commentators have pointed to significant differences with the EU Common Strategy.[10] In the new Foreign Policy Concept adopted in 2000,[11] relations with the EU are listed higher than those with all other countries bar the Commonwealth of Independent States (CIS). In the aftermath of the May 2002 EU–Russia summit, former President Gorbachev called for Russia to be involved in EU mechanisms of discussing and making decisions as an associate member.[12] The 2003 Iraq crisis has also given an extra impulse to EU–Russia relations as manifested by the unusual degree of unity between Russia, Germany, and France.

Certainly the EU is Russia's largest trading partner by far and the volume of trade in both directions is set to increase to around 50 percent of total trade after enlargement (see Philip Hanson, chapter 6 in this volume). The problem is that trade is asymmetric in character—fuel and raw materials make up the bulk of Russian exports whereas it imports finished industrial and consumer goods. Unlike Association Agreements, which provide for full economic integration, the PCA does little more than extend WTO rules to Russia, aimed at granting it most-favored-nation treatment and freedom of movement of capital. Russia is worried about the economic effect of enlargement, and much of the Russian effort in EU–Russia relations has concentrated upon pressuring the EU to support its membership of the WTO and to set up a common economic space. Membership in the WTO would make it possible for Russia to put in a claim for compensation if it could prove trade had been diverted as a consequence of enlargement. At the EU–Russia summit of May 29, 2002, as a largely political gesture, the EU granted Russia "market economy status" even though in practice Russia still falls short of being a genuine market economy. At the same summit, the two sides were unable to reach agreement on the thorny issue of the Kaliningrad enclave. The issue led to some bitter exchanges, but the parties managed to come up with a compromise package at the November 2002 summit.[13]

Paradoxically, in the long run, trade and economic issues may be more difficult to deal with than political issues. The EU and Russia share many concerns about regional security and stability. The two sides have already had practical experience in working together in Kosovo. At the Paris summit in October 2000, they agreed to strengthen dialogue and cooperation on security issues. Security is seen as a major component of the relationship with Russia. However, for the EU, the nonmilitary or so-called soft security aspects are paramount (and cannot be covered by other organizations such as NATO). These include "organized crime, insecure borders, ecological security, ethnic migration and the score of other threats to people living peaceful lives" (Solana 1999). For domestic reasons, President Putin has been more interested in linking security cooperation to the events of September 11, 2001, and ongoing terrorist threats. In economic relations, however, Russia has been slow in setting up the institutional framework essential for comprehensive and stable market reforms. In trade, the EU argues that Russia should adopt a framework based upon, or at least compatible with the relevant *acquis communautaire*. Indeed, Russia's Medium-Term Strategy reflects such an approach and implicitly accepts the notion of voluntary and gradual inclusion of the *acquis communautaire* into its legal framework. However, such incorporation should be selective, that is, limited to the core *acquis*. Russia should take advantage of the fact that it is not a candidate for EU membership. Adoption of the full *acquis* may not always be the optimal solution for emerging market economies. In some cases, simply applying the rule of law and best practices may suffice and insisting on transferal of the *acquis* may be seen not only as overly intrusive but even as distorting competition. Russia should therefore pick and choose those aspects of the *acquis* that will make its economy and regulatory framework, for instance in the banking system, less rigid and inefficient. Nevertheless, and despite positive progress reports from the High Level Group set up in May 2001 to study the concept of a single European economic space, numerous structural, institutional, and microeconomic problems remain to be addressed and the establishment of a common economic space between Russia and the EU may be quite a few years away.

There have been few substantial breakthroughs in EU–Russia relations despite the increasing number of institutional tools for an exchange of opinions and "dialogue." The same issues emerge again and again: security, the need to stimulate trade and investment (plus WTO accession), energy, environment, and nuclear safety. Nevertheless, and even though there is no foreseeable prospect of EU membership for Russia, both sides recognize that there is a common interest in developing close relations in a number of areas and ensuring that new lines are not drawn between East and West. And although there are few breakthroughs, a slow, incremental, two-steps-forward, one-step-back type of relationship is developing on the ground.

The inclusion of the EU High Representative in EU–Russia summits and the launching of a Common Strategy and increased emphasis on the Northern Dimension has institutionalized broader political and security aspects of the relationship (which had always been present; for instance, the Balkans or the conflict in Chechnya were certainly discussed at pre-Amsterdam Treaty summits but did not form part of the official competencies of the EU). Although Russia had initially tended to push the Organization for Security and Cooperation in Europe (OSCE) rather than the EU as its preferred forum for political dialogue,[14] contacts on stability and security are increasingly being channeled through EU institutional mechanisms. However, although Russia expects the EU to play a greater international role, it still recognizes that interacting with individual states directly "might be more efficient than waiting for the EU's joint position. In addition, the latter has a significant chance of turning out less energetic, unambiguous and action-oriented in comparison with the national positions" (Baranovsky 2002, 51).

Conclusion: Process vs. Strategy

Russia is obviously an important strategic partner for the EU, but our initial analysis has pointed out that EU–Russia relations reflect chiefly the EU strategy of institutional development. The evolving relationship between the European Union and the Russian Federation is not so much a matter of a grand strategy in the sense that it reflects power politics sui generis, but rather it is shaped to a large extent by what the EU itself is—a weak political actor in the traditional sense, but one that is trying to build itself up through the acquisition of new competencies. For the very reasons we have outlined above, that is, the multifaceted character of the EU, the lack of consensus about its basic aims and functions, and its institutional characteristics, the EU's relationship with Russia is rather different from a traditional bilateral relationship. The mechanisms used are many and varied, they often rely more on form than substance, but in the case of the EU they cross-cut communitarian and intergovernmental pillars and in the case of Russia they represent an institutionalized political relationship that goes beyond what it has with any other partner. The type of relationship that is developing with Russia ties in with what are gradually emerging as the cornerstones of EU foreign policy: an emphasis on rule of law and peaceful cooperation rather than coercive persuasion, multilateralism rather than unilateralism, and an emphasis on sustainable development in the broad economic, social, and environmental sense of the term.[15] It is a relationship that is aimed at integration in the EU without (as yet) the prospect of membership. Indeed, requests for membership that are unlikely to translate into concrete action in the foreseeable future may weaken rather than strengthen the EU's engagement with its neighbors to the east. Formal requests may raise unrealistic expectations leading the EU to become increasingly defensive, while countries left in the waiting room indefinitely will feel increasingly disaffected. However, the EU must seriously address its relationship with what is now being called its new neighborhood or Wider Europe. This cannot be limited to rhetoric on getting rid of dividing lines and spreading values and prosperity, but needs to be translated into action. It must result in greater access to the internal market, greater cross-border cooperation, access to and use of common policies, greater financial assistance, and better adapted programs.

Russia's importance for the EU will dramatically increase with the next wave of EU enlargement. New member states share with Russia not only a long border, but also a complex historical legacy. The inclusion of states from Eastern Europe will probably promote "Europeanization" in Romania, Bulgaria, Ukraine, Moldova, and Belarus. This is likely to have a positive spillover effect on Russia's relations with the EU. Russia could gradually be drawn in by the attractive magnetic pole on its Western borders. In this sense relations between Moscow and Brussels at the central level would be less important. More important would be the EU's demonstration effect on Russia and other countries in the region. In other words, Russia's integration with the European Union may well lead via Kyiv, Vilnius, and Warsaw rather than directly via Brussels.

The next wave of EU enlargement will probably also transform the EU into a kind of empire with fuzzy borders, divided sovereignty, and overlapping institutional arrangements. We have argued that this would make it easier rather than more difficult for Russia to integrate with the EU. Thus, although a "classical" form of membership is unlikely, in some functional fields such as trade, banking, economic regulation, or JHA cooperation and harmonization between Russia and the EU may become as intensive as if Russia were a full member state. New forms of partial or quasi-membership may develop. In due time, this dense web of mutual multifunctional relations are bound to have serious strategic implications for Europe and the outside world. As Stephan de Spiegeleire (2002) argues, the EU's strategy toward Russia "closely mirrors the neo-functionalist logic [. . .]: economic integration 'spilling over' in political and eventually in security integration."

Nevertheless, in its relations with Russia, the EU will not act like the United States does, no matter how ambitious its official foreign and security policy may be. This is because the EU is anything but a traditional state actor. The European Union's greatest international asset is its unique normative attraction combined with a sizable economic leverage and enormous geographic reach. The EU is and will remain militarily weak and lacking a clearly defined strategic purpose. The EU acts principally as a good administrator, regulator, and promoter of good governance rather than as a strategic ally. It slowly but steadily develops its competencies in new functional areas. It is more suited to low-key cooperation in various working groups than to delivering on grand strategies. Although it is sometimes pushed to take a leading role, for instance, as in Bosnia or Macedonia where special EU representatives/envoys have been appointed, it is the individual member states that make or break the deal. The EU itself, through its high representative and external affairs commissioner, tends to play a supporting role and tries to make optimal use of the policy instruments at its disposal. And those policy instruments have the potential for an integrated approach, including both "low politics" and "high politics" in an institutionalized and regulated political relationship. As the EU High Representative Solana and External Relations Commissioner Patten have claimed: ". . . [the EU is] the only institution capable of comprehensive action, ranging from trade, economic reform and infrastructure, humanitarian assistance, human rights and democratization, justice and police to crisis management and military security."[16] But this does not necessarily allow the European Union to act in a strategic manner as do the United States or other traditional state actors. In particular, this is not likely to result in any spectacular breakthroughs in EU–Russia relations, but it does provide the framework and structures for cooperation and dialogue on a regular basis at various official levels. It is the step-by-step, comprehensive, and incentive-geared approach typical of the EU. Sometimes this approach may look like a recipe for chaos or weakness, but if the European Union is indeed so weak why have so many European countries been gradually drawn into its sphere of influence? EU–Russia relations should also be seen from this broader systemic and historical perspective.

Notes

1. In the context of relations with Russia the EU is taken as the Council (in the form of the six-monthly rotating presidency), the European Commission (EC), and the European Parliament (EP). Since the entry into force of the Amsterdam Treaty it also includes the EU high representative.

2. See, for instance Patten (2002). Speech on EU–Russia Relations, European Business Club Conference on Shaping Russian–European Integration in the Twenty-first Century, Moscow, May 28.

3. In January 2001, a Political and Security Committee, chaired by the high representative, was set up that would have "a central role to play in the definition of and follow-up to the EU's response to a crisis" (Council Decision of January 22, 2001, European Foreign Policy Bulletin Database, Document 01/143). A Military Committee of the EU was also set up at the same time (Council Decision of January 22, 2001, European Foreign Policy Bulletin Database, Document 01/144).

4. One year later, in October 2001, the same committee assessed the progress achieved in the implementation of the CFSP and noted that the Council's monitoring reports prepared for the Goteborg European Council on the implementation of common strategies shows that they are "too broadly based and insufficiently geared to operational objectives" (European Parliament 2001, p. 18).

5. The preparation of the Common Strategy took place against the background of the war in Kosovo. During the parliamentary debate on a common foreign policy and an EU strategy toward Russia on May 4, 1999, Joschka Fischer, representing the Council presidency, stressed the importance of strengthening links with Russia in order to secure peace and stability in Kosovo. Recommendation of the European Parliament to the Council concerning the common strategy toward the Russian Federation—A4–0219/1999. See www.222.3.europarl.eu.int/omk/omnsapir.so/calendar.

6. See the Foreign Policy Concept of the Russian Federation; available at www.bits.de/EURA/russia052800.pdf [April 20, 2004].

7. The wording of successive joint declarations is illustrative of the lack of "deliverables": the Paris declaration on October 30, 2000, referred to "strengthening dialogue," and in Brussels one year later the title referred to "stepping up dialogue" while the Moscow summit of May 29, 2002, came up with "further practical steps in developing political dialogue." There is certainly intensive dialogue, but substantive cooperation always seems to be one step away.

8. It should be noted that the European Commission has since allocated some 20 million euros to support judicial reform in Russia under the TACIS program.

9. Available in (unauthorized) translation at the European Commission's external relations Web site at http://europa.eu.int/comm/external_relations/russia/russian_medium_term_strategy (April 20, 2004).

10. See for instance, Jensen (2001) and Vahl (2001). Baranovsky (2002) notes the Russian emphasis on "equality" and its "national interest" as the basis of its foreign policy. In the Medium-Term Strategy document this is linked to Russia's relationship with the CIS

and its intention to use the experience of EU integration to develop the integration process in the CIS.

11. The full text of the Foreign Policy Concept of the Russian Federation is available at www.bits.de/EURA/russia052800.pdf [April 20, 2004].

12. "Gorbachev Seeks EU–Russia Link," *Financial Times*, May 31, 2002. However, Russia's Medium-Term Strategy explicitly states that "partnership between Russia and the European Union will be based on the treaty relations, i.e., without an officially stated objective of accession to or 'association' with the EU."

13. See Joint Statement at http://europa.eu.int/comm/external_relations/russia/summit_11_02/js_kalin.htm [April 20, 2004].

14. In the early days of EU–Russia dialogue, Russian politicians strongly promoted the concept of a "pan-European security architecture" to replace structures inherited from the Cold War period, presumably downgrading the role of NATO and the EU, which was just starting to think about developing a common foreign and security policy and upgrading the OSCE.

15. See Pascal Lamy's speech on "Trade Policy, the Convention and External Relations: Some Lessons to Be Learnt," European Policy Center, Brussels, November 22, 2002. Not published but text available at www.europa.eu.int/comm./commissioners/lamy/speeches_articles/spla135_en.htm.

16. Ibid.

Bibliography

Arter, David. 2000. "Small State Influence within the EU." *Journal of Common Market Studies* 28, no. 5: 677–98.

Baranovsky, Vladimir. 2002. *Russia's Attitudes Toward the EU: Political Aspects.* Programme on the Northern Dimension of the CFSP, no. 15. Helsinki: Finnish Institute of Foreign Affairs.

Country Strategy Paper 2002–2006. National Indicative Programme 2002–2003. Russian Federation. Available at http://.europa.eu.int/comm/external_relations/russia/csp/.

De Spiegeleire, Stephan. 2002. "Recoupling Russia: Staying the Course Europe's Security Relationship with Russia." Paper prepared for IISS/CEPS European Security Forum, Brussels January 14, 2002, www.eusec.org/spiegeleire.htm [April 20, 2004].

Draft Treaty. 2003. Draft Treaty Establishing a Constitution for Europe submitted to the European Council meeting in Thessaloniki, June 20, 2003. Luxembourg: Office for Official Publications of the European Communities.

European Parliament (EP). 2000a. Report on the Implementation of the Common Strategy of the European Union on Russia (2000/2007 [INI]). Committee on Foreign Affairs, Human Rights, Common Security and Defence Policy. Rapporteur: Arie M.Oostlander. A5–0363/2000.

———. 2000b. Opinion of the Committee on Citizens' Freedoms and Rights, Justice and Home Affairs on the Implementation of the Common Strategy of the European Union on Russia. Draftsman: Margot Kessler. A5–0363/2000.

———. 2001. Report on the Progress Achieved in the Implementation of the Common Foreign and Security Policy. Rapporteur: Elmar Brok. A5–0332/2001.

Héritier, Adrienne. 1999. *Policy-Making and Diversity in Europe. Escape from Deadlock.* Cambridge: Cambridge University Press.

Jensen, Jens-Jorgen. 2001. "EU's relations with Russia-Issues-Pillars-Levels." Paper presented at the ECPR Joint Session, Workshop 23: Understanding the EU's International Presence, Grenoble, April 6–11.

Latham, Brigid, Rory O'Donnell, and Michael Smith. 2000. *Europe's Experimental Union: Rethinking Integration.* London and New York: Routledge.

Leshoukov, Igor. 1998. "Beyond Satisfaction: Russia's Perspectives on European Integration." ZEI Discussion Paper, no. 26.

Medium-term Strategy for Development of Relations between the Russian Federation and the European Union (2000–2010). Unofficial translation available at http://europa.eu.int/comm/external_relations/russia/russian_medium_term_strategy/index.htm [April 20, 2004].

Patten, Chris. 2001. Speech to European Business Club, Investing in Russia Conference, Brussels, October 2. Available at http://europa.eu.int/comm/external_relations/.

————. 2002. Speech on EU–Russia Relations, European Business Club Conference on Shaping Russian-European Integration in the 21st Century, Moscow, May 28. Available at http://europa.eu.int/comm/external_relations/.

Rummel, Reinhardt, and Jorg Wiedemann. 1998. "Identifying Institutional Paradoxes of CFSP." In Paradoxes of European Foreign Policy, ed. Jan Zielonka, pp. 53–66. The Hague: Kluwer Law International.

Solana, Javier. 1999. Speech on "The EU–Russia Strategic Partnership." Presented at the Council of the European Union, Stockholm, October 13. Available at http://ue.eu.int/solana/print.asp?docID=59417&BID=107 [April 20, 2004].

Treaty of Amsterdam. 1997. Luxembourg: Office for Official Publications of the European Communities.

Vahl, Marius. 2001. Just Good Friends? The EU–Russian 'Strategic Partnership' and the Northern Dimension. Brussels: Centre for European Policy Studies.

Zielonka, Jan. 2001. "How New Enlarged Borders Will Reshape the EU." Journal of Common Market Studies 39, no. 3 (September): 507–36.

8

European Union–Russia Relations
Transformation Through Integration

Stephan Kux

This chapter first explains that the multiple ties between Russia and the European Union (EU) have substantially deepened and broadened over the past five years. Today, based on the Partnership and Cooperation Agreement (PCA), the two neighbors entertain a complex and comprehensive partnership covering almost all policy areas and issues.

Second, while relations remain incomplete and political declarations have yet to be translated into action, the Russia–EU partnership has enormous political and economic potential and experiences a very dynamic development. Increasingly, the relationship goes beyond traditional transnational arrangements. The current state of relations and future projects such as the Common European Economic Space clearly take the form of integration. From a comparative perspective, this is not a surprise. In the hierarchy of the EU's relations with third countries, Russia takes a place in the second tier, comparable to Norway, Switzerland, or Turkey. As other cases of partial integration demonstrate, close interaction with the Single Market results in progressive adaptation of the associated state. In many respects, namely, in regard to market rules, Norway or Switzerland behave like EU member states without enjoying full-fledged membership. The dominant market logic and the substantial downstream pressures of European legislation reach beyond the geographic boundaries of the Europe of the twenty-five member states. There is no reason to assume that this empirical evidence should not apply in the case of Russia. Growing economic interaction thus will result in the increasing Europeanization of Russian institutions.

Third, if Russia is adapting gradually to European market rules in order to promote trade in goods, services, and capital and to reduce transaction costs, formal membership in European institutions is not the decisive cut-off point. Progressive adaptation and gradual integration are driven by structural and institutional factors, and not by deliberate choice. Moreover, formal membership in the European Union may take considerable time or never happen at all. It may be unattractive and undesirable for both sides. Nevertheless, Russia will have to adapt to the process of European integration in order to manage and to develop its economic and political ties with the European community of states. The

European Union has and will increasingly have a profound impact on the country's domestic transformation.

In the course of this project, various scenarios for integrating Russia into Europe have been discussed. One scenario assumes that Russia will eventually join the European Union and actually make use of the accession process to Europeanize its institutions (European integration via Europeanization). Another scenario envisages Europeanization without accession to the EU (Europeanization without European integration). This chapter makes the case that these two optimistic scenarios may happen simultaneously or in sequence. In any case, they will produce similar results regarding Russia's modernization.

Fourth, the real issue is not the form of and the path toward Europeanization. The issue is sovereignty and voice. How can Russia protect its interests and actively participate in shaping Europe during the process? Will it be at the receiving end, unilaterally adopting European rules, or will it actively participate in decision shaping and decision making on the future of the European project? Already today, Russia is adopting Single Market rules more or less voluntarily. European integration is characterized by strong downstream effects in the form of EU regulations and European court decisions set by the fifteen—soon twenty-five—member states and their institutions. Upstream, Russia has limited room for shaping European rules. The formal bodies of the relationship do not allow for co-decision. Russia's adaptation and integration is thus likely to face domestic problems of legitimacy and sovereignty in the future, just as in the case of Norway and Switzerland. The relationship is asymmetric, and Russia risks marginalization. Current activism reflected in the creation of an increasing number of task forces, working groups, and committees that act outside of the formal decision structures and legal frameworks of the EU are just covering up the fact that the distribution of power and influence between Russia and the EU is uneven. Moreover, Russia does not enjoy effective legal protection, while the EU can refer conflicts to the European Court of Justice. Given market power and sanctions, antidumping and other competition rulings can be enforced against Russia. A possible way out of the dilemma of integration without participation could be for Russia to submit a formal request for membership in the EU. While it is unlikely that Moscow will soon fulfill membership criteria such as democracy, state of law, functioning market economy, or efficient institutions, a membership request would set a clear point of reference—both at home and in relations with the EU, establish a more formalized relationship, and open doors for more active participation. After all, if Serbia and Turkey are considered fit to start membership negotiations in the near future, why not Russia?

An Ever Closer Relationship

The relationship between the EU and Russia has undergone a remarkable development over recent years unprecedented in European history. After a fifty-year period of Cold War confrontation and brinkmanship, within a few years Russia has turned into a regular partner of the EU just as Norway, Switzerland, or Turkey, third countries of similar status and economic importance to the EU. Relations are no longer defined by bilateral, sectoral agreements, but within a comprehensive multilateral framework. Following up on the 1989 USSR–EC accord, the two sides signed a Partnership and Cooperation Agreement (PCA) in 1994, which entered into force in 1997. The PCA not only covers trade and economic relations, but establishes a political dialogue, comprehensive technical cooperation, assistance to Russia's transition, and a common approach to problems of European security and stability.[1] The EU taxonomy distinguishes three policy areas or pillars, the first including the Single Market and Economic and Monetary Union, the second the Common Foreign and Security Policy (CFSP), and the third Justice and Home Affairs. The PCA covers mainly the first pillar, but includes cooperation in the second and third pillars as well.

Based on the PCA, a comprehensive institutional framework for bilateral relations has been established:

- Two *summits* take place each year, including the rotating EU presidency, the high representative for Common Foreign and Security Policy, the president of the European Commission, and the president of the Russian Federation.
- The *Permanent Partnership Council* at ministerial level, which meets several times a year.
- The *Cooperation Committee* at senior official level, which meets regularly.

Subcommittees (working level) deal with technical issues.[2] Numerous contacts take place on a regular basis between CFSP committees and working groups with their Russian counterparts. A *Joint Parliamentary Committee* unites members of the European Parliament and the Russian Duma to discuss current issues.

Based on the new provisions of the Amsterdam Treaty, the EU drafted its very first Common Strategy in 1999 on relations with Russia. The basic objective is to coordinate the EU's various external activities and relationships—of the European Commission, the Council of the European Union, and the member states—and to provide national strategies with a common roof.[3] In 2001, the European Commission passed a Country Strategy Paper for the period 2002–2006 including a National Indicative Program 2002–2003.[4] The focus is on supporting the Russian government's socioeconomic reform program, on building the legal, institutional, and administrative framework, on strengthening all aspects of civil society and free media, as well as the judiciary, and on promoting legislative, regulatory, and institutional convergence between Russia and the EU. The National Indicative Program is thus a key instrument to promote the Europeanization of Russian institutions.

At the 2001 EU–Russia summit, the two sides decided to go ahead with preparations to create a Common European Economic Space and to deepen the "strategic partnership."[5] A High Level Group (chaired by Commissioner Chris Patten and Deputy Prime Minister Viktor Khristenko) is drafting a program for economic relations in the medium term.

Moreover, there is a series of joint programs and activities including Technical Assistance to the Commonwealth of Independent States (TACIS), nuclear safety, energy, transportation, and environment. Finally, the EU and Russia participate in several joint regional initiatives including the Caucasus, Central Asia, Kaliningrad, and the Northern Dimension.[6]

The EU has not devised a special framework or specific relationship for Russia. The general approach follows the standard community method. Nevertheless, relations with Russia are the most elaborated and institutionalized ones the EU maintains with any third country, including those with Japan and the United States. Russia is best boy in the EU class, at least on paper. The main objectives are normalization, intensification, and integration.

A good sign of normalization is the consolidation of economic relations. After the turbulence of Russia's economic crisis, trade ties with the EU have stabilized to a large extent. Today, the EU (15) is Russia's most important trade partner (2002: 36.6 percent of total trade), followed by the thirteen accession countries (12.9 percent). Trade volume is growing rapidly. In 2001, Russia generated a surplus of 19 billion euros.[7] While the trade structure is still quite asymmetric with Russia mainly exporting energy and raw materials, the long-term trend clearly indicates a growing economic interdependence typical of European economic integration. After enlargement, the EU (25) is likely to absorb almost 55 percent of Russia's exports.

Increasing trade is both a source of normalization and a source of conflict and irritation. As a state trading country, Russia is far away from fulfilling the elaborate provisions of Single Market access. Nor is it a truly free market economy or a state of law. The potential of the PCA and Single Market access are not fully realized. In many cases, Russia is not using the assigned quotas or not taking advantage of the most-favored-nation advantages due to lack of economic strength. The PCA does not envisage a judicial procedure in case of trade conflicts comparable to the European Court of Justice or the World Trade Organization (WTO) panels. Conflicts are solved politically or decided unilaterally by EU bodies as in the case of antidumping and competition rulings. Russia has almost no legal remedies to defend its interests.

Compared with the state ten years ago, relations have widened and deepened beyond expectations. Many observers describe the relationship as mainly economic and technical in nature. In view of the comprehensive approach of the PCA and the Common Strategy and the width of current activities, this is an understatement. More important, current relations have profound political and strategic implications that will have a substantial impact on Russia's future role in Europe. The following arguments are based mainly on an EU perspective, on integration theory, and on experiences with the EU's relations with the East Central European accession countries and other third countries such as Norway, Switzerland, or Turkey.

Participation Without Integration?

Properly speaking, ties with Russia rank fourth in the EU's hierarchy of concentric circle relationships. At the core are the Europe agreements and the accession partnerships with the ten East Central European candidate countries plus Cyprus, Malta, and Turkey. The second tier includes the three European Economic Area countries Iceland, Liechtenstein, and Norway, which fully participate in the Single Market, enjoy highly institutionalized participation in decision making, and support the EU's Common Foreign and Security Policy. Candidate countries for the second tier are the post-Yugoslav countries Croatia, Bosnia-Herzegovina, Montenegro, and Serbia as well as Albania. At the Porto Karras European Council in June 2003, the EU offered the perspective of full membership and accession procedures. The third tier comprises the Lomé agreements with African, Caribbean, and Pacific (ACP) states. The EU has also concluded a PCA with Ukraine. Formally, the EU's relations with Russia can be compared to those with Switzerland, the Mediterranean countries (Euromed), or Latin America.

The main difference between the Europe agreements and the PCA is that the latter clearly does *not* envisage future EU membership. While the Europe agreements relate to accession, the PCA refers to an "appropriate framework of gradual integration" and deliberately speaks of a "larger area of European cooperation" (Article 1). It is a cooperation, and not an integration agreement. In these terms, the PCA does *not* imply Russia's integration into Europe. It is an intergovernmental agreement based on international law with relatively weak institutions. At the surface, the PCA does provide for Russia's participation in the process of European unification without integration. This may support Russian fears of exclusion, isolation, and division.

Integration is understood as (a) the transfer of competencies to supranational institutions and the application of European legislation (downstream effects); (b) participation in the decision making of European bodies (upstream effects); and (c) the adaptation or *Europeanization* of domestic institutions to the exigencies of European cooperation. Integration thus goes well beyond traditional international cooperation, namely, regarding the limitation of sovereignty and the impact on domestic institutions. This is the sui generis nature of the European Union as contrasted with the Association of Southeast Asian Nations, Mercosur, or the Commonwealth of Independent States (CIS). In the case of the EU, the degree of integration varies across policy areas. It is most elaborate in Common Market and monetary policy.

In the institutionalist view, the concept of Europeanization—in the narrow sense—is used to describe processes of institutional adaptation. It refers to the shifting relationship between, and within, different levels of government. Europeanization is here understood as how, and to what extent, the attempt to build joint institutions and capabilities at the European level, leads to changes in the relative importance between different levels of government, and to reorganization and adaptation within the various levels of government.[8]

The EU is often understood as a complex and open political system comprising a multitude of processes and actors at the local, national, and supranational levels of government. The concept of *multilevel governance* is frequently used to describe European network politics. The concept of multilevel governance is opposed to the traditional idea of hierarchy and a single, supreme authority. Instead, multilevel governance is understood as a system in which "there is a multiplicity of actors specific to each policy area: interdependence among these social-political-administrative actors; shared goals; blurred boundaries between public, private and voluntary sectors, and multiplying and new forms of action, intervention and control."[9]

Multilevel governance relates to the blurring, changing, downsizing, and rebuilding of institutional boundaries. Institutional boundaries is therefore a key concept in the current research on European integration. It defines who can participate in decision making, who has access to information, who bears the costs and enjoys the benefits, or who is subject to judicial review, monitoring, and sanctions. Institutional boundaries are increasingly blurred not only *within* the EU, but also *without*.

The most important institutional boundary is, as in most organizations, related to membership. In the EU, the concept is often treated as a dichotomy. Some states are members, others are not. And it is assumed that being a member matters. It is argued that in the EU there is a causal relationship between membership and the extent of institutional adaptation at the domestic level. That is, membership involves a strong pressure for adaptation of domestic institutions. Consequently, member states are likely to experience substantial changes in their political and constitutional systems, as well as shifts in their political discourse, beliefs, and understandings. According to this line of reasoning, nonmember states apparently experience less pressure to adapt. It is therefore assumed that member states and nonmember states have different leeway in designing their institutions and in balancing the relationship between effectiveness and legitimacy.

The study of nonmember states suggests, however, that institutional adaptation extends beyond the borders of the EU.[10] European countries such as Norway, Switzerland, or Turkey, which are not members of the EU, are affected by European integration. Consequently, they have to adapt their domestic institutions and policies in order to cope with the challenges they are facing. These countries have experienced a considerable change in administrative structures, elaborated new procedures for handling European issues, and assigned new resources and capabilities to these tasks.

The traditional way of drawing boundaries in the EU is challenged by a growing number of intermediary stages and patterns of integration. The concept of membership is not a dichotomy. In recent years, numerous European states have developed considerable formal and informal linkages to the EU. However, there are sectoral and institutional variations. In relation to some sectors and policy areas some of these countries could almost be considered full participants of the

EU. Norway, for instance, fully participates in the Single Market and transposes the *acquis communautaire* just as do member states such as Denmark or Sweden. This rethinking of the concept of formal membership is also consistent with the growing fragmentation and differentiation within the EU and the increased interest in flexibility, enhanced cooperation, and *Kerneuropa* as reflected in the limited membership in the European Monetary Union (EMU), the provisions of the Common Foreign and Security Policy, the Schengen rules on border controls, the gradual phasing in of the East Central European candidate countries, and the concept of enhanced cooperation introduced in the Amsterdam Treaty. The EU is gradually becoming more fragmented and heterogeneous. This is a result of a variety of factors such as the increase in the number of member states, the expanding agenda, or variations in domestic capability and willingness to participate in integrative efforts.

It would thus be an understatement to describe the current arrangements in the PCA framework just as an economic and technical agreement copying WTO trade rules at a European level. The PCA is comprehensive, ties the two sides closely together, and draws Russia into the dynamics of the Single Market described as *engrenage*. The PCA mainly covers trade in goods and services, and the planned Common European Economic Space will include all four freedoms of the Single Market (with restricted free movement of labor). The spillover or downstream effects are substantial. The PCA is based on the assumption of a free market economy, rule of law, and effective political and legal institutions. While Russia clearly does not fulfill these criteria, it will come under significant economic pressure to adapt. If Russian producers intend to export furniture to the EU, they have to comply with European safety norms and quality standards. If Russian export companies want to avoid antidumping rulings and increased custom duties, they have to respect European competition law. Thus, it makes sense for Russia to adopt European safety norms and quality standards in general and to pass laws that fully comply with European competition rules. These are just two examples of the downstream pressures the EU and its Single Market are exerting on the near abroad.

In Europe, all countries—EU members and nonmembers alike—have experienced significant pressures to adapt to Single Market rules, not only in the economic but also in the political sphere. Russia would be the first country to resist. Pressure for adaptation is implicit and gradual. Take competition rules: How can a country participate in the Single Market without adopting EU competition rules? With many costly antidumping procedures and fines, Russia is learning the hard way. Take participation in European research programs: Russian experts will sit in the administrative committees, and Russian research policy and administration will have to adapt to EU practices. If past experiences apply also to Russia, the PCA will have a double spillover, from the economic into the political realm, from the international trade into the domestic arena. Thus there is much more to the PCA than its 112 technical articles, ten appendixes, and two protocols.

Neighbors at Last

Enlargement will strengthen the case for closer EU–Russia relations. While Soviet Union–European Union relations have been facilitated by a certain distance covered by "buffer states," the EU and Russia have become direct neighbors with Finland's accession. The EU and Russia will move closer together with enlargement. They will share common borders in the Baltic Sea region or at least come close in the Black Sea region. Enlargement is of direct concern to Russia, mainly due to the Kaliningrad situation. Other concerns are primarily economic. There are justified fears that enlargement will bring higher trade barriers and result in a loss of markets for Russian products. Experience actually suggests that regional integration leads both to trade creation and trade diversion. Recently, Russian observers have also started to call attention to the political dimension of European integration, namely, the Common Foreign and Security Policy, which will tie in Russia's immediate neighbors and former allies.[11]

The difficult and lengthy process of enlargement will have a profound impact on EU–Russia relations. Already the first round of enlargement with twenty-five members is pushing the EU to its limits. Issues include institutional efficiency (consensus among twenty-five member states), equilibrium between micro-members such as Estonia or Malta and big players such as France, Germany, or Poland, disagreement about the *finalité* of the European project, limitations of free movement (opening up to the Russian or Ukrainian labor market), political capacity to deal with ten new members at the same time, and financial resources to promote cohesion among the very rich and the very poor. There are long-term commitments toward the new members, which cannot be abandoned and may force Russia and others into the background of the agenda. The agreed transition periods of seven or more years accorded to Poland and others indicate the time scales of implementing the first round of enlargement. The second group with Bulgaria, Romania, and Turkey will keep the EU busy as well. And the third group with Albania, Croatia, Bosnia-Herzegovina, Macedonia, Montenegro, and Serbia is just waiting outside the entrance.

The strategic task of enlargement may be a bit too heavy for the EU and its member states and may paralyze further developments for quite some time. Europe may rest divided into a core and a periphery, with the core finding new stability and prosperity and the periphery being locked out in poverty, trade barriers, and Schengen borders. Russia may be condemned to remain a hinterland and strategic resource reservoir. As an alternative, the EU may successfully pursue a strategy of concentric circles and flexible alliances around a core of integration based on the Single Market. This flexibility may offer various plug-ins for Russia. The distinction between membership, associated membership, and partnership (without immediate aspiration for membership) as currently applied in EU relations offers a way out. Russia may have an interest in closer involvement with the EU and its new member states in order to address neighborhood issues such as the role of Kaliningrad or the Northern Dimension.

Managing a Triangular Relationship

Finally, the EU's growing global role and the balance in the triangular relationship Russia–EU–United States may encourage Moscow to seek closer ties with Brussels. Russian commentaries still draw a line between a "good" EU and a "bad" NATO. The EU is perceived to form a third force, a counterbalance to U.S. unipolarism.[12] In this zero-sum logic, the political and security dimension of the EU is clearly underestimated. In recent years, the EU has made substantial progress toward a Common Security and Defence Policy. With the incorporation of the West European Union, the EU clearly moves closer toward a security alliance. And this is not in competition with NATO, but in cooperation as illustrated by the person of the former NATO Secretary General Javier Solana, who is now in charge of EU foreign and security policy.

Nevertheless, EU–Russia relations have to be viewed in a triangular context. Russia sees the EU as an influential, benevolent alternative to the United States, be it in international organizations, as a source of foreign aid, or as investor and trade partner. The privileged relationship with Russia, on the other hand, provides the EU with political leverage in its aspiration to become a global player. Thus, there is an increased or continued risk of EU–United States rivalry in their strategies toward Russia. This may relate to human rights or trade issues, or to differing regional interests in the Arctic or Baltic region, the Caucasus, and Central Asia. The conflict over the second Iraq war and the tacit anti-American alliance between France's President Jacques Chirac, Germany's Chancellor Gerhard Schröder, and Russia's President Vladimir Putin is just an example of bandwagoning in this triangular relationship.

Wider Europe vs. Marginalization

In the near future, some important decisions have to be made in EU–Russian relations. In late 2003, the High Level Group will present its Common European Economic Space concept. In 2004, the EU's Common Strategy on Russia has to be renewed. In 2004, the accession of ten new members will also require revision of relations with Russia. With Russia's WTO membership in 2004 or 2005, the PCA must also be adapted. Bilateral relations have to be viewed in the context of the EU's multilateral approach toward the near abroad.

In March 2003, the European Commission presented a new framework for relations over the coming decade with Russia, the Western Newly Independent States (NIS), and the Southern Mediterranean—countries that do not currently have a perspective of membership but will soon find themselves sharing a border with the European Union.[13] The objective is to offer a new perspective of neighborhood to the countries not included in the next round of enlargement. The concept proposes that, over the coming decade, the EU intends to develop a zone of prosperity and a friendly neighborhood—a "ring of friends"—with whom the EU enjoys close and cooperative relations—similar to that in the European Economic Area. It suggests that, in return for concrete progress demonstrating shared values and effective implementation of political, economic, and institutional reforms, all the neighboring countries should be offered the prospect of access to the EU's internal market. This will be accompanied by further integration and liberalization to promote the free movement of persons, goods, services, and capital (four freedoms) between the EU and Russia, Ukraine, Moldova, Belarus, and the Southern Mediterranean countries Algeria, Egypt, Israel, Jordan, Lebanon, Libya, Morocco, Palestinian Authority, Syria, and Tunisia.

Wider Europe thus forms a second tier around core Europe. The main intention is to avoid membership at the moment. Commissioner for External Relations Chris Patten noted: "Over the past decade, the Union's most successful foreign policy instrument has undeniably been the promise of EU membership. This is not sustainable. For the coming decade, we need to find new ways to export the stability, security and prosperity we have created within the enlarged EU. We should begin by agreeing on a clearer vision for relations with our neighbors."[14]

Given economic and political differences among these countries, this new European Economic Area will be implemented not on a multilateral, but on a bilateral basis. Depending on domestic progress, these countries will conclude a Neighborhood Agreement with the EU allowing for better access to the Single Market. This new policy of selective adaptation and differentiation meets the current aspirations of the Russian leadership.

Limited Participation

While EU–Russia relations are not yet fully developed, a fundamental change can be observed. Today, Russia is tied into a web of relationships that follow their own dynamics. This applies mainly to Single Market access and its spillover effects. EU–Russia relations are thus no longer subject to great power realpolitik or the ambiguous logic of historical legacies, but driven by factors of European integration common to most full or associated members of the Single Market. The impact on Russia's domestic transformation will be significant.

This does not mean that conflicts will be absent in the future, but they are of a different type. The EU has developed a solid mechanism to deal with trade conflicts. It will decide unilaterally, in accordance with its own rules, and based on the principle of equal treatment—even in the case of Russia. The main challenges will be deepening mutual understanding of European integration, implementing the substance of the PCA, managing the impact of enlargement, compensating the negative effects of closer cooperation within Russia and within the EU, and finding a new approach in the triangular relationship, EU–Russia–United States, at a regional level.

For the time being, limited participation and selective transposition of European rules seem to be a tailor-made strategy for Russia. First, it allows for negative integration without positive integration. Liberalization, regulation, and market access are not tied to participation in joint, supranational institutions, the pooling of sovereignty, and contribution to a common budget. Negative integration requires less coordination and less management, and remains at the level of intergovernmental cooperation. Second, within a given political and legal framework, Russia will retain considerable leeway about when and how to respond to the changing EU environment. Moscow has a certain veto, can assert her national prerogative, shape her own decisions within her own institutions, and implement tailor-made solutions. There is no automatism: Russia largely controls the time factor. Moreover, the current arrangements allow for transitional rules and exemptions in critical areas. There are filters, firewalls, and safeguards in order to protect certain industries such as energy, finance, or agriculture. Third, limited participation and selective transposition permit a country with scarce resources to reduce transaction costs and control its involvement. It is an efficient way for weak administrations to participate without being absorbed too much by day-to-day EU business. Finally, gradual adaptation helps to absorb external shocks and to protect fragmented, high-conflict societies in the difficult, controversial process of Europeanization. Policy toward the West is likely to remain one of the most contested and divisive issues in Russian politics. The Putin government is thus confronted with the difficult task of satisfying the expectations and exigencies of European integration and the veto positions of powerful domestic constituencies. Economic monopolies, vested elite interests, and center-periphery arrangements can be protected for a while. Deepening ties with the EU may have a significant impact on Russia's domestic cohesion. Experiences in ex-Yugoslavia, Hungary, or Poland show that regions close to the EU markets profit substantially more from trade liberalization than distant regions. This results in deepening regional cleavages. In the case of Russia, the Northern, Northwestern, and Western regions are clearly privileged. St. Petersburg will benefit more than Moscow. This may influence domestic balance and cohesion. A Europe from the Atlantic to the Urals may thus pose a challenge to Russian nation building.

However, we do not assume that the current outsider position of Russia is an optimal, sustainable status in European integration. One should not ignore that there are numerous and important differences between member states and non-member states in relation to Europeanization. First, transposition remains unilateral. This is a major restriction on sovereignty and self-determination. Relations between Russia and the EU remain intergovernmental, and the effects Russia experiences are supranational. Second, limited integration remains a restricted area in Russia's domestic politics. Only a limited number of political actors are involved, mainly mid-level administration and government officials. This technocratic approach and routine result in a depoliticization of integration policy. Third, the EU has developed a series of association ties with third countries. Moscow is unlikely to enjoy a privileged relationship with Brussels. In light of the demanding tasks of widening and deepening, the EU countries may pay increasingly less attention to Russia. Moscow may have to vie for attention and it risks marginalization and isolation in an increasingly overpopulated EU arena. Full integration may become a necessity to guarantee access and attention in the EU context. Fourth, enlargement and common borders may introduce new issues that may render EU membership more attractive. Finally, with the growing importance of the EU in the triangular relationship, Russia may require better access to EU Common Foreign and Security Policy than is possible within the current political dialogue.

The Case for Russia's Early EU Membership Application

Following these considerations, Russia is best advised to submit an application for full membership in the EU as early as feasible. Article 49 of the Treaty on European Union stipulates that "Any European State which respects the principles set out in Article 6(1) may apply to become a member of the Union." Article 6(1) simply states: "The Union is founded on the principles of liberty, democracy, respect for human rights and fundamental freedoms, and the rule of law, principles which are common to the Member States."

In order to join the European Union, states need to fulfill the economic and political conditions known as the Copenhagen criteria:

- stability of institutions guaranteeing democracy, the rule of law, human rights, and respect for and protection of minorities;
- the existence of a functioning market economy as well as the capacity to cope with competitive pressure and market forces within the Union;
- the ability to take on the obligations of membership including adherence to the aims of political, economic, and monetary union.

So far, only Morocco's application has been turned down, insofar as the country is not considered to be geographically part of Europe. All other applications have resulted in an application procedure that starts with an elaborate questionnaire regarding the economic, institutional, legal, and political conditions in a given applicant country, and the existing gap with the EU *acquis communautaire*. Based on the evaluation of the questionnaire, the European Commission gives an *avis* regarding the application pointing out basic questions and outlining the issues to be negotiated. The Council of the European Union then decides whether and when to start accession negotiations. These negotiations usually take several years. They specify which steps of approximation to the EU legislation and institutional framework have to be taken. In the phasing-in period, the EU assists the candidate country in taking on EU laws, and provides a range of financial assistance to improve institutions, infrastructure, and the economy. Negotiations result in an accession treaty that has to be ratified by the candidate country, the Council of the European Union, the European Parliament, and the member states.

This is not to suggest that Russia is willing or able to join the EU in the near future. Phasing in will take considerable time, and membership cannot be expected before 2015 or 2020. Yet a membership application would set a clear point of reference—both at home and in relation to the EU—establish a more formalized relationship, and open doors for more active participation. A membership application could close the current gap between mutual expectations and reality in EU–Russian relations. The EU and its member states would have to take a clear stance regarding whether Russia qualifies or not—just as in the case of Turkey.

It is the process of approximation that matters, not its results. The main criteria for membership—stability of institutions guaranteeing democracy, the rule of law, human rights, and respect for and protection of minorities; and the existence of a functioning market economy as well as the capacity to cope with competitive pressure and market forces within the Union—constitute the main challenges for Russia's democratic consolidation and economic transition. The process of approximation to EU standards would help to stabilize Russia. The ultimate decision whether to join or not has to be made by both sides at the end of the process—thus approximation is a no-regret strategy. Norway and Switzerland have fully adapted to European standards, but decided against joining the EU because they do not accept the economic and political constraints linked to membership. Their strategy is Europeanization in order to avoid membership—for the moment.

For sure, membership has its disadvantages. The EU is overregulated, the economy is down, its common foreign policy and security is a failure. The impact of enlargement on the EU's institutional capacity, its economic strength, and financial stability has yet to be experienced. Given Russia's size and difference in nature, accession would also change the character and the internal balance of the Union. One of the reasons is that EU bureaucrats and member state diplomats are rather reluctant to discuss the possibility of Russia's accession.

The requirement to adopt foreign rules and to accept constraints in domestic matters contradicts the persisting imperial attitude of the current Russian elite. The prospect of being a member of an organization presided over by an Austrian, Luxembourg, or Maltese president is probably not to the taste of Russia's geopolitical aspirations.

Yet does Russia or Europe have a choice? They are condemned to coexist and to find better ways of economic exchange and political interaction than exist today. With the disappearance of the "two-camp mentality," cultural proximity, political necessity, and economic interest will open the door for better relations. Today, the way of Europeanization is institutional. Democracy, rule of law, a functioning market economy, or good governance can be achieved only by accepting and adopting international rules and values as established in the World Trade Organization, the European Union, or the Council of Europe.

Despite its many difficulties and poor image, the EU is a success story. The

Single Market functions efficiently and effectively, the euro is reasonably stable, enlargement is on track, and the debate on a European Constitution enters its final phase. The EU stands for democracy, peace, growth, and social progress. The Russian population is taking notice. In its pragmatic approach, the Putin government has shifted its priorities to the EU.

Full integration may never happen. Nevertheless, Russia is already adapting progressively and integrating gradually. The European Union has and will increasingly have a profound impact on the country's domestic transformation. A membership request would set a clear point of reference—both at home and in relation to the EU—establish a more formalized relationship, and open doors for more active participation. It may not be the Russian government pushing for more integration, but Russian multinational companies such as Gazprom, Lukoil, Yukos, and some banks and insurance companies that are interested in a better regulatory framework and improved economic regulation.

Notes

1. *Official Journal* L 283, September 9, 1997, pp. 19–197.
2. See http://europa.eu.int/comm/external_relations/russia/intro/index.htm.
3. *Official Journal* L 157, June 24, 1999, pp. 1–9. See also European Commission, Communication to the Council and the European Parliament on relations with Russia, February 9, 2004, COM (2004) 1–06; available at http://europa.eu.int/comm./external_relations/russia/russia_docs/com04_106_en.pdf.
4. See http://europa.eu.int/comm/external_relations/russia/csp/index.htm [April 20, 2004].
5. *Bulletin EU*, June 2001, p. 135.
6. European Commission, Working Document on Nordic Dimension, SEC (2001) 552; Communication on Kaliningrad, September 18, 2002, COM (2002) 510 final; Centre for European Policy Studies (CEPS) (2000), *A Stability Pact for the Caucasus*, CEPS Working Document 145, Brussels.
7. See http://europa.eu.int/comm/external_relations/russia/intro/trade.htm.
8. Johan P. Olsen, "Europeanization and Nation State Dynamics," in *The Future of the Nation State—Essays on Cultural Pluralism and Political Integration*, ed. Sverker Gustavsson and Leif Lewin (London: Routledge and Nerenius & Santérus, 1996), pp. 245–85.
9. R.A.W. Rhodes, "The New Governance: Governing Without Government," *Political Studies* 44, no. 4 (1996): 652–67.
10. Bent Soetendorp and Kenneth Hanf, eds., *Institutional Adaptation of Small States—The Challenge of European Integration* (London: Longman, 1997); Stephan Kux, and Ulf Sverdrup, "Balancing Effectiveness and Legitimacy in European Integration: The Norwegian and the Swiss Case," ARENA Working Paper 97/31, 1997, Oslo.
11. Iris Kempe, Wim van Meurs, and Barbara von Ow, eds., *Die EU-Beitrittsstaaten und ihre östlichen Nachbarn* [The EU Accession States and Their Eastern Neighbors] (Munich: CAP, 1999); available at www.cap.uni-muenchen.de/download/2000/eubeitrittsstaaten.pdf.
12. Margot Light, John Löwenhardt, and Stephen White, (2000) *Russia and the Dual Expansion of Europe*, Economic & Social Research Council (ESRC) "One Europe or Several?" Policy Paper 02/00 (London: ESRC); available at www.one-europe.ac.uk/pdf/

LightP2.PDF; Igor Leshoukov, *Beyond Satisfaction: Russia's Perspectives on European Integration* (Bonn: Zentrum für Europäische Integration [ZEI], 1998), available at www.zei.de/download/zei%5Fdp/dp%5Fc26%5Fleshoukov.pdf.

13. European Commission, "Wider Europe–Neighbourhood: A New Framework for Relations with our Eastern and Southern Neighbours," COM (2003) 104 final.

14. See http://europa.eu.int/comm/external_relations/we/intro/index.htm. See also European Commission, European Neighbourhood Policy—Strategy Paper, May 12, 2004, COM (2004) 373 final; available at http://europa.eu.int/comm/world/enp/pdf/strategy/Strategy_Paper_EN.pdf.

9

Russia's Integration with the West and the States "in Between"

Oleksandr Pavliuk

The terrorist attacks on September 11, 2001, followed by the U.S.-led antiterrorist campaign and the war in Iraq have indeed affected many perceptions, policies, and priorities. A new international system is emerging; its principal features have yet to be comprehended.

From the perspective of this analysis, two dimensions of the post–September 11 change matter most. The first is a new dynamic in relations between the West (both America and Europe) and Russia. In the aftermath of September 11, the importance to the West of Russia's security and energy has increased, leading many to believe in the desirability (and possibility, given Putin's supportive response to the United States immediately after the terrorist attacks) of "integrating Russia with the West." Undoubtedly, the new security environment has created a larger Western (the United States, NATO, and the European Union) stake in cultivating "strategic" partnerships with Russia, although it remains to be seen how deep, broad, and sustainable these evolving partnerships might become. At the same time, Western accommodation with Russia, combined with a favorable situation for Russia on world energy markets (high oil prices have brought increased revenues to the Russian budget), has enabled Moscow to be a much more assertive and deliberate player in the post-Soviet space.

The second change has to do with the much accelerated pace of the European Union (EU) and NATO eastward enlargements. Brushing aside the remnants of earlier hesitation and doubt, NATO decided to proceed with "big bang" expansion. The alliance summit in Prague in November 2002 extended invitations to seven new members, all from the former "eastern bloc." In December 2002, the EU summit in Copenhagen set 2004 as the date for the first post-communist countries of Central and Eastern Europe to join the Union.

All this marks no less than the conclusion of a certain stage in the reconfiguration of Europe that began with the collapse of communism and disintegration of the Soviet Union.

At the same time, this new strategic landscape raises a number of questions about the future of Belarus, Moldova, and Ukraine—the three reluctant post-Soviet states squeezed between their former master Russia and the enlarging EU and

NATO. What should be their place in the emerging international order? Is Russia's integration or even an enduring partnership with the West possible without finding proper solutions for the countries "in between"? And does Russian policy toward these states help us better understand Russia's real goals as well as possible scenarios for Russia's own evolution?

Belarus, Moldova, and Ukraine: The Challenge of Being "in Between"

The fact of being "in between" has to a large extent affected the development of Belarus, Moldova, and Ukraine since the three countries became independent in 1991. Their transformations have been shaped by the influence of two opposing vectors or models of development: one of liberal economic reforms, rule-of-law and pluralist democracy based on European values and underpinned by an unequivocal European orientation, and another of limited economic reforms, corporate closeness of the state and controlled democracy (or even overt authoritarianism) aimed at concentration and consolidation of power by the ruling establishments. Both vectors or models of development have reflected the realities of and differences in transition processes in Europe and Eurasia. The former has been followed by the post-communist countries of Central and Eastern Europe; the latter has been chosen by the post-Soviet Commonwealth of Independent States (CIS). By virtue of their history and geography, Belarus, Moldova, and Ukraine have been caught in between these two vectors. Their response, however, has been different.

With a population of 10 million, Belarus has become an extreme embodiment of the "Eurasian" model of post-Soviet development. Since Alyaksandr Lukashenka was elected president in 1994 and especially after his position was consolidated as a result of the referendum in November 1996 (which approved a new constitution that significantly strengthened presidential power at the expense of the legislature), authoritarianism, violations of human rights, oppression of opposition and independent mass media, and a centralized and subsidized economy dependent on Russian energy supplies have become the permanent features of the country's domestic situation and international image. In foreign policy, Belarus (or to be more precise, Lukashenka) has opted for a union with Russia, although the implementation of the Union agreements has become part and parcel of Lukashenka's strategy aimed at consolidation and continuity of his rule. Russian political and economic support has in fact been a key factor in strengthening Lukashenka's power. Simultaneously, the November 1996 referendum, which the West refused to recognize as legitimate, has spoiled for good Minsk's relations with the West. The EU has substantially scaled down its ties with Belarus. Relations with NATO did not even have the chance to develop: Belarus vocally criticized NATO's eastward enlargement, while Lukashenka was denied an entry visa to attend the NATO summit in Prague in 2002. Belarus is the only European country to stay outside the Council of Europe. The main (if not the only) forum for Belarus–West interaction has been the Organization for Security and Cooperation in Europe (OSCE). But even there, for a long time the OSCE Parliamentary Assembly did not recognize the legitimacy of the Lukashenka-controlled parliament, while at the end of 2002 Belarusian authorities expelled (by not extending visas to diplomats) the OSCE Advisory and Monitoring Group (AMG) established in Minsk in 1998 to assist the country in the development of democratic institutions and monitor compliance with OSCE principles. Political pressure from the EU and U.S. (the two sides declared a temporary travel ban on Lukashenka and his senior officials) forced official Minsk to agree to the renewal of the AMG work, but with a weakened mandate. Lukashenka's dictatorial policies at home, his open hostility to the West, and his ties with "rogue" states have made Belarus Europe's most isolated, if not pariah, state.[1]

Tiny Moldova, with a population of 4 million is a neutral country according to its constitution. Since independence, it has been trying hard to cope with economic backwardness—Moldova is believed to be the poorest country in Europe—and domestic divisions. Its major problem has been Transdniestrian separatism, which led to a brief but bloody war in 1992, and which continues to endanger the country's territorial integrity and overshadow its development. In foreign policy, Moldova has worked to maintain its self-proclaimed international status. Being cautious about relations with NATO (but also refusing to join the Russian-led CIS Collective Security Treaty), Chisinau has been taking steps to develop closer ties with the EU. In June 2001, Moldova became the only former Soviet republic to be granted participation in the Stability Pact for Southeast Europe. But already in 2000, its poor economic situation, dependence on Russian energy supplies and markets, the new assertiveness of Russian policy vis-à-vis its immediate neighbors after Putin's accession to power, and the lack of sufficient interest in the West forced Moldova to move closer to Russia. The victory of the Communist Party in the parliamentary elections of February 2001 and election of a communist leader as the country's president have made Moldova the only country in Europe run by a communist government and strengthened the earlier policy trend of closer ties with Russia. Subsequently, Moldova has become more reluctant about cooperation within the framework of GUUAM—a group uniting five post-Soviet states (Georgia, Ukraine, Uzbekistan, Azerbaijan, and Moldova[2]), which attempted to coordinate their international politics and resist Russian domination in the CIS—and less pronounced about its European integration. Whatever the rhetoric though, the country's European prospect remains hostage to the unresolved Transdniestrian conflict.

With a population of 48 million, Ukraine, the largest of the three "in-between" states and a strategically vital country between Russia and Europe, has been, of all the CIS countries, the most vigorous and persistent in its European aspirations. Membership in the EU has for a long time been defined as Ukraine's long-term strategic goal, and as such it was officially fixed in a "Strategy of Integration with the European Union" adopted in 1998. In 1997, Kyiv endorsed NATO enlargement to the east, and negotiated its own Charter on Distinctive Partnership with the alliance. Of all the nonapplicants, Ukraine has developed the most comprehensive and substantive cooperation with NATO along a wide spectrum of military, security, and political issues. In May 2002, Kyiv made an important decision to seek membership in NATO, and at the alliance's summit in Prague later that year Ukraine and NATO signed a comprehensive Action Plan designed to strengthen mutual cooperation, albeit falling short of a Membership for Action Plan.

In the mid-1990s, Ukraine also looked the most promising among the CIS states as far as movement toward a pluralist democracy was concerned. It differed from (lagged behind) the more advanced Central European states, but it also did not fully resemble the CIS countries, constituting a relatively democratic "island" in the largely authoritarian CIS world. Yet as early as 1998–1999, Ukraine's political system and its system of governance became characterized by an overconcentration of presidential power, disproportional influence of shadow vested interests on key policy decisions, and entrenchment of opaque political and business culture. Leonid Kuchma's reelection as president for a second term in the fall of 1999 signified consolidation of that system. While the economic situation in the country was progressing with the beginning of economic recovery and growth in 2000–2001, Ukraine was in many ways regressing on a democratic scale. The country's basic political features and systemic characteristics were becoming increasingly Eurasian, despite progressive European rhetoric. Earlier hopes that Ukraine might speed up its reforms and catch up with Central European countries failed to materialize. Kyiv's European aspirations were set back.[3]

Negative developments at home affected the country's foreign policy, which was becoming increasingly "multivector" in rhetoric and amorphous in practice, and damaged Ukraine's relations with the West. As of the late 1990s, the latter began to express mounting criticism and bitterness regarding the state and pace of Ukraine's transition.[4] In 2000, the accumulated mutual frustrations in relations with the West on the one hand, and Putin's more concerted policy toward Ukraine on the other hand, pushed Ukraine's foreign policy pendulum toward Russia. This "eastward drift" culminated amid the political crisis and tape scandal (when audiotapes were released that implicated President Kuchma in the disappearance of journalist Heorhy Gongadze and other abuses of power) that swamped Ukraine in late 2000 to early 2001. The domestic turmoil further weakened the fragile country. While the West was voicing criticism over the lack of transparency and results in the investigation of Gongadze's murder, the Russian leadership was fast to offer support to the embattled President Kuchma. Pressured by domestic opposition and the West but courted by Moscow, the Ukrainian leadership pushed the country into Russia's "cynical embrace,"[5] as Ukraine's foreign policy became subordinated to the tasks of stabilization of the ruling establishment.

The September 11 attacks have dramatically changed the entire international setting, adding to international problems in Belarus, Moldova, and Ukraine. First, as foreign and security policy priorities of the West, especially those of the United States, were substantially revised, Western attention to Belarus, Moldova, and Ukraine considerably declined. And while Moldova and Belarus, being relatively small states on Europe's periphery, had been neglected earlier in Western discourse, for Ukraine, once defined as a "crucial factor" and "a key component" of regional and European stability and security, the change was particularly painful and difficult to manage. Second, the rapprochement between the West and Russia, which took place in the immediate aftermath of September 11, shattered the very background of foreign policies for the countries "in between." Through most of their independent existence their foreign and security policies had evolved in the context of West-Russia opposition. As this background began to disappear, the geostrategic situation of the countries "in between" changed. The new logic of international development challenged foreign policy foundations of all three: Belarus's persisting hostility to the West, Moldova's self-proclaimed neutrality, and Ukraine's ambiguous "multivector" policy.

To make things worse, Ukraine's relations with the West, in particular with the United States and NATO, suffered another blow in the fall of 2002, when Washington formally accused the Ukrainian leadership of sanctioning the supply of a sophisticated Kolchuga radar system to Iraq in violation of the existing international sanctions. Consequently, Ukraine–U.S. bilateral relations entered their most difficult period since 1993 and were characterized by a high-level American official as going through "a crisis of confidence at the senior level."[6] International media were putting Ukrainian leadership almost on a par with the leader of Belarus.[7]

Thus, regardless of different transition paths and foreign policy orientations since independence, by the end of 2002 the three countries found themselves in a largely similar position: weak at home and closer to Russia, and at a distance from the West on the international scene. Neither the ultimate result of their transitions nor their geopolitical future vis-à-vis Europe and Russia is certain. While the NATO summit in Prague and the EU summit in Copenhagen made crucial decisions on enlargement, both events have simultaneously fixed the marginal status of Belarus, Moldova, and Ukraine. As a new order on the continent takes place, the three countries "in between" with a combined population of over 60 million are being marginalized or even excluded from the mainstream process of European integration. If this tendency prevails and the doors to both institutions—particularly to the EU, which is overwhelmed with internal reorganization and the absorption of new members—are closed, Belarus, Moldova, and Ukraine might indeed become Europe's new "gray zone" or "black hole."[8]

The war in Iraq and Ukraine's decisions to send its radiological, chemical, and bacteriological protection battalion to Kuwait and then to contribute troops to the postwar stabilization in Iraq have brought a thaw in Ukraine's relationships with the United States and NATO and put Ukraine back on the radar screen of Western attention after a period of oblivion. It is, however, not mere policy correction, but real change, including in the leadership and the ruling elites, that is needed in Ukraine as well as in Belarus and Moldova. These primarily domestic reasons have so far prevented the three countries from taking advantage of the potentially promising opportunity presented by the EU and NATO approaching their borders.

For the moment, the non-European or Eurasian model of development, character-istic of all CIS states including Russia, has prevailed in Belarus, Moldova, and Ukraine. It is not only the poor quality of leadership but also the entrenched politi-cal and business culture, the existing (corrupt) systems of governance, and the nature of the political process (defined by the behind-the-scenes squabbling of a few vested interests and opaque deals between them) that differentiate these states from their European counterparts.

While the fundamental national interests demand meaningful reforms to ensure these countries' full-fledged participation in European integration and a decent place in the world of globalization, the narrow interests of those in power dictate protectionism and self-preservation and constrain the required change. Weak at home and compromised in the West, the ruling establishments in Ukraine, Moldova, and Belarus are becoming increasingly submissive to Russian pressure and depen-dent on Russian support in safeguarding their power, paying back with political and economic concessions that are starting to threaten the very independence of the countries "in between."

Without serious changes at home, Ukraine and Moldova, to say nothing of Belarus, will not have realistic prospects either for the ultimate success of their transitions or for adequate international roles.

Of the three, Ukraine has probably shown the greatest potential for change. A Western expert on the post-Soviet states observed in this regard:

> By comparison with the post-Soviet norm, civil society is becoming a reality in Ukraine. By comparison with Belarus . . . its [Ukraine] politics are vigorous, pluralistic, and very much alive. By comparison with the Russian Federation, with which Ukraine is almost always contrasted unfavorably, its citizens place a value on democracy and resent the unaccountability of the authorities; they are learning how to resist manipulation, and they attach far more importance to the decency of the state than its "effectiveness" or strength.[9]

Indeed, Ukraine has not only resisted the establishment of a "super-presidential" regime, which is common throughout the CIS (with the exception of Moldova), but also has originated a relatively strong democratic and Europe-oriented opposi-tion, both center-rightist and center-leftist, that presents an alternative to the ruling establishment. The latter's ability to manipulate public opinion and control the domestic political process has turned out to be limited. Despite the government's notorious widely applied "administrative resource" in the last parliamentary elec-tions (March 2002), voters spoke clearly against the authorities and supported political forces that championed reform and espoused a vision of and commitment to change and accountability.[10] The election outcome marked an important psy-chological and political shift in the electorate. In the opinion of a Moscow-based analyst, "These are all manifestations of another political model, different from ours [Russia's] and more 'European'"—a model that is worse when it comes to constructing an authoritarian state, but better for building a democratic society.[11]

The dynamics of change (albeit fragile and still uncertain) have thus been set into motion. These dynamics are not yet powerful enough to produce immediate political change or put Ukraine decisively on the European path, but they prevent Ukraine's final transformation into a Eurasian state.

The next, decisive battle, one of historic consequence for Ukraine, between those advocating real change and European integration and those, despite their declarations, working to maintain the existing political and economic systems, will take place during the next presidential elections, scheduled for 2004. The outcome of this battle will be crucial in shaping both the ultimate nature of the Ukrainian state and its geopolitical future, as it will determine what kind of decisive turn Ukraine will make: toward becoming a vibrant European state that holds its destiny in its own hands, or toward a Eurasian, oligarchic, and semidemocratic or even authoritarian country, detached from Europe and submissive to outside pressures and influences. The victory of "Europeans" and prevalence of the European model of Ukraine's development is probably in the interests of Ukraine's immediate neighbors, including Belarus and Moldova, the West, and Russia no less than it is in the interests of Ukraine.

A New Russian Foreign Policy?

For many, Moscow's response to September 11 came as a pleasant surprise. Putin showed personal vision and determination (sometimes against strong skepticism of some in the Russian political and military establishments) in shaping this response and laying down a new reference point in Russia's relations with the West. But what seemed to the West to be Russia's momentous decision may instead have been the result of a calculated, and best possible under the circumstances, policy choice that the Russian elite, or at least the most pragmatic part of it, had already been contemplating for quite some time before September 11.

The disintegration of the Soviet Union confronted Russia, more strongly than any other post-Soviet state, with an identity crisis. The old questions of what Russia is and where its place in the world is, were back on the agenda.

In the early 1990s, post-communist Russia made the first attempt to "integrate" with the West. The brief "honeymoon," however, ended in disappointment and was soon replaced by the conviction that Russia had always been and should remain a "great power." Under foreign and then prime minister, Evgenii Primakov, this conviction was embodied in the concept of "multipolarity." Russia's own ambition was nothing less than to become a separate pole in this "multipolar" world and a center of political, economic, military, and cultural gravity for its "near abroad." Two foreign policy components were central and closely interrelated in achieving this goal: (1) counterbalancing the West, that is, acquiring equal geopolitical weight in Europe and ensuring protection against U.S. dominance; and (2) consolidating the CIS space, regarded as a Russian natural "sphere of influence/interest." The second was seen almost as a precondition for achieving the first.

The problem, however, lay in the discrepancy between nurtured ambitions and available resources. In the CIS, where Russia was (and still is) a "superpower" compared to its much smaller and weaker neighbors, it lacked both attractiveness and the power to ensure reintegration to the desirable degree and scale. The practice was thus limited to bringing closer to the Russian fold those few former Soviet republics that for various reasons were more susceptible to Moscow's influence, and preventing others, especially Ukraine, from moving too far away. In this light, Ukraine's cooperation with the West was always perceived by Russia as a zero-sum game. Even less successful were Russian attempts to counterbalance, and occasionally even to confront) the West. Moscow failed to achieve most of its international goals, be it transforming the OSCE into a "main" European security institution, stopping NATO enlargement, or preserving Russian influence in the Balkans or in the Middle East. There was a growing realization among politicians and policy analysts that the concept of a "multipolar" world was misleading and harmful, in the first place for Russia itself. Instead, active participation in the process of globalization and "integration with the West" came to be seen as a necessary and the only reasonable alternative.[12]

Still, upon his accession to power, Putin started by continuing (with some modifications) the previous policy of shaping the "multipolar" world and building up "the Russian pole." The essence of the "early Putin" policy was best expressed in his programmatic presidential speech: "Russia was and will remain a great power. It is preconditioned by the inseparable characteristics of its geopolitical, economic and cultural existence. They determined the mentality of Russians and the policy of the government throughout the history of Russia and they cannot but do so at present."[13] But reflecting the existing power realities in the world, Russia's need to modernize itself, as well as his general pragmatism, Putin opted to avoid confrontation with the United States, as well as other major countries, relations with which could affect Russia's development and international standing. Moreover, even before September 11, Putin had started to look for closer ties with America and Europe to help Russia's modernization and to secure its larger role among the principal international bodies.[14]

Simultaneously, Putin's rise to power opened a new period of Russian assertiveness toward its periphery. Russia's domestic political consolidation was manifested in the significant centralization of presidential power and submission of dissent, and the beginning of economic growth (stimulated by high world energy prices), as well as the completion of large-scale privatization at home and the beginning of expansion of big Russian businesses to other post-Soviet states. These factors made possible Russia's conduct of a more assertive, purposeful, and differentiated policy vis-à-vis its much weaker CIS neighbors. In comparison with policy in the Yeltsin era, Russian policy has also become more sophisticated and skillful. This policy, which has often successfully combined the interests of a resurrected Russian state and Russia's expanding private sector, has played an instrumental role in Moldova's and Ukraine's foreign policy reorientations as of early 2000.

In this context, September 11 has provided Russia with an almost unique opportunity to pursue its goal of modernizing itself and attaining a place in the world "adequate to its [Russia's] potential" (and in the process to resolve some of its most burning security problems, such as curbing Islamic fundamentalism on its southern borders[15]) through cooperation with the West, rather than opposition toward it.

By placing security issues at the top of the international agenda, September 11 has raised Western, first of all the U.S., stake in cooperation with Russia: once an opponent, Russia turned into a security partner and a potential strategic energy supplier. This new American interest provided Russia with a chance to achieve desirable change in its relations with the West, and—most important—to achieve it on Russia's own terms. Putin acted fast seizing the opportunity to secure political accommodation with Washington and forge a new international role for Russia, which in turn could help rebuild the Russian economy and a strong Russian state. In a way though, he was also making a virtue out of necessity. For Russia, an alternative to cooperation with the West would have been to remain at the periphery of international politics and the global economy.[16] In this regard, while September 11 has fundamentally changed Western interests and perceptions, it remains to be seen whether and to what extent it has also affected Russian strategic interests and foreign policy goals. In other words, we have yet to see whether the proclaimed partnership and/or "integration with the West" has become Russia's genuine strategic choice, one that might ultimately help change the very nature of a Russian state, or whether it was just a tactical move, a new version of realpolitik aimed at grasping opportunities and evading perils. As the *Financial Times* asked, referring to Putin, "Is he trying to join the West, or is he trying to use it?"[17]

Moscow's post–September 11 policies and statements allow for different interpretations. On the one hand, Russia quickly aligned itself with the American-led antiterrorist coalition (a development that Russia has also used to link its own war in Chechnya to the international fight against terrorism), agreed to the (temporary) presence of U.S. troops in Central Asia and to U.S. missile defense plans, quieted (although did not revoke altogether) opposition to NATO enlargement, and pushed for setting up the NATO–Russia Council of "equals" to discuss a range of security issues. It is also seeking closer ties with the EU and has expressed interest in a strategic energy partnership with the United States. On the other hand, Russia continues to see itself as a self-sufficient country that wants to be an "equal" partner rather than a part of the West, and as a power that does not join alliances but creates its own.

The uncertain nature and unstable foundation of the current Russia–West partnership were highlighted during the recent war in Iraq. Russia threw its support to the anti-American position of France and Germany, which brought back memories of the old Soviet and Russian policy of trying to play Europe off against America, while reports appeared that Russia was sharing intelligence with and supplying military equipment to Baghdad. The rhetoric of a "multipolar world," which after September 11 seemed to be shelved, has returned with a spontaneous French–German–Russian "axis" being at some point defined in Moscow as "the first brick in constructing a multipolar world." Although Putin has embarked on mending fences after the war, the entire situation around Iraq has called into even greater question, rather than clarified, Russia's real intentions vis-à-vis the West. The future of Russia–West partnership, to say nothing of Russia's "integration with the West," remains hazy. Furthermore, the split of the "West" itself makes the entire task of such integration even more problematic and tricky.

September 11 and American preoccupation with combating terrorism also appear to have raised hopes in Russia that it can now conduct its hegemonic policy in the CIS, but this time without opposition or even much attention from the "friendly" West. As British analyst James Sherr aptly noted,

> Russia's first "foreign" priority has tended to be the neighbors which were so recently part of the Soviet Union and in most cases the Russian empire as well. We in the West often ignore this fact. We tend to divide our thinking about Russia into two categories: internal policy and policy toward the West. And Russians are very happy for us to do this, because to this day, they don't think that their policy toward their neighbors is our business."[18]

It is, however, the post–September 11 policy vis-à-vis its CIS neighbors—in particular Belarus, Moldova, and Ukraine—rather than toward the West, that may presently be more indicative of Russia's real interests, intentions, and direction of its own evolution. And it is this policy that reveals serious inconsistencies and contradictions in Russia's international behavior. The first such inconsistency is Russia's simultaneous pursuit of "integration with the West" and the attempts to reconstitute a Russian-led political, military, and economic bloc of the former Soviet republics (or at least some of them). As it had before, in the aftermath of September 11 Russia continued to define the CIS as its "number one" foreign policy priority.[19] The international fight against terrorism has in a way become a convenient tool for Moscow to step up efforts to consolidate its influence in the post-Soviet space and achieve the long-desired international "recognition/legitimization" of CIS-based intergovernmental structures.[20] The point is not that Russia has no legitimate "strategic interests" in the "CIS space," but that the Russian elites and many ordinary Russians continue to believe that the Russian state should exert hegemonic leadership throughout the region, or, as recently put by Anatolii Chubais, should aim at creating a "liberal empire."[21] Even those few in Russia who criticize Putin's policies from a "liberal" perspective are convinced that "Russia should restore a unified economic and military zone across the Commonwealth of Independent States."[22]

Moscow has reinvigorated efforts to breathe life into the Collective Security Treaty Organization, composed of Armenia, Belarus, Kazakhstan, Kyrgyzstan, Russia, and Tajikistan, seeing it as an advanced form of military-political integration in the CIS. In 2001–2002, Russia was also pushing hard for the newly created

Eurasian Economic Community (EEC) of five post-Soviet states, Belarus, Kazakhstan, Kyrgyzstan, Russia, and Tajikistan. At some point, the EEC seemed to be viewed by Moscow as a new nucleus for economic integration within the CIS that would develop in parallel with, and potentially as an alternative to, European integration. With Belarus already in, Moldova and especially Ukraine (relations with which are often defined in Moscow as a policy priority[23]) became the main targets for Russia's drive for the "westward enlargement" of the EEC. As a result, by the end of 2002, both Ukraine and Moldova were forced to accept observer status in the EEC, while still refusing to join as full members.

Moscow, nevertheless, seems to regard Ukraine's full-fledged participation as so critical to Russian integrationist economic and political projects that in early 2003 Putin, in a rather unexpected move, induced the leaders of Belarus, Kazakhstan, and Ukraine to sign a declaration on the creation of a single economic space (SES). Following a few months of nontransparent work by a special group of senior officials and powerful behind-the-scenes and open Russian pressure, an agreement on the establishment of the SES was signed by each country's president in Yalta on September 19, 2003, despite strong warnings and protests voiced by independent experts, many political forces, and even some members of the cabinet of ministers of Ukraine. If enforced in its current form, which bears the signs of a customs union, the agreement threatens to tie Ukraine closer to Russia, derail its accession to the WTO, and potentially thwart the country's European future. The document, however, has yet to be ratified by the parliaments, and its final shape remains to be seen. While Moscow would like to go as far as introducing a single currency and setting up a supranational governing body, Ukraine is reluctant to move beyond the establishment of a free trade area without exceptions and limitations; Kuchma signed the agreement with the reservation that it should not contradict Ukraine's constitution.

Such persistence in weaving Moldova and Ukraine into the Russia-led integration process, while simultaneously encouraging these countries' detachment from European integration, is a paradoxical position, if one assumes that Russia is serious about its own "integration with the West."

Hegemonic behavior is also evident in bilateral relations. Moscow does not hesitate to exploit the weaknesses of post-Soviet states to increase Russian influence, making its political support of their leaders dependent on economic and political concessions (creating favorable conditions for big Russian businesses in privatization, getting control over neighboring gas transportation and energy systems, etc.).[24] In Ukraine, Russian companies have, by means of frequently opaque deals often backed by the Russian government, acquired significant stakes in and control over key sectors of Ukraine's economy. Officially, Russia accounts for only 6.7 percent of overall foreign investment in the Ukrainian economy, but experts estimate that in some key sectors, such as energy, the Russian share might actually amount to 70 percent,[25] further increasing Russian influence in Ukraine. The danger of this growing influence was revealed recently when Russian oil companies and the Russian government joined forces in lobbying Ukraine to reverse (in Russia's favor) the use of the Odessa–Brody oil pipeline, thus trying to undercut Ukraine's efforts to ensure alternative energy supplies and serve as a strategic transport route for the delivery of Caspian energy resources to Europe.[26] In Moldova, the country's energy sector has been effectively put under Russian control. Belarus has been threatened with deprivation of Russian-subsidized gas supplies unless the country agrees to the introduction of a single (read, Russian) currency as of 2005—a move that, some experts believe would mean the "soft annexation" of Belarus.[27]

Moscow remains reluctant to demarcate the Ukrainian–Russian border, preferring to treat it as a political rather than a technical issue, the positive solution of which and the resulting better control of cross-border movement and migration are needed for the security of both Ukraine and Russia, as well as the EU.[28] Simultaneously, Moscow remains eager to keep its military presence in the "near abroad." Russia has hinted its intention to extend the current twenty-year lease of naval bases in Sevastopol. In Moldova, Russia has failed to deliver on its international commitment to pull out weapons and remnants of its "peace-keeping" troops from Transdniestria by the end of 2002 (the new deadline of 2003 is likely to be missed as well), and officially announced that it would maintain its military presence there even after the ammunition is withdrawn.[29]

Another and even more paradoxical and worrisome inconsistency in Russian policies toward Belarus, Moldova, and Ukraine is the fact that Russia's declared friendship with the West goes hand in hand with ongoing backing of the forces in these three states that are not known for being reform-minded and sympathetic to the West. The Russian leadership does not shy away from openly supporting stagnating and autocratic regimes, corrupt oligarchic groups, and retrograde political forces such as the communists.[30] For the ruling establishments in Belarus, Moldova, and Ukraine, Russia and its support have come to serve as the guarantee of their stability and possible continuity.

Russia continues to back the economically hardly sustainable but politically loyal regime in Belarus, including in international forums, such as the OSCE and the Council of Europe. Although there have been indications that the Russian leadership is becoming uncomfortable about having such an ally, the thinking in Moscow seems to evolve around making Lukashenka more manageable or even finding a more loyal (to Russia) replacement (who would be willing and able to ensure implementation of the Russia–Belarus Union on Moscow's conditions), rather than about encouraging fair elections and democratic change in Belarus. Sergei Karaganov perhaps best explains the essence of Russian policy in Belarus: "We [Russia and the West] should agree that Belarus keeps a regime that is liked by Russia. And that is it. If we see that without any clear reason this regime—which is quite unpleasant for Russia itself, but Russia has not yet found a better replacement—begins to collapse, this would mean that our relations with the United States are essentially hostile."[31] In Ukraine, the last parliamentary elections were marked by massive Russian interference in favor of pro-presidential parties and blocs and against pro-reform, democratic, and Europe-oriented forces. Russian experts, some politicians, and even high-level officials publicly voiced support for those political forces in Ukraine that "contribute to consolidation of Russian–Ukrainian relations."[32] Interference in Ukrainian internal affairs, including domestic politics, continues to date, apparently aimed at securing what Moscow considers a favorable result in the next, possibly decisive, presidential elections in Ukraine and keeping in power those political and financial groups that are loyal to and/or dependent on Russia, thus constraining democratic change in Ukraine.

Dominique Moisi, deputy director of the Institute of International Relations in Paris, noted that "President Vladimir Putin [is] looking westwards in terms of diplomacy, but eastwards in domestic politics."[33] It would not be an exaggeration to say that Russia is also "looking eastward" when it comes to its policy toward its post-Soviet neighbors. Russian political (and in some cases economic) support has helped entrench those elite groups in Belarus, Moldova, and Ukraine, whose policies and behavior derail these countries' democratic transitions and "Europeanization." In fact, to a large extent it is Russian influence that has helped consolidation in these states of Eurasian political and business culture.[34] The latter is in itself the best possible guarantee against European integration of Belarus, Moldova, and Ukraine and the best possible assurance that they will stick closer to Russia.[35]

A Role for the West?

Moscow's current policy toward Belarus, Moldova, and Ukraine indicate that so far Russia has opted for neither "integration with the West" nor liberal modernization. Rather, it goes the way of authoritarian modernization aimed at achieving the old goal of restoring a "powerful and mighty" Russian state dominating its neighbors and ultimately "counterbalancing" the West. While coming to understand that its future depends on its ability to modernize its economy and society and that this modernization will be overwhelmingly difficult (if possible at all) to achieve without support and assistance from the developed Western nations, Russia at the same time continues to play with great power ambitions and integrationist projects in the CIS space. In practice, Putin's foreign policy priority has been to regain and/ or strengthen Russian dominance in the "near abroad," taking advantage of Russia's improved economic situation and new dynamics in its relations with the West. Modernization is seen not so much as a goal in itself, but as a mean of renewing great power status, which inter alia presupposes a degree of control over neighboring states.

It is, however, Russia's liberal modernization (both economic and political) that is in the interests of all: Russia's immediate neighbors, Europe, the United States, and Russia itself (if it correctly perceives its own long-term interests). Without such modernization and a fundamental societal change along market-democratic lines, the Russia–West partnership (to say nothing of integration) would ring hollow. As long as Russia remains in its current state and sticks to its current goals, it will seek to benefit from any Western (both American and European) difficulties to enhance its own geopolitical influence, rather than to work together to resolve global and regional problems. Integration with the West (or even sustaining a long-term and stable strategic alignment) is possible mainly for those countries that are willing and able to develop "genetically similar" political systems and cultures, based on democratic principles and values.

At the same time, Russia's recent embrace of the West, if continued and based not only on a few intersecting security interests, but increasingly on economic interdependence and shared values, might actually prompt Russia to change its self-perception, reconsider its interests, and concentrate on its modernization—attaining functional democracy, economic prosperity, high living standards, individual freedoms for its citizens, and full-fledged integration into the world economy—rather than to claim special status or, in the words of Dmitrii Trenin, be "almost a minor planet sitting on the planet Earth."[36] If set as a genuine goal, strong partnership (if not integration) with the West would encourage democratic domestic reform and impose constructive constraints on Moscow's international behavior. Strategic and broadly based partnership with the West can embed Russia in a system of relatively transparent rules that are difficult and not beneficial to break.

Only such a Russia can become a reliable partner, if not a part, of the West. Russia itself must decide whether it wants to continue cultivating ambitions to be a "great power," a "Eurasian pole," an epicenter of post-Soviet integration, or to become a developed modern state, integrated into the world economy and, ideally, integrated with the West.

But the West can help Russia to make this crucial decision. Both America and Europe can play an important role in helping Russia to break what *Izvestiia* calls its "civilizational deadlock"[37] and to move along a liberal direction. This should not be a role aimed at trying to change Russia, but at creating conditions that encourage and facilitate Russia's liberal modernization and integration with the West. As once suggested by Zbigniew Brzezinski, "To be sure, neither America nor, even less, Europe can by itself seduce or transform Russia. Russia's epiphany must come from within. . . . But both America and Europe can help create not only a congenial but a compelling context for desirable change."[38] Joining forces in combating terrorism and the proliferation of weapons of mass destruction, deepening Russia's engagement with NATO, developing a strategic partnership with the United States, expanding trade and cooperation with the EU, and including Russia in the WTO are all necessary, but not sufficient, components of such a "compelling context."

To help ensure Russia's evolution into a liberal democracy integrated with the West, at least two other policy tasks are equally important:

1. considering the interests and addressing the situation of the countries "in between"; and

2. helping Russia understand that successful transformation and integration
   into Europe of Ukraine and Moldova (and in the longer run of Belarus) is
   as much in Russia's interests as it is in the interests of those countries, and
   hence encouraging Russia to welcome and support democratic change
   and the European aspirations of its Western neighbors.

The West, especially the European Union, has never had a clear conceptual
solution (the one that has been offered to the post-communist countries of Central,
and later Southeastern, Europe) for Belarus, Moldova, and Ukraine. The EU has
based its relations with all the CIS states on Partnership and Cooperation Agreements and refused to treat Belarus, Moldova, and Ukraine even as potential future
members; its financial and technical support to the three countries has been limited in comparison with that provided to Central Europe or to the troubled states of
the Western Balkans. At its summit in Goteborg in June 2001, the EU came closest
to a vision accepting the possibility of Ukraine's eventual membership. This approach, however, has failed to develop; on the contrary, the EU has moved backward from its declared position in Goteborg. This combination of EU indifference,
on the one hand, and of Russian persistence in keeping Belarus and bringing
Moldova and Ukraine back under its fold, on the other, has further aggravated the
domestic situations and complicated foreign policy choices of the countries "in
between." The United States and NATO were formerly more welcoming, in particular to Ukraine, but U.S. priorities shifted after September 11. Its decreased
involvement in Ukraine, the latter's domestic problems, and the Kolchuga scandal
delivered a serious blow to Ukraine–U.S. and Ukraine–NATO cooperation in 2002.
Although these relationships have begun to gradually recover since the Iraq war, it
will still take time and require strong political will and domestic change in Ukraine
and a vision from NATO for Ukraine to become a realistic candidate for membership in the alliance.

But as the EU and NATO proceed with eastward enlargement, the evolving
debate on the limits of Europe and the place for Belarus, Moldova, and Ukraine
will enter a new (and possibly decisive) stage. Once distant troubles, these weak
states, marginalized or even isolated by their own policies, Russian influence, and
Western neglect, are now on Europe's doorstep.[39] The three uncertain and unstable countries are not a desirable neighborhood for an expanding Europe. It is, in
fact, the unfinished nature of transition and remaining geopolitical uncertainty of
Ukraine and Moldova and the lack of a policy choice for Belarus that present a
potential risk for Europe's security. Instability on Europe's periphery will negatively affect Europe's own consolidation and development. Conversely, a democratic, prosperous, and stable Ukraine, Moldova, and Belarus will be a source of
regional security and stability, making it possible for the EU to concentrate on its
own development and policies rather than on the security of its eastern borders. As
the EU's immediate neighbors, these three countries have an important role to play
in combating the proliferation of weapons, trafficking in human beings, illegal

migration, and money laundering. Unstable at home and uncertain internationally, Belarus, Moldova, and Ukraine will not be good neighbors for Russia either. Russia itself is more likely to renounce the remnants of old geopolitics and become a truly democratic state and a long-term partner of the West if its immediate neighbors succeed in consolidating their independence and becoming vibrant states.

Possible options for the countries "in between" are very much defined by their geography. In the case of Belarus, Moldova, and Ukraine, those options might theoretically include: (1) staying on their own and balancing between Europe and Russia; (2) gravitating toward or even reintegrating with Russia; and (3) joining the process of European integration.

In today's world of global influences and interconnectedness, staying on one's own is increasingly difficult for any small or medium-sized state. For Belarus, Moldova, and Ukraine, three weak countries in unfinished transitions, this becomes an almost impossible task. Moreover, the very success of their transitions and the nature of their states depend enormously on the overall direction of their development—European or Eurasian. The past decade of their transformation vividly demonstrates that uncertainty and indecision about this direction delay and complicate domestic change and leave them on the periphery of a new world order and mainstream European processes. As suggested by Ukrainian political scientist Oleksandr Derhachov, in the case of trying to stay on their own, the result would still be a Eurasian/Russian model, but in a worsened form, in the absence of rich natural resources.[40]

Recreation of the post-Soviet economic and political space—in this or that shape—under Russian leadership does not present a positive alternative either. First, all CIS countries, including Russia, have scarce financial resources and very few new technologies to successfully pursue a serious integration project. Second, bilateral relations between Russia on the one hand and its Western CIS neighbors on the other are based not so much on national interests, mutual political benefits, and economic necessity, as on the links and partnerships (often informal) between ruling establishments and between influential political and business groups. The existing political regimes have little interest in the establishment of genuine democracy, freedom of media, rule of law, good governance, and civilized business culture.[41] Consequently, further strengthening of these partnerships and the realization of any kind of integration project based on them is very unlikely—contrary to some beliefs—to lead to more reforms, openness (e.g., establishment of WTO norms),[42] and economic growth, to ensure technological progress and evolution toward functional market economies, and to help overcome democracy deficits in the post-Soviet states involved. The inability of current EEC members to achieve that is indicative in this regard. On the contrary, willingly or unwillingly, such reintegration serves to "freeze" the existing underreformed and chaotic economic structures and consolidate nondemocratic political systems. Pursuing integration within the Collective Security Treaty, EEC, and SES will also increase the burden on Russia itself[43]—a burden that might well become too heavy for Russia's still unstable economy, and that risks derailing Russia's own modernization. Russia's current and still unresolved "civilizational deadlock" might thus become a dead-lock for Belarus, Moldova, and Ukraine as well.

No doubt, were Russia to succeed in modernizing itself, this would have had a major positive impact on its neighbors. But will Russia be able to change the centu-ries-long paradigm of its development and transform itself into a democratic modern state? Will Putin be able to deliver, even if one assumes that such a Russia is indeed his ultimate goal? The answers to these questions remain uncertain. It is also not clear how long Russia's modernization might take and, as Lilia Shevtsova wonders, "what price it [Russia] will have to pay for its final break with the past" (see chapter 6, p. 102). Under such circumstances, it is at best unwise for the countries "in be-tween" to make their destiny dependent on Russia's ability to succeed.

To ensure the progressive development of Belarus, Moldova, and Ukraine, the three countries should be given an appealing and attractive alternative. Such an alternative is needed both to facilitate democratic internal change and to put an end to these countries' remaining geopolitical uncertainty. Domestic democratic and reformist forces will be more likely and prevail more rapidly if there is such an alternative, and if they can demonstrate that this alternative is not only a necessary but also a realistic prospect (even if in the distant future).

It is the option and prospect of European integration that can present such an alternative. It is the EU, not Russia, that has served as a pole of attraction for practically all post-communist countries in Europe. European integration and en-largement—the EU's and NATO's most powerful diplomatic and political tool for the post-communist countries—has been instrumental in ensuring the success of transition in Central Europe; it has proven successful in stabilization of the Balkans; and it could become the single most important instrument for changing the bal-ance of forces, stimulating the consolidation of democratic elite groups, and break-ing the deadlock in Belarus, Moldova, and Ukraine. In fact, after the EU and NATO had announced their plans for eastward enlargement in the mid-1990s and practi-cally all post-communist states of Central and Eastern Europe had applied for membership, any positive alternative to European integration for Belarus, Moldova, and Ukraine has largely ceased to exist. Their evolution over the past several years, both domestic development and international standing, has only proven this lack of a positive alternative. For the countries "in between" today, European integra-tion is not so much about membership as it is about the direction and model of their future development; it is about their historical and civilizational choice.

At the moment, however, Ukraine and Moldova, and even less so Belarus, are not prepared for full-fledged participation in the process of European integration, and the EU and NATO are not ready to accept them. On the one hand, the leaders of the three countries have proved unwilling and unable to deliver the domestic change necessary for their nations to become truly European. They themselves have begun to be viewed as a "fundamental problem" on their countries' way toward Europe.[44] On the other hand, there is still a question of whether NATO and especially the EU would be willing to take a more embracing stance vis-à-vis Ukraine, Moldova, and Belarus, even if the desired domestic change does take place. It is already clear what these countries have lost in terms of European integration by lagging with domestic reforms. It is, however, not yet clear what chance (if any) they might have for European integration if the required change is mastered.[45] A conceptual solution, one that is appealing and stimulating, has yet to be found and articulated for Belarus, Moldova, and Ukraine. The latest EU initiative "Wider Europe–Neighbourhood: A New Framework for Relations with our Eastern and Southern Neighbours" designed to guide relations between the enlarged Union and its immediate neighbors, while offering few positive incentivès and practical steps to be taken, does not provide such a solution either, in its attempt to construct one general framework for the EU's very different eastern (Russia, Belarus, Moldova, and Ukraine) and southern (North African and Mediterranean) neighbors.[46]

In the long run, the prospect of EU and NATO membership linked to domestic change and stimulating that change should not be excluded for all three states. The philosophy of inclusiveness and an "open door" policy should be continued, and membership prospects should be explicitly recognized for Belarus, Moldova, and Ukraine. As long as the EU remains institutionally and functionally what it is today, anything less than membership, such as offers of some status "in between" (be it a "new neighbor," a "ring of friends," "more than partnership and less than membership," or "sharing everything but institutions") will not serve the purpose. For the time being, it is not membership per se but the prospect of membership, a clear alternative to their current situations, the possibility of being treated and becoming "like Poland, Lithuania, or Romania," that matter most for Ukraine, Belarus, and Moldova. European integration is an essential guideline to the overall societal development of European post-communist countries, and as such it is strongly needed by Belarus, Moldova, and Ukraine. The task of becoming democratic, strong, and stable will take much longer to accomplish or might even become impossible for the three countries "in between" if their European aspirations are ignored and they are left on their own. Failure to make the European alternative clear and feasible will strengthen their stagnation and uncertainty, reduce their ability to cope with internal and external challenges, increase instability, and lead to more international alienation and isolation. The risk of being excluded from European integration is in fact the main risk that Ukraine, Moldova, and Belarus face. But this is also a risk for Europe.[47] If weak and failed states present one of the main security threats in today's world (as many in the West believe), then the exclusion of Belarus, Moldova, and Ukraine is the shortest way to make them weaker.

The short- to mid-term policy options should be different in each case, reflecting the differences in these countries' past transition experiences, current balance of domestic forces, and foreign policy aspirations. For Belarus, this could be constructive cooperation with the OSCE and attaining membership in the Council of Europe. International attention should be given to promoting democratic institution building and civil society development in Belarus. In Moldova, the international community should continue efforts to find a solution to the country's main problem—the unresolved Transdniestrian conflict. The priority should be to secure the soonest possible withdrawal of the remaining Russian troops and ammunition. It is critical that the final settlement of the Transdniestrian conflict is done in a way that facilitates democracy building in both Moldova and Transdniestria. Increased involvement of the EU will be helpful, including in providing post-settlement security guarantees. The Action Plan for Moldova, which the EU has yet to prepare in the framework of the "Wider Europe–Neighbourhood" initiative, could contain measures whose implementation would lead Moldova to the conclusion of a Stabilization and Association agreement, similar to those signed between the EU and countries participating in the Stability Pact for Southeast Europe.

In the case of Ukraine, a Western strategy in the next few years can be based on two main pillars, with both NATO and the EU playing a role. NATO should work with Ukraine to fully implement the Action Plan agreed at the NATO summit in Prague in 2002. This can be followed by Ukraine's enrolling in NATO's Membership for Action Plan, paving the way for the country to become a candidate for the next wave of NATO enlargement. The EU Action Plan for Ukraine to be elaborated in 2004 should aim at bringing the country to the conclusion of an associate agreement with the prospect of future membership in the EU. Supporting Ukraine's accession to the WTO should be another goal, as progress in this regard will be a powerful engine for bringing more openness and transparency to the country's economic structures and consequently to its political system. The immediate task, however, is to help ensure free and fair presidential elections. The chance that the 2004 election will be free would be greater if the West keeps a close eye on the election (including the election process), and ideally links its outcome with certain (meaningful) progress (or the lack of it) in Ukraine's European integration. Ukraine's success can then become a powerful example and incentive for Moldova and Belarus.

For all three countries, it is important to ensure that EU enlargement and the introduction of tighter controls and visa regimes on the new eastern borders of the enlarged Union do not disrupt these countries' ties with their neighbors to the West and the development of their civil societies and NGO sectors.[48] Intensifying various exchange programs and twinning processes, increasing support to NGOs, independent media, and other segments of civil society, and actively engaging all agents of democratic change should become priority tasks for the enlarged Europe in the coming years.

In conceptualizing and shaping its policies toward Ukraine, Moldova, and Belarus, the West, especially the EU, should more actively and substantively involve these countries' immediate Central European neighbors. Poland, Hungary, Lithuania, and some other Central European states are the direct and most interested stakeholders in the development and future of their eastern neighbors. Their knowledge of the "East" should be as indispensable for the West/EU, as their experience of the "West" (experience of European integration) should be relevant for Ukraine, Moldova, and Belarus.

The West should also help Russia understand that the progress and ultimate success of Belarus, Moldova, and Ukraine with European integration is in its own interests. Bilateral relationships of these countries with Russia will, no doubt, be an advantage if Russia also moves in the same direction of European integration. It is, however, important to understand that the final goal of that movement is different for Ukraine and Moldova (and potentially for Belarus) on the one hand, and Russia on the other. While Ukraine and Moldova aim at EU accession in the future, membership in the EU is not on Russia's agenda; Russia rather sees itself as a political, economic, and security partner of the EU.[49] For Russia, a relationship with the EU is about "equal" partnership in resolving issues of mutual concern and interest. For Ukraine, a relationship with the EU is about adaptation and integration. Consequently, the model of Russia–EU relationship will not be appropriate and adequate for Ukraine's (and Moldova's) relations with the EU (also considering the obvious difference in geographic size, economic potential, and international weight between Russia and its three western neighbors). Therefore, the slogan of moving to Europe "together with Russia," which has recently been championed in Russia and by some politicians in Ukraine, inasmuch as it might sound attractive in theory, in practice imposes a serious limitation on Ukraine's integration with the EU. For Ukraine to succeed, its relations with Russia should be subordinated to the main goal of European integration.

What is important though is to find a way to combine in a positive way the interests of the countries "in between" the West and Russia. This should not be an attempt to couple EU policy toward Ukraine (as well as Moldova and Belarus) with EU–Russian policy, but rather a pragmatic and practical goal of enforcing transparent and mutually beneficial energy supplies from Russia via Ukraine to the EU, and joining forces in combating illegal migration and other new security threats, including the development of adequate border control and infrastructure on Ukraine's borders with Russia and Belarus. Moscow's post–September 11 rapprochement with the West provides a sufficient and necessary basis for such a "trilateral" approach.

In this regard, the evolving West–Russia partnership presents a rare opportunity to address in a nonconfrontational and friendly manner the relations of Ukraine, Moldova, and Belarus with NATO and the EU, as well as the nature of Russian policy toward its immediate neighbors. The level of West–Russia closeness and the sincerity of Russia's declarations on its "integration with the West" should also be measured by the essence and practice of Russian policies toward the countries in between. Russia's support or the lack of it for the European and Euro-Atlantic integration of Ukraine, Moldova, and Belarus (if the latter opts for it) is the best litmus test for Russia's own long-term intentions vis-à-vis the West and for the prospect of Russia's liberal modernization. Russian continued support of undemocratic and anti-Western forces in Belarus, Moldova, and Ukraine significantly derails domestic change and "Europeanization" in these countries, and it also slows down Russia's own modernization, thus narrowing the foundation for Russia's durable partnership (or even integration) with the West and threatening its ultimate failure. It is only the success of transition in Ukraine, Moldova, and Belarus and—should they wish to do so—European integration that can ensure their stable, equal, and friendly relations with Russia and help the emerging partnership between Russia and the West to achieve its full potential.

Notes

1. For more on Belarus's domestic development and international standing since independence, see *Belarus at the Crossroads*, ed. Sherman W. Garnet and Robert Legvold (Washington, DC: Carnegie Endowment for International Peace, 1999); *Independent Belarus: Domestic Determinants, Regional Dynamics, and Implications for the West*, ed. Margarita M. Balmaceda, James I. Clem, and Lisbeth L. Tarlow (Cambridge, MA: Harvard Ukrainian Research Institute, Harvard University Press, 2002).

2. Uzbekistan's present status within GUUAM is uncertain. Having joined the group in 1999, three years later, in 2002 Tashkent announced it was "suspending" its membership. Recently, however, Uzbek representatives have renewed their participation in some of GUUAM's meetings.

3. For more on Ukraine's post-communist transition and nation building see *State and Institution Building in Ukraine*, ed. Taras Kuzio, Robert S. Kravchuk, and Paul D'Anieri (New York: St. Martin's Press, 1999); *Ukraine: The Search for a National Identity*, ed. Sharon L. Wolchik and Volodymyr Zviglianich (Oxford and Lanham, MD: Rowman and Littlefield, 2000).

4. On the evolution of Ukraine–West relations see Oleksandr Pavliuk, "An Unfulfilling Partnership: Ukraine and the West, 1991–2001," *European Security* 11, no. 1 (2002): 81–101.

5. Adrian Karatnycky, "Ukraine's Rogue President," *Wall Street Journal*, October 9, 2002, www.freedomhouse.org/media/100902wsj.htm.

6. *International Herald Tribune*, November 9–10, 2002 p. 6.

7. "The Least Wanted" as the two presidents were referred to in *Newsweek*, December 9, 2002, pp. 4–5.

8. A definition given by an official of the European Commission. See Stefan Wagstyl, "Vilnius Looks to Its Future Frontier Role with Unease," *Financial Times*, December 3, 2002, p. 3.

9. James Sherr, "Ukraine's Euro-Atlantic Choice: Is Failure Inevitable?" in *Ukraine: Our New Neighbour*, ed. Rikke Kierulff-Jorgensen (Copenhagen: Danish Institute of International Affairs, Report no. 13, 2002), pp. 25–26.

10. For the first time since independence, the election was won not by the Communist Party, which lost its place as the largest faction in the parliament, and not by the pro-presidential bloc, which received less than 12 percent of the vote on party lists, but by democratic forces. The pro-reform bloc of centrist and right-wing parties, Our Ukraine, led by popular former prime minister Viktor Yushchenko came in first, receiving support from 23.57 percent of the voters. Another 7.26 percent voted for the representative of the right-wing and openly anti-Kuchma bloc, charismatic Yulia Tymoshenko. To compare, in 1998 the only unequivocally pro-reform party elected to the parliament was Rukh with a mere 9.4 percent of the vote. The difference in the Ukrainian situation is even more striking, if one compares Ukrainian results with the outcome of the last parliamentary elections in neighboring Moldova (in February 2001, 49.9 percent of the vote went to the Communist Party) and Russia (in December 1999, the winner was the Communist Party with 24.3 percent, second was the pro-presidential bloc Unity, with 23.2 percent, while the liberal Union of Right Forces and Yabloko received 8.6 percent and 6 percent, respectively.

11. Dmitrii Furman, "Kuchme dostalsia ne tot narod," *Moscow News*, no. 40 (October 15, 2002), www.mn.ru/issue.php?2002-40-14.

12. See, for example, Iurii Fedorov, "Krizis vneshnei politiki Rossii: kontseptual'nyi aspekt," *Pro et contra* 6 (Winter–Spring 2001): 31–49; Dmitrii Trenin, "Nenadezhnaia strategiia" *Pro et contra* 6 (Winter–Spring 2001): 50–65.

13. "Rossiia na rubezhe tysiacheletii" (Russia at the Turn of the Millennium), December 1999, www.e-government.ru/government/government1/press-centre/briefings/archieve/1999/12/28/imported-news53.htm.

14. A policy that sometimes is described in Russia as "Putin's doctrine," *Vremia MN*, July 26, 2002, p. 3.

15. Today it has almost been forgotten that these were Western (rather than Russian) policy makers and experts who, long before September 11, had been trying (in vain) to convince Russians that a real threat to their security was coming not from NATO expansion, but from instability in the south and Russia's inability to cope with overwhelming problems along its southern flank.

16. The author of this chapter is also of the opinion that Russia's post–September 11 rapprochement with the West was not (contrary to some beliefs) a "one-man show," but rather a reflection of the consensus of a part of the Russian elite (both its major business groups and part of the political class) on the need to rebuild a powerful Russian state able to protect and promote their interests, including on the international scene and global markets.

17. See Robert Cottrell, "Putin Policy Shift Is Bold But Risky," *Financial Times*, April 15, 2002, Survey on Russia, p. i.

18. James Sherr, "After 11 September: A New Russian Policy?" (Speech to annual conference of the Atlantic Council of the United Kingdom and the Trades Union Committee for European & Trans-Atlantic Understanding, *Grantham*, February 8, 2002), p. 3.

19. See Putin's Address to the Federal Assembly on April 18, 2002 (www.president. kremlin.ru/text/appears/2002/04/28876.shtml) and Putin's Address to the Federal Assembly on May 16, 2003 (www.president.kremlin.ru/text/appears/2003/05/44623.shtml). Foreign Minister Igor Ivanov's article "Oriientiry vneshnei politiki Rossii" (The Landmarks of Russia's Foreign Policy), *Kommersant-Vlast*, no. 22 (June 11, 2002), www.kommersant.ru/k-vlast/get_page.asp?page_id=20022248–15.htm.

20. Vladimir Socor, a senior fellow at the Washington-based Institute for Advanced Strategic and Policy Studies, argued in one of his articles that September 11 raised Russian hopes that the alignment with the West might earn Russia tacit Western acceptance of its "bloc-rebuilding agenda." See his article, "Unfinished After 1991, Renewed After September 11," *Wall Street Journal*, September 13, 2002, p. A9.

21. See *Pravda.ru*, September 25, 2003. According to the well-known Russian sociologist Iurii Levada, Russian society still finds it difficult to accept Ukraine's independence, with about 70 percent of Russians believing that Ukrainians and Russians are one nation. See Levada's interview "Slov'ians'koho svitu nemaie i nikoly ne bulo" in *Den'*, July 2, 2003, www.day.kiev.ua/2003/110/nomer.htm.

22. Boris Berezovsky, "The Problem of Putin," *Financial Times*, May 28, 2002, p. 14.

23. In a recent article, for example, Foreign Minister Ivanov emphasized: "In Russian foreign policy the Ukrainian vector was and remains an absolute priority. It is constantly in the field of vision of the top leadership of the Russian Federation." See "No Alternative to Russian-Ukrainian Strategic Dialogue," *Dialog*, December 2002, 222.ln.mid.ru/brp_4.nsf/e78a48070f128a7b43256999005bcbb3/3l9f4131874e0e6d43256c8c0028688b?OpenDocument.

24. In the fall of 2002, Grigory Yavlinsky, leader of the Russian liberal party Yabloko, recognized that "Russian president Vladimir Putin takes advantage of the current political crisis in Ukraine to get maximum benefits for Russian interests while Ukraine's president Leonid Kuchma is weakened." See his interview for the BBC, Ukrainian Service, *Ukrains'ka pravda*, October 21, 2002.

25. *Den'*, December 10, 2002, p. 2.

26. The six largest Russian oil companies signed a collective letter to the prime ministers of Russia and Ukraine calling on them to ensure the reverse use of the Odessa–Brody pipeline, while Russian prime minister Kas'ianov openly linked the signing of an agreement on oil supplies via Ukraine in 2004 with solution of the Odessa–Brody issue.

27. Sophie Lambroschini, "Russia/Belarus: Putin, Lukashenka Struggle to Put on Happy Face After Talks," *RFE*, September 16, 2003, www.rferl.org/features/2003/09/16092003163855.asp.

28. Statement by Russian First Deputy Foreign Minister Valerii Loshchinin, *UNIAN*, April 24, 2002, www.unian.net.

29. A statement by the Ministry for Foreign Affairs of the Russian Federation, *Interfax*, January 2, 2003, www.interfax.ru.

30. Vladimir Socor, "Putin's Easy Pickings, So Far," *Wall Street Journal Europe*, April 19–21, 2002, p. A13.

31. From an interview by Sergei Karaganov in *Nezavisimaia gazeta*, April 8, 2002.

32. Such statements were made by the head of Putin's administration, Aleksandr Voloshin, and ex-prime minister and current Russian ambassador to Ukraine, Viktor Chernomyrdin. Voloshin, for example, listed among those forces the pro-Kuchma bloc For a United Ukraine, the oligarchic Social Democratic Party of Ukraine (United), and the Communist Party of Ukraine. On the eve of the elections, Putin granted an audience to the Ukrainian communist leader Petro Symonenko, which was widely covered by TV.

33. Dominque Moisi, "Why Russia seeks a welcome in the West?" *Financial Times*, October 21, 2002, p. 17.

34. Dmitrii Furman of the Moscow-based Institute of Europe observed in this regard that Moscow supports Kuchma to "build in Ukraine a system analogous to the one in Russia."

35. During one of his meetings with Putin, Kuchma applauded the fact that he and Putin understand each other and speak the same language, both figuratively and literally: "We do not need to try to convince one another about many matters—while at the same time, in our conversations with our Western colleagues they often do not understand us . . . we have different problems, different mentalities" (*Ukrains'ka pravda*, December 9, 2002); see also Taras Kuzio, "Ukrainian President Orchestrates Oligarchic Takeover," *RFE/RL*, December 13, 2002, www.rferl.org/newsline/2002/12/131202.asp#5–not.

36. Dmitri Trenin, *The End of Eurasia: Russia on the Border Between Geopolitics and Globalization* (Washington: Carnegie Endowment for International Peace, 2002), p. 18.

37. *Izvestiia*, December 20, 2002, p. 1.

38. Zbigniew Brzezinski, "Living With Russia," *National Interest*, no. 61 (Fall 2000), http:/www.globalpolicy.org/nations/future/0228bzki.htm.

39. Christian Caryl, "Trouble Next Door," *Newsweek*, August 12, 2002, p. 16.

40. See his interview for *Den'* December 27, 2002.

41. Oleksandr Derhachov, "Za zavisoiu" [Behind the Curtain], *Dzerkalo tyzhnia*, no. 50 (425), December 28, 2002–January 10, 2003, www.zn.kiev.ua/ie/show/425/37223/.

42. It is indicative that the latest survey by the *Foreign Policy* journal suggests that Russia, which claims that participation in the EEC would help its members to join the WTO, is actually behind Ukraine in degree of globalization (forty-fifth place vs. forty-second) and on scale of integration into the world economy (fifty-first place vs. thirty-fifth). "Ukraina bil'sh hlobalizovana, nizh Rosiia, ale menshe, nizh Kytai," *Ukrains'ka pravda*, January 10, 2003, www2.pravda.com.ua/archive/?30110.

43. According to Russian estimates, Ukraine's participation in the EEC or SES and the resulting establishment of a free-trade area would cost the Russian budget around US$450 million annually. As stated by Russian First Deputy Prime Minister Viktor Khristenko, "We understand that Russia should pay for economic integration, and we have already taken

such a political decision," Serhii Syrovatka, "Zona napivvil'noi torhivli," *Den'* June 24, 2003, www.day.kiev.ua/2003/107/nomer.htm.

44. "Eastern Approaches," *Financial Times*, January 2, 2003, p. 8.

45. At some point, both EU Commissioner for Enlargement Günter Verheugen and Commission President Romano Prodi flatly and unconditionally refused an EU membership perspective for Belarus, Moldova, and Ukraine. Prodi stated in the fall of 2002 that Ukraine, Moldova, and Belarus, as well as Russia and the Mediterranean countries, would never become EU members, unlike the Balkan states. See *La Stampa*, October 15, 2002, and *Ukrains'ka pravda*, November 27, 2002, citing his interview in the Dutch newspaper *Volkskrant*. For Günter Verheugen's remarks see *Financial Times*, September 18, 2002, www2.pravda.com.ua/archive/?archive2002ukr.

46. Available at www.europa.eu.int/comm/external_relations/we/intro/ip03_358.htm (April 20, 2004).

47. For more discussion of this see Oleksandr Pavliuk, "Ukraine and the EU: The Risk of Being Excluded," in *Beyond EU Enlargement*, vol. 1: *The Agenda of Direct Neighbourhood for Eastern Europe*, ed. Iris Kempe, (Gütersloh: Bertelsmann Foundation, 2001), pp. 65–84.

48. According to some estimates, since Slovakia imposed a visa regime on its border with Ukraine (July 2000), the number of Ukrainians visiting Slovakia has decreased threefold: from 750,000 annually to 250,000. See interview with Borys Tarasiuk, Chairman of the Committee on European Integration, Verkhovna Rada of Ukraine, in *Za vil'nu Ukrainu*, January 7, 2003. Poland and Hungary have become the last two Central European countries to decide to introduce visas for Ukrainians as of October 1 and November 1, 2003, respectively. It was, however, agreed that Polish and Hungarian visas for Ukrainians would be free of charge, while their citizens would be able to travel to Ukraine without visas.

49. See, for example, an interview with Sergei Rogov, director of the Institute of USA and Canada Studies of the Russian Academy of Sciences in *Den'* February 25, 2003, www.day.kiev.ua/2003/35/nomer.htm.

10

"Greater Central Asia," Russia, and the West

Challenges and Opportunities for Cooperation

Rajan Menon

The Road to Engagement

The question of whether the United States had vital interests—ones on which Americans would spend much blood and treasure and undertake protracted obligations—in Central Asia was debatable, and debated, until recently. My own assessment was that, for several reasons, we did not. With deep and longstanding strategic commitments in other regions (Europe, Northeast Asia, the Persian Gulf) the opportunity costs of assuming additional ones were high for the United States. Most Americans knew little and cared less about Central Asia and remain wary of strategic choices that yield swamps that are hard to emerge from. Assuming big commitments in Central Asia, a new and unfamiliar theater with poor infrastructure to support operations, would also have required spending sizable sums of money, and for purposes that were hardly clear. Together, these considerations seemed to rule out deep U.S. engagement in Central Asia—until recently.

However reasonable the grounds for eschewing deep commitments in Central Asia might have once been, they have been upended by a sudden, unexpected event of the sort that sometimes reorders the strategic calculus of major powers. The massacres of September 11, 2001, were precisely such a bolt from the blue. They transformed the American strategic environment, took the United States into a "war on terrorism," and into greater Central Asia, which I define here as the five post-Soviet states of "greater Central Asia" (Kazakhstan, Kyrgyzstan, Tajikistan, Turkmenistan, and Uzbekistan, plus Afghanistan and Pakistan) in contradistinction to Central Asia "proper" or simply "Central Asia." The actions that the United States has taken in greater Central Asia following what is now called "9/11"— basing agreements, implied (or explicit) security obligations to local regimes, military construction, and training programs—leave little doubt that there has been a reassessment of greater Central Asia's salience in Washington and in the capitals of other leading NATO powers. The Bush administration's war to bring down the regime of Saddam Hussein shows that engagements that were once thought improbable no longer are, and this leaves open the possibility that the American engagement in the region could become wider and deeper.

Some suggest that the West's (for it is not just American troops that are involved in Afghanistan but those of other NATO members as well) present engagement in greater Central Asia could turn out to be a flash in the pan. The American military, their argument goes, has a deep-rooted fear of distant quagmires after Vietnam; the Bush administration abhors nation building; the Taliban is history; al-Qaeda is on the run; and its Western European allies will depart the Central Asian scene the moment the United States does. This view is flawed logically and dubious empirically.[1]

The faulty reasoning stems from conflating intentions with outcomes: were they one and the same, the world would be a different place. States often do not get what they want, what happens is other than what they expect, and unanticipated events lead them in unexpected directions. As for empirical evidence, the Western military presence in greater Central Asia (the International Security Assistance Force in Afghanistan, the infrastructure being built to house it, the agreements that have been signed between the West and Central Asian governments, and the anti-terrorism operations being launched from Pakistan) suggests that what we are witnessing is not a fleeting visit. Deriding "nation building" may have been a catchy campaign slogan, but, having gained the presidency, George W. Bush is engaged precisely in nation building in Afghanistan and in Iraq, for that is what "regime change" entails. Toppling governments without creating stability thereafter is not statecraft; it is demolition. More important, as I show below, conditions in Central Asia will not allow the West, particularly the United States, the luxury of an early departure.

Central Asia's Abiding Strategic Salience

Washington's current strategic engagement in greater Central Asia is rooted in three circumstances. First, the region was the best perch from which to supply and train the Northern Alliance (whose base was chiefly in the Tajik and Uzbek areas of northern Afghanistan and the Hazara zones in the central parts of that country) and to gather intelligence on the ground and from the air. The Northern Alliance rode to victory, but that has not settled the question of what sort of political order will emerge in Afghanistan—or, indeed, if there will be any long-lasting order at all. The new administration in Kabul, headed by Hamid Karzai (a Pushtun), faces many problems, ranging from internecine squabbles, coup and assassination attempts, disorder in much of the country, reign of regional strongmen (such as Ismail Khan and Abdul Rashid Dostum) who pay it scant heed, a flood of refugees returning from Pakistan, and a less than overwhelming inflow of reconstruction aid from the West, despite grand promises. These difficulties do not mean that renewed civil war in Afghanistan is inevitable (few things in life are), but it is certainly not a prospect that sensible policy makers in the United States can fail to anticipate and prepare for, especially in Afghanistan, where so much of what happens depends on one man, Hamid Karzai, who has already once been an assassin's target.

Pakistan is nearly as shaky.[2] Its leader, Pervez Musharraf, has alienated the radical Islamists by helping the United States destroy the Taliban regime and by aligning with the West in the ensuing war on terror, and in parts of the country, notably in the part of the Northwest Frontier Province (NWFP) near the Afghanistan-Pakistan border, Bin Laden remains a popular figure and al-Qaeda can count on assistance and sanctuaries. As for Pakistan's secular political opposition, chiefly Benazir Bhutto's People's Party and the Muslim League headed by former Prime Minister Nawaz Sharif, whom Musharraf deposed in a 1999 coup, they abhor Musharraf's regime. They see it as yet another of Pakistan's thinly veiled military dictatorships, complete with constitutional amendments achieved by fiat, an emasculated parliament, and a rigged referendum to prettify the usurpation of democracy with a patina of popular consent. The fact that the United States supports this government in no way legitimizes it in their eyes. Aside from the armed forces and the intelligence services (the ISI), then, it is not clear what Musharraf's base of support consists of, and even these two institutions contain factions that question whether facilitating the ouster of the Taliban and joining the war on terror—which they see as part of a war on Islam—was proper from the standpoint of either principles or practical interests.

There are, in short, deep divisions in Pakistan regarding the American war on terrorism, and they will shape politics even more strongly now that the Islamist parties demonstrated in the 2002 elections that they can do more than organize street rallies. What this means is that the United States and its allies can hardly assume that Pakistan can be the principal platform from which to bring order to Afghanistan and to continue the war against al-Qaeda. It follows that Central Asia, which offers multiple points of access to Afghanistan—from Uzbekistan, Tajikistan, and Turkmenistan—will remain important to operations against al-Qaeda in South and Southwest Asia.

The second circumstance that illuminates the nature of the strategic commitments the United States and its European allies have made in Central Asia involves al-Qaeda itself. While that organization is in tatters and on the run in Afghanistan and Pakistan's tribal areas, it has not been put out of commission. Al-Qaeda is not a one-country organization; it is akin to a multinational corporation, with affiliates in many countries in the Muslim world. With the destruction of the Taliban, a new headquarters will be reestablished, and geography makes Central Asia proper an attractive location, and it is easy to see why if one considers the region's profile. Its governments are despotisms to one degree or another (Turkmenistan at one end and Kyrgyzstan at the other mark the continuum). Poverty is pervasive, especially in the rural areas. Corruption is ubiquitous. Birthrates are high and the population is young, which means that there are plenty of unemployed, but educated, young men—the classic raw material for millenarian movements. And oil and gas revenues, so often portrayed as the panacea for Central Asia's ills, could actually aggravate these problems. Economic development strategies based on hydrocarbon exports tend to generate social inequalities, corruption, wasteful spending, and militarization; and they are rarely accompanied by reforms to foster democracy and economic efficiency.[3]

Islam, never expunged in the Soviet era, is making a comeback in the form of mosques, *madrassahs*, literature and cassette tapes, underground political movements, and the inflow of money and activists from the wider Muslim world.[4] The appeal of a radical and politicized Islam (based on so-called *Salafi* interpretations) will grow given the anomie and the vacuum in values that abound in Central Asia following the collapse of the communist order. There are other conditions that could give opportunities for radical Islam to emerge. The region contains disputed boundaries and regional rivalries. The polities are run by soon-to-be-gone authoritarian, ex-communist leaders, two of whom (Uzbekistan's Islam Karimov and Turkmenistan's Saparmurat Niazov) have survived assassination attempts in recent years. And gun running and drug trafficking are well established. These problems can create a context for political mobilization, and Islam will be among the vehicles.

In short, Central Asia is prime real estate for al-Qaeda. The local regimes are weak and ill-equipped to infiltrate and disrupt a major terrorist organization, which can gain recruits because there are so many deep-rooted problems and discontented young men. Russia, while it sees itself as having a rightful and preeminent position in Central Asia, is too poor and distracted (not least by Chechnya) to act as an effective hegemon that offsets the weakness of local regimes by providing reliable security. And, in any event, intervention by Russia or another European state could improve the recruitment prospects of radical Islamist movements who can portray it as part of the infidels' war against Islam.

What is worse, these sources of instability are structural: that is, they cannot be made to attenuate, let alone disappear, rapidly because they flow from deeper historical, political, and economic forces. They are not the product of transitory influences such as election results, commodity prices, or bad weather. In addition, they have a pernicious synergy that will generate instability for years to come. In theory, the United States could wash its hands of such a perilous region and avoid entrapment by doing so; in practice, having established a strategic position in Central Asia following 9/11, it cannot easily quit when the going gets rough—unless it wants al-Qaeda to reconstitute its central apparatus of command in this proximate, porous setting, to plan acts of terror from there, and to use it to subvert the Kabul and Islamabad governments. The United States and its allies manifestly do not want any of these outcomes.

The third circumstance that helps us understand the strategic environment that the West faces in Central Asia is the atrophy of Russian power, something I have already alluded to. While Russian nationalists are incensed that America has ensconced itself in the only region where Russia could claim hegemony, Russia is in no position to take on the job of stabilizing a Central Asia that could face upheaval and become the operating zone for a major terrorist organization like al-Qaeda. What this means is that the option of waging the war on terrorism while subcontracting Central Asian security to the Russians is not a viable one for the United States and its allies. Nor would most Central Asian states welcome such an arrangement for fear that Moscow would use the cover of partnership with the West and the legitimacy of a division of labor in the war against terrorism to construct hegemony from the ruins of empire. That Russia is bound to fail in this endeavor by virtue of its weakness comes as cold comfort to Central Asians. By contrast, America and Western Europe, in Central Asian minds, are geographical and historically distant. Moreover, with their wealth and technology, they have much more to offer than Russia, which promises hegemony with few offsetting gains. There is, therefore, no comparable Central Asian animus toward the West (although that could change if the United States and its allies become enmeshed in the region). The reason is that, unlike Russia, the United States and Western European states never ruled the region. For Central Asians, one of the appeals of a strategic alignment with the West is that it is a way to loosen Russia's 150-year embrace.

With its geographical proximity, plethora of vital interests, and historic familiarity with Central Asia, Russia can be a valuable complement to American strategy, but it cannot supplant the United States or substitute for its labors. Russian President Vladimir Putin, a man who detests fighting the inevitable and is adept at turning necessity into acts of statesmanship, has (reluctantly) come to terms with this reality for now, even if all his fellow citizens have not.

Russia is left with two choices in Central Asia. The first is to oppose and subvert a Western emplacement in its long-time sphere of influence, even if that means making Central Asia a source of friction with the United States—an outcome that could adversely affect Russia's prospects for building closer ties with Western Europe (although a Western Europe-Russian alignment against the United States cannot be ruled out). The second is to accept the diminution of its power and to develop a long-term and cooperative relationship with the United States and Western Europe in Central Asia based on a common interest in creating stability and extirpating terrorism. Russia's calculation in the latter instance would be that widening and deepening the agenda of cooperation with the West will slowly alter the political-psychological aura of its relationship with the United States and Western Europe so that Cold War legacies and suspicions on both sides are buried and Russia receives tangible gains—in the economic and security realms—down the road. In short, it means using the Western entry into Central Asia as an opportunity rather than seeing it as a threat.

Russia's Worries: What the West Can Do

In the abstract, it would seem axiomatic that Russia should make the second of the choices just mentioned. But the prospect of an entrenched American-led Western military presence in Central Asia proper (and, to a lesser extent, in the South Caucasus) evokes apprehension in Russia for at least four reasons. The first stems from simple geographical realities. Central Asia is connected directly to Russian territory; what happens in that region—be it the drug trade, the operations of criminal syndicates, ethnic wars, or upheaval created by radical Islamist movements—cannot be, and in the minds of Russian strategists is not, seen as separate from Russian's politics and national security. Russia is heir to the continental empire forged by the Romanov tsars and, unlike the European maritime imperial powers (Britain, France, Belgium, Portugal), cannot disengage in the face of upheaval that proves unmanageable. Nor can Russia retreat to the homeland as the United States did in Vietnam in 1975. Central Asia may matter to the West now; but to Russia, it will matter forever: geography and history have decreed this. And because of the legacy of the Cold War, Russians will not quickly and easily take the view that Western aims in Central Asia are benign and beneficial to Russia.

Second, Russia has dominated Central Asia for 150 years. Even after the end of empire, the marks of empire remain. Some 20 million ethnic Russians live in the region (particularly in Kazakhstan, where they make up a third of the population and in Kyrgyzstan, where they account for a quarter); there are numerous north-south links, whether roads, railway lines, and energy pipelines; military installations; and Central Asia's ruling elite is still more at home in Russian than in their indigenous languages, even though the latter are now in vogue thanks to post-independence nationalism. Aside from propinquity therefore Russia has many stakes and a deep historical footprint in Central Asia—and that makes retreating inward infeasible. The question for Russia is not whether to remain engaged in the area, but how, with whom, and to what end?

Third, Russians of all political persuasions realize that all facets of Russia's power have atrophied. In such circumstances, the erosion of Russian influence in Central Asia, the sole remaining region in which Moscow can claim predominance, adds to the angst created by declining power and stature—all the more so when the reason for the accelerating loss of influence is an expanding American presence. Whatever the intentions behind Western military deployments in Central Asia, they will be received suspiciously by Russians given the state of their country, the imbalance in power between it and the West, and the baggage of the Cold War. Retreating from, or playing second fiddle in, Central Asia will seem like yet another installment in the ongoing saga of their homeland's loss of power and stature. Americans caught up in the triumphal "unipolar moment" may find this hard to understand, but that does not mean it is any less important.

Fourth, Russians view the American military presence in Central Asia, a projection of power onto Russia's doorstep, within a broader strategic context, not as a single event. It is, to them, part of a pattern that includes the expansion of NATO (which has even incorporated the Baltic states), moves to turn Caspian energy pipelines westward and thus away from Russia, and the Bush administration's determination to build strategic missile defense (with or without Russian consent) if need be by opting out of the Anti-Ballistic Missile treaty. One need not be a Russian given to conspiracy theories to wonder whether there is a larger design at play.

Therefore, no amount of verbal assurances about the well-meaning and constructive intent guiding Western policy in Central Asia will cut ice with Moscow. The effects of the Western emplacement in Central Asia on Russian politics and foreign policy will depend not on what is said by Washington, but on what is done. What is said is not unimportant, however, and a cost-free and easy step that the United States and its allies can take is to ensure through public pronouncements and private diplomacy that the West realizes how and why Central Asia matters to Russia and that it is prepared to work with Russia to develop avenues for cooperation on the many common goals that both sides have in Central Asia and its immediate environs.

The nature of Western policy in Central Asia (or any other region for that matter) will hardly determine Russia's political trajectory, and assertions that Russian democracy's fate hinges on Western policies are both naïve and narcissistic. Yet the way in which the West deals with Russia can shape that country's internal balance of forces; the cumulative effect on elite and mass opinion in Russia of Western words and deeds is significant enough to warrant care. The balance of forces within states, as Otto Hintze among others has stressed and history has demonstrated time and again, is shaped by the strategic environment. And while Russia's strategic environment depends on many things, one of them is certainly what the West does in regions that are critical to Russian national security.

Beyond declarative diplomacy, there is much more that can be done to fashion a Western policy for Central Asia in cooperation with Russia and in ways that are regular and supported by institutions meant to promote consultation and joint efforts. There are, moreover, good reasons why such an approach will prove mutually beneficial:

- The United States and its allies are newcomers to Central Asia and the experience and expertise that they can muster is limited. Yet, for reasons noted in the next section, this region is littered with traps and minefields; it would be foolish not to tap into Russia's far more extensive knowledge of the region's history and strategic terrain.
- Central Asia is a good place to inaugurate a post–Cold War relationship with Russia that rests on mutual security and joint problem solving. Central Asia's major problems—potential separatist and irredentist conflicts, millenarian Islamist movements, terrorist networks, the narcotics trade, and the security of energy infrastructure—threaten Western and Russian security, and neither side, even the West, has the wherewithal to address them independently and unilaterally.
- It now appears that the United States is in for a long stay in Central Asia. But, given its military commitments elsewhere and the possibilities of war in other parts of the world (the Middle East and the Korean peninsula come to mind), a partnership with Russia is a hedge against overextension and unexpected

contingencies. If the United States is forced to redeploy the forces it now has in Central Asia to other turbulent locales, it makes sense to have in place a security arrangement with Russia so that the region does not face a security vacuum and U.S. forces are not stretched too thinly.

- Training and reequipping Central Asian police and military forces are best carried out in cooperation with Russia. The language barrier can be overcome that way. The training and force structure of regional military and security forces have been shaped by the Soviet legacy such that building from an existing foundation, rather than starting from scratch, is more efficient and less expensive. Moreover, training and modernization programs that are funded by the West but that involve Russian personnel and equipment could play a small role in ameliorating the Russian military's penury and demoralization, which are themselves threats to Russia's nascent democracy.
- At the end of the day, the United States is far removed from Central Asia and, if the antiterrorist war winds down, it will have few compelling reasons to remain in Central Asia. Russia, by contrast, will always have major interests in Central Asia, and the region's regimes are fated to deal with Moscow. Thus a Western policy in Central Asia that bypasses Russia, gives it little more than a token role, or seeks to marginalize it, is shortsighted because it will make the states of Central Asia less, not more, secure. Even if Russia's current weakness limits its ability to compete with the United States and its allies for positive influence in Central Asia, Russia's ability to exert negative influence, to act as a spoiler, is considerable.

On Tails Wagging Dogs and Other Hazards

The shock of September 11 pushed the United States and its allies into Central Asia with a speed and resolve that no one imagined (though many will doubtless claim now to have foreseen), and Central Asia's leaders eased the entrée by throwing down the welcome mat. They have compelling reasons to draw the United States and its allies in deeper, to pump up Central Asia's value in the fight against terrorism, and to try and ensure that we do not simply use them and depart, leaving them to contend with the messy aftermath. In short, the flip side of Western engagement in Central Asia is entrapment. And multilateral approaches to regional security, ones that feature active Russian participation in their design and implementation, are a way to reduce its risks and costs.

At the head of the welcoming line was Uzbekistan, which long peddled the idea that it is the natural strategic partner for the United States—partly to counter Russian influence, partly to acquire the legitimacy and resources needed to further its self-image of being Central Asia's natural leader. Karimov's sales pitch made little headway for many reasons. But 9/11 brightened his fortunes; ironically, militant Islam, which Karimov has used to justify his slow but steady strangulation of civil society and democracy (both had weak roots in any event), has, in the form of al-Qaeda, been Karimov's unwitting ally: it raised Uzbekistan's strategic value to the United States. When asked what the United States can gain by aligning with him, Karimov now has a compelling answer; he can also expect his undemocratic regime to be viewed with even greater tolerance.

The main reason is that Islamist movements will be even more prominent in Central Asia's political landscape. (Recall the earlier discussion about the pernicious synergy among poverty, the vacuum in values, the lack of opportunities for political participation, and demographic trends.) That will help Karimov to strengthen ties with the United States. But even Uzbeks who favor Karimov's gambit do not want to become the lightning rod for wrathful Islamists, to be condemned for consorting with the gendarme of *Dar al-Harb*, to be left defenseless and in an even more vulnerable state because the United States conducts the military equivalent of a stopover in Central Asia. The same calculation applies to Kyrgyzstan and Tajikistan, which have also put their military bases at the West's disposal. Given the vulnerability of Central Asian regimes to militant Islam and the importance of Islamic radicalism in Russian conceptualizations of security, a long-term Western policy toward Central Asia should be crafted together with Russia. A joint policy—but one that does not endorse or facilitate a Russian sphere of influence in the region—toward radical Islamist movements would be an opportunity to show in concrete terms that Russian and Western security interests do converge and that the West's goal is not to evict Russia from Central Asia.

Rivalries within Central Asia will also induce local regimes to draw the United States and its allies into a long-term commitment. The idea that Uzbekistan could be the principal beneficiary of September 11 in Central Asia is unpalatable to Kazakhstan, but it is downright frightening to Kyrgyzstan and Tajikistan. Both are weak states that have experienced Uzbekistan's budding hegemony in the form of unauthorized military exercises on their soil, suspensions of gas supplies, and various forms of interference in their internal affairs. The best way for them to counter Uzbek dominance is to sign on to the U.S. war on terrorism and to leverage their strategic value to obtain U.S. commitments and resources to counterbalance Tashkent. The point is not that the Central Asian states are not fearful about the Islamic Movement of Uzbekistan, Hizb ut-Tahrir al-Islami, and al-Qaeda. They are—and for good reasons—but that in no way precludes their pulling the United States into their neighborhood for reasons that have nothing to do with Islamic radicalism and that flow, rather, from regional rivalries.

A regional arrangement that fosters joint approaches to security and creates a system of confidence-building measures could also help reduce the likelihood of regional conflicts. Because Russia is part of the Central Asian strategic landscape, any effective regional security system must draw Moscow in. Russia can help create a more stable regional balance because of the influence it has with Kazakhstan and Kyrgyzstan, with which it has deep and strengthening economic and security ties. Russia can also reassure weaker states that would-be regional hegemons will be unable to act with impunity and trample the interest of smaller states. By undertaking military-to-military contacts and joint military exercises and by pursuing "confidence-building measures" within a multilateral framework, the West can also reduce the mistrust that the Uzbeks in particular feel toward Russia. A Russian role in Central Asia that is played out alongside the West will be much more reassuring to Central Asians.

The dangers that entrapment poses for the United States and its allies in Central Asia should be clear by now. Over the next decade (i.e., before 2013), the actuarial process (if nothing else) will bring about political successions in every Central Asian state, and there is no guarantee that they will be peaceful, and it is quite likely that they will not. This not only makes Central Asia's political ground shaky; it also poses the risk that the United States and its Western allies could be sucked into local power struggles—not because we want to, but because we will have acquired stakes that may have to be defended. This pattern will hardly be unfamiliar to those who have considered the history of Western involvement in other regions. A go-it-alone Western approach in Central Asia—one that is not coordinated with Russia—will make entrapment more likely and more costly.

The economic and social conditions of Central Asia that were mentioned earlier make it quite likely that radical Islamist movements (it should be stressed here that fundamentalism is only one of several ways in which Islam and politics mix) will be among the forces that mobilize people politically. The West (with Britain being an exception) is not well equipped to walk through the minefield given its limited experience in Central Asia. Its knowledge of the region is slim: there are few American or European experts who have spent considerable time in the regions (I mean doing fieldwork and living in the region for prolonged periods rather than consorting with ruling elites during brief visits), who know the local languages, or who are not intellectual arrivistes that descended on the region seeking fresh pastures after the collapse of the Soviet Union. A generation of younger, well-qualified Western experts is emerging, but that will take time. Moreover, access to policy makers will continue to favor better-connected senior experts, knowledge and influence being separate attributes. None of this means that the United States and its allies should flee Central Asia; it does mean that our leaders need a clear picture of the hazards that accompany our deepening involvement. That awareness will grow with time, but it can also be fostered by working with Russia and resisting the temptation to sideline it.

Policy Assumptions and Recommendations: Central Asia

- The West, led by the United States, should cooperate with Russia to promote an environment in Central Asia that is more stable and better defended against the ravages of terrorism. Citizens in the West, Russia, and Central Asia should be made to understand that such cooperation is not equivalent to allowing Russia to determine, much less veto, the means and ends of Western policy, but rather, a way to make Western policy more effective.

- A cooperative approach would acknowledge Russia's vital interests in Central Asia; it would seek to benefit from Russia's special knowledge of this part of the world; and it should build on the security concerns shared by Russia and the West to facilitate collective action, to reduce the burdens and dangers of unilateralism for the West, and to foster a new post–Cold War relationship that alters the pattern of zero-sum competition between Russia and the West.
- Cooperation with Russia should take diverse forms and it should be a long-term endeavor. It should involve intelligence sharing on problems ranging from terrorism to narcotics trafficking and money-laundering; regional confidence building and security arrangements; regular and institutionalized consultations between the West, Russia, and Central Asia at the ministerial level; programs for training and reequipping Central Asian security and military forces; and regular NATO–Russia consultations (which have expanded since 9/11) on Central Asian security that draw Russia into cooperative approaches so that its role in NATO is substantive rather than symbolic.
- Military-to-military contacts between Russia and NATO states should give explicit attention to the exchange of views on Central Asia. This would reduce the distrust that the West's recent strategic emplacement in Central Asia has created in the Russian armed forces and increase the awareness that the West is mindful that both Russian interests in Central Asia and emerging threats in the region affect Western interests.
- Multilateral (NATO–Russia–Central Asia) task forces should be formed to fashion joint policies and institutional (rather than intermittent and ad hoc) responses to terrorism; the drug trade; organized crime; the security of energy installations; and smuggling involving the raw materials, expertise, or parts needed to make weapons of mass destruction. The goal should be to create (slowly) the architecture needed for a multilateral and comprehensive approach to security that breaks with Cold War postulates and practices.
- A multilateral (NATO–Russia–Central Asia) organization should be established to promote the coordination of intelligence and the training of forces geared toward combating terrorism, and joint operations should become a routine practice.
- The living conditions, equipment, and morale of Russian border guards serving on the Tajik–Afghan border should be bolstered through Western assistance as part of a larger effort to improve local responses to regional security. Russian units should ultimately share responsibilities with Western forces for guarding the Afghan border, and with Central Asian units that gradually acquire the capacity to assume the principal burden. The same approach can be adopted toward the recent Russian decision to deploy security forces in Kyrgyzstan at the base in Kant: these Russian units should be joined by Western and Central Asian forces to make the operations originally envisaged multilateral.

Extending Cooperation to greater Central Asia

By this point in the discussion it should be obvious that the traditional conception of Central Asia—the five post-Soviet "-stans"—is outmoded.[5] It may once have been convenient to treat Central Asia as a self-contained region, but it is less and less appropriate now that the fate of the region is connected in so many ways to what happens in Afghanistan and Pakistan. The spirit of the cooperative proposals outlined here should, therefore, be carried over into a "greater Central Asia" where Russia and the West have several common interests, among them: preventing the fragmentation of a nuclear-armed Pakistan; rooting out al-Qaeda facilities and operations in Afghanistan and Pakistan; creating an Afghanistan that, at long last, settles into a life free of war, terrorism, and warlordism; preventing an India-Pakistan confrontation over Kashmir; disrupting the financial operations of terrorist networks and the flow of weapons in and through Afghanistan and Pakistan.

The scope for including Russia in a collaborative scheme for greater Central Asia is more limited than in the case of Central Asia proper. There is much mistrust between Russia and Pakistan, and it is not clear what Russia can offer to alleviate Pakistan's urgent economic problems. But Russian cooperation is certainly required for realizing plans, which have been resurrected now with the demise of the Taliban, for a gas pipeline from Turkmenistan's Daulatabad fields to Pakistan's coast through Afghanistan. And if the line were extended to supply the Indian market, it would constitute a small step toward recasting the India-Pakistan relationship. Since Russia's policy has been to bottle up Turkmenistan's gas exports (by limiting access to Russian-controlled pipelines that run to Europe and thus forcing Turkmenistan to export gas to cash-strapped Ukraine and Georgia), Moscow would not necessarily welcome the trans-Afghanistan pipeline project. But its assessment could be changed by giving Russian companies a role in constructing the pipeline. Were an international force needed to protect construction routes—pipeline construction is a distinct prospect given Afghanistan's instability—Russian forces could be included. They could be deployed, together with units from NATO, in sectors just south of the Turkmenistan-Afghanistan border, where, unlike in the eastern and southern (predominantly Pushtun) parts of Afghanistan, a Russian military presence would be more politically acceptable.

The prospects for stability and the war on terrorism in greater Central Asia depend greatly on whether Pakistan can avoid plunging into anarchy. That disastrous outcome could occur in many ways, but one would be as a consequence of an India–Pakistan war over Kashmir that results in Pakistan's defeat and humiliation. While India would resist internationalizing the Kashmir dispute—which Pakistan claims as the nub of the core of the problem between it and India—there are steps that can be promoted by the United States and its NATO allies to reduce the risk of war in South Asia even if the Kashmir problem remains unresolved. They include increasing bilateral political contacts (to build on the promising developments in this field that began in the spring of 2003), increasing economic and cultural exchanges, and exploring confidence-building measures that ease each side's fear about sudden or accidental war, especially one involving nuclear weapons. Even though the United States and India have redefined their testy relationship since the Cold War era and are now embarked on an array of discussions to foster closer cooperation, Russia retains considerable trust in India, particularly on the political left and in national security circles, and could be brought into a Western effort aimed at moving New Delhi and Islamabad toward a more stable relationship.

Finally, the ad hoc consultations between Western and Russian intelligence agencies on Afghanistan and on the links that Islamist movements in Central Asia proper have with organizations in greater Central Asia should be institutionalized and regularized so that they add yet another bit of substance to collaboration in the war on terrorism. There is already a base to build on, but increased cooperation will not occur simply because some joint work has begun.

Conclusion: Knowing the Pitfalls

The proposals made here for cooperation between Russia and the West in greater Central Asia are based on the assumption that there are, in fact, some convergent interests between the two sides in this region. A further assumption is that the process of defining what these convergent interests are and working out together specific and long-term ways in which they have to be moved from plans to practice will itself contribute to replacing the competitive motif of East-West interactions of the Cold War and laying the political and psychological groundwork for a new and productive relationship. These gains are quite separate from the operational questions of who does what with whom and for whose benefit. But if the process of collaboration is not to degenerate into vapid conferences and symbolic contacts, actual collaboration in peacekeeping, intelligence sharing, and planning must start and expand. And the benefits—greater security at a smaller price—must become apparent to both parties, not just to one side.

The collaborative approach suggested here faces at least six obstacles. First, there remains considerable distrust between the national security organizations of East and West, and it is fair to say that such feelings run particularly deep in the Russian military and intelligence agencies. This sentiment has deep roots and will not disappear quickly. It will also remain a formidable barrier to cooperation in greater Central Asia.

Second, economic constraints will limit severely what Russia can contribute in tangible form to some of the cooperative ventures I have mentioned. If the result is that Russia essentially plays a minor or largely symbolic part in collective efforts, it will not attain the security and confidence that come with joining others on an equal footing.

Third, in much of Central Asia the increased role of the West in regional security is seen as a way to reduce dependence on Russia, not to increase Russia's role. The degree of enthusiasm in Central Asia for multilateral approaches to security in which Russia plays a central role will vary. This is not an insurmountable problem, but it needs to be recognized up front.

Fourth, once the actual on-the-ground cooperation begins, the West will have to face the problem posed by the dismal state of the Russian military. Programs will have to be developed—and funded—to ensure that Russian units that work alongside Western ones have the equipment and training they need to do the job.

Fifth, for historical reasons, any direct and visible Russian role in Pakistan and Afghanistan risks the danger of a backlash. It will therefore have to be carefully calibrated and carried out as part of a multilateral venture in which the West participates. (By contrast, in India, which is increasing its profile in Central Asia and whose relationship with Pakistan directly affects the environment in which the war on terrorism will be waged in South and Southwest Asia, the Russian role could be much greater—and more welcome.)

Sixth, the recommendations I have made in this analysis hinge on Russia's political and economic trajectory because they require that there be sufficient political support within Russia for multilateral programs in greater Central Asia and that Russia acquire the economic capacity to make significant contributions. Yet Russia's efforts to expand and consolidate a democratic polity—one based on more than the routine of elections—and a market economy are inherently difficult and therefore also uncertain. If Russia's efforts fail, much of what I have proposed here will prove infeasible—but then the West will have far greater problems to worry about.

Notes

Rajan Menon is Monroe J. Rathbone Professor of International Relations at Lehigh University and a Fellow at the New America Foundation. This chapter is part of a book project supported by a 2002 Carnegie Scholar award from the Carnegie Corporation of New York.

1. Rajan Menon, "The Restless Region: The Brittle States of Central and South Asia," in *How Did This Happen? Terrorism and the New War*, ed. James F. Hoge and Gideon Rose (New York: Public Affairs, 2001), pp. 97–108.

2. Owen Bennet Jones, *Pakistan: Eye of the Storm* (New Haven: Yale University Press, 2002).

3. Robert Ebel and Rajan Menon, eds., *Energy and Conflict in Central Asia and the Caucasus* (Boulder, CO: Rowman & Littlefield, 2000).

4. See Mehrdad Haghayeghi, *Islam and Politics in Central Asia* (New York: St. Martin's Press, 1995); Roald Sagdeev and Susan Eisenhower, eds., *Islam and Central Asia: An Enduring Legacy or an Evolving Threat?* (Washington, DC: Center for Political and Strategic Studies, 2000).

5. See Rajan Menon, "The New Great Game in Central Asia," *Survival* 45, no. 2 (Summer 2003): 187–204.

11

Russia–European Union–Germany
After September 11 and Iraq

Alexander Rahr

Russia's foreign policy seems to be directed toward a fast return to "Western civilization." Russia is focused on quick integration into the World Trade Organization (WTO) and the closest possible partnership with such Western institutions as the European Union (EU) and NATO. Russia needs Western assistance in order to restructure its economy. The question remains whether President Vladimir Putin is a genuine believer in European values or whether he is following a hidden agenda that was once characterized by Tsar Peter the Great as follows: "Today we need Europe to modernize our state and economy, but later we will turn our back on Europe." (A.W. Just, "Russland in Europa," Berlin, 1950, S. 221).

Toward a New World Order

Russia's foreign policy must be evaluated in the context of the dramatic changes in world politics following September 11, 2001 (9/11). The greatest changes in the aftermath of 9/11 occurred in the United States and in U.S. policy versus the world. The events provoked the United States to interfere more vigorously in the process of shaping the world's new order. For the first time since Pearl Harbor, the United States felt vulnerable to outside attack. Over two years, the United States conducted regime changes in two "rogue states" in the Middle East and voiced a strong political intention to revamp the political chart of the Arabic world. The democratization of the Middle East and the fight against worldwide terror will create the foundation of the new world order in the twenty-first century. The stability of the entire world now depends on the success of this policy.

The events of 9/11 gave an additional boost to Europe's search for its own foreign and security agenda. The EU has become heavily involved in strengthening its military component, creating a European army, and addressing perceived threats. The EU is in the middle of discussions about future peace-keeping missions, military interventions in regional conflict areas, and even preemptive strikes against terrorists. The EU is flexing its muscles vis-à-vis the outside world. Russia, which is the EU's strategic partner, seems partly irritated by the EU's striving for military strength and new political ambitions. Moscow tended to view the EU only as an economic alliance, never as a competitor for the role of one of the world's future superpowers. Issues such as Kaliningrad (visa regime), the EU's tough stance, even reluctance, to grant Russia early entry into the WTO, the war in Chechnya, and EU plans to conduct peace-keeping operations on the territory of the former Soviet Union have put Moscow on the defensive vis-à-vis the EU.

Changes have also hit Germany. In 1999, the German public and elites were still protesting against Germany's participation in the Kosovo war. The overall German perception was antiwar and pacifist due to the historical experience of the recent past. Now German troops are fighting in Afghanistan and conducting peace-keeping operations in the Balkans. Germany is regarded as a leading NATO power, almost on a par with the two nuclear European powers, Great Britain and France.

An element of the new world order is, of course, Russia. Thirteen years since the demise of the Soviet Union, Russia is vehemently knocking at Europe's door, demanding full acceptance as a key actor on the European continent. Russia wants to participate in shaping the future European economic and security architecture. It wants to be respected in the same manner as Russia had always been in the course of recent European history since Peter the Great. But since the future of the European continent is being designed on the basis of an EU–Europe, the enlarged EU is not yet prepared to accept Russia in its newly founded family of nations. Russia risks being cut off from the historic integration processes in Europe, which would risk the danger of isolation and, consequently, of a change in the present reform drive toward Western-style reforms.

The World Order After the Iraq War

Germany, France, and Russia created a common alliance against the U.S.-led war in Iraq at the beginning of 2003. Although the tensions were clearly reduced in the aftermath of U.S. victory in the Iraq war, the potential for some sort of resistance to U.S. unilateral policies remains, particularly if U.S. policy in Iraq fails. Germany and Russia, in particular, have improved their relations with the United States. The German Chancellor Gerhard Schröder and Putin share the same view that in the present world a policy directed against the interests of the only superpower—the United States—would be counterproductive and even dangerous. In order to participate in shaping the new world order, full cooperation in the U.S.-led antiterror alliance was necessary. A repetition of a U.S. war without a clear UN mandate against a country like Iran, Syria, or North Korea could, however, prompt criticism and opposition from these three countries. Such an "alliance" in Europe against the United States seemed completely impossible a year ago.

Before the Iraq war, Russia tried all it could to be on the winning side and believed working with the German–French antiwar coalition to be the best way to achieve this goal. Evidently, Russia's priorities no longer lay with the development of the successfully initiated post–September 11 strategic partnership and antiterror coalition with the United States, but rather with the prevention of

America's breakthrough to sole world domination. Russia was executing an increasingly difficult balancing act in the Iraq conflict. On the one hand, Moscow was showing itself as staunchly antiwar, and on the other hand, it was simultaneously making an effort to continue a pragmatic partnership with Washington. The Russian defense minister, Sergei Ivanov, explained that Moscow objected to the Iraq war not for economic reasons, but rather for fear of negative consequences for the global world order. "Saddam is not our friend, nor our brother, and he will never repay us his debts," said Ivanov (*Komsomol'skaia pravda*, April 1, 2003). But for the Russians it was about setting a precedent: "Today the Americans do not like Iraq, tomorrow Syria, then Iran, North Korea, and finally, what—all the rest?"

According to critical voices in Russia, Putin's turn toward the Americans after September 11 did initially allow Moscow to envisage the unique perspective of a new historic and strategic partnership with the United States. But afterward, the American side did not keep its promise. The United States Congress has not lifted the ominous Jackson-Vanik clause, a remnant of the Cold War that imposes trade restrictions on Russia, despite George W. Bush's personal intervention. It was the British, not the Americans, who with BP made the largest foreign investment in Russia this year. The highly praised American–Russian energy alliance exists for the time being only on paper and is forcing Russian oligarchs to turn their sights in the direction of Asian markets once again.

For many liberal politicians, however, the Russian position in the antiwar coalition against the Americans was too aggressive. According to them, the openly displayed *Schadenfreude* over the Americans' military problems at the very beginning of the war in Iraq was damaging to Russia's long-term national interests. In the *Moscow Times*, the political scientist Andrei Piontkovskii asked what Russia would gain from an American failure, which according to surveys had been hoped for by 80 percent of the population. Were Iraq to win, contrary to expectations, the danger of Islamic fundamentalism would increase, particularly for a country like Russia, weapons of mass destruction (WMD) would be aimed at Russia, America would devote itself to isolationism, and the vacuum in world politics would be filled not by Russia, but by China. Other Moscow liberals questioned whether Putin's "foreign-policy revolution," which he carried out after September 11, 2001, through swift accession to the American antiterror coalition, turned out in retrospect to be nothing more than tactical finesse to strengthen Russia's status in world politics with America's help in the short term, in order later, heeding its own reflexes and xenophobia, to continue to develop Russia's superpower position again through a rivalry with America.

Hardly noticed by the outside world, shortly before the start of the Iraq war, two important events took place in Russian domestic policy, which also left their mark on Putin's behavior. In Russia, the power constellation changed through government restructuring. The Federal Security Service (FSB)—the former Committee for State Security (KGB)— acquired the position of power it had in Soviet times by amalgamating other services. The Ministry of the Interior was also politically fortified.

The strengthening of "the Putin system" before the presidential elections in 2004 continues (see the most recent study on Russia by Deutsche Bank Research). Russian intelligence services, which are taking part in creating Russian foreign policy as at no time before in Russian history, were never supporters of Putin's turn toward George W. Bush. The oligarchs, who have lately been actively calling for an orientation toward America, have been weakened.

The second significant event was the referendum in the Chechen Republic, by means of which Russia is trying once and for all to legitimize its second Chechen campaign. The Russian government assessed the voting at the end of March as broad Chechen approval of remaining in the Russian Federation. As both the EU and the United States acknowledged the referendum, Moscow felt strengthened to repudiate future criticism of its treatment of the Chechen problem, and that at a time when America in bombing Baghdad and setting up internment camps was applying the same tactics in the Iraq war as Russia is in the Chechen war.

Both developments strengthened not the liberal, but rather the great power politicians in the Kremlin. For the latter it was humiliating to be condemned to insignificance, while the former archrival, the United States, enlarged its position of power in world politics by means of a war. Putin may have felt that he had moved too far away from his establishment's traditionally critical views of America and that a stubbornly continued pro-American course during an unpopular war could maneuver him into dangerous isolation on the domestic front. Some Western and Russian observers believed that during his term of office Putin had already taken enough revolutionary steps in the politics of his country, such as the legalization of private property and the recently begun communal reform, to name two. He did not want to take any unnecessary risks so soon before the presidential elections and in an election campaign likely to play on antiwar sentiments, which helped his political partner Gerhard Schröder to election victory in Germany.

The Path to an Antiwar Coalition

Until Putin's trip to Berlin and Paris in February 2003, it seemed as if Russia, in view of the advantages awarded by the strategic partnership with America in the international antiterror coalition, would not make use of its veto in a vote on the Iraq war in the UN Security Council. The Bush administration was sure that the perspectives of cooperation in the newly created NATO–Council of 20 in a global energy alliance (which was to replace OPEC), as well as in controlling the nonproliferation of WMD, were more important for Putin than the risk of confrontation over Saddam Hussein. With satisfaction, Washington took note at the end of January 2003 that Putin, during his trip to Kyiv, had warned the Iraqi dictator about obstructing the work of the UN inspectors.

However, in February 2003, Schröder and Jacques Chirac of France managed to win Putin over to a common antiwar stance. In Berlin, Putin was still warning of anti-American sentiments in Europe, but it was from French soil that he first threatened the Americans openly with a veto. At the end of February, Moscow, having previously been rather passive in the Iraq question, developed a lively diplomacy. The Kremlin sent the former prime minister and head of intelligence services, Evgenii Primakov, on a secret mission to Baghdad, as during the first Gulf War twelve years earlier. Presumably Primakov was to discover under what circumstances the dictator would go into exile or accept an increased UN inspector regime for his country.

At the same time, Putin sent his influential head of the presidential administration, Aleksandr Voloshin, to Washington, where he met with the American leadership. According to Kremlin adviser Sergei Karaganov, Voloshin, who is higher placed in the Kremlin hierarchy than the foreign minister, Igor Ivanov, was to assure the Americans of Putin's interest in a continued pragmatic partnership in the world after the Iraq war. Moscow feared incurring greater losses for its own economy as a result of the war: oil prices would drop in the long term, Russia would lose the oil-production and industry-delivery contract that it had signed with Saddam Hussein, and, all in all, Russia's losses due to a regime change in Baghdad would amount to US$48 billion (*Nezavisimaia gazeta*, March 27, 2003).

Besides Voloshin, the chairman of the Foreign Affairs Committee of the Federal Council, Mikhail Margelov, attempted at the end of February 2003 in Washington to win support for the continued existence of the antiterror coalition in the Middle East, also involving the NATO–Council of 20. Meanwhile, Schröder came to Moscow on a quick visit, in order to continue working on Putin in person to take the antiwar course, for the French were becoming skeptical about Putin's true position and feared a change of heart. Simultaneously, in Beijing, Foreign Minister Ivanov tried to convince the Chinese to move toward a veto-wielding stance as well, so that Moscow did not run the risk of standing on its own with its objection in the Security Council. Finally, the chairman of the Duma's Foreign Committee, Dmitrii Rogozin, traveled to Berlin to assess the German antiwar stance. The Kremlin could not resist the temptation to join the surprisingly open German–French antiwar front against the archrival United States.

Russia at the Lead of the Antiwar Coalition

In the Kosovo war, Boris Yeltsin formed the sole opposition to the war in the UN Security Council, which in turn led to Russia's fatal self-isolation. After the Kosovo war, Russia was not even assigned its own sector in the international peace-keeping mission. In the Iraq war, Putin managed, with the help of Germany and France, to isolate America in the Security Council. Spurred on by traditionalists in the Kremlin, he may have dreamed of installing, in the future, together with the two strongest powers of the old continent, a regime of "soft containment" of the United States.

Specifically, Russia, alongside Germany and France, wants to work toward strengthening the UN Security Council in the world order after the Iraq war, in order to prevent the United States, by means of the UN, from unilaterally controlling Iraq, as well as to take advantage of its own economic interests in Iraq. Furthermore, on the European continent, Russia wants to work toward weakening NATO as well as strengthening the independent European Security and Defense Policy, which would include Russia's participation. Moscow's calculation is as follows: as a consequence of a longer U.S.- and U.K.-led war, hostilities would become so extensive, that the entire Arabic world could revolt against the war coalition. The Americans may have proved victorious in the disempowerment of Saddam, but Russia could pocket the peace dividend. Should Russia, together with France, Germany, China, and other members of the Security Council, nevertheless manage, against the will of the Americans, to gain a foothold economically after the end of the war and take over the peacekeeping with their own UN peace keeping troops, the coup would be perfectly executed. In these endeavors, Russia counted on having Germany and France by its side, or else the change of course would be senseless. The German chancellor's speech on the Iraq crisis at the beginning of April at the Bundestag strengthened Putin in this belief.

But has this change in course actually taken place? While Foreign Minister Ivanov was attacking America, Putin did not want a conflict with the United States. On April 3 in Tambov, he declared that he would remain in the antiterror coalition with the United States. A failure of the United States in Iraq would have devastating consequences for the Russian economy. Putin stressed that the United States and Russia, being nuclear powers, had the responsibility to secure stability in the world. Previously, the United States accused Russia of having supported Saddam Hussein with military supplies, in disregard of UN sanctions. Moscow sharply repudiated the accusations. The leadership of the Federal Council and the Duma, which are under control of the Kremlin, initially did not allow a conviction of the United States in their chambers, but the Duma nevertheless did not ratify the new nuclear disarmament treaty with the United States.

The Iraq War Divides the Commonwealth of Independent States

The Iraq war not only divided the UN Security Council, NATO, and the EU, but the Commonwealth of Independent States (CIS) as well. Some Caucasian and Central Asian countries, as well as Ukraine, envisaged an opportunity to open the door to NATO by swearing allegiance to Washington. The political elite of these countries sees the United States, rather than Russia, as their future protecting power, despite the fact that Putin in past months had initiated an economic union with some of the countries willing to reintegrate, among them Ukraine, and had also revived the collective defense alliance of the CIS, which was considered dead, with its central command in Moscow.

At the end of February 2003, Russia, Belarus, Kazakhstan, and Ukraine signed a declaration on the creation of a common economic union in Novo Ogarevo near Moscow, where back in 1991, the transformation of the Soviet Union into a confederation was decided. According to the heads of state who signed the declaration, it is supposed to "become the highest level of integration in all post-Soviet history" (*Ukrains'ka*, February 23, 2003). Earlier, Putin managed to transfer the presidency of the CIS Council to the Ukrainian president, Leonid Kuchma, and thus bind Ukraine closer to the community.

Foreign Minister Ivanov particularly praised two achievements of Russian foreign policy of the past year in an article in *Rossiiskaia gazeta* (December 30, 2002); the new strategic partnership with the United States; and the reinforcement of the Shanghai Organization for Cooperation (ShOS), in which Russia, China, Kazakhstan, Kyrgyzstan, and Tajikistan fight side by side against Islamic fundamentalism. The latter is meant to promote Russia's integration in Asian security policy structures. Moscow has been lobbying for a long time for India and Pakistan to join the alliance. That would allow Moscow to strengthen its role as middleman in the Indian-Pakistani conflict. At the end of February 2003, during his visit to China, Ivanov declared the ShOS "a crucial supporting pillar of a future multipolar world order,"(Russian Federation Embassy in China, February 27, 2003) as an important partner of the UN in the international fight against terrorism. Should the ShOS, according to Ivanov, become a new edition of Primakov's triangle "Moscow–Beijing–New Delhi," besides the European axis "Berlin–Paris–Moscow," an Asian component of the policy of "soft containment" of the United States?

With some suspicion, Russia has observed that the U.S. military bases in Central Asia, which were used on a short-term basis for the war against the Taliban and al-Qaeda in Afghanistan, were not shut down after completion of the successful military operation, but rather have settled in the region. In the meantime, Moscow was able to break Kyrgyzstan and Tajikistan partly out of the American alliance. On the Iraq question, Bishkek and Dushanbe supported Moscow's stance. Russia has now stationed its own military units in Kyrgyzstan. Attempts by Russia to undermine U.S. cooperation with strategically important Uzbekistan have failed. The United States "compensated" Uzbekistan with $200 million, which Russia could not pay. Meanwhile, the United States has reinforced its presence in Georgia, where it is training Georgian Special Forces for the fight against terrorism. To Moscow's indignation, American spy planes are patrolling the Georgian-Russian border. In the Kremlin it is feared that in a possible conflict over the rebel Republic of Abkhazia, the United States might help Georgia and thus become drawn into direct confrontation with Russia.

This turmoil could have fatal consequences for the sensitive oil region of the Caspian Sea. In the past year it seemed as if Russians and Americans had renounced the so-called Great Game and wanted to jointly establish this region as an alternative to oil deliveries from the Persian Gulf. As a result of the Iraq war, the American–Russian rivalries in the Caucasus and in Central Asia could once again vehemently come into play, much to the regret of Europeans.

Russia's Policy Toward the European Union

Putin's first tenure as president has ended. His presidency has been marked by success. The West applauds Russia's economic performance. A liberal reform program has been gradually introduced. From the point of view of internal stability, Russia is a different country than the one Putin inherited from Yeltsin in 1999. In foreign policy, Russia has partly returned to the so-called Kozyrev era (1990–1994), which was characterized by a close and trustful partnership with the West. Russia has accepted America's dominant role in world politics and is prepared—for the time being—to play the role of junior partner in order to play in the first league of world politics. However, Putin succeeded in safeguarding some of Russia's essential national interests and did not surrender his foreign policy agenda entirely to the United States. Russia has regained its second rank on the world's international arms market and continues—despite U.S. criticism—to cooperate on nuclear issues with Iran. Russia continues to promote the idea of reintegration in the post-Soviet space—a policy that always raises Western suspicion about the Kremlin's true intentions.

Putin's foreign policy follows two goals, which sometimes seem to contradict each other. On the one hand, Russia demonstrates its intentions to integrate with the West. On the other hand, Putin seeks to revive Russia's great power status. Should Russia use its new economic potential to boost its geopolitical ambitions, he might collide with Western interests very soon. So far, Putin has attempted to combine his two priorities in one single strategy, which he successfully sells to the West. The creation of the common economic space with Ukraine, Kazakhstan, and Belarus is being presented as an effort to build an "EU–East" to facilitate the CIS countries' cooperation with the EU.

When Putin came to power, he conducted enormous efforts to improve Russia's relations with the European Union. At the beginning of his presidency he even sent signals of his country's desire for membership in NATO and the EU, causing a stir in the West. Concrete and pragmatic talks with the EU focused on the creation of "common spaces"—in the economic, cultural, informational, and security fields. The talk of "common spaces" substituted for the idea of EU membership, which the West could not offer to Russia. Putin used the economic partnership agenda to foster Russia's integration into the world economy.

The events of 9/11 provided Putin with the unique chance to switch tactics. Integration with the West could now be achieved not through an economic angle but by following a clear security agenda. While having a hard time convincing the EU of the necessity to integrate Russia's economic potentials with those of Europe, particularly in the energy sector, Putin could now portray his country as an indispensable ally for the United States in fighting the new global threats. Through security and intelligence cooperation with the United States, Putin strengthened his country's geopolitical ambitions.

While the U.S.–Russia security agenda increasingly improved, EU–Russia relations suffered some heavy blows. Issues such as Kaliningrad or the failure to start a Russian–European energy dialogue became serious barriers to rapprochements. Russia must have felt a psychological problem emerging in its dealings with the Europeans. EU expansion, which began with the widening of the Schengen zone deep into Eastern Europe, may soon be perceived in Russia as more harmful to Russian interests than NATO expansion. In Soviet times, Moscow could not care less about the EU. In the 1990s, Russia learned to regard the EU as an economic power. Now, since the EU started flexing its political and military muscles, speaking with Russia from a position of strength, pushing forward ideas of an international court on Chechnya, and resurrecting the visa barrier along Russia's western borders, Russia has begun to understand that the EU may soon become a strong competitor for superpower status in world politics, too.

The future of Russian–EU relations will also be determined in Brussels. The EU must choose whether to keep a low partnership profile only in areas where cooperation is absolutely necessary, while in reality keeping Russia at a distance. Or it may choose the strategy of incorporating Russia into Western structures. A historical opportunity to follow the latter course exists. Even a change in the composition of the Duma will not seriously change Putin's foreign policy. The crucial moment will come after Putin steps down—in 2008. Then it will be important to have a successor in the Kremlin who will follow Putin's policy for another eight years—until 2016. By that time, Russia may have met the conditions required to become a member of the present EU and NATO.

Germany–Russia: A Solid Strategic Partnership

Germany plays a key role in Russia's foreign policy strategy. In 2003, two German–Russian summits were held: in April in Saint Petersburg and in October in Ekaterinburg. On both occasions, it was stated that the relations between the two countries "had never been so good in the past 100 years." Germany remains Russia's main strategic partner for the country's integration with the West, despite Putin's obvious foreign policy priority shift from the European Union toward the United States after 9/11. Germany is Russia's key foreign trade partner outside the CIS. Germany may even become a strategic partner, whom Russia would like to see as an ally not only in European but also in global affairs. In turn, the German business community has finally discovered Russia as a lucrative investment market. The improvement of Russia's international credit ranking has accelerated the move of German business to the east.

The present German–Russian relationship is based on a solid foundation that was created back in the 1990s. Germans remain thankful to Russia for Mikhail Gorbachev's stance in favor of German reunification and Boris Yeltsin's quick removal of Soviet troops from East Germany. During the Yeltsin era the economic dividends of the relationship proved greater than the political dividends: besides being the single largest investor in Russia, Germany regularly provided loans to

Moscow, as it had during the Soviet era. Russia does not regard Germany's new assertive foreign policy toward the east as a threat to Russian national interests. Russians do not suspect geopolitical ambitions behind Germany's foreign political agenda vis-à-vis the post-Soviet space. Therefore, Russia has allowed Germany, as the first NATO country, to conduct military transportation over Russian territory into Central Asia and Afghanistan, where German elite forces have been stationed in the war against terrorism.

When Gerhard Schröder assumed office in 1998, he made it clear that his relations with Russia would be measured by Russia's compliance on the foreign debt issue. Since Putin came to power, Russia has punctually cleared its debts toward the Paris and London clubs. By 2003, the largest portion of former Soviet and Russian debt to Germany and other Western countries had been repaid. Moscow had not even asked for a restructuring of the debt. As a result, new trust was built in German–Russian economic relations. Russia has invited German business to participate in some projects that are crucial for the country's revival of energy and transportation. Russia often refers to Europe's growing dependence on Russian mineral fuels.

Schröder and Putin have met more than twenty times in the past four years. The relations between the two politicians have become the driving force behind historical rapprochement of their two countries. Putin enjoys conducting parts of the talks in German, without interpreters or aides, which often infuriates German diplomats and goes against protocol. Since Schröder's relations with the number-one man in the United States remain frosty as a result of German opposition to the U.S. war in Iraq, the chancellor welcomes the opportunity to improve his foreign political standing on the platform of Russian diplomacy. The dramatic changes that have taken place in the first years of the new century in world affairs are characterized by the situation that the Russian president enjoys more trustful, better relations with the U.S. president than the German chancellor does.

Could Germany, together with France, take the lead in creating a common European strategy directed toward a more clear-cut integration of Russia into Europe?

Russian–United States Rivalry over the CIS

The West remains in a certain dilemma toward Putin's second foreign policy priority, namely, the reintegration of the post-Soviet space. The new EU strategy of "direct neighborhood" or "near abroad" (terminology taken over from "imperialist" Russia) translates into a closure of the EU's membership list. The West, on the one hand, exercises pressure on Georgia, Ukraine, Uzbekistan, Azerbaijan, and Moldova (GUUAM), South Caucasus, and the Central Asian states to integrate into regional alliances, but, on the other hand, criticizes Russian attempts to create its own integration structures with immediate neighbors, such as Ukraine.

Obviously, an "EU-East" is unrealistic at the present time. The CIS countries have no common political need to revive a union in the post-Soviet space. All former soviet republics seek integration with Brussels, not with Moscow.

The real struggle on the territory of the former Soviet Union is being fought in the south. The revival of the ancient Silk Road has become the gateway of the Caspian states to the West and to Asia. The United States, the EU, and Asian big powers such as Japan and China share in the enthusiasm about the revival of the Silk Road and have given broad support to one of the most exciting developments in the post-Soviet space. In fact, the Silk Road revival policy has become an essential part of large-scale geopolitical developments in the Caspian region, which has been labeled "the new Great Game." The Great Game, in its modern form, is a fierce competition among regional states, middle, and large powers over control of Caspian Sea strategic assets and rich energy resources.

The main competitors in that Great Game are the United States and Russia. They have opposing goals in the Caspian region. Post-Soviet Russia seeks to restore its hemisphere on the territory of the former Soviet Union. The United States wants to prevent Russia from rebuilding its empire. Tsarist Russia and the Soviet Union had always kept the Caspian region in artificial isolation. Transportation and communication corridors were built only in the north–south direction. Links for the Transcauscasian and Central Asian republics to Europe and Asia through west–east corridors were not constructed.

The United States and Russia have succeeded in forging some coalitions or alliances of countries to foster their goals. The idea of reviving the ancient Silk Road—which is exactly the strategy of creating a west–east corridor—is being whole-heartedly supported by Turkey, the EU, Japan, Pakistan, Ukraine, and other states that have founded the so-called GUUAM alliance. The GUUAM alliance is another "pillar" of the Silk Road revival-strategy.

Russia's alliance looks much weaker than that of the Silk Road revival-group. It consists of Iran and Armenia, and in some aspects Kazakhstan, China, and India. Kazakhstan, China, and India, however, do not support the idea of the Silk Road itself. Their cooperation with Russia is founded on different reasons, mainly common economic and security considerations.

The Great Game has not yet reached its culmination point. The struggle intensifies over future railway, pipe, and communication lines. Different organizations and political structures are emerging throughout the region—each with its special aim in mind: to construct the political, economic, and security infrastructure along either the north–south or the west–east axis. The will of the two opposing actors in the Great Game is manifested through demonstrations of military strength, the fight over military bases, control of peace-keeping missions, border control, and air space control. In future years, the United States and Russia are likely to stage a fierce battle over the succession processes in the Caucasian and Central Asian countries.

The rebirth of the Silk Road requires not only political will but also economic and financial power. Russia has lately succeeded in dramatically improving its economy. President Putin has made Russia again a "bridge" between Europe and

Asia. Goods are again being transferred between the two continents along the Trans-Siberian railroad. The Caucasus and Central Asia risk becoming marginalized as transit countries—the idea of reviving the Silk Road may never be implemented. On the other hand, the Baku–Ceyhan pipeline will soon be constructed. It will be the second pipeline carrying Caspian oil to Western markets, circumventing Russia, and breaking Moscow's monopoly.

In order to better understand the essence of the Great Game it is worthwhile examining the various political, economic, and security organizations that have been created in the region. The organization-building process exceeds even that in the EU. Because Moscow has finally realized that it cannot revive the CIS, it has created several smaller unions within the CIS. The new Common Economic Space is a sort of Eastern EU composed of Ukraine, Kazakhstan, and Belarus. Moscow succeeded in reviving the Collective Defense Treaty—the former Tashkent Treaty involving the CIS countries that did not join the GUUAM alliance. Together with China, Russia has installed working mechanisms for the Shanghai Organization for Cooperation. Together with Kazakhstan, Russian has built a Euro-Asian Union— another counterforce to GUUAM. Russian industrial-financial groups have "invaded" the economies of Caucasian states and essentially of all GUUAM.

However, the United States and the EU have not surrendered their positions on the southern rim of the ex-Soviet space. The ongoing NATO Partnership for Peace Program helps to prepare the necessary conditions for the long-term stationing of Western antiterror forces in the regions. Some observers do not exclude the possibility that America will offer GUUAM quick access to NATO in the next round of NATO expansion.

While in the past year the EU has been overburdened with its inner reform and expansion to East Central Europe, it has lately returned as a potential actor in the Great Game. There are indications that the new European Security and Defense Policy (ESDP) may get oriented in the post-Soviet space. The EU may be willing to take over peace-keeping missions in the autonomous republics of Transdneistr, Abkhazia, and Nagorno-Karabakh. The operations are not likely to be conducted without Moscow's consensus. But the new Western security agenda since 9/11, to which Russia fully adheres, may indeed offer new opportunities. An ESDP engagement in GUUAM would boost the idea of the revival of the Silk Road.

There are two perspectives for the revival of the Silk Road. One is a positive scenario, the other is a negative one. The positive outcome is a successful integration of the Silk Road states into a larger Transatlantic-European community. The security aspects of the integration process will probably prevail over economic considerations. The war against international terrorism will almost certainly continue under George W. Bush or any other U.S. president. The United States will need allies for that task and the present NATO may not be enough. Russia, it seems, has decided to commit itself firmly to the antiterror alliance, following the slogan: "if you can't beat them [the United States and NATO in the Great Game]—join them." Such a development will make the Silk Road an important strategic link between allies in arms and a frontier road at the edge of two civilizations, between the northern and the southern worlds.

The negative scenario is the open outbreak of conflicts between the United States and Russia along the Silk Road, the consequences of which would be unforeseen and could even end in the establishment of new nuclear powers, such as Iran, in the region. Failure to make the Silk Road a peaceful path toward stability would lead to the incursion of Islamic extremist forces into the entire region. The present example of Iraq—which has become a failed state where control may end in the hands of Islamist extremists—could well become a model of Pakistan. The Great Game may then extend beyond its present borders. The Silk Road would receive a different strategic significance. It would carry no material and financial goods or democracy and wealth from the West and Japan into the region, but would be used for drug-trafficking, illegal migration, Islamic rebel infiltration, and weapon smuggling to the Western hemisphere.

Prognosis

If the opinion becomes firmly established in Russia that with the global antiterror coalition the United States is less concerned with fighting potential terrorist structures than with claiming hegemony and unilateral world power at the cost of the UN, the country may fully withdraw from a strategic partnership with Washington. Then Moscow may attempt, together with Germany, France, China, and India, to form a counterweight to the United States. Such a development would create, parallel to the transatlantic community, a Eurasian partnership, which few in Germany have faith in, but which seems to have supporters in Russia and France.

Are we standing at the threshold of radical political change in Europe? On what basis could the axis "Berlin–Paris–Moscow" last in the world after the Iraq war anyway? How can the partners support each other? Were Putin to fall out with Bush over Iraq, Russia would in future have to depend solely on European help to modernize its economy.

Schröder views close German–Russian crisis management on the Iraq question as "forward looking." First of all, Europe's energy supply could be extended with Russian gas and oil. Second, Schröder seems to have discussed the idea of founding an EU–Russia Security Council, which would complement the existing NATO–Russia Council, and in case of the eventual marginalization of NATO, even replace it. Sergei Nedoroslev, head of the airplane group Kaskol, spoke about a Russian–European alliance in airplane production. But how would the rest of Europe react to Germany and France turning toward Russia? Could Berlin, Moscow, and Paris even assert themselves against the America-oriented remainder of Europe, without risking a serious divide within NATO and the EU?

The idea that the United States would give up its protective power function for Germany and France, as president of the European Commission Romano Prodi recently hinted, and that both countries would place their fate in the hands of the other nuclear power, Russia, seems absurd. It is clear that for Germany and France, the traditional allies of the United States, it will be less difficult to reestablish solidarity with Washington. Russia on the other hand, runs the risk of suddenly becoming completely isolated and gambling away all its options for integrating into the West.

However, should the United States base its antiterror alliance on cooperation with the UN and transatlantic tears be mended again, Putin the pragmatist will not hesitate for long to return to the strategic partnership with America, which, to be precise, he never left. Besides the long-term goal of securing peace in the Middle and Far East, another delicate topic awaits a solution: North Korea. Disarmament of this regime, in view of the possibility of enemy use of atomic weapons, cannot be brought about according to the Iraqi model. In this case there is no alternative to close cooperation and an alignment of interests of the powers of the United States, Russia, and China.

In its new study, Deutsche Bank Research concludes that Russia has no alternative to the current modernization course. That course can be conducted only if Russia refrains from its ambitions to become a superpower at all costs. Russia must strengthen its international position with economic arguments. A renunciation of its traditional role in world politics would, however, harm Putin's authority inside the country.

No Clear Answers

The Partnership and Cooperation Agreement (PCA), as a working instrument in the EU–Russia partnership, has lost its interest for Moscow. Instead of focusing on the PCA, EU–Russia relations could be based on another agenda, proposed in the Russian–EU strategy of October 1999—the first foreign political document prepared by Putin in his capacity as prime minister for the EU summit in Helsinki. There Russia already spoke of security cooperation between the EU and Russia and suggested introducing the euro instead of the U.S. dollar in trade relations on the European–Asian continent.

Russia is concentrating on inclusion in the WTO, which will open the way for full-fledged integration into the global economy. Entrance into the WTO will become Putin's major foreign political achievement of two presidencies.

New efforts should be considered to develop a future "common security space" between the EU and Russia. Cooperation in this sphere has several aspects. The cooperation between intelligence services that has been rather successful should be extended to military ties between Russia and the ESDP. Military-technological cooperation is feasible on the basis of the new European Centre for Emergency Situations, which has a clear counterpart in Russia—Sergei Shoigu's institution, the Russian Ministry for Emergencies.

The ESDP could aim toward new initiatives with Russia and develop joint diplomatic approaches for regions of conflicts, such as the Middle East, North Korea, or the South Caucasus. The EU's problem is that, overburdened with its own integration processes, it has failed to develop a proper ESDP approach to Russia—a tactical mistake, which may prove fatal in future.

Russia's relations with the West will remain ambiguous for some time. In specific areas, U.S.–Russian and German–French–Russian relations may, however, enjoy strategic significance. Putin has made a clear choice. He has selected the United States as Russia's main security partner, and retained the EU as its main modernizing partner.

12

Russia, the European Union, and NATO After September 11

Challenges and Limits of a New Entanglement

Sophia Clément-Noguier

During the early 1990s, the relationship between European security institutions and Russia was meager. The European Union (EU), entangled in its Balkans quagmire, was obsessed by its own internal developments and reforms, essentially looking at the United States and NATO to fill the gap on security. NATO and the United States essentially considered Russia a security risk in spite of the rapprochement initiated by the Clinton administration.[1] In the second half of the 1990s, various attempts to integrate Russia into the West were made. But they remained timid rather than proactive. In the Balkans, the EU viewed Russia as a precious mediator with the Slavs and Russian military presence as a counterweight to American policy, which often opposed European interests. Russia participated in peace-keeping operations and was closely associated with negotiation processes. The EU as a main soft-security actor developed a special relationship with Russia through the strategic partnership, worried by a spillover of Russian instability on European territory. NATO established a similar relationship in the Balkans by associating Russia with crisis management operations in Bosnia and Kosovo and by granting Russia the Cooperation Partnership Council (CPC) in 1997. But in essence, Russia was left out of the major changes affecting the European strategic setting such as the development of the European Security and Defense Policy (ESDP) and NATO reform. The Chechnya issue was severely criticized by both Europeans and Americans as a major case against human rights.

The geopolitical changes since September 11 (9/11) have led to a new strategic alliance between the United States and Russia, a Russia–NATO rapprochement, and a redefinition of Russia's relations with the EU. These changes have opened new windows of opportunity for all actors and especially for Russia to engage with the Western community. President Vladimir Putin immediately supported the U.S. war against terrorism and showed his determination to integrate Russia into the West. Moscow had been steadily following this policy of rapprochement since the beginning of the 1990s after the collapse of the Soviet empire. It has invariably attempted to regain power on the international scene either bilaterally

United States or regionally in its immediate periphery and traditional zones of interest. Hence, September 11 has accelerated the pace of Russia's rapprochement with the West and boosted America's bilateral relationship as well as NATO–EU cooperation with Russia, rather than introducing a change in nature.[2] Western willingness to further integrate Russia was an opportunity for Moscow. However, distinctive features of Russian foreign policy clearly persist. Moscow pursues its self-interest at both regional and global levels, in the near abroad, in the Middle East, in Asia, and with the United States. Similarly, for Western allies a rapprochement with Russia is made necessary by geopolitical and economic reasons for Europeans, and by the war against terrorism for the United States. Hence, at this moment, the rapprochement has not led to further substantial institutionalization of the relationship.

This chapter will examine the evolution of EU and NATO relations with Russia through a brief historical perspective and a particular focus on the current period after September 11 and Iraq. We will analyze EU and NATO security relations with Russia in a broader European security and defense context, namely, the evolution of the ESDP, reformed NATO, and enlargement. We will also deal with the degree to which Europe has, or is likely to have, a role to play in security issues and whether this role facilitates or impedes Russia's integration and transformation. In so doing, we will attempt to underline the major changes and their motivations and to assess the long-term dynamics and significance of such trends and their consequences for the nature of Russia's relation with European security as a whole.

The Evolution of the European Security Setting During the 1990s and NATO–EU Relations with Russia

Europe's strategic environment has dramatically evolved with the end of the post–Cold War era and the collapse of the Soviet bloc. European security institutions were in transition. In 1991, the EU was not militarily prepared to address low-intensity conflicts on its own continent. It developed political and military tools during the Yugoslav conflicts when left alone without American and NATO participation. The Common Foreign and Security Policy (CFSP) was initiated only in 1992. Having devolved its security to NATO during the Cold War period, it did not possess adequate military tools, decision-making mechanisms, and the common political will to address them. In addition, European partners appeared divided politically on the way to go forward in security and defense as well as operationally in the Balkans. The EU partners entangled in the Balkan quagmire were focusing on their own internal developments and reforms. Until the Dayton agreement in 1995, which ended the Yugoslav wars, NATO did not intervene in the Balkan crisis. It was not adapted to low intensity conflicts or prepared for "out of area" missions, and the United States, its main contributor and guarantor, was supporting a disengagement from Europe in favor of other domestic and external priorities.

After that period, the United States used NATO as a privileged framework to intervene (air strikes in 1994 and 1995, and peace enforcement in Bosnia). NATO was faced with a range of new challenges (low-intensity conflicts, ethnic hatred, and spillover). As the sole organization for collective defense in Europe, it adapted to the new regional environment. It identified new potential threats, extended the nature of its missions to non-Article 5 operations, and developed crisis management mechanisms, all embedded in its New Strategic Concept in 1999. The United States, through its political and military participation in crisis management in the Balkans, imposed itself as a power and as a key actor in Europe in ensuring the stability of the European continent. Euro-American divergences emerged on ways and means to address crisis management in the Balkans. For Europeans, burden sharing in NATO had to be based on more equity, shared responsibilities (strategic control, military guidance), and risks (deployment in theater). In Kosovo, where EU partners acted under NATO's chain of command together with the United States, Americans resented strategic constraints on operational conduct and military guidance. Russia on its side looked at the absence of a UN mandate as proof of U.S. unilateralism and lack of cooperation and integration in dealing with European security. Above all, it rejected the Kosovo operation as a precedent that would legitimize external interference in domestic policies.

During the early 1990s, cooperation between European–Atlantic security institutions and Russia was low. There was no real actor strong and coherent enough to address Russia in any security sense at all. In addition, attitudes toward Russia were ambivalent. The EU, although relieved by the disappearance of the enemy at its borders, feared a spillover of instability from a Russia in transition. NATO, still led by traditional Cold War thinking, feared the nostalgic mentality of Russia's political and military establishments. Thus, the feeling of relief was not sustained by a willingness to get too close to Russia. Finally, a major part of the Russian military and elite establishment looked reluctantly at any form of cooperation with the former enemies. Through that period, Russia's relations with NATO alternatively experienced periods of tension and cohabitation. In spite of the Clinton administration's promotion of democratization and pro-Western policy for Russia, there were tensions over a number of issues, notably, Kosovo, NATO enlargement, Chechnya, and Russia's policy toward "rogue" states. On the one hand, the allies still considered Russia as a security problem because of the uncertainty of its transition, the evolution of the military-industrial complex, and its stance in the Balkans and Chechnya. This excluded in-depth institutional or operational cooperation. On the other hand, Russia, in the pure Soviet tradition, continued to view NATO transformation and American predominance within it as a threat to its influence in Europe and to its relations with former satellites. Moscow feared that an extension of NATO's functional missions such as non-Article 5 missions and Partnership for Peace or a NATO/U.S. intervention in the Balkans might have consequences: it would lead to growing U.S. or allied interference in Russia's internal affairs, notably Chechnya, the immediate periphery, and old areas of interest such as the Caucasus, Central Asia, and the Balkans. Hence, Russia's participation in the diplomatic process led by the allies in Kosovo (Rambouillet accord) and in peace-keeping missions in Bosnia and Kosovo at the end of the decade did not prevent tensions on a number of issues such as the nature and zones of Russian military deployment in Bosnia or the attitude toward local allies (notably in Kosovo).

It is only in the second half of the decade that various attempts to integrate Russia into the West were made both by NATO and the EU. This approach had many implications for Russia's transformation and integration into the West. Allies favored the association rather than the marginalization of a stable and democratic Russia, which was also an important partner in crisis management in the EU's immediate periphery. Consequently, Russia was invited to participate in the diplomatic process led by the allies in Rambouillet in 1998 and to peace-keeping missions in Bosnia and Kosovo at the end of the 1990s. In particular, the EU partners pushed to integrate Russia rather than marginalize it. Russia was geographically closer, and interested in economic cooperation with the EU. Its positions in the Balkans were also closer to European ones on border intangibility, multiethnic integration, the use of force, and the role of the UN. The EU was also more worried about a spillover of Russia's instability than was the United States. An important part of Russia's establishment, influenced by traditional Soviet perception of the Alliance, continued to view NATO transformation and American predominance as a threat to its influence in Europe and in former "satellite" territories. It feared that an extension of NATO's functional (non-Article 5 missions, Partnership for Peace) as well as geographic missions, with a NATO/U.S. intervention in the Balkans, would lead to growing U.S. or allied interference in Russia's internal affairs (Chechnya), in its immediate periphery, and in traditional areas of interest (Caucasus, Central Asia, Balkans).

The Founding Act on Mutual Relations, Cooperation and Security in May 1997[3] led to NATO's creation of a Permanent Joint Council (PJC) in 1997 between Russia and NATO to develop common approaches to European security and political problems. It allowed consultations and joint initiatives and could make joint decisions and take actions on a range of issues. But relations remained essentially low due to disagreements on the Balkans. The Kosovo campaign and Russia's opposition to the use of force interrupted bilateral relations and loosened the partnership with the West. Still, Russia's association with the diplomatic process and the peace-keeping efforts underlined its commitment to European security. In addition, Moscow recognized that militarily NATO remained the organization able to undertake a military operation in high-intensity contingencies, to combine multilateralism and power projection, and to ensure that diplomacy was backed by an adequate military threat. Politically, unity of action was achieved through consensus among the allies despite strong divergences. Kosovo allowed a bridge between a "European Europe" and the NATO–Atlantic security community. Under President Putin, NATO was no longer considered to be a threat or a priority for Russian foreign policy.[4] The PJC was perceived as a forum to influence developments within the alliance. In 2000, Putin revitalized Russia–NATO relations as he recognized the existence of a new NATO with an expanding role, membership, and missions.

Still, at the end of the 1990s, Russia was not an American preoccupation due to increased asymmetry between the internal and external situations of the two countries. Arms control, the traditional channel of dialogue between them, was no longer the sole structural factor. When it came into power, the Bush administration created a pause in the U.S. relationship with Russia. This ended with the first Bush-Putin meeting in Ljubljana in June 2001.

Russia, United States, NATO, and the EU After September 11

The Priority of Multilateralism with the United States

The events of September 11 have changed the principles of European security. They brought to the fore U.S. political and military supremacy, bolstered the creation of a new strategic framework with Russia, and a global redistribution of alliances. Russia whose strategic importance has increased steadily, despite the presence of nuclear armaments, has integrated those multiple constraints. This was evidenced by Moscow's support of Bush's war against terrorism, the extensive U.S. military presence in Central Asia and the Caucasus, and the definition of a new strategic framework with the United States. The latter requires political cooperation with Russia in some Central Asian countries, military cooperation in containing terrorist networks inside Russia/Chechnya, and information exchange in the field of intelligence. President Putin has strategically decided to orient Russia toward the West despite the opposition of the military and part of the political elite. He intends to modernize, integrate, and obtain guarantees of Russia's security. He has implicitly recognized American predominance and Russian inability to oppose enlargement. He sees the war against terrorism as a springboard to initiate transformation of the old antagonistic relations between NATO and Russia. For Washington, Russia is no longer a threat and the global strategic framework will be less and less influenced by the Russian–American relationship. Russia remains a key partner in the war against terrorism, beneficial notably in the nuclear and chemical areas and missile defense, as a strong stabilizer in its former zone of influence, and as a counterweight to China.

Consequently, since September 11, and in spite of American renunciation of the Anti-Ballistic Missile (ABM) Treaty, a new framework for cooperation was developed between the United States and Russia along two major axes.

Strategic Armaments Reduction

The Crawford summit in November 2001 initiated cooperation in the war against terrorism, proliferation of weapons of mass destruction (WMD), and a closer association of Russia with NATO. The two countries signed an agreement in May 2002 at the Bush-Putin summit in Moscow. However, divergences remain: on strategic disarmament, especially on verification and transparency, Russian military assistance to Iraq (nuclear, biological, and chemical missiles), and Russian arms sales to Iran as well as the construction of a nuclear plant. In addition, both countries have different approaches. Russia favors institutional formalization of offensive weapon numbers within a legally constraining framework, which shows Russia's continued suspicion. The United States favors transparency and flexibility, which indicates its desire to maintain room for maneuvering. In addition, the Bush administration has based its missile defense strategy on a dialogue with Russia.

Cooperation on Counterterrorism

Interests and priorities converge on a preemptive approach to eradicate terrorist activities inside and outside of national territories. The United States wants bases and allies in Central Asia and the Caucasus and needs Russian cooperation at its borders. Consequently, a joint working group on Afghanistan, intelligence sharing, and the presence in Georgia of American military trainers to help Georgian special forces in their fight against the Chechen connection were created. U.S. support for Russia's entrance to the G-8, President Bush's loan of $20 billion to help Moscow dismantle its strategic weapons, and the American offer to support Russia's accelerated membership in the World Trade Organization demonstrate U.S.–Russian mutual interests.

At the global level, the United States focus is on bilateral relations. The upgrade of the U.S.–Russian relationship has clearly become a priority for Russia as Moscow seeks equal status at the global level with the United States since the end of the Cold War. Moscow deals on a par with the United States at the global level, especially in common areas of interest such as the Caucasus and Central Asia, where cooperation with Russia is unavoidable for Washington. At the regional level, the war against terrorism brings stability in Central Asia, in particular, with the end of the Taliban regime, and in the Caucasus, and reduces potential spillover to Russian Muslim territories. By assimilating Chechens to terrorism and supporting a preemptive approach to address it, Washington's approach also legitimates Russia's military policy against terrorist networks in Chechnya and Georgia. Finally, it supports the diversification of Russia's interests away from Europe toward the Middle East, notably with Turkey and Iran, and toward Asia, notably with China. Russia has also offered an alternative for oil and gas supply. Like the United States, Moscow's interests are multiple and diversified, based on a complex web of bilateral and flexible relations and alliances. In turn, Russia's cooperation is beneficial to the United States in Central Asia and the Caucasus, and Moscow is not a threat as long as it does not interfere with American foreign policy. In this perspective a NATO-Russian rapprochement could provide the backbone of Euro-Atlantic security in the Central Asian "arc of crisis." It could also facilitate the redeployment of American forces in the region for future ad hoc coalitions.

Hence, for Russia, this bilateral relationship, although situational, takes precedence over other security issues such as multilateral relations with the EU and NATO and enlargement, and over a potential convergence with its immediate neighbors. All important matters have already been addressed bilaterally in a direct and parallel way without the constraints and slowness of the NATO–Russia Council, called "NATO at 20." It also takes precedence over enlargement to the Baltic states whose contributions to global security issues remain comparatively lower. In addition, this global status for Russia also increases its room for maneuver at a regional European level, especially since Washington no longer considers a Russia–EU rapprochement as a threat. This bilateral relationship could also boost debates, work within the NATO–Russia Council, and help to develop relations with the EU through the development of new channels for cooperation. In other words, there could be a spillover of the benefits of a flexible bilateral U.S.–Russian consultative and operational relationship toward more institutional frameworks such as the EU and NATO, thus leading to greater institutionalization and multinationalization of Russia's relations with the West.

A Global NATO as a Complement

The new NATO–Russia relationship is developing within the new global strategic context described above. Moscow's attempt to further develop those relations and American pressures to integrate Russia into NATO are the outcome of these evolutions. Russia's relationship to NATO is determined by a series of variables: NATO's future shape, NATO's attitude toward Russia's integration in the European security framework, and the U.S. approach to both NATO and Russia.

The events of September 11 have deeply modified the nature of the NATO–Russia relationship, which introduced a new rationale and is based on the mutual benefits of a closer association. NATO's secretary general (1999–2003), Lord Robertson, clearly stated in his speech in Volgograd the necessity for a coalition of countries that share the same convictions and work together.[5] The United States, which has largely defined the NATO agenda toward Russia since September 11, has strongly backed Russia's rapprochement and further institutionalization of relations with NATO as a reward for Russia's support in the war against terrorism and Putin's "silence" on missile defense and the U.S. withdrawal from the ABM Treaty (both were strongly criticized internally). NATO is seen as the facilitator of a rapprochement and as a springboard and forum for permanent long-term dialogue and interaction. Within the new strategic context, Washington's preoccupation is to modify Russian perceptions that NATO is still a threat, which can only be achieved through increased interaction with the West. However, the nature of the Russia–NATO relationship is dependent upon a number of factors such as Russia's geographic, political, and military perceptions of the American establishment toward Russia as well as NATO, the evolution of the organization itself—toward a toolbox or collective security—and the fluctuations of the Russian–American relationship itself. Hence, this relationship appears to be mostly political. But Russia's "integration"—in the broad sense—into NATO is more likely than integration with the EU because NATO essentially remains a military alliance that is flexible. Therefore, whether Russia's development into a democratic state lies in closer interinstitutional links with the West or in the development of a web of bilateral alliances with the United States and regional countries remains to be seen.

Russia was a founding member of the North Atlantic Council of Cooperation in 1991, and joined the Partnership for Peace in 1994, where it developed cooperation in specific military and technical areas. A Russian mission to NATO was established in 1998 to facilitate cooperation and communication. And a Military Liaison Office was established in Moscow in 2002 to increase transparency and cooperation. The decision was made to upgrade Russia's status.[6] The NATO–Russia Council, NATO at 20, was created in May 2002 at the NATO–Russia summit in Rome and replaced the PJC established by the Founding Act on Mutual Relations, Cooperation and Security in May 1997.[7] It is headed by NATO's secretary general. A preparatory committee of NATO at 20 and a "secretariat" initiates work. Specific work at the expert level will be conducted by NATO at 20 within appropriate NATO committees, including the Military Committee. Decisions are taken by consensus (co-decision) and the members of the Joint Council bear equal responsibility for their implementation.

Russia is considered an equal partner in key areas for cooperation such as the war against terrorism, crisis management, and nonproliferation of WMD. Other areas of cooperation include peacekeeping, reform of the defense sector, search and rescue, civil emergency plans, and theater missile defense. Decisions are taken by NATO at 20, thus ending the 19 plus 1 of the PJC, and are based on consensus. If the resort to precoordination is considered to be an exception rather than a rule, certain safeguarding principles have been defined to prevent Moscow from having a veto right on the alliance's decisions at 19: possibility for an NAC independent action, for precoordination at 19 after an ally's request and the right for each ally to take back an issue discussed at 20 within the framework at 19. The Theater Missile Defense is the most advanced item. The U.S. withdrawal from the ABM Treaty and the new strategic relation with Russia lifted the constraints that existed on U.S. missile defense. Consequently, European allies' capacity to invoke Russia's opposition to a U.S. proposal to protect their territories against enemy missiles has also disappeared. In the near future, Russia could even be associated with NATO Theater Missile Defense programs to protect its troops during operations. In reality, these new procedures only provide for a general framework to promote common decisions and actions. The real dynamic and ambition of the NATO–Russia relationship will be evaluated through the concrete work of NATO at 20. Russian participation in NATO operations in the Balkans, the Implementation Force (IFOR) and Stabilisation Force (SFOR) in Bosnia, and Kosovo the Force (KFOR) in Kosovo after 1999 has been one of the major achievements. Russia's contribution has been the most important of all non-NATO countries. It has also shown the capacity to work together operationally and to share responsibility at the political level. Intensified cooperation against new threats is another key issue that has been addressed through numerous and regular work and conferences at the expert level.[8]

Still, perceptions of the new NATO–Russia relationship are subdued. Most NATO European allies initially feared a dilution of NATO if Russian membership was enhanced.[9] They feared that closer NATO–Russia rapprochement would weaken the alliance's collective defense mission, especially since Afghanistan and the nonactivation of Article 5 to the benefit of ad hoc coalitions. They, especially France, feared that an extension of NATO missions to terrorism would also raise soft security issues with Russia that could be better handled within the CFSP-ESDP framework (peace-keeping missions, civil emergency planning). The new Russia–NATO/ U.S. relation could have negative strategic and political consequences for them. Even the American establishment was divided on the nature of the association, although a consensus existed on its necessity.[10] Russian perceptions of NATO itself and the PJC have evolved as well. Suspicion of the West, notably the U.S. and Euro-Atlantic security institutions of the 1990s, has ended. NATO is no longer a threat or a priority for the United States, and thus not for Russia either. It is marginalized by the United States, has lost its central role, and tries to find a new raison d'être as it did in the 1990s through enhanced relations with Russia. In Afghanistan, the United States did not activate Article 5 and preferred unilateral action. Cooperation with Russia on terrorism and especially intelligence sharing did not occur at a multilateral level and is difficult even among allies.[11] In addition, key issues such as counterterrorism and intelligence are essentially addressed at a bilateral level between Moscow and Washington. Furthermore, NATO enlargement will dilute the alliance and turn it into a political forum with no military means,[12] which will further complicate a decision-making process based on consensus.

Therefore, Moscow privileges bilateral relations, which are more flexible and adaptable than collective institutional frameworks. It also opts for a definition of national interests that is more global and less Western. Finally, if NATO's membership expansion raises only regional problems for Russia, it is different in the context of expansion of alliance missions and areas of responsibility. These affect Russia more globally in regions of key strategic significance for Russian national interests and in various functional fields (permanence of peace-keeping missions in its near abroad).[13] Consequently, the nature and range of NATO's crisis management strategy become important in terms of Russia's association with NATO and in light of Russian security interests regarding conflict points at its periphery. Russia can therefore become either a partner in substantially cooperating with NATO or a "serious obstacle . . . in constructively balancing inadequate or openly aggressive NATO actions in Europe" or elsewhere.[14]

However, Russia's association with NATO remains important for Moscow. In a fluctuating world situation, NATO as a permanent multilateral framework of continued shared interests among allies guarantees Russia's role and participation in the long run, and anchors and ties Russia to the West. NATO supported Moscow's hostage crisis in October 2002 within the framework of the war against terrorism thus legitimizing Moscow's action. It ensures the continuity of the political cohesion of its members and an American presence in Europe. It provides security guarantees in times of peace. It also appeared that NATO had its merits for the United States as well. It is a unique reservoir of forces for ad hoc coalitions, guaranteeing a certain level of interoperability through day-to-day interaction, joint exercises, and operations. It remains at the core of American policy in Europe, Russia's anchorage in Europe, and a springboard toward the Black Sea and Central Asia, especially with enlargement.

Russia can influence American policy orientations although it cannot set any limits on it. The current Russian government can also downplay its internal opposition by arguing that NATO is not a threat due to active Russian participation through the PJC. As for the ESDP, Russia must participate actively in the process under construction to have its say and avoid marginalization in European and global security issues with major partners. In addition, the PJC is the body where Russia can present its positions, for instance on enlargement or sea rescue operations. The PJC, presided over by NATO's secretary general, thus gaining credibility and efficiency, has met regularly and intensively and has debated a number of issues. There are benefits of enhanced cooperation as shown by the joint civil-military crisis response exercise in September 2002, simulating a terrorist attack against a chemical plant in Russia to test multinational coordination levels during a disaster where Russia could call in NATO. Such exercises could lead to enhanced institutionalization or more permanent procedures. Russia can only benefit from NATO's experience in training and planning at an operational level essential for crisis management. It has adopted a joint document on peace-keeping operations of Russia and NATO that defines political control for such joint operations. It has also launched debates on missile defense, military reform, civil planning, cooperation in space, and the evaluation of terrorist threats for the Euro-Atlantic area. Moscow would also "balance" China's request for a rapprochement with NATO.

Above all, the reformed alliance since the Prague summit has become a key asset in long-term commitment to the war against terrorism and the necessary expansion of sustainable courses of action. As a consequence, there is renewed American interest in an organization able to address new challenges.[15] The objective has been to rationalize the alliance's structures to give it more flexibility and deployability and to enlarge its missions and ambitions. Concretely, the reforms include: the expansion of NATO's functional missions, including new threats such as WMD and terrorism, already present in the 1999 Strategic Concept; force protection against chemical, biological, radiological, or nuclear attacks[16] and global missile defense (forces, populations, territories); the creation of a NATO Response Force; a rationalized capabilities process, Prague Capabilities Commitment (PCC); and the reform of the command structure. In addition, NATO is present in Russia's zones of interest in Afghanistan and Iraq, explicitly implementing "out of area." Within the war against terrorism, the United States pushes for a global NATO. Washington needs bases and political allies in an enlarged Europe, which borders areas in turmoil such as Central Asia and the Caucasus. The rapprochement between Russia and NATO could extend the backbone of Euro-Atlantic security in the direction of the "arc of crisis" in Central Asia. It could also facilitate the deployment of American forces in Central Asia or the Caucasus for future operations. NATO has also started a dialogue with China on Eurasian security. For most allies NATO remains, in spite of debates in both the United States and Europe on its rationale and efficiency, a unique multilateral security forum for Euro-Atlantic dialogue. It has integrated structures that allow operational conduct and interoperability between forces. It will possess a pool of forces for NATO or ad hoc coalitions in and around Europe as well as globally. Such competition on parallel processes· (rapid reaction force, capabilities) could weaken the ESDP.

The ESDP and Russia: Cooperation Postponed

Russia's rapprochement with Europe is primarily a Russian-led process voluntarily initiated in Moscow.[17] The EU is a long-term asset in a changing world and a regional challenge at Russia's immediate periphery. Russia's economic and commercial interests lie with Europe. But as Moscow must balance multiple priorities, its interest is not to focus exclusively on the EU. To the EU, Russia is important both regionally and in soft security terms. It is a regional neighboring power, bordering the now-enlarged Union, especially the Baltic states and Poland. It is a country with a strong potential for instability at its borders and its internal developments and regional policies are a cause for EU concern. Consequently, Russia is both an ally to be sought and a preoccupation. The EU–Russia relationship appears to be more institutionalized and legally framed than it is with NATO. But because of Russia's geographic location and the nature of the EU integrative process, Russia remains a distinctive actor. Russia's full integration into the EU would alter the balance between deepening and enlarging, imply a revision of the nature of the EU deepening process in favor of enlargement, and finally lead to an in-depth revision of the EU endgame. Hence, the most likely perspective at this point would instead be continuing rapprochement of the EU with Russia with the development of current links and a renewed strategy toward Russia.

However, the EU has aimed at "integrating" Russia rather than marginalizing it to avoid a spillover of instability and economic migration, especially since enlargement brings EU borders next to Russia. Hence, EU preoccupations with Russia are essentially regional. This process has been progressive, multifaceted, and long term. It has followed the rationale behind European integration in terms of functionalist spillover from economics into politics and security.[18] Consequently, the focus has initially been on economic issues. Russia was also the first country to benefit from the EU "common strategy" tool within the newly established CFSP. The Common Strategy, although fairly ambitious on paper, remains loosely defined, not legally binding, and therefore dependent on the political will of both parties to implement it.[19] The EU intensified relations with Russia through the EU–Russia October 2001 joint statement and through the European commission. Commission communication of March 2003 on the Western newly independent states—Ukraine, Moldova, and Belarus—and the Russian Federation.[20]

In the military and defense areas, achievements are meager. While the Agreement on Partnership and Coordination signed in 1994 provides only for a political dialogue aimed at defining converging positions on international issues of mutual interest, it essentially deals with economic and commercial issues. The Common Strategy for Russia in 1999 is the first document addressing security issues. Although objectives are broadly defined in terms of Russia's democratization, economic integration, and cooperation to ensure stability, it proposes an EU strategic vision for Russia and identifies common interests between them: a permanent political dialogue on European security through joint initiatives, participation in joint conflict prevention and crisis management operations, and the adoption by Russia of European values and principles such as the market economy and the rule of law. The Russian answer to the Common Strategy, the Medium-Term Strategy for Development of Relations Between the Russian Federation and the European Union until 2010, elaborated at the end of the 1990s clearly reveals the Russian position and dilemmas when it comes to European security. Contrary to the EU's "integrative" approach, it underlines Russia's geopolitical uniqueness, its special role in Europe and elsewhere as a global power, and hence a nationally defined foreign policy. Russian–EU relations are envisaged within the overarching European security system as a counterweight to NATO's American predominance. But it remains clear that, since his election in 1999, and notably at the EU–Moscow summit in May 2000, President Putin remains committed to his choice of integrating Russia into Europe and the West both economically and politically.[21] The EU integration process is perceived as a model for integration of the Commonwealth of Independent States. It is also a model for multilateralism on Euro-Atlantic security and defense issues. In addition, the EU does not present a threat to Russia's security as it does not embed a strong defense dimension. NATO remains the cornerstone of collective defense and now of collective security in Europe and beyond, and Russia's rapprochement with it is favored by all allies. The EU and Russia share a common position: they view each other with regionally focused interests.

In practice, achievements have been limited. Divergences over the Chechen conflict, Moldova, the Caucasus, or Belarus have underlined ideological differences and the inability of the EU to influence Russia's foreign policy in its near abroad. What has prevailed is the absolute necessity for European security in view of future enlargements to integrate Russia rather than marginalize it. Russia and the EU have also attempted to coordinate their positions on issues of common interest such as the Balkans or the Middle East, notably in the Quartet (United

States, Russia, UN, EU) and through common declarations. They share similar positions on the use of force and the role of the UN, and making them public jointly has had some influence. After the Kosovo crisis, institutional linkages to the emerging ESDP have been developed in order to strengthen dialogue and co-operation with Russia on political and security matters in Europe. The Nice Council in 2000 elaborated proposals for the participation of Russian troops in EU crisis management operations, which were again clarified in June 2002. Russia–EU dialogue must be intensified in times of crisis, with Russia informed of an EU operation and invited to participate, once the EU has achieved its operational planning.[22] The European Union Military Staff (EUMS) in charge of operational guidance provides some military coordination for crisis management with Russia, notably in the field of joint planning and civil emergency operations. A Russian liaison officer ensures the exchange of information.

The issue of Russia's relation to the ESDP is important for security and stability in Europe. The Balkans experience has shown how fruitful cooperation can be. The development of EU strategic capabilities, especially on strategic airlift, could benefit from Russian participation. Furthermore, historical, cultural causes as well as geopolitical challenges differentiate Russia from other EU countries.[23] They limit the acceptance of the whole range of European values and EU constraints. They also influence Russia's perception of its place and role in Europe. Consequently, Russia's policy toward the EU remains more pragmatic than ambitious. The EU remains a channel to counterbalance U.S. positions and force Washington toward more multilateralism (on the UN, on Iraq) where European and Russian positions converge. It is also a stable long-term ally in uncertain times. In the area of capabilities, various possibilities are under discussion for the eventual cooperation and participation of Russia. They concern strategic lift, which is one of the ESDP's major shortcomings, space, notably with the development of the European Galileo Program. But they stumble on political difficulties, costs, and the quality of Russian capabilities. Since September 11, terrorism has become a central issue between Russia and the EU. They have engaged in increased cooperation and information exchange on terrorist activities.[24] The handling of the Chechen conflict and the Russian forceful and preemptive approach has caused some tensions.

However, the ESDP has developed considerably over the past five years since the Saint Malo summit in 1998, which boosted the development of European defense after the UK-France rapprochement. The EU has created the necessary institutional and decision-making mechanisms to deal with crisis management: permanent political and military structures,[25] a rapid reaction force (the Headline Goal[26]) to implement Petersberg missions,[27] including civilian crisis management, and provide for the development of strategic capabilities command and control, intelligence and strategic lift, in particular, with the A-400M. In spite of the massive NATO presence after 1995 in peace-keeping operations all over the Balkans, EU countries are already contributing the bulk of the military presence and especially of the financial burden in the Balkans. This contribution has increased with the EU decision to take over from NATO peace-keeping operations in Macedonia (in March 2003), in Bosnia in 2004, and maybe in Kosovo in the future. This phenomenon underlines two realities: the leading role of the ESDP in crisis management on the European continent, despite shortcomings; the fact that NATO is not the sole multilateral organization with a role to play in crisis management in Europe. The announced reduced American presence in the region in 2004 and the current redefinition of NATO's missions and ambitions will definitely enhance those trends. Russia might then become an important partner for Europeans in providing additional support troops on the ground. In other words, all European partners have in one way or another advanced EU-specific interests and responsibilities in their own geographic space: the proximity of conflicts that influence threat perception (spillover risks), the existence of a large spectrum of tools that allow the EU to act prior to or post-conflict (economic, diplomatic, and humanitarian tools, and military deployment), and the logic of integration (in different forms and scopes) toward the rest of the European continent.

In addition, the so-called Berlin plus agreement in 2003 gives the EU access to NATO means and capabilities in certain planning. Furthermore, the EU has force projection: major European countries participated in the Gulf War coalition in 1991, in the air strikes in Kosovo in 1999, and undertook crisis management operations in Africa (Operation Artemis in the Congo for France, in East Timor for the United Kingdom and France, and on the Ivory Coast for France). European partners have currently agreed to create a permanent planning cell within the EU Military Staff in Brussels to deal with future EU crisis management operations. Finally, the ESDP is part of a global political project aimed at integration in Europe involving various levels and areas, namely, economic, political, legal, and now, defense. It has no Article 5-type commitments for nations but has developed appropriate civil-military tools and concepts of use of force (forces and planning capabilities) as well as a whole range of tools to intervene before, during, and after a crisis, in a much larger framework than NATO.

Still, the ESDP remains weak. Since September 11, NATO reform has overshadowed European defense efforts. The adaptation of NATO at the level of strategy and doctrine (the nature of missions including terrorism, de facto "out of area"[28]), and at the operational level (increased flexibility, unique reservoir of forces, capabilities, integrated civil emergency planning procedure, interoperability) inevitably interacts with the EU capability process and could further weaken the ESDP. Internal economic problems, the absence of political will, and the lack of consensus impede the development of joint procurement programs, the creation of new mechanisms, and the increase of defense budgets. The Iraqi crisis showed divergences among partners on the use of force and the role of the UN, and also revealed to some partners the importance of the relationship with the United States for defense in the global setting. Central European countries as well as some older members like Spain and Italy privilege NATO under American leadership for their security, fearing that a too strong ESDP might exclude the United States from Europe and create duplication that would weaken NATO.

Finally, the EU needs to define its political goals and strategic ambitions and there lies a problem with Russian perceptions. Concretely, this means the interpretation of the Petersberg tasks (the whole spectrum for France to essentially the lower end for the United Kingdom) and the necessity to define the range and geographical limits for force projection. In other words, how broad can the geographic area be? Should the EU conduct operations close to the European territory, at its immediate periphery, or beyond at a global level in Africa, the Middle East, the Caucasus, or Central Asia? How should it proceed: autonomously, borrowing NATO assets, or preferably in ad hoc coalitions led by NATO or the United States? The answers to these questions are central to Russia's security policy in Europe and will define the nature and degree of its cooperation with the ESDP. Currently, the EU focuses on robust peacekeeping, as in the Balkans, an area where Russia has a lot of experience and has cooperated in the past. But the EU rapid reaction force has, in principle, no geographical limitation and can project around Europe over 3,500 to 4,000 km. It could therefore reach Russian areas of interests, blur the distinction between external and internal dimensions of crisis, and interfere with Russia's "internal" affairs. This was one of the main Russian arguments against the Kosovo campaign.

The second argument was the absence of a UN resolution, which, however, is not the case for the ESDP at this moment. This is one of the major dilemmas for ESDP–Russian relations as neighboring countries like Russia, Ukraine, or Belarus are simultaneously potential risk factors—a place where the ESDP might have to intervene—as well as potential partners in crisis management.[29] Matters are even more sensitive with Russia concerning the Caucasus. In addition, political considerations can lead to some ambiguity, for example, on the Chechen issue or on Abkhazia. Finally, the developments between NATO and the ESDP are considered with suspicion. The ESDP is not a threat because it remains weak. The possibility for the EU to borrow NATO assets for crisis management is another development that could be directed against Russia. Only the balance created by the Russia–America relationship and the convergence of both countries on the definition of terrorism constitute a relief for Russia in this respect.

Hence, at least in the mid-term, a preventive approach on the soft security issue is important. The EU has at its disposal a whole spectrum of varied and specific tools in the economic, financial, political, security areas, and these embrace a combination of possible actions ranging from conflict prevention to financial support, post-conflict reconstruction, confidence-building measures, and diplomacy. In addition, in the area of foreign policy, Russian and European approaches often correspond (UN, Iran, ABM Treaty). Addressing security in a broader sense (cross-border control, legal migration, control of mafia network, trade, etc.) is more appropriate than pure defense matters, at least at present, and adapted to the nature of the needs of the periphery and Russia.[30] The EU has also provided for the development of privileged relations with its periphery embedded in the EU strategy for Russia and for Ukraine. Enlargement brings the Baltic states into the EU. These states will benefit totally from the EU *acquis communautaire* and will lead Brussels to enhance cross-border relations between the newcomers and their immediate periphery. Finally, geography has its say. The EU is de facto an actor in Europe, a natural area of interest, in the long run. For the EU, Europe is not simply an option but a natural outlet and an imperative. Its own security is dependent on and subordinated to the stability of its immediate surroundings. This trend will be enhanced with the upcoming new geographic division of labor since September 11, as the EU remains the main actor in Europe.

The Impact of Enlargement

The November 2002 Prague NATO summit and December 2002 Copenhagen EU summit, which accelerated enlargement, did not affect Russia. Since September 11, the international environment has changed and Russia's priority is clearly its bilateral relationship with the United States within the framework of the war against terrorism. The next round of EU enlargement to Romania will considerably expand the EU's eastern border with Russia and Ukraine.[31] In addition, the Central and East European states, the newcomers, are uneasy in dealing with Russia for obvious historical reasons and they appear more defensive than proactive as part of the new EU border with Russia. The extent to which they will affect relations with and between Russia, Ukraine, and the three Baltic states remains to be seen.

It can be argued that both enlargement processes strengthen Russian security. They create a zone of peace and stability and a shift from military to soft security issues. As such, they will provide stability around Russia's borders and promote cooperation. They will ensure protection of Russian minority rights within the EU legal framework. They will more generally enhance the security of their neighbors by providing a secure area and a web of multilateral frameworks, by expanding the area of mutual trust and shared values and by developing stronger economic ties (trade, investment, regional cooperation). In addition, they will constitute an example for Ukraine or Belarus in internal and external transition processes. They will limit Russia's ambitions regionally and press for internal change and reforms toward democratization. The future of the EU and Russia is geostrategically linked as they share a common border. An enlarged EU therefore remains the best forum to cooperate with Russia on a range of soft security issues and tools developed by the EU.

Still, enlargement processes are negatively perceived by part of the Russian military and political establishment. They establish a new dividing line on the European continent that excludes Russia. Russia is left out of economic, political, and social developments because it is not directly associated. Above all, the accession of Poland and Lithuania separates Russia from Kaliningrad for which it did not get a special status or compensations. Moscow feared its rights over Kaliningrad would be diminished as the Schengen regime would have consequences for Russian mobility. This limits Russia's capacity to rule this part of its territory and obliges the Russian population to transit through foreign EU borders, although the EU–Russian summit achieved a Russian transit agreement. Still, EU enlargement is less feared because it is free of a strong defense dimension. Furthermore, enlargement increases the strategic value of the Baltic states and Poland and strengthens economic competitiveness and defenses against Russian penetration.[32] NATO remains the enemy and enlargement increases the threat against Russia, which complicates effective cooperation.[33] Hence, perceptions of NATO are mitigated. The current Russian establishment does not wish to join NATO but only to be associated closely with all issues that matter within the new NATO–Russia Council. But it fears being excluded from current developments in Europe with which many other countries will be more or less closely associated (from the Baltic states to China). This paradox could constitute a major driving force toward internal reform and democratization and closer association with EU policies. The weakness of the ESDP removes any threat perception. EU enlargement weakens the ESDP's strategic awareness in its immediate periphery as it becomes more and more difficult to strengthen and deepen in an expanded area of responsibility. In addition, accession countries entrust their security to NATO and American leadership.

However, the necessity to respond to new challenges could enhance the ESDP. For both the EU and NATO, there are challenges ahead. On the one hand, enlargements expand the area of stability in Europe and help to acquire precious allies, politically and militarily, to address new challenges. On the other hand, NATO and the EU will have to address illegal migration, drug trafficking, organized crime, weapons proliferation, and terrorism as well as environmental problems, nuclear pollution, and social problems (AIDS epidemics) for which there is no real approach from the West. As Steven Blank notes, there is a need to decommission nuclear submarines in the north, attack sources of pollution from nuclear materials, and reduce nuclear weapons through the Cooperative Threat Reduction program.[34]

The EU and NATO have opted for an "open door" process, allowing the possibility for further geographic expansion. It raises the dilemma of how to relate to neighbors and the immediate periphery. For the EU, regional instability will become a specific EU problem. It therefore needs to identify different levels of integration and cooperation in all fields. EU enlargement also means extension of the geostrategic interests and crisis management missions of the EU at its periphery. The EU Petersberg missions are not geographically limited. A European priority is to deal with crises around its borders in order to avoid spillover inside, and to share the burden with the United States in and around Europe as well as globally, either autonomously, using NATO assets, or jointly with the United States in an ad hoc coalition. It will considerably increase interdependence in the security field.

The EU has been cautious about enlargement to the East Central European states. It feared halting the EU deepening process and internal reforms. U.S. pressure for rapid enlargement of the EU by integrating East European countries was perceived by EU partners as a willingness to dilute the integration process and its security and defense dimension. It was also seen as an attempt to establish a parallel between both enlargements so as to subordinate EU mechanisms and include Turkey, an American ally, by definition.

Perspectives

Rather than integrating Russia, the EU and NATO are opting for a certain level of institutionalization of bilateral relations because new threats must be addressed through long-term and stable policies. In addition, their approaches are progressive. They provide for concrete cooperation on common specific issues that will progressively expand. Soft security issues with the EU remain a priority while defense is only secondary. It is dealt with by NATO at present but, above all, at the national and bilateral levels with the United States. However, security and defense will always be defined nationally in both Washington and Moscow. Russia seeks its own interests, which lie long term both with the EU and the United States but imply different challenges and show an implicit division of labor between America and Europe: with Europe handling long-term soft security interests, and the United States handling hard policy, political international status, oil, zones of influence, and external competition.

How can this role facilitate or impede Russia's integration and transformation? Can we determine the degree to which those relations amount to integration and foster or hinder Russia's domestic transformation in NATO itself (new NATO, enlargement), in the EU ESDP and after EU enlargement? Our main thesis is that all these parallel processes (EU, NATO, U.S. rapprochement) imply different types of transformation of Russia and integration into Europe. It is therefore necessary first to reject a deterministic approach between integration and transformation and delink them as those relations facilitate, impede, or slow Russia's integration and transformation. Second, it is imperative to clearly define integration, which may differ in each case.

The U.S.—Russia Rapprochement since 9/11

From a European perspective, this relationship delinks integration from transformation for Russia. Based on realpolitik premises ("grand politics," areas of interest), Russia's integration to the West as a strategic partner of the United States occurs independently of Russia's internal reforms and transformation (as defined by the editors). Actually, in current global politics and in the war against terrorism, what is needed according to newly defined standards is a strong Russia militarily able to ensure security inside and outside its territory against the common threat. President Putin's strong policy against the Chechens (theater attack, Chechnya) is therefore welcomed in view of the reversal of moral principles since 9/11 as compared to the recriminations of the West against Russia last year for its poor handling of human rights in the Chechen case. In addition, this relation has an exclusive bilateral dimension, with no multilateral and integrative character (including new direct and exclusive channels of cooperation in Afghanistan, on the ABM Treaty, on U.S. bases in Central Asia, and on cooperation on North Korea and Iraq). The Russian–U.S. relationship is based on both continuity and change. Slower reforms in Russia and further internal radicalization will not constitute obstacles to bilateral integration because Russia better serves U.S. interests in the war against terrorism if it is stronger rather than weaker. Although this new relationship should by no means be overidealized insofar as its own limits might increase in the future (refer to chapter 13 in this volume, by Angela Stent), it nevertheless remains an issue of preoccupation for European partners as it could have strategic consequences for them (strategic objectives, armament reductions, oil) and halt the terms of real transformation (as defined by the editors of this book) in Russia, a priority from a European point of view.

Rapprochement with NATO

This enhanced cooperation also does not imply a direct linkage between integration and transformation. Integration, although reinforced as well as a part of the learning process of cooperation, is institutionally and politically limited to a range of specific issues related to terrorism, and is not subordinated to any specific transformation process. In addition, due to the sensitive nature of most of these issues, the "real matters" will not be addressed multilaterally (intelligence, Special Forces position, etc.) but at a bilateral Russia–U.S. level, if at all. This is not a specific attitude toward Russia but an already existing limit to enhanced multilateralism within NATO. Furthermore, the U.S. agenda remains independent, and the military-industrial complex still strongly opposes any closer rapprochement (refer to chapter 14 in this volume, by Dmitri Trenin). Of course, increased movement in favor of Russia's further integration into NATO might not be excluded in the future, for example, in the event of more terrorist events or a need for consolidation of the partnership. But it would imply many conditions such as U.S. willingness, the Russian establishment's willingness, and profound doctrinal change of NATO. Undoubtedly, Russia should be closely associated with European and Western strategic interests. But it should not occur at the expense of NATO's credibility and efficiency either. For Europeans, a strong NATO is also a way to "tie in" the United States, to ensure minimal political control, and preserve some kind of multilateralism. The tiny balance should be found between a valorization of the NATO–Russia relation and the developing EU–Russia strategic dialogue. While the new NATO–Russia relation should not turn NATO into a "Euro-Atlantic security forum" to the detriment of its military dimension, Russia should be seen as a counterpart and an essential long-term partner.

Relationship with the EU

This relationship reveals the closest linkage between integration and transformation due to established EU mechanisms (e.g., conditionality, definition of EU strategy). Since 1991, EU partners have viewed Russia's transformation process as a boost for the country's further integration to the West. Political, institutional, and economic support of Russia is motivated by the need to have a democratic Russia at its borders rather than a radical and marginalized country as well as by the existence of common interests and preoccupations (e.g., border control, managing enlargement, cooperation in the Balkans, counterweight to exclusive Russia–U.S. relations). The fact that the EU's internal integration process does not extend to Russia, because of its geographic position and size, represents a limit on the nature of EU–Russia relations, but does not prevent their positive development. In other words, the Russia–EU relationship might finally prove to be more stable, more in depth, and longer term on a broader range of issues (including function, geographic substance, and linkage between integration and transformation). In substance, they will match the terms of real transformation as they have been defined in Part I of this book. Their results will depend upon the willingness of the EU to deepen and give substance to this special relationship, which remains to be defined by European partners (see chapter 8 by Stephan Kux and chapter 7 by Ania Krok-Paszkowska and Jan Zielonka).

Consequently, Russia should not underestimate the importance of its relationship with the EU. There are common interests, the dynamic created by September 11 could change, and the Russia–NATO rapprochement might have its own limits and should not be confused with integration as such. However, in the meantime the EU should clearly define its strategy toward Russia to engage more bilaterally on all issues in order for the EU to better achieve its own security interests, to support Russia's transformation, to "balance" potential excessive trends of the U.S.–Russia relationship. Since the Balkan crisis, Europeans are convinced that it is better to bring Russia closer to European institutions to avoid its marginalization, ensure better democratic control, and thus guarantee stability.

Only then will it be possible to assess whether the relationship is heading toward:

- Partnership: Russia must be engaged to ensure its democratic development and attachment to the West.
- Alliance: Russia is considered to be necessary for crisis management at the periphery. (This could lead to progressive associationand to further integration in certain specific areas).
- Détente: Russia is rewarded for good behavior. This scenario is already outdated but it could occur in case of change of government and internal instability in Russia.
- Dissociation: This presupposes an absence of interest (return of the Russian Grand Strategy and reevaluation of short-term gains versus national strategic goals that would lead to a reorientation of priorities).

Notes

1. See chapter 13, in this book, by Angela Stent "America and Russia: Paradoxes of Partnership."
2. Dov Lynch, intervention at the Carnegie conference on Russia's integration to the West in Paris, Maison des Sciences de l'Homme, October 16, 2003.
3. Founding Act on Mutual Relations, Cooperation, and Security Between the North Atlantic Treaty Organisation and the Russian Federation, NATO–Russia Summit, Paris, May 27, 1997.
4. Dov Lynch, "Russia Facing Europe," Chaillot Paper, no. 60 (May 2003), p. 32.
5. Lord Robertson, "NATO and Russia: A Special Relationship," November 21, 2001 [www.nato.int].
6. The Prague Summit and the Transformation of NATO. NATO 2003. pp. 43–44.
7. Ibid.
8. Ibid., p. 46.
9. France and the UK underline the necessary development of confidence to obtain real added value. Italy had proposed to host the NATO–Russia summit in Rome in spring 2002. Germany, fearing a dilution of the alliance initially supported co-decision and common action but within the previous CPC framework. The strongest opposition came from the Netherlands, Turkey, and the three new members from Central Europe, which only backed a slow rapprochement to avoid weakening the alliance.
10. The Pentagon favored a minimal association (essentially status quo and association of Russia to certain decisions) and feared enhanced membership for Russia would be hampered by Russian instability and unpredictability and would weaken NATO (at 19 with ad hoc association). The State Department held a mid-way position arguing for closer association in certain fields without granting Russia a veto in the decision-making process (at 19+1). The White House was backing a maximalist approach, essentially for political reasons, to "reward" Russia for its support against terrorism (at 20).
11. Lynch, "Russia Facing Europe," pp. 36–37.
12. Ibid.
13. Dmitri Glinski-Vasiliev, "NATO Eastward Enlargement as a Russian and European Security Problem," in *Russia and European Security Institutions: Entering the 21st Century*, ed. Dmitri Trenin (Moscow: Carnegie Moscow Center, June 2000).
14. Yekaterina Stepanova, "Russia and NATO's Post-Cold War Crisis Management Strategy," in *Russia and European Security Institutions: Entering the 21st Century*, ed. Dmitri Trenin (Moscow: Carnegie Moscow Center, June 2000).
15. Identification of necessary capabilities to fight terrorism that would focus on a few key fields such as communications, transport, biological issues, TMD protection; addressing the absence of adequate European capabilities.
16. Chemical, biological, radiological, and nuclear.
17. Dmitri Trenin, "A Russia-Within-Europe: Working Toward a New Security Arrangement," intervention at the IISS/CEPS European Security Forum, January 14, 2002.
18. Stephan de Spiegeleire, "Recoupling Russia: Staying the Course Europe's Security Relationship with Russia," intervention at the IISS/CEPS European Security Forum, January 14, 2002.
19. Igor Leshoukov, "Russia and the European Union: A Strategy of Interaction," in *Russia and European Security Institutions: Entering the 21st Century*, ed. Dmitri Trenin, (Moscow: Carnegie Moscow Center, June 2000).
20. Wider Europe–Neighbourhood: A New Framework for Relations with Our Eastern and Southern Neighbours, Commission Communication COM (2003), Brussels, March 2003.

21. Angela Stent, "American Views on Russian Security Policy and EU-Russian Relations," intervention at the IISS/CEPS European Security Forum, January 14, 2002.

22. Report of the Presidency on ESDP, annex 4 on Russia. 10160/2/02 REV 2, June 22, 2002.

23. Alexander J. Motyl, "Ukraine, Europe and Russia: Exclusion or Dependence," in *Ambivalent Neighbors: The UE, NATO and the Price of Membership*, ed. Anatol Lieven and Dmitri Trenin (Washington, DC: Carnegie Endowment for International Peace, 2003), pp. 15–43.

24. See the Brussels Declarations on International Terrorism, EU–Russia summit, October 3, 2001, and November 11, 2002.

25. The Political and Security Committee (PSC) ensures the political control and the strategic direction for EU operations. The EU Military Committee (EUMC) gives recommendations and military advice to the PSC and provides the military direction of EU military operations. The EU Military Staff (EUMS) provides early warning and strategic planning.

26. Declared operational in 2003, it can deploy a force of 60,000 men within sixty days for a least a year.

27. Humanitarian aid, population evacuation, conflict prevention, separation of forces, and crisis management.

28. NATO in Afghanistan supporting ISAF with planning capabilities following Germany's and Turkey's requests. NATO possible planning support in an eventual operation in Iraq after UK request.

29. Stefan Froehlich, "(Geo)strategic Implications of Euro-Atlantic Enlargement," Woodrow Wilson Center and Stanley Foundation, Washington, DC Conference Proceedings, December 19, 2002, p. 41.

30. See recurrent chapters in this book.

31. Froehlich, "(Geo)strategic Implications of Euro-Atlantic Enlargement," p. 37.

32. Steven Blank, "The Baltic States and Euro-Atlantic Enlargement," Woodrow Wilson Center and Stanley Foundation, Washington, DC Conference Proceedings, December 19, 2002. p. 93.

33. William D. Jackson, "Encircled Again: Russia's Military Assesses Threats in a Post-Soviet World," *Political Science Quarterly* 117, no. 3 (Fall 2002).

34. Steven Blank, "The Baltic States and Euro-Atlantic Enlargement," p. 98.

13

America and Russia

Paradoxes of Partnership

Angela E. Stent

When the Cold War ended, the United States' overriding goal was to ensure that post-Soviet Russia would not pose a threat to American interests around the world. Whereas the Soviet Union was perceived as both an ideological and a military threat—especially its nuclear capabilities—America saw the new potential Russian threat as a product of Russia's weakness, its inability to control nuclear weapons and materials, and its possible disintegration as a functioning state with dangerous spillover beyond its borders. A major concern initially was that the Yugoslav catastrophe would repeat itself in the vast, ethnically diverse Russian Federation. Thus, the primary driving force behind American policy toward Russia was containing the potential global fallout from Russia's weakness.

During the first post-communist decade, Russian–American relations fluctuated between a tentative and a more robust partnership. Neither side was fully committed to seeking Russia's integration in the West, nor did either country agree on what form that integration might take. Whereas both sides were rhetorically committed to Russia's transformation into a democratic, market-oriented, post-imperial state, only sporadically did their bilateral relations engage Russia's domestic evolution. For the United States, unlike for the European Union, partnership with Russia was focused primarily on Russia's external behavior, including Russia's relations with its neighbors, with Europe, with "rogue" states, and with the United States itself. Russia's domestic situation was not a key determinant of American policy. For Washington, "hard" security concerns remained predominant during the Yeltsin era. This began to change after Vladimir Putin came to power.

This chapter will examine the evolution of U.S.–Russian relations by placing them in a historical and contemporary perspective: discussing the background of American attempts to influence the Soviet Union's domestic evolution, the Soviet response, and the change in American policy post-1991. It will highlight the similarities and differences in the approaches to Russia under presidents Bill Clinton and George W. Bush, suggest ways in which the U.S.–Russian partnership might develop in the future, and examine the extent to which it might affect Russia's domestic evolution.

In contrast to Europe, which sees Russia as a regional neighbor, the United

States views Russia through a global lens; hence its interest in Russia's transformation and integration is of a different kind than is that of the European Union (EU). Because the EU and Russia are neighbors, and because what happens in Russia can easily impact the EU—particularly now that it includes Russia's neighbors, the Baltic states and Poland—the EU is more concerned about Russia's domestic developments than is the United States. The U.S.–Russian relationship is more flexible and less dense than is the EU–Russian relationship, which involves a complex network of ties. Russia's integration with the West involves membership in multilateral organizations, some of which include both the United States and European countries. The United States and the EU are in reality not alternatives for Russia, but complement each other. Thus, one should not confuse temporary "coalitions of the willing" with the longer-term interests of Russia, the United States, and the European Union. If Russia is to become a fully modern liberal democratic country, it will have to become more integrated with both Europe and the United States.

Cold War Linkages

The debate over whether the West should seek to change Russia's domestic situation has influenced American policy for decades. Throughout the Cold War, American policy toward the Soviet Union vacillated between a limited realpolitik strategy of containment and a broader interventionist policy that sought to change Soviet domestic behavior as well as influence its foreign policy. This dualistic policy survives in the post-communist world. Americans are still divided over whether the United States should legitimately intervene in Russia's domestic transformation or whether America's role should be limited to engaging Russia on a variety of foreign policy issues that serve American interests, including offering it a role in Euro-Atlantic institutions. Indeed, the policies of the Clinton and Bush administrations highlight the contrast between, on the one hand, a commitment to influencing Russia's domestic transformation, and, on the other hand, the focus on engaging Russia on pragmatic foreign policy issues—particularly the war on terrorism—and eschewing attempts to influence domestic politics.

After 1945, there were essentially two schools of thought among American policy makers: those who believed that the lethal combination of communist ideology and traditional Russian messianic expansionism necessitated a "long-term vigilant policy of containment," otherwise the Soviet Union would inexorably seek to expand its influence; and those who viewed the Soviet Union as a traditional great power whose foreign policy behavior was influenced more by the international framework than by communist ideology.[1] From 1945 to 1969, the containment school prevailed, and little attention was paid to trying to change Soviet domestic behavior. However, with the onset of détente, the American debate changed. President Nixon and Secretary of State Kissinger realized that behind Brezhnev's moves toward rapprochement lay concrete goals—fear of a resurgent China, and the desire to improve Soviet economic performance. The Republicans in 1969 subscribed to a realpolitik school that believed it was possible to modify Soviet foreign policy behavior through a series of linkages that tied economic incentives to Soviet international behavior.[2] Kissinger explicitly rejected the premise that America should try to change Soviet domestic behavior.[3] However, Democratic opponents led by Senator Henry Jackson, thought otherwise. They insisted on linking Soviet behavior on human rights to trade privileges. The passing of the Jackson-Vanik Amendment (which remains on the books in 2004), tying the granting of most-favored-nation status to emigration, was the first formal American attempt to change Soviet domestic behavior.[4]

Under the Carter administration, the linkage policy continued. There was more economic legislation designed to punish the Soviet Union for its treatment of dissidents. Technology sanctions were imposed on the Soviet Union after it jailed a number of prominent critics. The policy of negative leverage—using punitive economic levers to express dissatisfaction with Soviet behavior—contrasted to the European preference for using trade inducements to encourage positive change in the Soviet Union.[5] Indeed, the 1975 Helsinki Final Act of the Conference on Security and Cooperation in Europe (CSCE) institutionalized the linkage between the political, economic, and human rights "baskets."[6]

By the time the Soviet Union collapsed, the Cold War linkage legacy remained in dispute. Although the United States was skeptical about the utility of the CSCE process, most European nations argued that it was precisely this form of multilateral linkage—tying foreign policy concessions to domestic behavior thereby opening up East European societies to Western Europe—that had helped undermine communism. Some attributed the fall of communism to internal Soviet rot; others to the Reagan administration's deliberate policy of forcing the Soviets to spend more on defense and challenging Soviet policy in Eastern Europe by actively supporting anticommunist groups, especially in Poland. Whatever one's view of the reasons for the collapse of the Soviet Union, there was no consensus in the United States about the role that Washington could or should play now that communism was over. During the Gorbachev period, tentative attempts at encouraging the Soviet Union's integration into the West—primarily by inviting Gorbachev as an observer to the G-7 meeting in 1991—were made at the end of his tenure. But the question of integration was raised more systematically after Gorbachev departed from the Kremlin.

Post-Soviet Russia: A New Challenge

The collapse of the Soviet Union presented the United States with tremendous opportunities and challenges. In place of the familiar—albeit antagonistic—Soviet Union came fifteen new states, most of which had never existed in this form before and all of which were undergoing revolutionary transformation as they renounced the communist model. A huge and ailing society had shaken off seventy-four years of communism almost serendipitously, and was in the throes of a major transformation into something else—but it was unclear what that was or could be. Because it was so unexpected, and because many Americans, like their major European allies, had sought to keep Gorbachev in power and prevent the breakup of the Soviet Union, it was at first difficult to form a coherent policy.[7] There was no consensus on what American goals in post-communist Russia should be, let alone a road map for how to reach them. Expectations for Russia were widely disparate: at the most optimistic end of the spectrum were those who believed that Russia was capable of a rapid triple transition to a post-imperialist, democratic, market economy. At the most pessimistic were those who believed that Russia's 1,000-year history of autocracy and communism doomed it forever to authoritarian rule, corruption, economic backwardness, and imperial ambitions toward its immediate neighbors. These American views reflected Russian debates on Russia's transformation. Indeed, since the collapse of the Soviet Union, there has been a constant interplay and mutual influence between Western and Russian discussions about the nature of Russia's transformation and integration.

One problem that has confronted analyses of Russia's transformation and integration, both in the United States and Russia, has been the frequent absence of an appropriate comparative framework. Is it realistic, a mere decade after the collapse of communism in a country that had no prior experience of democracy and the rule of law, to judge Russia's transformation by the standards of a developed Western democracy? Should one, rather, compare Russia's progress to previous Soviet regimes, or to Asian or third world countries?[8] Depending on the comparative framework in which one places Russia, one's assessment of Russia's progress to date can vary widely. It is this absence of an agreed comparative starting point that has given rise to widely varying evaluations both of American policy and of Russian developments and has often made civilized discourse on these issues extremely difficult. The truth is that Russian society remains a heterogeneous patchwork, a hybrid system with areas where there has been demonstrable progress toward a modern, democratic market society and areas where little has changed since Soviet times.

The Clinton Administration: The Liberal-Internationalist View

During the 1990s, American policy toward Russia wrestled with the issue of how to balance traditional realpolitik concerns versus a liberal-internationalist outlook. Should Washington focus primarily on Russia's foreign and security policy or should it become more actively involved in shaping Russia's post-communist political and economic transformation? When the Soviet Union collapsed, President George H.W. Bush and his advisers adopted a cautious—some would argue overly cautious—approach toward the new Russia, focusing primarily on the need to contain the potential catastrophe that large numbers of uncontrolled nuclear weapons might cause. Economic assistance was an afterthought.[9] There was no consensus on what the United States thought should happen domestically in Russia or how it might go about encouraging those changes. The Bush administration convened an international conference on assistance to Russia in the summer of 1992, passed the Freedom Support Act to bolster democratization in October 1992, and formed the North Atlantic Cooperation Council, a NATO-led forum for all the post-communist states, in December 1992. These represented, at most, preliminary moves in support of economic reform and links to NATO. Beyond that, little attention was paid either to integration or to Russia's domestic transformation. It was left to the Clinton administration to initiate a dual strategy of supporting transformation and integration that, by the end of its tenure, had not achieved either goal.

Even before he was sworn in as president, Bill Clinton argued that what was happening in Russia was "the biggest and toughest thing out there. It's not just the end of communism, the end of the cold war. That's what's over and done with. There's also stuff *starting*—stuff that's *new.* Figuring out what it is, how we work with it, how we keep it moving in the right direction: that's what we've got to do."[10] From the beginning, therefore, the Clinton administration adopted the view that the United States should legitimately become involved in Russia's domestic transformation as well as its integration into Western structures. It adopted a much more interventionist approach than had Bush, combining realpolitik with the belief that Russia's democratic evolution was a prerequisite for a more benign foreign policy. In other words, Clinton and his advisers believed that integration without transformation would ultimately fail.[11] President Clinton called for "strategic alliance with Russian reform," warning that "The danger is clear if Russia's reforms turn sour— if it reverts to authoritarianism or disintegrates into chaos. The world cannot afford the strife of the former Yugoslavia replicated in a nation as big as Russia, spanning eleven time zones with an armed arsenal of nuclear weapons."[12]

Clinton's Russia policy was based on seven major premises:[13]

- Democracies do not go to war with each other. Hence it was imperative to encourage the growth of democracy in Russia and directly influence Russia's transformation.
- Economic and political liberties are inextricably linked, and a market society based in private property ultimately produces a more democratic polity.
- The West should promote an American neoliberal economic model, rather than a more statist or social democratic European economic model.
- The major security danger was Russia's large arsenal of nuclear weapons and weapons of mass destruction (WMD) materials not under full control by the central authorities. The United States' primary goal was to support programs that diminished the threat of proliferation.
- Russia's weakness and unresolved questions of post-imperial identity meant that it had the potential to destabilize the post-Soviet space. American policy should support the independence of the post-Soviet states and contain Russia's ability to undermine their security.

- The return of communists to power was the greatest danger facing Russia. Thus, support of Boris Yeltsin, for all his idiosyncrasies, was imperative.
- As compensation for Russia adapting to its new, reduced international role, the United States would offer Russia some of the trappings of a major power, for instance, membership in the G-8 and later on a partnership with NATO. The promise of integration into Euro-Atlantic institutions was, therefore, designed to reinforce Russia's domestic transformation by offering concrete rewards in major Western clubs.

The desire to engage in reconstructing a post-communist Russia and a belief in the possibility of large-scale transformation drove U.S. policy during much of the 1990s. The large Soviet military arsenal and the possibility of disorder or conflict on a large scale in the post-Soviet space cemented this commitment. The Clinton administration pursued a variety of policies and programs designed to bolster Russia's transformation: promotion of free-market economics both by American advisers and by the International Monetary Fund; assistance for the construction of civil society and democratic parties; a Comprehensive Threat Reduction program dedicated to dismantling nuclear weapons, eliminating nuclear materials, and retraining nuclear scientists, offering alternative employment to selling their know-how to would-be third world nuclear states or terrorist organizations; assisting the transformation of other post-Soviet states in an effort to bolster their independence from Russia. It encouraged Russia's integration by offering Russia associate membership in a number of international organizations, such as the G-8 and the NATO–Russia Permanent Joint Council (PJC), and selectively consulting with it on foreign policy issues, such as the Contact Group dealing with the wars in Bosnia and Kosovo.[14]

The outcome of these policies remains controversial both in the United States and in Russia.[15] As one group of scholars concluded, "The Russian political class acted as if it was promoting market and democratic reforms, and the West acted as if it believed that this was happening."[16] In general, both critics and supporters have overestimated America's influence on Russian developments and underestimated the impact of decisions taken independently by Russian political and economic elites. It is clear in retrospect that there was a conflict between Russia's major foreign and domestic goals as it dealt with the United States. While the Yeltsin administration accepted in principle the goal of becoming a market democracy, it also sought to preserve as much as it could of Russia's great power status, which strained Russia's resources and bolstered the waning influence of the antireformist military-industrial groups. This produced a paradoxical situation, whereby great power ideology continued to cement Russian society at a time when democratic values had not taken hold broadly within society and there was no consensus on post-communist national identity.

In terms of integration, under Clinton, Russia began to join Euro-Atlantic institutions. Russia's acceptance as a partial member of the G-8 grouping of industrialized countries enabled Yeltsin to attend the political, but not the economic, meetings at the annual summits. While these meetings gave Russia a voice in global deliberations, including strategic issues of direct importance to Russia, the G-8 served only as a partial forum for integration since with a shrinking GDP, Russia was not in the same league economically as the other members. Membership in the Council of Europe, supported by the United States (although America itself is not a member), was potentially more significant in terms of Russia's domestic behavior, but it is unclear how much membership in this parliamentary body has influenced Russia's domestic transformation. The other major Clinton-era integration initiative, the 1997 NATO–Russia Permanent Joint Council, offered as a consolation prize for the first round of NATO enlargement, also had mixed results. In terms of military relations, on the ground NATO–Russian cooperation in Bosnia and even Kosovo after the wars there ended were arguably more conducive toward the transformation of Russian military attitudes than were the difficult PJC discussions themselves.

While most commentators would agree that American policy toward Russia's integration was at least partly successful—especially in the security sphere—there is no consensus about the impact of the Clinton policies on Russia's domestic transformation. At one extreme, as the Cox Report, a Congressional Republican attack on Clinton policies produced for the 2000 U.S. presidential election, claimed, the Clinton policies had been responsible for "Russia's road to corruption." The United States had pursued policies that had corrupted Russia and led to the impoverishment of its people—in other words, U.S. policy had actively sabotaged Russia's domestic transformation into a modern democratic state.[17] Some academics echoed this view, arguing that U.S. policy was deliberately designed to undermine Russia's transformation and was "the worst foreign policy disaster since Vietnam."[18] Others argued, to the contrary, that the United States had encouraged Russia's development in the right direction, had ensured that the communists did not return to power, and had supported reforms that would admittedly take many decades to complete.[19]

While one can point to the many flaws in Russia's domestic evolution in the 1990s, as other authors in this book already have, it is ahistorical only to stress Russia's failings and to assign major blame to the United States for these problems. By the end of the Yeltsin administration, Russia was a pluralistic, imperfect market society, an electoral democracy with relatively free media, where power had been decentralized chaotically and there was considerable freedom of expression. There were also widespread corruption, vast disparities of wealth between the rising oligarchs and the rest of the population, and little political or economic transparency. The Clinton administration supported the market reformers, but they, and not the United States, had made the crucial decisions about the most controversial policies—voucher privatization and loans-for-shares. The Clinton administration had unwaveringly backed Yeltsin because it considered that, given the alternatives, he represented the best hope for transformation. However one comes out on these issues, it is incontestable that both Russians and Americans have overestimated America's influence on Russia's domestic development. Ultimately, Russian officials and business people acted on their own interests, invoking American advice when it suited them.

By the end of the Yeltsin–Clinton partnership, U.S.–Russian relations had reached a low ebb. Russia's untransparent and controversial economic evolution—symbolized in the loans-for-shares program that ensured Yeltsin's 1996 reelection—NATO enlargement, the Kosovo war, and the second Chechen war had soured both sides. At this point, the Clinton administration had distanced itself from attempts to influence Russia's domestic situation and confined itself to Russia's foreign policy. The agenda became increasingly negative—Russia's nuclear assistance to "rogue" states and disputes over the United States plans to build a missile defense system reinforced existing strains. The attempt to support Russia's transformation into a modern, democratic state had not turned out the way it was initially conceived.

From Clinton to Bush

The Bush administration came into office vowing to "normalize" relations with Russia, review all previous policies, and cease treating Russia as a special case. In particular, it promised to eschew policies that involved the United States in managing Russia's domestic affairs. It was a classic realpolitik view—one should engage Russia where necessary over security issues, but leave Russia to its own devices and let it decide whether it wanted to become a democracy and be integrated into Euro-Atlantic structures. Inasmuch as Clinton's policies were explicitly rejected, the Bush administration emphasized the need to downgrade relations with Russia and not to pay as much attention to the country's evolution as had the Democrats.

Despite this policy of distancing, however, when Bush first met Putin in Ljubljana in June 2001, he appears to have decided that, contrary to what all of his advisers had said during the election campaign, he favored a close personal relationship with the Russian president. Ironically, this may partly have resulted from his difficult encounters with European statesmen in his NATO and EU meetings prior to meeting Putin. Thus, the condescending manner in which some European leaders—and particularly their elites—treated him contrasted to the more welcoming and respectful reception he received from President Putin.

This personal encounter reinforced what has subsequently become clear—that Vladimir Putin, as he himself has often stressed, had decided early on in his presidency that if modernizing Russia was his top priority, Russia must become integrated with the West, at least in terms of institutional ties. The question of domestic transformation is clearly more complex, as his millennial piece shows.[20] Closer ties to the EU and individual European states were a major part of his plan. But the United States was also important—and, unlike the EU, it could still validate Russia's role as a great power. If Russia were to play in the top league, so to speak, the United States was a key partner. In this sense, September 11 provided a major opportunity for Putin to engineer a rapprochement with the United States.

September 11 and After

The terrorist attacks offered the United States and Russia the chance to redefine their relationship and move beyond the impasse of the late 1990s. Putin was able to argue convincingly that fundamentalist Islam represented a threat to both Russia and the United States and to present Russia as an ally by agreeing not to hinder American plans to set up military bases in Central Asia to launch their attacks on al-Qaeda. As the antiterrorist campaign developed, America's new ally reacted with relative equanimity to the same issues that had so plagued the U.S.–Russian relationship under Clinton—the announcement to abrogate the Anti-Ballistic Missile Treaty, the commitment to further NATO enlargement, and continued criticism of Russia's role in facilitating WMD proliferation to states that formed what was later termed the "axis of evil." Suddenly, the atmospherics and rhetoric of the U.S.–Russian relationship had improved beyond what any informed observer might have imagined a few months before. As President Bush seized the opportunity to enlist Russia as a partner in the antiterrorist campaign, talk of "normalizing" relations with Russia or downgrading them evaporated. In allying with Russia against terrorism, the Bush administration committed itself to limited integration for Russia—forming a partnership against fundamentalist Islam. It did not, however, commit itself to participation in Russia's domestic transformation. In this sense, the new Russian–American relationship has reverted to classic realpolitik, an alliance against a common enemy, but not necessarily based on shared interests or values beyond antiterrorism. It is a return to the Nixon–Kissinger view of relations, rather than a Reaganite or Clintonite view.

The current U.S.–Russian relationship is based on the following premises:

- ꝰ Russia's prime importance lies in its ability to assist the war on terrorism by facilitating U.S. military operations in Central Asia and providing intelligence for the campaign. Conversely, Russia could act as an obstacle to these operations if it so chose.
- In return for support for the U.S. war, and under the slogan that those who fight terrorism are the United States' friends, the United States has been virtually silent about Russia's domestic situation, from the Chechen war to the limitations on media freedom to the selective assault on oligarchs. Indeed, it has virtually endorsed the Russian claim that the Chechen war is driven by rebels linked to al-Qaeda. The administration does not view active government-sponsored democracy promotion as a task for the United States.[21]
- In return for Russian support, the United States is willing to facilitate Putin's primary goal—economic modernization and integration into the global economy—by offering to accelerate World Trade Organization (WTO) membership, by urging Congress to graduate Russia from Jackson-Vanik, and by engaging Russia actively on a number of other economic fronts, particularly energy production and exports.

- Despite the new antiterrorist alliance, the United States continues to press Russia on issues of ties to Iran and North Korea and on Russia's role in facilitating WMD proliferation. Russia and America disagreed over the war in Iraq but have begun to reach compromises on Russia's future role in Iraq's reconstruction.
- Despite criticism of Clinton-era assistance programs, the Bush administration has retained most of them and even increased some. In addition, although the administration abolished the Gore–Chernomyrdin Commission, it has de facto recreated significant parts of it by sponsoring bilateral working groups on a variety of issues, particularly strategic questions and energy.
- For the time being, and despite serious differences over Iraq, Putin is seen as a reliable partner. In this antiterrorist alliance, the United States and Russia share a common enemy and some common interests.

The Limited Alliance

The Bush–Putin summits of 2002 and 2003 and the NATO–Russia summits reveal the modest dimensions of Russia's new ties to the West. The 2002 summit products—a short arms control treaty that enables either side to withdraw on three month's notice and permits both sides to store, not destroy, the warheads that they cut; a joint declaration on energy, on the Middle East, and on general partnership; and a NATO–Russia Council that enables NATO to withdraw issues from the table if it appears that Russia will obstruct discussion—suggest that this remains a limited partnership. American willingness to encourage investment in the Russian private sector and promote Russia's integration into the world economy could facilitate closer ties between Russia and the West, and encourage the growth of a more forward-looking middle class, but this is still some time off. Closer association with NATO is also no guarantee that Russia might move in a more democratic direction. And even the most explicitly domestic aspect of the Bush administration's policy—the business-media dialogue—has done little to curb Putin's restrictions on critical media or his pressure on certain representatives of big business, particularly the arrest of Yukos CEO Mikhail Khodorkovsky.

The limits of the U.S.–Russian partnership became clear in the run-up to the Iraq war. Washington understood Russia's economic stake in Iraq—the $8 billion in debts owed to it and potential future energy contracts—and its preference for action legitimized by the United Nations Security Council, the only international body where Russia still enjoys a status equal to that of the United States and can veto American proposals. However, the Bush administration, while it did not anticipate active Russian support for the war, did not expect active opposition either. As France led the opposition to the war, the United States was taken unawares by Moscow's robust support for Paris and Berlin, in what became the "coalition of the unwilling."

While a history of this war and its diplomacy remains to be written, it is notable that the Bush administration chose not to woo Russia—and many other countries —actively in order to change their minds and lessen their opposition to the war. There were no high-level visits to Moscow to discuss Iraq, nor were there feelers to engage Putin directly, aside from a brief visit to Washington before the war broke out by his chief of staff Aleksandr Voloshin. Russia's support of the UN resolution to lift sanctions on Iraq was the first sign that ties could be improved. The 2003 St. Petersburg and Camp David summits represented an attempt to restore the partnership after Iraq. However, the dispute over Iraq and over the exercise of American military power revealed the fragility of the post–September 11 partnership and raised questions about how robust the substance of this relationship was.

For the foreseeable future, therefore, American policy is likely to be limited to securing Russia's continuing assistance in the war against terror and trying to persuade Russia to change its relations with Iran and North Korea. Greater democracy in Russia might be desirable, but it is not at the forefront of American goals. Conversely, Russia hopes for more concrete economic benefits from the relationship with the United States and for continuing treatment as an important partner. President Putin reiterates that he has always wanted Russia to be part of the West. But, as far as one can tell to date, his definition of being part of the West does not include Russia's transformation into a liberal democracy.

Russian Views of the U.S.–Russian Relationship

Russian attitudes toward the U.S.–Russian relationship have varied as much as have American views, and there is no consensus within Russia about the desirability of ties with America or about integration into Western institutions. This reflects profound disagreements within Russian society about the domestic direction post-Soviet Russia should take. For centuries, the Russian intelligentsia has debated whether Russia is part of Europe, whose destiny lies in the secular, post-Enlightenment, materialist West, or whether it is a unique Eurasian country, whose natural allies are to be found in the East and South. Even those Russian rulers like Peter the Great, who favored looking West to reap the benefits of Europe's technological prowess, said, "We need Europe for a few decades. Later, we must turn our back on it."[22] In the post-Soviet era, pro-Western Russians, also known as Atlanticists, have included the United States as a model, although they acknowledge the differences between American and European democracy. Some pro-Western Russians argue that, given their size, ethnic heterogeneity, and economic endowments, America and Russia have more in common than either do with Europe, but this is a minority view.

Since 1991, the pro-Western Atlanticist Russians have argued both for domestic transformation and for integration into Euro-Atlantic structures. As Andrei Kozyrev, the first post-Soviet foreign minister (1992–1996) put it, "Our aim is to

enter the community of civilized nations of the Northern Hemisphere. Our choice
. . . is to progress according to generally accepted rules. They were invented by the
West, and I'm a Westernizer in this respect. . . . The West is rich, we need to be
friends with it. . . . It's the club of first-rate states Russia must rightfully belong
to."[23] On the opposite end of the spectrum, Eurasianists, communists, and nationalists alike have rejected both transformation and integration: "Democracy is pro-
foundly inimical to our national culture, it tramples down everything it comes into
contact with, in the name of some world order or another. And in general all these
phenomena—democracy, globalism, Zionism and cosmopolitanism—are identi-
cal twins."[24] In between these opposites, some Russians have favored slower transformation, partial integration, and a "multipolar" foreign policy that looks to the
United States and Europe, but seeks to balance a pro-Western policy with one that
aligns Russia with China, India, and other Asian countries. Indeed, Evgenii
Primakov's tenure as foreign minister represented a synthesis between the Atlanticist
and Eurasianist views. He argued that Russia should cooperate with the West where
appropriate, while seeking a selective, pragmatic, and "equal" partnership in the
world economy.[25]

Igor Ivanov, foreign minister from 1998 to 2004 and now head of the Security
Council, has articulated a cautious but supportive view of U.S.–Russian relations,
stressing that these relations can only prosper "through equal partnership and by
taking each other's interests into account, and only within the context of broad international cooperation."[26] He has highlighted nuclear weapons reductions, nonprolif-
eration, economic relations, and "pragmatic cooperation" as the key aspects of
U.S.–Russian relations. Ivanov articulates the thrust of Russia's official "Foreign
Policy Concept of the Russian Federation." Nowhere is the concept of Russia's "in-
tegration" into Western structures mentioned in this document. Relations with the
United States receive minimal attention, and it is clear that the Ministry of Foreign
Affairs view is that relations with Europe and the United States should not involve
Western attempts to influence Russia's domestic political or economic situation.[27]

When one moves beyond the official statements, Russian views on relations
with the United States express a wide diversity of views along a spectrum from
strong optimism to deep pessimism, from praise to profound criticism. President
Putin appears to be in a class by himself. Domestically, his emphasis during his
first term was on stability; during the second term it is on consolidated growth.
Having taken the bold step of supporting President Bush after September 11, against
the advice of most of his colleagues, he has continued to articulate a positive vision
of U.S.–Russian relations, while his foreign and defense ministers, and other officials, have been more cautious or even critical. Even as he opposed U.S. policy
during the run-up to the Iraq war, he urged caution against anti-Americanism. Russian experts have argued that Putin's pro-American policy has been largely a one-
man show, that he has relied on a small group of advisers, and has not fully explained
the reasons for his pro-American stance to his population. Despite his support of
closer ties to America, however, Putin has made it clear that the United States,

while it should become more involved in the Russian economy, should stay out of Russia's domestic political situation, particularly the war in Chechnya. From Putin's point of view, America should provide support for Russia's economic reforms and for its economic modernization, but should not interfere with its domestic politics. Putin favors closer ties with the EU and wants Russia to join the WTO as soon as is feasible, and in this sense he supports Russia's economic integration into global and Euro-Atlantic institutions. His pragmatic policies foresee ties with the United States that bolster Russia's significance as a global and regional player, but are based on realpolitik, leaving him to pursue his "managed democracy" at home.

Within Russia, only a small group of liberal intellectuals favors a U.S.–Russian relationship that moves beyond bilateral cooperation in foreign policy to influencing Russia's domestic situation in the direction of greater democracy. The scholar Dmitri Trenin lays out such a vision in his book, *The End of Eurasia,* where he rejects the concept of Eurasianism and advocates that America and Russia "turn this relationship into a vehicle for Russia's integration within the American-European security community."[28] Liberal Russian commentators by and large believe that institutional integration into Euro-Atlantic structures will ultimately promote Russia's domestic transformation. They are less concerned about whether the improved U.S.–Russian relationship since September 11, 2001, has brought Russia commensurate rewards, and more focused on the longer-term goal of Russia's rapprochement with the West in such a way that will prevent a return to Russia's illiberal and undemocratic past.

Other pro-Western commentators support closer U.S.–Russian ties for the foreign policy benefits they bring Russia, particularly membership in the various Euro-Atlantic "clubs," and less for the potential benefits of integration.[29] Many question what the antiterrorism alliance has brought Russia concretely, and bemoan Russia's junior status in that partnership. The agenda in the U.S.–Russian relationship remains largely a product of American, not Russian, concerns, given the asymmetry between American and Russian power and influence. Thus, a lingering Cold War mentality that continues to view U.S. and Russian interests as naturally opposed (such a mentality also exists in the United States) means that even liberal commentators view the relationship with the United States with considerable ambiguity.

When one moves beyond the pro-Western commentators, there are plenty of Russians, both inside and outside the government, who continue to view the United States with suspicion, not only because of its overwhelming international power but also because they view democracy and capitalism negatively. For many, the fact that the United States believes that it "won" the Cold War, coupled with the disintegration of the Soviet Union, remains a source of humiliation and disgrace. The indisputable predominance of U.S. power further exacerbates these negative views. During the 1999 Kosovo war and again during the Iraq war, these feelings were evidenced in growing popular anti-American sentiment, demonstrations against the United States, and charges that America was trying to force Russia to act against its own interests. These sentiments, echoed in official Communist Party pronouncements, as well as those from nationalist "patriotic" groups, reflect, to varying degrees, the wholesale rejection of integration with the West and greater democracy. The December 2003 Duma elections saw the rise of a new party, *Rodina,* that is outspokenly nationalistic. Anti-Western themes were echoed in the election campaigns of the victorious United Russia Party and in the failure of the small democratic parties Yabloko and Union of Right Forces to gain the 5 percent of the vote necessary for seats in the parliament.

Nevertheless, for the past decade, Russia has been ruled by leaders who eschew anti-Western views, and, as long as President Putin remains in power, Russia is likely to continue to seek membership in Western "clubs." Indeed, barring some major economic downturn, it is difficult to imagine scenarios under which Russia's foreign policy course could dramatically change. After all, as long as economic modernization remains a key Russian goal, Moscow must continue to pursue closer ties to the United States and Europe. The question is, with which Europe should Russia align itself?

United States–Russia–EU: The Divided West

Since the end of the Cold War, the United States and EU countries have increasingly diverged over a number of issues—the Kyoto protocol, the death penalty, military spending, the use of force, the welfare state vs. unbridled free-market capitalism—but the Iraq war has crystallized and sharpened this "values gap." Europeans have grown increasingly critical of what they view as American unilateralism, and, although they agree that global terrorism presents a major security threat, they disagree about the concept of using military force to deal with this threat. Moreover, Europeans and Americans hold diverging views of the role and utility of the United Nations.[30] Thus, despite a common commitment to democracy, markets, and the rule of law, the transatlantic relationship has become increasingly contentious in the absence of a Soviet threat to bind the alliance together. During the Iraq war, transatlantic strains were further complicated by the split within Europe itself. In the words of U.S. Defense Secretary Donald Rumsfeld, "old Europe"—led by France, Germany, and Russia—opposed the war and refused to provide a UN mandate for the use of force.[31] In contrast, "new Europe," led by the UK, Italy, Spain, and Central Europe, supported the war. While these countries had different reasons for supporting or opposing the war, the split within Europe has further complicated the process of developing a common European foreign policy and the repercussions on the transatlantic relationship have been serious and will continue to be so for some time.

Despite talk of a new "Paris–Berlin–Moscow axis" this triangular coalition of the unwilling during the Iraq war was a limited phenomenon. Yet it illustrated a number of paradoxes in the Russian position. On the one hand, President Putin, in the words of a seasoned commentator, "once again played a lousy hand of cards with extraordinary skill."[32] The Russian relationship with Europe's leading powers improved, high-level summitry in the run-up to the war raised Putin's international profile, and Russia's opposition to the Iraq war played well at home. Yet the disputes over the Iraq war reinforced a new reality: Russia might have to choose with which "West" to integrate.

After the war was over, Putin paid a state visit to the UK and spent part of his vacation with the Italian prime minister, thus showing that he could cultivate ties with both "old" and "new" Europe. Moreover, despite Russia's opposition to the war, President Putin was able to restore his relationship with President Bush, whereas the White House continued to distance itself from the leaders of France and Germany. On the other hand, despite Putin's ability to enjoy close personal ties with the leaders of France, Germany, Britain, and the United States (a seemingly unique accomplishment), Russians themselves were unclear what this diplomatic maneuvering had brought them in concrete terms. Indeed, many Russians recognized that, in contrast to the Cold War years, it is not necessarily in Russia's interest to face a divided West. Given Putin's desire for economic integration with the West and increased international status for Russia, it is more productive to deal with a West that is more united. As Foreign Minster Igor Ivanov noted during the height of the Iraq controversy, "the preservation of a unified Euro-Atlantic community, with Russia now part of it, is of immense importance."[33]

The impact of the U.S.–Russian partnership on European Union–Russian ties has so far been marginal. Whereas many EU countries were far more wary of the concept of the "war on terror" than was Russia, the EU continued to pursue its relations with Russia—a much denser network of ties than that involved in the U.S.–Russian relationship. However, Putin's focus on the United States after 9/11 represented a shift away from a primary focus on the EU to a more balanced relationship with the United States and Europe. After all, it is easier to talk about joint interests in combating Islamic fundamentalism than it is to negotiate the intricacies of Schengen visa regimes in Kaliningrad with the unbending Brussels bureaucracy. Putin's frustration with dealing with the EU has apparently led to a renewed interest in America as an alternative partner and to dealing with individual European leaders, as opposed to the EU. Yet the United States can never replace Europe in terms of Russia's economic interests. Europe is simply far more important economically for Russia than is the United States. Conversely, the Moscow–Berlin–Paris "axis of opposition" during the Iraq war did not indicate a qualitatively new Russia–EU relationship. It was a tactical alliance that brought Russia only short-term benefits. Thus the U.S.–Russian partnership should complement, not compete with the EU–Russia relationship.

Transatlantic divisions over Iraq and other issues should not, however, obscure the fact that the United States and the European Union by and large agree on what needs to be done in order to integrate Russia into the West. America and the EU hold regular consultations on Russia, and Russia is also a topic for bilateral discussions between Washington and individual European allies. America and Europe may themselves disagree over a range of important issues, but they concur that

Russia should become a more transparent market democracy and that its relations with its neighbors—whether Russia chooses to pursue a benign or an imperial policy—are an important measure of its commitment to become more integrated into the West. In the longer run, therefore, Russia is an issue over which there could be more future transatlantic cooperation.

Impact of the U.S.–Russian Partnership on Russia's Integration

Where is the U.S.–Russian relationship headed? As it now stands, the bilateral partnership—essentially an alliance to combat international terrorism—will have a limited effect on Russia's integration into Western institutions. America will continue to promote the NATO–Russia Council, and its deliberations could widen to include joint theater-missile defense and closer military-to-military cooperation. The greatest hindrance to Russia's closer relationship with NATO remains the ambivalence of the Russian military toward cooperation with NATO. This is reflected in the fact that Russian officials who are stationed at NATO and Russian military personnel who serve with NATO units in the Balkans are not promoted when they return home. The Russian government needs to make the decision to reward, not punish its officials for service with NATO. Military and intelligence cooperation between the United States and Russia in the antiterror war could also serve as a means to integrate Russia into Western military structures. However, the key decisions remain to be made by the Putin administration. Military reform is an essential element of Russia's move toward a more modern, democratic state. So far, despite publicly recognizing the need for military reform, little has been done, partly because of opposition within the military and partly because of the high cost of moving from a conscript to a professional army. Partnership with NATO and the United States can serve to encourage military reform, but the Kremlin itself will have to make tough decisions and then ensure that they are implemented before the Russian military becomes more modern.

It is unclear to what extent the current U.S.–Russian partnership can or will promote Russia's integration. America is actively encouraging Russia's WTO accession. WTO membership would impact on Russia's domestic economic reform, but, as the Chinese case shows, one can be a member of the WTO without being a democracy. America will continue to support NATO–Russian ties, but they represent the promise of gradual integration, and only if Russia itself is willing to promote that integration. As long as the main American focus remains fighting terrorism and pressuring Russia on WMD proliferation, the impact of this partnership on integration will remain limited.

Could this partnership retard Russia's move toward modernity? Inasmuch as any such partnership endorses the status quo, because it deals with the current government, one might argue that the partnership is not designed to move Russia's modernization forward. Indeed, Washington's caution in criticizing Putin's domestic policies and its quasi-endorsement of the campaign against Chechen militants has, in the opinion of some critics, helped Putin consolidate his system of rule. Nevertheless, one has to acknowledge the limits of any outside country's influence on Russian domestic developments. While the U.S.–Russian partnership may not move Russia's transformation forward, it cannot retard it either. The transformation is Russia's, and Russia's alone, to make.

As it now stands, the U.S.–Russian partnership will remain in place as long as global terrorism threatens both the United States and Russia, and as long as both the American and Russian governments assign a high order of priority to that struggle. In effect, that means as long as Putin remains president, because any American government for the foreseeable future will remain committed to this war. The partnership is therefore sustainable under these circumstances for the next few years, but it will remain limited and will have only a marginal impact on Russia's integration and no perceptible impact on its transformation.

Beyond the Limited Partnership?

Could the United States move beyond this limited partnership and devise policies that might facilitate Russia's integration or even transformation? America could play a part in encouraging Russia's greater integration only if its current policy is modified from one of a limited partnership in the antiterrorist war to a policy of long-term, active engagement with Russia based on the premise that Russia can one day be part of Euro-Atlantic civilization. This is a far cry from the current policy of alliances "à la carte" and coalitions of the willing.

If the United States were to rethink its policies—and to find a receptive Russian ear—then there are a variety of ways in which closer economic and political ties could eventually promote both greater integration and also domestic change in Russia.

The starting point for Washington would be integration, rather than transformation, given the current demands of the war on terror and the disinclination to remake Russian society. There are a number of areas where Russia and the United States could cooperate more closely that would encourage Russia to adopt norms of behavior that are more consistent with Western values. Three have considerable potential to promote integration.[34]

- *European Security:* The new NATO–Russia Council has the potential to involve Russia much more closely in enhancing European security. The council is already more productive than many had thought it would be. The key to overcoming the problems that the PJC had is to start with modest joint projects that can build trust and develop into larger projects. Inasmuch as these projects—counterterrorism, search-and-rescue operations, missile defense—involve close cooperation between the Russian military and NATO, they could serve over time to reorient the mentality of the Russian military in directions that are more compatible with Western military values. If the NATO–Russia

Council could also deal with issues directly related to Russian military reform, then it could have a more significant domestic impact in Russia. Thus, at its most productive, the NATO–Russia Council could serve both to encourage Russia's further integration into NATO structures and Russia's domestic transformation away from a Soviet-era military mentality.

- *Security in the Post-Soviet Space:* From a foreign policy perspective, if the antiterrorism campaign is to succeed in the long run, there needs to be multilateral cooperation in Eurasia in order to achieve peace and stability. The United States and Russia will have to work with China and other neighbors, as well as the EU, to establish a new framework for security in Central Asia and beyond. If Russia were willing to become a guarantor of stability in Eurasia, instead of being tempted to act as a spoiler, that would also alter Russia's perception of its identity as a great power. A more forward-looking role in Eurasian security could reinforce these beliefs and ultimately could have an impact on the domestic expressions of Russia's national identity.

- *Energy Cooperation and Global Markets:* One of the most promising avenues of current U.S.—Russian cooperation is in the energy field. The U.S. administration believes that Russia has the potential to become a major stabilizer of the volatile oil markets.[35] Russian energy entrepreneurs, seeking to build their reputations as responsible corporate players, are playing a key role in the new U.S.–Russia energy dialogue. While there is no direct correlation between greater energy cooperation—including joint projects—and either integration or transformation, there is a potential indirect connection. However, greater energy cooperation will also depend on how the Russian authorities resolve the situation with Yukos and whether they are willing to encourage more foreign participation in the energy sector.

There are also two possible ways in which the current U.S.–Russian relationship could develop a partnership that could affect Russia's domestic transformation more directly:

- *New Security Issues:* Despite the current preoccupation with traditional security issues, U.S.–Russian relations will become increasingly concerned with problems that are of more recent vintage, but have grave security implications for Russia and its neighbors. These "new" security issues include infectious diseases, especially tuberculosis and HIV/AIDS, both of which are reaching epidemic proportions; trafficking in drugs and people; and organized crime. If the United States and Russia were to intensify cooperation to deal with these problems, including both governmental and nongovernmental organization support, then habits of cooperation and a diminution of Russian suspicions about American motives would follow. It is in America's long-term interest to create a more benign security environment in Russia, and cooperation on nontraditional security issues will involve Russian society as well as its political elites.

- *Targeting the New Generation:* Generational change in Russia will be an important aspect of Russia's attempts to become a modern democratic state. The United States could do much more to target these younger "cadres," through exchanges for students and young professionals, assistance to small entrepreneurs and local politicians. In the most optimistic scenario, if one assumes that there is a spillover effect from these forms of cooperation onto Russian domestic developments, then a longer-term American partnership involving both bilateral and multilateral institutional cooperation could go some way toward encouraging the development of democratic institutions, rule and law, and civil society in Russia beyond their current state. But history has few examples that provide a road map for this kind of engagement. America's ability to democratize postwar West Germany or Japan was premised on their defeat in war and on their occupation by the United States. These conditions do not apply to Russia.

In order to promote integration and transformation, American policy would have to accept a long-term commitment to multifaceted engagement with Russia both internationally and domestically. Russia would also have to reciprocate this engagement and respond appropriately to it. Given the current domestic and foreign policy priorities of both governments, this appears to be an unlikely scenario in the next few years. However, it is a goal toward which both countries should be encouraged to move. The current pragmatic partnership based on foreign policy cooperation would not per se affect Russia's domestic development. However, at the margins, the projects outlined above could encourage more far-reaching change in Russia. But Putin will find that integration with Western institutions will ultimately be limited if Russia is not willing to undergo a more far-reaching domestic transformation. Ultimately, Russia's integration into Euro-Atlantic structures is a project for decades, a process that will evolve for much of this new century.

Notes

1. These two schools, the "Riga" and "Yalta" axioms, are discussed in Daniel Yergin, *Shattered Peace: The Origins of the Cold War and the National Security State* (Boston: Houghton Mifflin, 1977), chapters 1, 2. George Kennan, who first articulated the containment policy in his "Sources of Soviet Conduct" article, epitomized the Riga axioms.

2. For a broader discussion of the evolution of American views of linkage strategies, see Angela Stent, "East-West Economic Relations and the Western Alliance," in *Trade, Technology and Soviet-American Relations*, ed. Bruce Parrott (Bloomington: Indiana University Press, 1985), pp. 283–90.

3. Henry Kissinger, *Years of Renewal* (New York: Simon and Schuster, 1999), chapters 8–10.

4. Paula Stern, *Water's Edge: Domestic Politics and the Making of American Foreign Policy* (Westport, CT: Greenwood Press, 1979).

5. For a fuller discussion of these policies, see Angela Stent, *From Embargo to Ostpolitik: The Political Economy of Soviet-West German Relations, 1955–1980* (Cambridge: Cambridge University Press, 1981).

6. The CSCE Final Act committed all its signatories to recognize the borders of Europe (although peaceful change was permitted), to increase economic contacts and to implement policies that respected human rights.

7. The Bush administration was initially divided over how far to support Gorbachev once the Soviet Union unraveled. For an analysis of Russian–American relations during Yeltsin's tenure, see Angela Stent and Lilia Shevtsova, "Russia's Elections: No Turning Back," *Foreign Policy* 103 (Summer 1996): 92–111.

8. For the view that Russia should be compared to other middle-income capitalist economies, see Andrei Shleiter and Daniel Treisman, "A Normal Country," *Foreign Affairs* 83, no. 2 (March/April 2004): 20–38.

9. See Angela Stent, "Russia's Economic Revolution and the West," *Survival* 37, no. 1 (Spring 1995): 121–43.

10. Cited in Strobe Talbott, *The Russia Hand: A Memoir of Presidential Democracy* (New York: Random House, 2002), p. 42.

11. See James Goldgeier and Michael McFaul, *Power and Purpose* (Washington, DC Brookings Institution Press, 2003).

12. President Clinton's Annapolis Naval Academy speech, April 1, 1993, cited in Gail W. Lapidus, "Transforming Russia: American Policy in the 1990's," in *Eagle Rules?* ed. Robert J. Lieber (New Jersey: Prentice Hall, 2002), p. 103.

13. The Bush administration showed these premises, but the difference between Bush and Clinton was that the latter believed it could have a decisive impact on Russia's domestic situation, whereas the former did not.

14. Between 1992 and 1999, the United States gave Russia $7.67 billion in assistance. Russia also received $8.89 billion in commercial financing and insurance from the U.S. government. See Esther Brimmer, Benjamin Schreer, and Christian Tuschoff, "Contemporary Perspectives on European Security," *German Issues* 27, American Institute for Contemporary German Studies, Johns Hopkins University, Washington, DC, 2002.

15. For contrasting views, see Lilia Shevtsova, *Yeltsin's Russia: Myths and Realities* (Washington, DC: Carnegie Endowment for International Peace, 1999); Peter Reddaway and Dmitri Glinsky, *The Tragedy of Russian Reform* (Washington, DC: U.S. Institute of Peace, 2001); Leon Aron, *Yeltsin, A Revolutionary Life* (New York: St. Martin's Press, 2000); and Strobe Talbott, *The Russia Hand: A Memoir of Presidential Diplomacy* (New York: Random House, 2002).

16. Manfred Hueterer and Heidi Reisinger, "Von den Illusionen der neunziger Jahre zu einem neuen Realismus," in *Der Schwerfaellige Riese: Wie Russland den Wandel gestalten soll*, ed. Olaf Hillenbrand and Iris Kempe (Guetersloh: Bertelsmann, 2003), p. 263.

17. *Russia's Road to Corruption: How the Clinton Administration Exported Government Instead of Free Enterprise and Failed the Russian People*, Report of the Cox Commission, Washington, DC, 2000.

18. Stephen S. Cohen, *Failed Crusade: America and the Tragedy of Post-Communist Russia* (New York: Norton, 2000), p. 9.

19. On this, see Talbott, *The Russia Hand* and also Leon Aron, *Making Sense of a Revolution* (American Enterprise Institute for Public Policy Research, September 2002; see www.aei.org/publications), which argues for evaluating Russia's progress in the past decade in terms of its communist past, not on the basis of some hypothetical contemporary democratic ideal.

20. See Putin's "Russia on the Eve of the Millennium," at www.government.gn.ru, December 28, 1999.

21. However, Secretary of State Colin Powell directly addressed Russia's democratic deficits in his article, "Partnership Under Construction," *Izvestiia*, January 26, 2004.

22. Cited in Angela Stent, *Russia and Germany Reborn: Unification, the Soviet Collapse and the New Europe* (Princeton: Princeton University Press, 1999), p. 4.

23. Interview with Andrei Kozyrev, *Moscow News* June 7–14, 1992, p. 14; Kozyrev quoted in Moscow *Interfax*, November 25, 1992, in FBIS-SOV-92–229.

24. *Sovetskaia Rossiia*, July 4, 1992.

25. For a discussion of these issues, see the round-table discussion on national interest and foreign policy, "Natsional'nie interesy vo vneshnei politike Rossii," *Mezhdunarodnaia zhizn'* 3, 1996.

26. Igor S. Ivanov, *The New Russian Diplomacy* (Washington, DC: Brookings Institution/Nixon Center, 2002), p. 111.

27. "Foreign Policy Concept of the Russian Federation," reproduced in Ivanov, *The New Russian Diplomacy*, pp. 165–82.

28. Dmitri Trenin, *The End of Eurasia* (Washington, DC: Carnegie Endowment for International Peace, 2002), p. 323. For a further discussion of these views, see Angela Stent, "Russia: Farewell to Empire?" *World Policy Journal* (Fall 2002): 83–89.

29. See, for example, the press conference with Sergei Rogov, Director of the Institute of USA and Canada Studies, March 28, 2003 (2003–03–FNS); and press conference with Duma member Andrei Kokoshin, March 24, 2003 (2003–03–24 ITA).

30. For a full discussion of these issues, see *Transatlantic Trends 2003*, a public opinion survey conducted by the German Marshall Fund of the United States (Washington, DC: 2003).

31. See Anne Appelbaum, "Here Comes the New Europe," *Washington Post*, January 29, 2003.

32. Quentin Peel, "Putin Delivers a Lesson in Political Survival," *Financial Times*, April 8, 2003.

33. *Financial Times*, February 14, 2003.

34. For a fuller discussion of these issues, see Angela Stent, and Lilia Shevtsova, "America, Russia and Europe: A Realignment?" *Survival* 44, no. 4 (Winter 2002–3): 121–34.

35. See Edward Morse and James Richard, "The Battle for Energy," *Foreign Affairs* (March–April 2002): 16–32.

14

Russia's Security Integration with America and Europe

Dmitri Trenin

Vladimir Putin's post–September 11 strategic choice has withstood the test of Iraq. Integration with what is still commonly referred to as "the West" has ceased to be an ideological and philosophical issue in Russia. Instead, it has become a very practical one. Russian elites discuss the terms of various economic, political, and security "joint ventures" with the West. However, it has become clear that Russia's integration is above everything else the product of its internal transformation, the development of a market system, based on the rule of law, that boosts the formation of a civil society and leads toward political democracy. There have been ups and downs along that path.

Russia's "national idea" has recently been interpreted as achieving a degree of competitiveness and success in the century that has started. Thus, Russia's business should be Russia, and its modernization and transformation ought to be "the way." This would call for engagement with the outside world, in particular, with its more advanced members. The parameters of that engagement and the domestic implications are still being fought over, but this is a fight of tactics and possibly strategies, but not principles. Within a few years, Russia will accede to the World Trade Organization (WTO). Some kind of a free trade area between Russia and the European Union (EU) is likely to emerge soon thereafter, maybe styled as a Common European Economic Space. Politically, Russia has been anchored by means of its membership in the G-8 (the former "G-7 plus Russia," which is due to hold its first meeting in Russia in 2006), a privileged relationship with Washington, and an institutionalized dialogue with the European Union.

Still, there are important limitations. First of all, thirteen years after the fall of communism and the collapse of the Soviet Union, it has become clear that, in contrast to most countries of Central and Eastern Europe, Russia is not a country in relatively short "transition" from communism to democracy and the market system. As a result of its history, Russia's route will not only be longer, its "end station," if such a thing exists in transformation processes, is not yet in sight. Second, Russia is not on the way to becoming—even in the very long-term future—a member of the European Union. It will stay apart, probably wielding economic and political influence in those former Soviet states that will not be admitted to the

EU. Third, Russia is likely to continue in the twenty-first century as a free-standing strategic player, maintaining close contacts with America and Europe, but also interacting with China and India.

In terms of security, Russia's cooperation with the United States and Europe is currently inspired by the common struggle against international terrorism and is practiced in the framework of the NATO–Russia Council. In many ways, Russia has been able to preserve its autonomy and some freedom of action without alienating itself from the United States or Europe's leading nations.

During the 2003 Iraq crisis, for example, Moscow opposed the U.S./UK military action, but it did so without leaving the Western orbit altogether. One might (as this author does) question the wisdom of threatening the use of veto in the UN Security Council or the formal joining of the Franco-German "coalition of the unwilling,"[1] but one has to admit that Putin's handling of the crisis over Iraq was a far cry from the 1999 Kosovo imbroglio. Of course, it can be argued that the only difference between Kosovo and Iraq was that in the former case NATO allies had stood united, and Russia opposed the West as a whole, whereas in the latter one the Western alliance split on the war issue, which left Moscow in the "European" company of Paris and Berlin, and even then in the role of a follower. This argument, however, can be reversed. Had there been no split between the United States and "old Europe," Russia, in all likelihood, would have desisted from openly opposing the United States alone.

This is anything but surprising. A nation that only a dozen years ago or so was proudly carrying the title of one of the world's two military superpowers; that still keeps the second largest nuclear arsenal; where Victory Day in World War II has been the closest to national day, whether under communist rule or after its downfall—this nation cannot be expected to join the happy band of other post-communist states in remodeling their militaries within NATO's Partnership for Peace program. Indeed, Russia's problems with NATO and its enlargement in the 1990s are typical of a major military power that needs to come to terms with both a more benign external environment and its own much reduced status.

For a long time, Moscow has been trying to fashion a relationship with the alliance that would at least appear as one of equals. Initially, and utterly unrealistically, it even sought to have a parity-based relationship between NATO and the post-Soviet Commonwealth of Independent States (CIS), which Russia dominated. In the mid-1990s, Moscow politicians fulminated about Russia having "fewer rights in relations with NATO than Iceland," or about Moscow being placed, under the Partnership for Peace Program, in the same category as Tallinn. In fact, Russia did not want to become a "regular NATO ally." It was determined to be first among equals, with the only possible exception of the United States. But this, of course, could not be.

September 2001 was a turning point in Russia's relations with the West. Essentially, Putin used the occasion to discontinue the pointless and burdensome rivalry with the United States in the fields of strategic nuclear arms and conventional geopolitics. Russia joined the U.S.-led antiterrorist coalition and tolerated U.S. military presence in parts of the former Soviet Union (Central Asia and Georgia); its reaction to NATO's second wave of enlargement, involving the Baltic states, was muted and relaxed. Indeed, Russia itself upgraded its relationship with the alliance to a special council in which all twenty nations were participating on an equal footing. Moscow's new ambition was to become Washington's principal ally in the struggle against terrorism.

This latest ambition was anything but universally shared. The vast majority among Russian elites did not want to see their country become America's "patsy." They watched Tony Blair's handling of the Iraq crisis and its consequences and evidently did not envy Britain. However, those among them who dared to think more imaginatively about the prospects for U.S.–Russian military collaboration had to conclude that any such collaboration demanded a fundamental overhaul of the Russian military system, not merely tinker with it. No meaningful cooperation is possible between the United States and Russia unless and until the Russian forces become adequate to the new world inside and outside their country.

Modernization, however, is not merely or solely a foreign policy exigency. This is part and parcel of the Russian domestic reform agenda. So far, the military has been spared a serious reform effort. Despite everything they say, neither the elites nor the public see national defense as a priority. Consequently, they turn their backs on the armed forces. The former do this by essentially avoiding making hard decisions; the latter, by going to great lengths to protect their sons from doing military service. As a result, the essentially Soviet army that Russia has inherited has been dying a slow and silent death. It has taken longer than most outside observers had expected, but the process of "withering away" of the once mightiest military force in Eurasia has virtually become unstoppable and irreversible.

Under Putin, the issue of military reform has again risen in the public eye. Initially a corollary, almost an afterthought of the economic reform plan, it was put into stark relief by the 2000 Kursk submarine disaster, and kept alive by the unprecedented public row on defense priorities between then Defense Minister Igor Sergeiev and Chief of the General Staff Anatolii Kvashnin. Yet, despite major reorganizations and bold promises, little of substance was accomplished in the first presidential term (2000–2004). Closer to the 2004 elections, Putin declared the military reform completed and ruled out further major personnel reductions. Reform was to be succeeded by a more normal "force development."

At the end of Putin's first mandate, there were basically three options for proceeding with the current Russian military establishment, which is essentially beyond "reform" as commonly understood.

Option One is essentially doing nothing, leaving "reform" in the hands (or, rather, the mouths) of the military high command. This choice, first made by Boris Yeltsin for purely political reasons, rejects the need to modernize, and allows the Russian military establishment to continue along the downward path. For more than a decade, this is what was de facto practiced. Fortunately, this is not the likeliest choice under the present circumstances. The demographic situation in the country, as well as the general thrust of the government's economic policies (to name just two salient factors), militate against this.

Option Two means recognizing the long-term need to modernize, but balancing that against the short-term political costs. It would entail partial adjustment of the Russian military establishment to some of the existing domestic and international environments. This "handle with care" option is anything but revolutionary. Caution is the watchword. It pays tribute to the national military tradition and reaches out to an acceptable compromise with the military top brass. At present, this option stands the most chance of being accepted.

Option Three would reject caution as strategy, while prudently keeping it as a tactic. It would mean achieving a fundamental transformation of the Russian military, in line with Russia's economic transformation and the profound changes in the international strategic environment. One thing that distinguishes this option from the first one (explicitly) and the second one (implicitly) is the clear and unambiguous replacement of the notion of a threat from the West, on which the current military doctrine, strategy, deployment pattern, mobilization requirements, and education/indoctrination systems are based. Thus, it sees the problem not so much as reforming the military, but as replacing the current one with a fundamentally different entity. This option, seen as too radical by the Kremlin for now, is a way to the future.

No Reform

The first option has in fact been exercised since the collapse of the Soviet Union, and, to put it more broadly, since the official launch of "military reform" under Gorbachev/Iazov in 1987. The Soviet and Russian military have experienced most drastic changes in that period, but have undergone no reform worth the name. What passed for reform was drastic downsizing and very crude restructuring. Underlying this refusal to reform was the deep conviction of much of the political class and nearly the entire military establishment that Russia in the 1990s was experiencing only "temporary difficulties" and that it would bounce back relatively soon in essentially the same capacity as before 1985–1987. Politically, this option rested on an informal understanding between President Yeltsin and the military top brass, reaching as far back as the fall of 1991, which guaranteed the latter's loyalty to the nominal commander-in-chief in exchange for the president allowing his generals to run the army the way they saw fit.

If one were to succeed in actively resisting changes to the still essentially Soviet military organization of Russia, the following conditions would need to be met. Politically, a conservative, even reactionary agenda must prevail in the Kremlin. Reversing the policies of the past dozen years, the government, supported by both houses of parliament, would have to map out an essentially isolationist course. The economic part of the new agenda would have to contain a version of the "mobilization economy," meaning self-reliance, near-autarky and widespread renationalization of industrial and other key economic assets. In foreign policy, the post–September 11 decision to withdraw from geopolitical and strategic competition with the United States would have to be revised, and likely reversed. In fact, opposition to "American hegemony" and "unipolar world order" would have to be much more than rhetoric. Russia would have to see itself as a next U.S. target after Yugoslavia, Iraq, and the other members of George W. Bush's "axis of evil." This new worldview would provide a degree of political mobilization and unification, at the expense of suppressing all opposition, dissent, and so forth. Ideologically, the stress would have to be placed on a xenophobic form of patriotism, a crudely concocted version of the "Orthodox (really meaning anti-Western) values," and so on.

In reality, Option One can be conceived in two versions, "soft" and "hard." The softer one would be conservative, slowing down the pace of economic reform, reverting Russia's foreign policy to the late-1990s "multipolar world model," that is, actively seeking to balance U.S. preponderance with a system of axes and alliances, and leaving things in the military much the way they are now. It would be a major step back by comparison to where Russia has been standing since September 2001. The hard-line version would actually be reactionary and irresponsible, aimed at a rollback of reform rather than its slowdown. The closest model for this version would be Alyaksandr Lukashenka's Belarus.

Whether multipolarist or Lukashenkian—though the difference between the two is not a trifling matter, Option One would essentially view Russia as a distinct civilization, equidistant from both the East and the West. It would also posit that Russia's current and future problems are largely with the West, in particular the United States. American political hegemony, its economic might, and military dominance per se would be perceived as a threat. NATO enlargement, American military presence in Central Asia and the Caucasus, and the use of U.S. military force, either direct as in Iraq, or in the form of threat, as regards Syria, Iran, and North Korea, as well as the new doctrinal tenets of preventive strikes and usable "nukes," would be seen as embodiments of the threat. Naturally, the U.S. and NATO armed forces (despite the transatlantic tensions), as well as those of Japan, South Korea, and Pakistan would be designated as Russia's potential likely adversaries.

This threat assessment would require Russia to "lean on the East" to improve its position vis-à-vis the West. In the name of "multipolarity," in fact a code word for geopolitical anti-Americanism, Russia would need to cultivate close strategic ties to China, North Korea, and Iran. Belgrade and Baghdad, earlier candidates for this "united front" membership, have undergone "regime change," and India, an early hopeful in this "countervailing" political strategy, has made it clear after September 11 that it prefers close political and military ties with the United States to any potential ganging up on America. The hard-line version would go further. Having lost such clients as Milosevic and Saddam Hussein, its remaining hope would be to pursue an aggressive arms transfer policy in the third world, both to gain money and make life more difficult for the United States.

This would have the following implications for the Russian military:

- Restoring a "strong nuclear posture." That would mean revising the 2001 decision to slash the Russian nuclear arsenal and to downsize/downgrade the Strategic Rocket Force (SRF). Under the new policy, the SRF would again become the mainstay of the Russian military. Citing the U.S. withdrawal from the Anti-Ballistic Missile Treaty, Russia would feel free to re-MIRV (multiple independently targetable reentry vehicles) its ballistic missiles. More extreme measures would include withdrawing from the Intermediate Range Nuclear Forces Treaty and resuming the production of intermediate range missiles; abandoning the moratorium on nuclear testing and engaging in the production of more advanced nuclear weapons.
- Giving priority to the conventional forces facing NATO. This would mean implementing the 1999–2000 decisions to create large formations in Russia's European part to ward off a "Balkans-type aggression" by NATO[2]; turning Kaliningrad into a forward defense base; creating a joint military command with Belarus; "strengthening the borders" with the Baltic states; deploying tactical nuclear weapons along the "line of confrontation" with NATO.
- Prioritizing information warfare and other asymmetrical means of hitting the sophisticated military/civilian infrastructure of the Western countries.
- Focusing military education and training on updated scenarios of war against the West.
- Continuing to procure a broad range of nuclear, conventional, and nontraditional items designed primarily for a war against the United States and its allies. Entering into joint research, development, and production ventures with China and, possibly, Iran.
- Abandoning plans for an all-contract-based military. Instead, nullifying the exemptions from draft and making it more difficult for serving officers and academy graduates to resign from military service.
- Making the military even more opaque for the public and parliament alike. Restoring a Soviet-type military propaganda machine for internal brainwashing and creating a "positive image" of the military in society at large.

An attempt to implement this option would immediately run against a number of constraints. The first and most obvious one is the lack of resources. Russia's GDP is about 5 percent of the U.S. level; Russia's defense expenditure is $12 billion as against $400 billion in the United States (which in turn is roughly the size of the Russian GDP); Russia's population is less than three-fifths of America's, is declining at the rate of between 750,000 and 1 million per year, and the health situation, including the creeping HIV/AIDS epidemic, is abominable. Military science and the degraded, but unreformed, defense industry are in a shambles. Many of the best and the brightest have left the country, a large number of them for the United

States. A reversal of Russia's transformation would spark off another massive exodus. To hope for a reversal of these trends is to daydream. To hope for achieving strategic parity with the United States through mobilization of the available resources is sheer lunacy.

The second constraint is the opposition of wide sections of Russian society to remilitarization. Within the economic elite, it can only be supported by the less enlightened parts of the nuclear and defense industry and by the more backward quarters who abhor opening up to the world economy; others, starting with, but by no means limited to, the oil and gas companies, would be cashing out and even leaving the country. Part of the economic and political elite at national and regional levels would see their interests threatened by the advent of a state security state, and would either resist it or go into exile. Even more important, the wider public would resist a government attempt to apply much stricter conditions for military service.

The third constraint would be the likely reaction of other countries, both in the West and in Russia's neighborhood. Self-isolation would come at a horrendous cost, which would soon be felt by the entire population.

The result would be keeping a large, but increasingly obsolete and ineffective (nuclear forces apart) military. It would mean mismanaging still further the meager resources at the disposal of the Russian political-military leadership. This will not help to deal with the real threats and risks that Russia is likely to face in the military sphere: concentrating on the virtual "threat from the West" will not make these real threats disappear. As a result, in reality no priorities will emerge, and no clear strategy would be developed. Finally, this will strengthen the obscurantist streak in the Russian military and strategic thinking, pushing still further away the moment when a meaningful reform can start.

Hesitant and Partial Modernization

The second option is the careful adaptation of economic reforms to the still largely untouched military sphere. This choice is a major step forward by a national leadership that has become convinced that economic modernization is the sine qua non for Russia's development in the twenty-first century. Putin has said that Russia's goal is to become a competitive nation in an increasingly globalized environment. This view logically places the economy at the very top of the national agenda ("It's the economy, stupid!") and derives foreign, security, and defense policies from that principle. The foundation for that approach was laid in early 2000 by President Putin embracing the liberal reform program presented by German Gref, the minister of trade and economic development, and it was much solidified by Putin's calling off the traditional rivalry with the United States. The underlying philosophy of that approach can be summarized as "Russia's business is Russia." This has one important qualification. Political control comes first, even ahead of the economy, and democracy needs to be managed.

To pursue modernization in earnest, one has to start by accepting that Russia is no longer a traditional military-heavy great power, but an essentially different player in the throes of a fundamental transformation; that its national interests should be radically reinterpreted, so that foreign policy becomes a resource for development, and not the tool of ambitions for which resources are lacking; that the U.S. preeminence is a fact, but not a threat, since Russia's interests overlap much more than they conflict with those of the United States, especially in the security field. Thus, to begin with, the modernization agenda posits Russia in the same league as China, India, and Europe as a first-tier member of the U.S.-centered world order. In terms of affinities, it places Russia between America and Europe, with an all-important caveat that relations with China are of paramount importance to Moscow.

The strategic worldview of the supporters of this group is marked by the following tenets. Any confrontation with the United States is damaging to Russia's interests and must be avoided. To the extent possible, Russia should cooperate with the United States and NATO in the field of security. Yet, Russia should not surrender its sovereignty and continue as a discreet strategic unit. Its political and security cooperation with the West, moreover, should be conducted without prejudice to Russia's emerging partnership with China. The principal military threat to Russia comes from the south, and it comes from nonstate actors. This presently ranges from local separatism to international terrorism to domestic instability and ethnic and religious conflicts. Increasingly, there is growing understanding of the dangers of nuclear proliferation and the spread of missile technology, in particular in Northeast and South Asia and the Greater Middle East.

The implications of the modernization approach include the following:

- Phased reduction of the strategic nuclear weapons arsenals to around 1,000 by 2010.
- Reduction of the military personnel to just under 1 million in the armed forces and by 15–20 percent in the "other forces."
- Reduction of the too heavy conventional forces structure. Emphasis on leaner, meaner forces capable of rapid deployment to the areas of conflict on Russia's periphery.
- Restructuring and consolidation of the defense industry. Giving priority in defense procurement to less modern advanced equipment over larger orders of Cold War-type weapons.
- Gradual replacement of the current draft-based system with an all-volunteer force. Reform of the military education system by bringing it closer to the post–Cold War realities.
- Streamlining the money flow within the Ministry of Defense (MOD).
- Introducing a nominally civilian leadership at the head of the Ministry of Defense.

- "Civilianizing" the other "power structures" (the Ministry of the Interior, the Federal Border Service, the security community) by turning them into mainly civilian-run and civilian-organized agencies.

The principal feature of the modernizing-without-integrating option is the *defense tous azimuts*. This can be seen as a strength, in terms of "keeping all options open." It certainly appeals to the deeply held view within the strategic and policy community. At the same time, failing to anchor Russia firmly within a security community with the West (to which, incidentally, France always belonged despite the withdrawal from NATO's integrated military organization) creates a possibility for a reversal of the country's strategic position. It is striking how Russian political figures and military leaders can swiftly move from talking partnership with the West to warning about a still existing threat of a military conflict with NATO and the United States This leads one to conclude that partnership within the antiterrorist coalition is a temporary marriage of convenience, reminiscent of the many short-lived war alliances of the past.

Even those Russians who called, in the fall of 2001, for a close security collaboration with the United States based their argument on the reemergence of a common enemy, almost 1941–1945 style. However, such argumentation failed to highlight the deeper change in Russian–Western security relations, leading to their demilitarization. It also implied that once the new threat was dealt with, the former allies would fall out again.

Indeed, the failure of the Russian leadership, including Putin himself, to debunk the notion of a Western (actually, American) threat, even after 2001, is the single most important impediment to both the transformation of the Russian military security establishment (because the threat assessment is flawed) and the country's political rapprochement with the United States and Europe. The continuing existence of outdated threat scenarios and their embodiment in force structure, exercise scenarios, and the like, helps preserve Russia's image in the West as a potentially adversarial power, definitely *not one of us*.

Many of the resource constraints still applying, "strategic independence" would also make Russia pay an increasingly high price for keeping its defense industry viable and ensuring that its military's needs are fully met. To achieve this, Russia will have to enter into cooperative projects with others, mostly in the West, but some elsewhere. This "diversification" would create ambiguities and allow for political manipulation.

The result of this modernization effort would be positive but limited, and, more important, not firmly secured. Russia would be able to overcome the worst effects of the fifteen-year crisis of its military system, but the roots of the crisis will not have been properly dealt with. There would also be a danger of slipping back to the first option. Even as the current Russian administration is pursuing the second option, the difficulties it encounters are rising. The choice is essentially between abandoning the modernization effort altogether while recognizing defeat, and moving further.

Modernization and Integration

The third option treats modernization in conjunction with security integration. In other words, the pragmatism of the second scenario becomes subordinate, as a method, to the larger goal of integrating Russia with Europe and the Atlantic alliance in the field of military security as well as in all other relevant fields. By definition, this means viewing military transformation as part of the larger transformation agenda whose objective is to make Russia a modern European society. Thus, economy is joined by other important aspects, such as democracy and the rule of law, civil society and human rights, and so forth.

The third option demands, as its crucial element, a full and permanent demilitarization of Russia's relations with America and Europe, so that a military conflict between them becomes as unthinkable as the one between Germany and France. Unlike a clear presidential order to the MOD/General Staff to discontinue planning against a Western attack scenario, this is not a prerequisite to transformation; rather, this could be its long-term outcome. Neither is Russia's formal membership in NATO or the EU a must or even an objective ready to be stated. The formula, which in the fall of 2001 sounded as Russia's "alliance with the (NATO) alliance," in the words of Alexander Vershbow, the U.S. ambassador to Moscow, could be termed security partnership with the United States in addressing the dangers of terrorism, WMD proliferation, and instability in the Greater Middle East, and a more comprehensive economic and political relationship with the EU, with security as an integral part of it.

Russia would be joining with America and Europe not so much against a new enemy in the south, be it international terrorism or Islamist extremism. Unlike in Option Two, this would not be a situational coalition but an organic security community built on common long-term interests and a set of increasingly common values. This would mean that Russia will come to share a threat perception that bears little resemblance to either the Cold War environment or the earlier balance-of-power pattern that so many Russians readily accepted in the mid-1990s.

This will amount to nothing less than a revolution in Russia's military affairs. America and Europe will be viewed as *permanent* allies and/or partners. Gone will be the fixation on their military capabilities. Russia will seek a form of permanent association with the EU within a "wider Europe" and a Eurasia-wide security partnership with the United States. This relationship will be formalized in the special institutions uniting Russia and its partners, such as the NATO–Russia Council or a similar arrangement with the EU security wing, as it emerges. Rather than badges of exclusiveness and clearing shops for mutual grievances, these institutions will be used as vehicles for an ever deeper inclusion and involvement of Russia in the common councils with the West, while at the same time helping Russia accept those councils and their agendas as Russia's own.

In the strategic stability area, Russia will set to work on a new agenda with the United States. The Cold War notion of strategic stability would be replaced by a new one, featuring joint efforts to address WMD and missile proliferation, third-country nuclear crisis management, missile defense and so forth. Russia will still keep a sizable nuclear arsenal, but eventually its nuclear relationship with the United States would resemble the one between France and Britain.

The reform of the armed forces, as a key component of military reform, will feature replacement of draft by contract. This will make quality of the military personnel, rather than its quantity, the main asset of the future Russian military. From recruitment to education and training to procurement policies to housing to pay and retirement benefits, this will wholly transform the Russian military organization.

Preferring quality over numbers would mean, on account of the country's rather limited resources, a much smaller all-volunteer military force, perhaps numbering around 500,000. However, this army will not have to defend Russia from an invasion from the West. Recruitment and retention of personnel would have to be the main concerns of the MOD and the military leadership.

Reform of military education is the starting point and the prime vehicle of the systemic transformation. The aim would be to give officer cadets and more senior students a broad civilian education (including, inter alia, English as one of the majors) and special military training, to stimulate their independent thinking, resourcefulness, and initiative. At the same time, civil servants dealing with defense, military, and security issues would be receiving courses in these issues. No serious reform can be implemented without a large body of people who understand it and work to advance its goals.

The functions of the Ministry of Defense and the General Staff would have to be redefined, and the areas of responsibility delineated. The MOD would require a strong body of top-level civilian managers, financiers, economists, and the like. The General Staff would need to adapt itself to the post–World War II strategic environment. There is a strong argument against the continued existence of the General Staff (GS) in its present form.

At lower levels of the military establishment, administrative reform would have to be as fundamental as at the top. Priority must be given to joint and special commands. This would call for abolition of the military-districts structure and refashioning the missions of service headquarters. The structure of military units and formations will be revised, emphasizing lighter units and giving preference to variable configuration-type rather than permanently fixed formations.

The missions of the armed services will need to be reassigned. Thus, the army would emphasize special units and airmobile forces. The air force needs to stress its airlift capabilities. The navy will shift the emphasis from blue to brown water.

Military reform affects, besides the MOD/GS and the armed forces, all other government agencies that keep military formations as well as the defense industry. The general principle of the reform should stipulate that there will be only one army in the country. The Ministry of Interior would undergo civilianization. Its military arm, the Interior Troops, will be transformed into a national guard, more like heavily armed and highly capable police than a lightly armed army. The Border Troops of the Federal Border Service would be similarly transformed into frontier guards, more competent in immigration and cross-border trafficking issues than in defending against an armed incursion. The emphasis throughout should be on good training of personnel and proper technical equipment.

The absence of a world war scenario from defense planning makes it possible to abolish the "mobilization requirements" (i.e., keeping vast spare production capacities), which still are a very heavy burden. Military industrial cooperation will be fundamentally reinterpreted. Instead of standing for arms sales abroad, this will be a way to integrate sections of the Russian defense industry, such as the aircraft industry, with that of Europe.

In the sphere of civil-military relations, strict constraints on servicemen's political activity must be imposed and maintained. The "legal culture" of military personnel needs to be dramatically improved. Of particular importance is the observance of national legislation and international humanitarian law. The defense budget and the budgets of other power ministries would have to be made fully transparent (with very few reasonable exemptions), with the parliament receiving the right of oversight. A fundamental revamping of the promotion system would be a priority.

Getting from Here to There

Option One is not very likely but cannot be fully ruled out; this is a default position for the Russian political and military establishment. Option Two is currently being attempted, but without a game plan, a team of committed reformers, and a set of techniques. Option Three, the optimal one, is, at best, for the future. Russia's improved relations with both the United States and the European Union create an incentive and a range of opportunities to bring the future forward.

Of key importance is the new NATO–Russia Council. If orphaned by the politicians and left to the diplomats and military officers, it will become a latter-day version of the ill-fated Permanent Joint Council, which will compromise the very idea of turning an exclusive relationship into an inclusive one. If, on the other hand, the political fathers of the project develop a work plan and achieve significant results relatively soon, this can create a new momentum. The critical factor is finding the right people for the job.

Should Russia's personnel policy change, many "new people" can be trained within a few years in various NATO, U.S., European, or joint educational projects. The George C. Marshall School in Garmisch-Partenkirchen, the NATO School in Oberammergau, the NATO Defense College in Rome, American war colleges, *die Bundesakademien*, and so forth, can take in a number of Russian officers and civilians. The problem is to see their training not as tourism and not to regard them as "tainted" once they come home, but instead to promote them and place them in charge of Russia's security cooperation with NATO, the EU, and the United States.[3]

A short answer to the question of what Russia needs (or may get) from its new relationship with NATO is: the doing away with the residual Cold War heritage and help with military reform at home.

However, the bulk of the task will have to be dealt with by the Russians themselves. The key ingredient will have to be strong political will at the top level. A commander-in-chief, bold enough to repair Yeltsin's "original sin" of leaving the top brass to run military reform, would need to start his reform effort at the top level by creating a civilian-military defense ministry and a new military command headquarters. A group of top class professional managers would be needed to evaluate the inheritance of the Soviet/early Russian Federation years, and radically redesign the civilian side of the MOD. A number of these people can be seconded by the business community. Some of the military's best and brightest could be brought over to the new military command headquarters, which may still be called the General Staff, but whose function will be altered away from the World War II/Cold War model.

To provide the military establishment with a growing group of modern thinking professionals, a National Security Academy needs to be established, under the patronage of the commander-in-chief. Its graduates will form the expanding team of leaders of Russia's military transformation. At lower levels, new-look military academies and schools need to be launched to attract some of the country's bright young people willing to serve in the new army.

Within the armed forces structure, those elements that might be usable in creating a new force for the twenty-first century will be reformed and constitute a core force. These would include, for example, nuclear forces, special forces, airborne troops, parts of the navy and the air force, and so on. Others will have to be phased out. Outside the armed forces structure, the new security establishment would contain the National Guard and the Border Guard. A program of such a scale is unlikely to be implemented within one or two presidential terms. Underlying it must be a consensus among the principal political forces in Russia that in the twenty-first century traditional defense has to be subsumed within a modern security system.

A transformed Russian military force would be a much more useful partner to U.S. and European forces. Conversely, international cooperation projects may speed up transformation. Ballistic missile defense cooperation with the United States and Europe at global and theater levels, multilateral operations with NATO and the EU, and regional military cooperation in Central Asia can add both to international security and military transformation. There is no single "West" to integrate with, and no Russian desire to enter into an entangling security relationship with either America or Europe. However, through transforming the Russian military establishment to meet the new challenges and collaborating with both of its principal Western partners, Russia would remove a massive roadblock on its path toward integration with the more advanced segment of the world system.

Notes

1. Particularly unhelpful was the notion, which Igor Ivanov sought to promote, of Russia, France, and Germany forming a permanent alignment, a new *entente cordiate*. See his piece in the *Financial Times*, February 14, 2003.

2. Cf. Dmitrii Afinogenov and Viktor Eesin, "V plenu ustarevshikh stereotipov," *Nezavisimoe voiennoe obozrenie, NVO*, no. 14 (2002), p. 4.

3. A number of interesting proposals on that score are contained in a recent RAND-ISCRAN report, released in April 2002.

Conclusion

Integrating Russia into the West

The Challenges Before the United States, Russia, and Europe

Alexander J. Motyl, Blair A. Ruble,
and Lilia Shevtsova

Any consideration of Russia's integration into Western institutions must begin with the importance of the terrorist strikes of September 11, 2001. The good news is threefold. First, the terrorist attacks led President Vladimir Putin openly to align Russia with the United States. In turn, American policy makers appear more willing to heed Russian concerns with respect to previously contentious issues such as the National Missile Defense and NATO. Second, the U.S.-led war on terrorism may be leading to a major shift in geopolitical alignments. Russia's possible transformation from a regional problem to a strategic asset may facilitate closer economic relations with the European Union, promote a deeper Russia–NATO partnership, and enhance Russia's cultural links with the West in general and the community of liberal democratic states in particular. Third, the likelihood of continued instability in the Middle East means that Russia necessarily becomes an increasingly more reliable and more important supplier of energy resources to the West, at least to Europe.

But the bad news is no less striking. America's extension of the war on terrorism to Iraq divided the international community over whether such a war was necessary and desirable, over the appropriate place of the U.S. "hyperpower" in the international community, and over the best means to deal with weapons of mass destruction. Russia vehemently opposed the war, openly sided with France, and alienated the United States. France, Germany, and many other traditional U.S. allies also opposed the war. The result was a fracturing of the international community and a sharp worsening of U.S. relations with Russia, France, Germany, and indeed the European Union (EU).

Moreover, the Franco-German rejectionist stance forced the East Central Europeans and smaller EU states to choose between the Franco-German alliance that could do little for their security concerns and the American hyperpower that could do much. Not surprisingly, many sided with Washington. By the same token, Russia's alignment with France's opposition to the war not only alienated the United States but also terrified the East Central Europeans. In the end, the Iraq war resulted not in the deepening of Europe, but in the deepening of the divisions that had historically been papered over by the EU.

Despite considerable acrimony before and during the war in Iraq, it is striking that, as soon as coalition forces seized Baghdad, virtually all the opponents of the war began making overtures to Washington. Even Washington began making conciliatory gestures toward the United Nations and its advocates, including Russia. Clearly, then, one lesson of recent months must be to caution against viewing any policy choice as either "inevitable" or "permanent."

And yet the fact remains that, even if, as is likely, U.S. relations with Europe and Russia eventually normalize, the West has become distracted and divided. The United States is, and will long remain, preoccupied with the war on terror and the reconstruction of Iraq. Russia, though still important, will be a less pressing issue for Washington, and promoting its integration into Western institutions will in all likelihood be placed on the U.S. government's back burner. And what can talk of Russia's integration into Europe possibly mean if Europe ceases to be a coherent political-economic entity, and, in the worst case, even breaks apart into a set of squabbling states? If neither the United States nor Europe is interested in or able to provide the Russian leadership with incentives to abandon authoritarianism and pursue democracy, then the logic of our argument suggests that Russia will abandon the democratizing route and necessarily become more authoritarian and, over time, less modern.

While the case for pessimism is robust, the Iraq crisis presents the United States, Europe, and Russia with an opportunity to transcend limited visions of their interests and work toward mutually satisfactory solutions. A win-win-win scenario *is* thinkable, we argue, but only if all three sides do their best to pursue one. As we explain below, that means several steps.

- The United States will have to maintain and strengthen its security partnership with Russia and thereby allay its fears of irrelevance and marginalization.
- A Russia reassured and taken seriously by the United States need not act in a hegemonic manner vis-à-vis Ukraine, Belarus, and Moldova, thereby reassuring the East Central Europeans who are now inclined to look to the United States—instead of the EU—for their security needs.
- A European Union less concerned with east-west differences can self-confidently pursue its institutional development, play a more responsible role in world affairs, extend a hand to Russia, Ukraine, Belarus, and Moldova, and serve as a complementary force to the United States.
- The United States will in turn develop partnerships with Russia and Europe, on the basis of which it will be able to address world problems on a more cooperative, and hence more effective basis—without necessarily having to abandon its own preeminent position of power.

America's Choice: Partnership or Isolation?

Throughout the Cold War, American policy toward the Soviet Union vacillated between a limited realpolitik strategy of containment and a broader interventionist policy that sought to change Soviet domestic behavior as well as constrain its foreign policy. This dichotomy survives in the post-communist world. Americans are still divided over whether the United States should legitimately try to mold Russia's domestic transformation or whether America's role should be limited to engaging Russia on a variety of foreign policy issues that serve American interests, including offering it a role in Euro-Atlantic institutions. Indeed, the policies of the Clinton and Bush administrations highlight the contrast between, on the one hand, a commitment to influencing Russia's domestic transformation, and, on the other hand, a focus on engaging Russia on pragmatic foreign policy issues—particularly the war on terrorism—and eschewing attempts to influence domestic politics.

For the foreseeable future, American policy may be limited to securing Russia's continuing assistance in the war against terror. But, we argue, such a partnership does not preclude America's treating Russia as a serious and reliable partner, and thereby assuage Russian anxieties about their status in the world and enable them to deal with Europe, both East and West, from a position of security and self-confidence. More important, despite America's current sense of omnipotence, it is clearly the case that even "hyperpowers" need friends, and Russia can, as we suggest below, be an excellent and indispensable friend of the United States.

There are a number of areas in which Russia and the United States could cooperate in the months and years ahead.

- *European Security:* The NATO–Russia Council has the potential to involve Russia much more closely in enhancing European security. The key to overcoming the problems that the earlier troubled Permanent Joint Council had is to start with modest joint projects that can build trust and develop into larger projects. Inasmuch as these projects—counterterrorism, search-and-rescue operations, missile defense—involve close cooperation between the Russian military and NATO, they could over time serve to reorient the mentality of the Russian military in directions that are more compatible with a modern professional military. If the NATO–Russia Council could also deal with issues directly related to Russian military reform, then it could have a significant domestic impact in Russia. Thus, at its most productive, the NATO–Russia Council could serve both to encourage Russia's further integration into NATO structures and Russia's domestic transformation away from a Soviet-era military mentality.

- *Security in the Post-Soviet Space:* If the antiterrorism campaign is to succeed in the long run, there needs to be multilateral cooperation in Eurasia in order to achieve peace and stability. The United States and Russia will have to work with China and other neighbors, as well as the EU, to establish a new framework for security in Central Asia and beyond. If Russia were willing to become a guarantor of stability in Eurasia, instead of being tempted to act as a spoiler, that would also alter Russia's perception of its identity as a great power. President Putin has indicated, through his alliance with the United States, that he eschews Soviet imperial nostalgia, accepts the limits of Russia's influence, and is willing to play the role of a junior partner. A more forward-looking role in Eurasian security could reinforce these beliefs and ultimately affect domestic expressions of Russia's national identity.

- *Strategic Partnership in the War on Terror:* Central Asia is a good place to inaugurate a post–Cold War relationship with Russia that rests on mutual security and joint problem solving. Central Asia's major problems—potential separatist and irredentist conflicts, millenarian Islamist movements, terrorist networks, the narcotics trade, and the security of energy infrastructure—threaten Western and Russian security, and neither side, even the West, has the wherewithal to address them independently and unilaterally. Russia has two choices in Central Asia. The first is to oppose and subvert a Western emplacement in its long-time sphere of influence, even if that means making Central Asia a source of friction with the United States and its allies. The second is to accept the diminution of its power and to develop a long-term and cooperative relationship with the West (and China) in Central Asia to create stability and extirpate terrorism. Russia's calculation in the latter instance would be that widening and deepening the agenda of cooperation with the West will slowly alter the political-psychological aura of its relationship with the United States and Western Europe so that Cold War legacies and suspicions on both sides are buried. In that case, Russia would receive tangible economic and security gains down the road. In short, it means using the Western entry into Central Asia as an opportunity rather than seeing it as a threat. The United States and its allies must ensure through public pronouncements and private diplomacy that the West realizes how and why Central Asia matters to Russia and that it is prepared to work with Russia to develop avenues for cooperation on the many common goals that both sides have in Central Asia and its immediate environs.

- *Energy Cooperation and the World Trade Organization:* One of the most promising avenues of current U.S.–Russian cooperation is in the energy field. The United States believes that Russia has the potential to become the stabilizer of volatile energy markets. Russian energy entrepreneurs, seeking to build their reputations as responsible international corporate players, are playing a key role in the new U.S.–Russia energy dialogue. If Russian energy oligarchs were, despite the Khodorkovsky affair, to continue to embrace more transparent modes of corporate governance as they become more involved with international companies, energy cooperation could have a beneficial impact on Russia's domestic economic reforms. Equally important for cementing Russian–American relations is strong U.S. support of Russia's entry into the World Trade Organization.

- *New Security Issues:* Despite the current preoccupation with traditional security issues, U.S.–Russian relations will become increasingly concerned with problems that are of more recent vintage, but have grave security implications for Russia and its neighbors. These "new" security issues include infectious diseases, especially tuberculosis and HIV/AIDS (both of which are reaching epidemic proportions in Russia); trafficking in drugs and people; and organized crime. If the United States and Russia were to intensify cooperation to deal with these problems, then habits of cooperation and a diminution of Russian suspicions about American motives would follow. It is in America's long-term interest to create a more benign security environment in Russia, and cooperation on nontraditional security issues will involve Russian society as well as its political elites.

Note that U.S. cooperation with Russia in all these areas furthers both Russian and American interests, without negatively affecting the interests of other states. Our suggestion that the United States extend a hand to Russia does not in any way presuppose a reduction of American power or an aggrandizement of Russian power. Instead, we have in mind a pooling of resources for the pursuit of mutually beneficial ends. Such a pooling will, on the one hand, enable Russia to adopt a more constructive role toward its neighbors and thus promote European integration, and, on the other, provide the United States with incentives not to isolate itself from its friends and partners around the world.

Russia's Choice: Europe or Hegemony?

The task before Russia is twofold. First, Russia must embrace policies that allow the pragmatic pursuit of advantageous relations with Europe and the United States. Second, Russia must allay the security fears of the East Central Europeans—and it can do so most effectively by acting more responsibly toward their immediate neighbors, Ukraine, Belarus, and Moldova. As long as their suspicions remain strong, Russia must realize that East Central Europeans will naturally look to the United States for security. And as long as East Central Europeans prefer American power to Franco-German high-mindedness, Europe may well remain divided.

Indeed, the European Union appears to be in crisis. The United Kingdom has allied itself with the United States, while France and Germany are determined to assert their primacy. Many other Europeans, in both the West and East, oppose Franco-German hegemony, fear Russia, and see no alternative to siding with the United States. An EU Common Foreign and Security Policy—more a plan than a reality—now seems more distant than ever. Europe's identity as a set of like-minded democratic states committed to settling the problems of the world with "soft power" as opposed to "hard power" is under strain. The EU's Constitution may become a nobly worded document that will create as many tensions as it hopes to resolve. Europe's claim to represent an alternative to American hyperpower appears at best premature.

As Europeans squabble among themselves and with the United States, Russia could follow in the Soviet Union's footsteps and play off the Europeans against the Americans and try to reap advantage from the discord. President Putin has refrained from pursuing this course: for the first time in Russian history a Russian leader has understood that a divided West is not to Russia's advantage. Or Russia could show genuine vision by seizing on these divisions as an opportunity to act as an honest broker and try to reintegrate Europe as a step toward its own integration into Europe. A Russia that serves as a strategic partner of the United States in the war against terror should have the self-confidence and vision to play such a peacemaking role. Thus far Russia has failed to take advantage of this unprecedented opportunity and effectively play the role of mediator between America and Europe.

Russia's post–September 11 policy vis-à-vis its neighbors in the Commonwealth of Independent States (CIS)—and in particular toward Belarus, Moldova, and Ukraine—also reveals serious inconsistencies in Russia's international behavior. The first such inconsistency is Russia's simultaneous pursuit of "integration with the West" and the attempts, at least on the part of the Russian political class, to reconstitute a Russian-led political, military, and economic bloc that includes its immediate neighbors as a counterbalance to the West. The point is not that Russia has no legitimate strategic and economic interests in the "near abroad," but that many Russians believe that the Russian state should exert hegemonic leadership throughout the region. The international fight against terrorism has become a convenient tool used by some Russian elites to step up their efforts to consolidate Russia's influence in the post-Soviet space.

Moscow has attempted to breathe life into the CIS Collective Security Treaty (composed of Armenia, Belarus, Kazakhstan, Kyrgyzstan, Russia, and Tajikistan), seeing it as an advanced form of military-political integration in the CIS, and to transform it into an "international regional organization." The recently signed accord on the creation of a single economic zone consisting of Belarus, Kazakhstan, Russia, and Ukraine is a step toward economic integration within the CIS that develops in parallel with, and potentially as an alternative to, European integration.

The hegemonic temptation is also evident in bilateral relations. Moscow does not hesitate to exploit the weaknesses of its neighbors to increase Russian influence, making its political support of their leaders dependent on economic and political concessions. In Ukraine, Russian companies have, by means of frequently opaque deals backed by the Russian government, acquired significant stakes in and control over key sectors of Ukraine's economy. Officially, Russia accounts for only 6.7 percent of overall foreign investment in the Ukrainian economy, but experts estimate that in some key sectors, such as energy, the Russian share might actually amount to 70 percent. Russia has also exercised leverage elsewhere in the region. In Moldova, for example, Russia is already in breach of its international commitment to pull out weapons from Transdniestria by the end of 2002, despite serious grounds for believing that the arms depots in this self-proclaimed but nonrecognized entity have become important to international smugglers and terrorists.

To be sure, the involvement of Russian capital can also help reanimate local industry, and Russian investment is, in and of itself, a good thing. It is only when Russian capital is purposefully directed at promoting oligarchic trends that its effects are worrisome. Unfortunately, the Russian leadership does not shy away from openly supporting stagnating and autocratic regimes, corrupt oligarchic groups, and such retrograde political forces as the communists in Belarus, Ukraine, and Moldova. Although no easy generalizations can be made about the overall effect of these developments, it is clear that Russia's declared friendship with the West is inconsistent with its continued backing of antireform and anti-Western forces in these three states.

Russia, like Europe, is thus at a crossroads. Russia has to choose between attempting to preserve or restore hegemony over its neighbors or establishing mutually beneficial relations within its own region and integrating with the West. If Russia opts for hegemony, then it will inflame East Central European fears and promote Europe's divisions. Russia may then be able to engage in great-power posturing, but to what effect? Although the United States sees Russia as an ally in the war against terror, it is unlikely to accept Russia's efforts to promote Euro-Atlantic divisiveness with equanimity. In the end, Russia could lose its partnership with the United States and its chances of integrating into the West in exchange for achieving hegemony over impoverished and weak countries in its backyard. No less worrisome, hegemony will also derail the democratic modernization of Ukraine, Belarus, and Moldova, thereby impeding Russia's own transformation and integration into the West and contributing to a long-term division of Europe into a rich and democratic West and an impoverished and nondemocratic East.

Europe's Choice: Russia or Irrelevance?

Disagreement in Europe about the U.S.-led war in Iraq has starkly brought into focus the difficulties of creating a cohesive Common Foreign and Security Policy within an institutional framework in which national interests are still paramount. Yet, paradoxically, such disagreement highlights both the weakness and the strength of the European project in which sovereignty is "pooled" rather than surrendered. The European Union's most important foreign policy commitment, enlargement to include ten new members, occurred on schedule. Under the European Security and Defense Policy, the EU has just launched its first military operation in Macedonia. Notwithstanding deep and wide policy differences on Iraq both within the current EU and among the candidate states, EU leaders recently pledged continued work on the "Lisbon Strategy" to boost European competitiveness. In other words, disagreement is business as usual in the European Union.

As these events demonstrate, despite recent divisions among member states,

the EU overall continues to act principally as an administrator, regulator, and promoter of good governance. Through its high representative and external affairs
commissioner, it tends to play a supporting role and tries to make optimal use of
the policy instruments at its disposal. Such policy instruments have the potential
for an integrated approach, including both "low politics" and "high politics" in an
institutionalized and regulated political relationship. While not likely to result in
any spectacular breakthroughs in EU–Russia relations, this core characteristic of
the EU provides a framework for cooperation and dialogue.

The EU's policies toward Russia and other actors are thus driven by institutional rather than political or economic logic. This has at least two important implications. First, the EU acts toward Russia only when equipped with a mandate
and a treaty. The EU is not geared toward ad hoc or rapid responses to political or
economic developments. Second, how the EU responds to political and economic
developments concerning Russia is determined by its internal institutional characteristics.

The irony should be apparent. Just as Russia seeks to define appropriate relations with the West, so too the West—or, more precisely, Europe—must confront
its own institutional self-limitations. After all, integrating Russia into Western institutions means, above all, integrating Russia into Europe. Although the European Union has no intention of expanding beyond the states of East Central Europe
in the foreseeable future, it is vitally important that its door remain open. Notwithstanding the obstacles represented by the EU's notoriously bureaucratic rigidities,
the decisions adopted at the December 2000 EU summit in Nice point to a way of
addressing this problem. Because groups of EU members will effectively be able
to pursue varying degrees of institutional cooperation, the EU may, over time,
develop into an institution consisting of concentric circles of cooperating countries. Once concentric circles are possible *within* the institution, then it becomes
easier to envision further concentric circles extending *beyond* the institution, thus
blurring the rigid line between insiders and outsiders.

Naturally, NATO should be equally attentive to this issue. If Russia's post–
September 11 strategic partnership with the United States were, as we suggest, to
deepen, then it is not inconceivable that Russia could at some point be brought into
the alliance. To be sure, enlarging NATO to include Russia would entail a quantum
reorientation of NATO strategically—from an alliance that is focused on European security to one that is willing and able to engage itself in the geopolitics of all
of Eurasia. Russia would not be averse to such a redefinition, and the United States
might also welcome it. The Europeans would at present greet it with nothing short
of alarm. But, if the war on terror continues, the possibility of extending the bounds
of Europe's security eastward would increase. As NATO then becomes more important, so too would the prospect of Russia in NATO appear less preposterous.

The fact of the matter is that integrating Russia into Western institutions and
thereby promoting Russia's democratic transformation is primarily a task for the
European Union. Russia and Ukraine are Europe's immediate neighbors—indeed,

they arguably are a part of Europe—and Europe's soft power is precisely what can best facilitate their institutional integration. The United States, whatever the extent of its hard power, is both too far away and too preoccupied to concern itself with the institutional integration of Russia beyond where its interests are most affected—in NATO and the WTO, for example. Moreover, the United States may soon become overstretched and thus incapable of pursuing an activist agenda. Europe, in contrast, has little choice but to act as the great power it claims to be. If its institutions, values, and ethical standards are really as important to it as European leaders insist, then the EU has no choice but to extend its zone of benign influence to the countries east of the Schengen divide.

In sum, if Europe seeks to play the role of great power—and it is a role that we strongly endorse—the European Union can no longer claim that its institutional peculiarities prevent it from doing so. If the United States is to restrain its power and Russia is to restrain its ambitions, then Europe has no choice but to increase both its power and its ambitions. Europe must act as the powerhouse that it has in fact become, just as both America and Russia must learn to act with some forbearance. All sides can win if the United States engages Russia in a long-term security partnership; if Russia takes this unprecedented opportunity to promote intra-European and transatlantic amity by refraining from dusty imperial projects vis-à-vis its near abroad; and if Europe extends its institutions to Russia and its neighbors.

For the United States and Russia, the task is to pursue wise policies. For Europe, the task is much more formidable—to transform itself institutionally and exhibit the leadership it claims it wants. This should include adopting a more flexible approach to the development of a Common European Economic Space involving Russia—in particular, reducing its own protectionism and not considering the wholesale adoption by Russia of EU legislation and regulations as necessary to this project.

The time is therefore ripe for the United States to translate its hard power into the basis for a cooperative strategic partnership with Russia; for Europe to translate its soft power into the basis for Russia's rapprochement with Western institutions; and for Russia to act responsibly toward its neighbors. Were all three sides to act in this manner—a manner that we believe is fully consistent with their self-interest—the result would be a win-win-win. Russia's modernization would be more likely to be democratic and hence successful; the European Union would be more likely to be able to proceed with its own deepening and broadening; the United States would be more likely not to find itself alone in a hostile world. Last but not least, Russia would serve to bridge—and not exacerbate—differences between the United States and Europe.

Conclusion

We are fully aware that, as most of the articles in this book suggest, the win-win-win scenario sketched out above is practically unrealistic at this point in time.

304 ALEXANDER J. MOTYL, BLAIR A. RUBLE, AND LILIA SHEVTSOVA

Even so, the scenario remains reasonable, sensible, beneficial, and plausible; it does not, after all, recommend something intrinsically impossible. Indeed, the scenario is not even all that far-fetched—especially if one assumes that the alternatives can only fail.

Untrammeled unilateralism cannot succeed and the United States will at some point realize that it needs reliable partners. Neo-imperialism will diminish Russia's security and Russia will, like all post-imperial states, come to appreciate that external hegemony is no substitute for good governance at home. Irresponsible isolationism by a potential great power is a recipe for global instability and the European Union will have no choice but to assume its fair share of the world's burdens.

Naturally, it will take time for these realities to sink in. But as they do, however slowly and fitfully, wise Russians, Americans, and Europeans would do well to keep in mind that they can only win from closer cooperation and responsible behavior.

Index

Dubrovka hostage crisis, 85
Duma International Affairs Committee, 143

East Timor, 251
Economic and Monetary Union, 172
economic development, 162
Edinaia Rossiia (United Russia), 78, 81
Egypt, 179
Enlightenment, 60, 64, 67
  post, 270
Estonia, 21, 23, 139, 177
Eurasia, 302
European Bank for Reconstruction and
  Development (EBRD), 125
Eurasian Economic Community (EEC),
  195, 200
Euro-Asian Union, 234
European Business Club, 92, 95
European Centre for Emergency
  Situations, 236
European Commission (EC), 132–137,
  152, 154, 156, 158, 161, 172, 249
European Constitution, 96
European Convention on Human Rights, 88
European Council, 154, 156
European Court of Human Rights, 88
European Court of Justice, 171, 173
European Economic Area (EEA), 132–133,
  135, 137, 174, 179
European Free Trade Association (EFTA),
  136
European Galileo program, 250
European Investment Bank, 142
European Monetary Union (EMU), 176
European Parliament (EP), 157–160, 162,
  181
European Security and Defense Policy
  (ESDP), 153, 157, 160, 234, 236–239,
  246–247, 250–252, 254–255
European Union (EU), 4, 11, 46, 49, 54–57,
  85–86, 88, 90–91, 94–97, 117,
  121–122, 125, 127–128, 131, 133–137,
  139, 140–144, 157, 199, 201–204,
  223–224, 228, 233–239, 241–242, 244,
  248–257, 260–261, 273–274, 281, 290,
  292–293, 295–296, 301–303

European Union (EU) *(continued)*
  Constitution, 299
  enlargement/ expansion, 20, 139, 144,
    151–152, 160–162, 165–166, 177,
    181, 203, 231, 253–255
  federalism, 50
  High Representative, 164
  legal culture, 50
  movement of people, 132
  policies toward Russia, 151–167
  relations with Russia, 170–183
  Russia's incompatibility with, 34
  Russian policy toward, 230
European Union Military Staff (EUMS),
  250–251
European Union (EU)-Russia summit,
  Vladimir Putin, 159
Europeanization, 51, 52, 157, 165, 174,
  180, 182, 197, 204
  of Russian institutions, 170–171
Eurozone, 141

Fatherland-All Russia and Unity, 91
Faustian bargain, 104–105
Federal Security Service, 9, 225
Foreign Affairs Committee of the
Federal Council, 83, 91, 227
Federal Border Service (FBS), 28, 292
  illegal immigration, 29
  terrorism, 29
Federal Migration Service (FMS), 27
  immigrant workers, 28
Federation of Internet Education (FIE),
  89
Fedorov, Nikolai, 93
fertility rates, 23
Feshbach, Murray, 23
Finland, 139, 142, 157–158
Foreign Affairs Committee, 191
Foreign Direct Investment (FDI), 141
foreign investment, 128, 131, 300
  Cyprus, 123
  McDonald's, 131
foreign trade, 125
Founding Act on Mutual Relations,
  Cooperation and Security, 241

Russia's Engagement
with the West

Russia's Engagement with the West

with the West

Transformation and Integration in the Twenty-First Century

Alexander J. Motyl, Blair A. Ruble, and Lilia Shevtsova, Editors

M.E.Sharpe
Armonk, New York
London, England

Copyright © 2005 by M.E.Sharpe, Inc.

Library of Congress Cataloging-in-Publication Data

Russia's engagement with the west : transformation and integration in the twenty-first century
/ Alexander J. Motyl, Blair A. Ruble and Lilia Shevtsova, editors
   p. cm.
Includes bibliographical references and index.
   ISBN 0-7656-1441-3 (hardcover : alk. paper); ISBN 0-7656-1442-1 (pbk. : alk. paper)
   1. Russia (Federation)—Foreign relations. 2. Russia (Federation)—Foreign relations—
Europe. 3. Europe—Foreign relations—Russia (Federation) 4. Russia (Federation)—Politics
and government—1991–5. North Atlantic Treaty Organization. I. Motyl, Alexander J.
II. Ruble, Blair A., 1949– III. Shevtsova, Lilia Fedorovna.

DK510.764.T73 2004
327.4704′09′0511—dc22   2004005787

Printed in the United States of America

BM (c) 10   9   8   7   6   5   4   3   2
BM (p) 10   9   8   7   6   5   4   3   2

Contents

List of Tables and Figures

Tables

Figures

About the Editors and Contributors

Pilar Bonet has been the correspondent in Moscow of the Spanish newspaper *El Pais* from 1984 until 1997 and again since 2001 when she returned to Russia after four years as *El Pais* correspondent in Germany. She has been at the Kennan Center as a research scholar and has published three books on Russian topics, one of which, *Figures in a Red Landscape*, has been published in English. Bonet has degrees in Spanish literature from Barcelona University and in journalism from Barcelona Autonomous University.

Sophia Clément-Noguier teaches International Relations at the Institut d'Études Politiques in Paris. Earlier, she worked at the Delegation of Strategic Affairs of the French Ministry of Defense and was a senior fellow at the Institute for Security Studies of the (Western) European Union in Paris. She has published on crisis management and transatlantic security issues, notably "Tensions between Unilateralism and Multilateralism in U.S. Policy within the NATO Alliance" in *International Perspectives on U.S. Unilateralism and Multilateralism*, ed. David Malone and Yuen Foong Khong.

Philip Hanson is emeritus professor of the political economy of Russia and Eastern Europe, University of Birmingham, UK, and associate fellow of the Royal Institute of International Affairs, London. Previously, he has worked at the British Treasury, the Foreign and Commonwealth Office, the United Nations Economic Commission for Europe, Radio Free Europe/Radio Liberty, and at the universities of Michigan, Harvard, and Kyoto. His books include *From Stagnation to Catastroika* (1992), *Regional Economic Change in Russia* (co-edited with Michael Bradshaw, 2000), and *The Rise and Fall of the Soviet Economy* (2003).

Ania Krok-Paszkowska has a PhD in political science from the University of Leiden. She has been a visiting fellow at the Robert Schuman Centre for Advanced Studies (European University Institute in Florence). Her current work focuses mainly on the European Union and enlargement. Her recent publications include a report on "The Political Dimension of Enlargement" (2001), "Public Attitudes towards the EU in Candidate Countries" (2003), and "Poland's Road to the European Union" (with Jan Zielonka, 2004).

Stephan Kux is delegate for European affairs of the Canton of Zürich (Switzerland) and senior lecturer in political science at the University of Zürich. Educated at Columbia University and the London School of Economics, he has specialized in Soviet and Russian affairs and European integration. His current work is on domestic adaptation to European integration and transformation of political systems in the east and south in a comparative perspective. Kux has published several books on Soviet federalism and revolution, foreign affairs, and the fall of the Soviet empire.

Rajan Menon is Monroe J. Rathbone Professor of International Relations at Lehigh University and a fellow at the New America Foundation. He is also a senior fellow at the Council on Foreign Relations, and a senior adviser and academic fellow at the Carnegie Corporation's International Peace and Security Program. His chapter is part of a book project supported by a 2002 Carnegie Scholar award from the Carnegie Corporation of New York. His most recent publications include *Russia, the Caucasus, and Central Asia: The Twenty-First Century Security Environment* (1999) and *Energy and Conflict in Central Asia* (2001).

Jerzy Maćków is chair of comparative politics (Central and Eastern Europe) at the Institute for Political Science at the University of Regensburg. His fields of interest include the theory of totalitarianism and authoritarian rule, post-communist transformation, and country studies (Belarus, Poland, Russia, Ukraine). His recent publications include *Die Konstruktion politischer Stabilität. Polen und Russland in den Umbrüchen der achtziger und neunziger Jahre* (1998) and *Parlamentarische Demokratie und Autoritarismus. Erfolge und Misserfolge der postkommunistischen Verfassunggebung* (1998).

Alexander J. Motyl is professor of political science and deputy director of the Center for Global Change and Governance at Rutgers University-Newark. He is the author of six books, the latest of which is *Imperial Ends: The Decay, Collapse, and Revival of Empires*, and he is the editor of *The Encyclopedia of Nationalism*.

Oleksandr Pavliuk is an expert on European security. He has published widely on security in the post-Soviet space, Ukrainian foreign policy, and implications of EU and NATO enlargement. He is editor of the recent volume *The Black Sea Region: Cooperation and Security-Building* (2004) and co-editor of *Building Security in the New States of Eurasia* (2000).

Alexander Rahr is program director of the Körber-Centre for Russian and CIS Affairs of the German Council on Foreign Relations. He is also coordinator of the Council's EU–Russia Forum. Before joining the Institute in 1994, he was senior analyst at the Research Institute of Radio Free Europe/Radio Liberty, Munich, and project manager at the Federal Institute for East European and International Studies, Cologne. He has published biographical studies of Mikhail Gorbachev (1986) and Vladimir Putin (2000), and is co-author of the Trilateral Commission Report on Central Asia (2000). He was educated at the University at Munich.

Blair A. Ruble is director of the Kennan Institute for Advanced Russian Studies of the Woodrow Wilson Center in Washington, D.C., where he also serves as co-coordinator for comparative urban studies. He received his MA and PhD degrees in political science from the University of Toronto, and his undergraduate degree from the University of North Carolina at Chapel Hill. His book-length works include *Leningrad: Shaping a Soviet City* (1990), *Money Sings! The Changing Politics of Urban Space in Post-Soviet Yaroslavl* (1995), and *Second Metropolis: Pragmatic Pluralism in Gilded Age Chicago, Silver Age Moscow, and Meiji Osaka* (2001).

Yuri Senokosov is director of the publishing program of the Moscow School of Political Studies. He is editor-in-chief of *Obshchaia tetrad'* magazine and co-editor of the London-published, English-language tri-quarterly *Russia on Russia*. A graduate of the history department of Moscow State University, Dr. Senokosov served on the editorial board of the journal *Voprosy filosofii* (Problems of Philosophy) and is author of a book *Vlast' kak problema* (Power as Problem).

Lilia Shevtsova has been senior associate at the Carnegie Endowment for International Peace since 1995 and was on the faculty of the Moscow State Institute for International Relations from 1997 to 2003. Shevtsova is a member of the editorial boards of the journals *Polis*, *Pro et Contra*, *Journal of Democracy*, *Demokratizatsiia*, *Megapolis*, and *Moscow News*. She is a member of the Women in International Security Advisory Board, the Executive Council of the Russian Political Studies Association, the Council for Central and Eastern European Studies, and the Board of the Institute for Human Sciences at Boston University. Shevtsova is author and co-author of several books, including *Yeltsin's Russia: Myths and Reality* (1998) and *Putin's Russia* (2003), and co-editor of *Gorbachev, Yeltsin, and Putin: Political Leadership in Russia's Transition* (2001).

Angela E. Stent is director of the Center for Eurasian, Russian, and East European Studies and professor of government and foreign service at Georgetown University. She has published widely on U.S.–Russian relations and on Russia's relations with Europe. She has served as National Intelligence Officer for Russia and Eurasia on the National Intelligence Council and on the Policy Planning Staff of the U.S. Department of State.

Elizabeth Teague is an analyst of Russian politics with the UK Foreign and Commonwealth Office, currently on secondment to the UK Ministry of Defence. Earlier, she worked as an analyst of Soviet affairs with Radio Free Europe/Radio Liberty Inc. in Munich, as an advisor to the OSCE High Commissioner on National Minorities in The Hague, and as an analyst for the Jamestown Foundation. The views expressed here are her own and should not be taken as representing those of the British Government.

xii ABOUT THE EDITORS AND CONTRIBUTORS

Dmitri Trenin is a senior associate at the Carnegie Endowment for International Peace and director of studies at the Carnegie Moscow Center. Prior to his retirement from the Russian military in 1993 he served as a liaison officer with the Western allies in Germany, staff member of the Soviet delegation to the Nuclear and Space Talks in Geneva, and was the first senior fellow at the NATO Defense College. He has authored several books on Russian foreign and security policy, including *The End of Eurasia: Russia on the Border between Geopolitics and Globalization* (2001, 2002) and *Russia's Restless Frontier* (2004).

Jan Zielonka is Ralf Dahrendorf Fellow in European Politics at St. Antony's College, University of Oxford. He previously taught at the European University Institute, Leiden University, and the University of Warsaw. His books include *Explaining Euro-Paralysis* (1998), *Europe Unbound* (2002), and two volumes on *Democratic Consolidation in Eastern Europe* (2001).

Russia's Engagement
with the **West**

Introduction

Russia's Reintegration into the West
The Challenges Before Russia

Alexander J. Motyl, Blair A. Ruble,
and Lilia Shevtsova

How can Russia become prosperous, well governed, and socially equitable—a country that is, to use the Western social-science parlance, "modern"?[1] The answers to this question—whether proposed by Russians or by analysts outside Russia—often fall into the two mutually exclusive camps already defined by similar debates in previous centuries. One side claims that Russia can become modern only if it adopts liberal values and democratic practices. The other insists that Russia must go its own way, relying on the national values, authoritarian traditions, and institutions that have both defined and been defined by Russia's history and culture.

This question and the answers are not new, and the fact that they have characterized debates over Russia's future for the past two hundred years strongly suggests that this binary opposition, while useful as a way of imagining stark historical alternatives, may have outlived its utility as a signpost for developing policy-relevant approaches to Russia's future. Accordingly, the Center for Global Change and Governance at Rutgers University-Newark, with the sponsorship of the Carnegie Corporation of New York, convened a group of U.S., European, and Russian observers of Russia to discuss how Russia's relationship with the West, broadly defined, has changed in recent years.[2] This effort was predicated on an assumption that President Vladimir Putin's support for the United States in the post–September 11, 2001, war against terrorism may have represented a sea change in how Russia interacts with the West, at least on the level of state-to-state relations. What new options did Putin's post–September 11 embrace of the West create for Russia's internal development? How does pursuit of those domestic options influence Russia's relationship with the world beyond its borders?

While the choices facing Russia and the West are rather more complicated than the binary opposition of Westernizers and Slavophiles would suggest, we do believe that Russia can become modern only if it proceeds along a democratic path—one that, naturally enough, must take into account Russia's historical and cultural

3

specificities. This is so, not because nondemocratic paths to modernity—prosperity, good governance, and social equity—are impossible, but because the peculiar conditions of Russian's post-communist institutional development virtually guarantee that a nondemocratic path to modernity will not only fail but also produce a dysfunctional, polarized, and ultimately impoverished country. While we acknowledge that the choice of democratic modernization must be made first and foremost within Russia itself, we believe that the West—the United States and the European Union—can facilitate democratic paths most conducive to economic growth and Russia's well-being.

This perspective explicitly shapes our evaluation of developments within Russia over the past decade and a half. Russia has experienced wrenching change over that period. A new state, political regime, economic order, and society have emerged in what was, in retrospect, a fairly orderly manner. The Russian Federation has neither collapsed nor broken apart. It avoided social revolution or widespread turmoil and has so far escaped harsh dictatorial rule. Indeed, the new Russia has many achievements to its credit, including having succeeded in stabilizing itself and generating economic growth. After years of uncertainty, most Russians have realized that they cannot attain general prosperity, social equity, and good governance—or modernity—without integration into Western society. Moreover, the Russian transition is still short-lived, under way only slightly more than a decade.

While Russian society appears ready for a dramatic breakthrough toward democratic principles, Russian elites remain unable to shake off the past. Most important, Russia's political system, however democratic its trappings, rests on personified power, bureaucratic measures, and the fusion of political power with business. In the years of Boris Yeltsin's stewardship, Russia became a democratically legitimated, paternalistic, and inefficient bureaucratic system. Under President Putin, Russia's democratic tendencies have weakened and its authoritarian ones have strengthened. In a word, Russia is moving away from the only kind of system that can succeed in making it modern.

Although the nature of Russia's system precludes the easy pursuit of democracy, the piecemeal introduction of democratizing measures is both possible and far more likely to succeed than centralization or authoritarianism, whether hard or soft. But a democratic form of modernization can work only if Russia is first weaned off its current authoritarian predilections. Insofar as the Russian government is unlikely to make the first move, the West could have an important role to play in this aspect of Russia's transformation. As we argue in the conclusion, the United States is ideally positioned to address Russia's "hard power" concerns and maintain a strategic partnership with it. But we believe that it is also time for the European Union (EU) to exert its "soft power" and reach out vigorously to Russia. Despite the many divisions that appeared within Europe as a result of the Iraq crisis, the European Union—if it is genuinely serious about becoming an influential global actor—has no choice but to settle its internal differences and reach out to Russia and its neighbors.